Beyond CHARITY

Reformation
Initiatives
for the Poor

Carter Lindberg

Fortress Press, Minneapolis

BEYOND CHARITY
Reformation Initiatives for the Poor

Cover and interior design: McCormick Creative
Author photo: Matthew Lindberg
Interior photos: Roger H. Baumann

Library of Congress Cataloging-in-Publication Data

Lindberg, Carter, 1937–
      Beyond charity : Reformation initiatives for the poor / Carter Lindberg.
          p.   cm.
      Includes bibliographical references (p.   ) and index.
      ISBN 0-8006-2569-2 (alk. paper)
      1. Church work with the poor—Europe—History—16th century.
2. Reformation.   3. Church work with the poor—Europe—History.
4. Church work with the poor—Europe—History—16th century—
Sources.   5. Reformation—Sources.   6. Church work with the poor—
Europe—History—Sources.   I. Title.
BV639.P6L543   1993
261.8'325'09409031—dc20   92-29963
                                                                                        CIP

Manufactured in the U.S.A.   AF 1-2569

97   96   95   94   93   1   2   3   4   5   6   7   8   9   10

To my mother
Esther Bell Lindberg
and
in memory of my father
Harry G. Lindberg
(1910–1990)

Contents

Introduction

Part One: Reformation Initiatives for the Poor

Chapter 1

Chapter 2

Chapter 3

Chapter 4

Part Two: Sources on Poverty and Social Welfare

Chapter 5

Chapter 6

Chapter 7

Illustrations

Preface

IS POVERTY the result of defects in the personal character of poor individuals or in the social and economic structure of society? Are the rich the elect and the poor the reprobate? Is the cause (for some, the sin or crime) of poverty individual or communal? Are welfare programs destructive of the poor person's character? Are welfare programs destructive of the social and economic fabric of society itself? Is provision for the incapacitated (however incapacity is defined) really support of the unfit? Does welfare suffocate initiative or is it necessary in order that everyone in society may breathe more freely?

In common with all who have served on boards and committees of social ministry, I have been acutely aware of the passionate intensity with which these questions concerning poverty and social welfare are debated today. As a historian, I was startled to discover that these same concerns, albeit with marked variations in perspectives, existed during the late Middle Ages and Reformation. Indeed, some of these earlier perspectives seem more advanced than our own, while others are clearly the original expressions of contemporary attitudes. It is my hope that the following narrative of the origins of modern social welfare, and the accompanying anthology of documents, will contribute to a greater understanding of social welfare policies.

My motivation is hardly unique. All church historians hope that their work in examining the past will constructively inform the present church. Over a century ago, Gerhard Uhlhorn contributed the first—and to date, the only—comprehensive study of the history of Christian charity. Uhlhorn recalled in the foreword to the second edition that it was Theodor Fliedner, the "father" of the modern deaconess movement, who inspired his work. In a summer evening's conversation, Fliedner stated to Uhlhorn: "You should write a history of charity for such a book could serve to awaken and increase widespread interest for Christian love."[1]

In many ways Uhlhorn's work has been not only an inspiration but a comfort to me. The conversation with Fliedner that initiated Uhlhorn's work took place in 1863, but the collecting and choosing of materials and the writing of his study was no easy task, and thus his first volume did not appear until 1882. Since my own work on this subject began in the mid-1970s, I take no small comfort in knowing of the length of Uhlhorn's labors. Of course, this present study is a minor work compared to Uhlhorn's. Although I hope to supplement it in the future with further studies on social welfare in the early and modern church, I am deeply aware of the wisdom of Bernard of Chartres's comment that we are but midgets standing on the shoulders of giants.

As important as literary inspiration is to one involved in a long-term project, it is always the personal encouragement and support that keeps one going. The students in my seminar "Church Care of the Poor" have contributed to and stimulated this project in innumerable ways, as have also the participants in my seminar "Luther on Property and Poverty" held during the Seventh International Congress for Luther Research.[2] Gregory Miller, Ph.D. candidate at Boston University, has provided helpful suggestions along the way. I also wish to express my appreciation to the Graduate College of Boston University for a seed research grant for the summer of 1986, and to the School of Theology for the sabbatical year that provided time for writing. Finally, I am especially grateful to both the Association of Theological Schools and the Ella Lyman Cabot Trust for the grants that made my sabbatical year possible.

1. Gerhard Uhlhorn, *Die christliche Liebesthätigkeit*, 3 vols. in 1, 2d ed. (Stuttgart: Gundert, 1895), 3. The first volume originally appeared in 1882 and was translated into English with the title *Christian Charity in the Ancient Church* (New York: Scribner's Sons, 1883). The other volumes have not been translated. The second edition was reprinted in 1959 (Neukirchen). Uhlhorn's major contributions to theological ethics are sketched in the introduction to his *Schriften zur Sozialethik und Diakonie*, ed. Martin Cordes & Hans Otte in collaboration with Elke Rothämel (Hannover: Lutherische Verlagshaus, 1990), 11–37.
2. Oslo, Norway, August 1988. The seminar report is in *Luther-Jahrbuch* 57 (1990), 251–53.

Abbreviations

ARG	*Archiv für Reformationsgeschichte*
CW	*The Collected Works of Thomas Müntzer.* Peter Matheson, trans. & ed. Edinburgh: T. & T. Clark, 1988.
LQ	*Lutheran Quarterly*
LW	*Luther's Works.* St. Louis: Concordia; Philadelphia: Fortress, 1955–1986.
MM	*Miscellanea Mediaevalia*
Mollat	Michel Mollat, ed. *Études sur l'histoire de la pauvreté.* 2 vols. Paris, 1974.
PL	*Patrologia cursus completus, series latina.* Ed. P. Migne. Paris, 1844–1855.
Riis I	Thomas Riis, ed. *Aspects of Poverty in Early Modern Europe,* vol. 1. Stuttgart: Klett-Cotta, 1981.
Riis II	Thomas Riis, ed. *Aspects of Poverty in Early Modern Europe,* vol. 2. Odense: Odense University Press, 1986.
Sehling	Emil Sehling, ed. *Die evangelischen Kirchenordnung des XVI. Jahrhundert.* 15 vols. Tübingen: Mohr, 1902–1980.
SCJ	*The Sixteenth Century Journal*
StA	*Martin Luther Studienausgabe.* Berlin, 1979ff.
TRE	*Theologische Realenzyklopädie*

WA	D. *Martin Luthers Werke*. Kritische Gesamtausgabe. Weimar, 1883ff.
WA Br	D. *Martin Luthers Werke*. Briefwechsel. Weimar, 1930ff.
WA DB	D. *Martin Luthers Werke*. Deutsche Bibel. Weimar, 1906–1961.
WA TR	D. *Martin Luthers Werke*. Tischreden. Weimar, 1912–1921.

Beyond
CHARITY

Introduction
Relieving Misery, Preserving Social Order

POVERTY AND POOR PEOPLE are the subjects and generators of sharp political and social controversy in our time. This controversy is vividly expressed in the conflicting images of ex-President Jimmy Carter involved in rehabilitation of housing[1] and ex-President Ronald Reagan justifying reduction of federal support of the school lunch program on the basis that ketchup is a vegetable. These actions are symbolic of the unresolved tensions coexisting in modern social welfare: relief of misery, preservation of social order, regulation of the labor market, and mobilization of political power.[2]

Controversy over the conflicting goals of welfare and the means to attain them is by no means limited to political parties but is equally present within and between churches. Such divisions are most clearly seen on the regional and international levels of ecclesial organizations. The World Council of Churches and the Lutheran World Federation, for example, have been active for some time in development programs as well as in theological reflection

1. See Millard Fuller with Diane Scott, *No More Shacks* (Waco, Tex.: Word Books, 1986), 73ff.
2. These specific expressions of an analysis shared by various scholars are from Michael B. Katz, *In the Shadow of the Poorhouse: A Social History of Welfare in America* (New York: Basic Books, 1986). See also the works by Frances Fox Piven and Richard A. Cloward, such as *Regulating the Poor: The Functions of Public Welfare* (New York: Vintage Books, 1971) and *Poor People's Movements: Why They Succeed, How They Fail* (New York: Vintage Books, 1979).

1

on poverty and welfare.[3] Liberation theology, with its "preferential option for the poor" and its method of theological reflection from "the underside of history," has spread quickly from its initial Roman Catholic Latin American base to ecumenical if not universal acceptance.[4] These various expressions, although by no means agreed on specifics, share perspectives that reject blaming the victims for their poverty and look to structural and systemic social changes as means for developing rights for the poor and measures for preventing poverty as well as relieving misery.

Alternative ecumenical—that is, trans-ecclesial—perspectives reject calls for structural social and economic changes on the basis that each individual is self-responsible. In this view religion is to be concerned with spiritual values rather than material well-being. The more extreme expressions posit divine support for laissez-faire capitalism, with the concomitant argument for a divinely ordained cause-and-effect relationship between cultural and material prosperity and biblical obedience. The "underside" of this theology is the conviction that poverty is God's means of punishing and controlling the disobedient and heathen.[5]

In short, the question of the relationship of values, attitudes, and ideologies to both the development and evaluation of welfare policies continues to be a lively one among social scientists, philosophers, historians, and theologians.[6] The various conflicting judgments depend not only upon empirical observation but upon nontestable assumptions held by social sci-

3. See, for example, the three volumes written and edited by Julio de Santa Ana, *Good News to the Poor: The Challenge of the Poor in the History of the Church* (Geneva: World Council of Churches, 1977), *Separation without Hope? Essays on the Relation between the Church and the Poor during the Industrial Revolution and the Western Colonial Expansion* (Geneva: World Council of Churches, 1978), *Towards a Church of the Poor* (Geneva: World Council of Churches, 1979), and Béla Harmati, ed., *Christian Ethics—Property and Poverty* (Geneva: Lutheran World Federation, 1985).

4. For a brief discussion of how the spread of liberation theology has led to a new theological methodology, see Per Frostin, "The Hermeneutics of the Poor—The Epistemological 'Break' in Third World Theologies," *Studia Theologica* 39 (1985), 127–50. On the importance of historical studies with regard to the urbanization and industrialization process in Third World countries, see the comment by Bronislaw Geremek in his *Truands et misérables dans l'Europe moderne*, 1350–1600 (Paris: Gallimard, 1980), 218, 240.

5. See, for example, George Gilder, *Wealth and Poverty* (New York: Basic Books, 1981); David Chilton, *Productive Christians in an Age of Guilt-Manipulators* (Tyler, Tex.: Institute for Christian Economics, 1982); Larry Christenson, *Social Action, Jesus Style* (Minneapolis: Dimension Books, 1976). This combination of evangelical individualism and an attack on the secular humanism of governmental social welfare programs was also espoused by the popular theologian and preacher Helmut Thielicke. Cf. Warren Holleman, "Welfare Reform, Helmut Thielicke, and Secular Humanism," *Dialog* 28 (1989), 289–92. For opposing evangelical views, cf. Ronald J. Sider, *Evangelicals and Development: Toward a Technology of Social Change* (Philadelphia: Westminster Press, 1981). For a Roman Catholic argument that charity rather than structures of justice and rights should be the primary focus of Christian concern, see Gordan Graham, *The Idea of Christian Charity: A Critique of Some Contemporary Conceptions* (Notre Dame, Ind.: Univ. of Notre Dame Press, 1990).

6. See, for example, David Rochefort, "Progressive and Social Control Perspectives on

entists, policymakers, welfare workers, historians, and theologians about the nature of humans and society.[7] Our perspectives, values, and commitments are as important as our perceptions in the process of determining how poverty may be addressed.

The importance of perspective is not a modern phenomenon, but rather has been expressly present in the history of welfare since the late medieval–early modern period.[8] It was then that the relatively undifferentiated roles of family, community, church, and government with regard to welfare began to be distinguished. The major responsibility for welfare shifted from the church to governmental and economic institutions; the attitudes, values, strategies, tactics, and policies engendered by this early modern shift continue to affect the present. The attitudinal shift is reflected in the stark contrast between the medieval canonical statement that "poverty is not a kind of crime" and the early modern development of punitive houses of correction for the poor.[9]

Until recently the historical origins and development of what we today call social welfare and social work have been little studied.[10] The last two decades have seen a marked increase in studies of early modern theories on poor relief and the legislative actions of specific urban centers, but a comprehensive study is yet to be done.[11] As Thomas Riis recently stated:

If one were merely to summarize existing publications, little more than an annotated bibliography would result. On the other hand, as most publications on Early Modern poverty refer to restricted areas—usually individual towns or provinces—broader comparisons are desirable. Seldom has more than one aspect of poverty been considered, moreover, so that an understanding of the problem in all its complexity awaits an

Social Welfare," *Social Science Review* (Dec. 1981), 568–92; James Douglas, *Why Charity? The Case for a Third Sector* (Beverly Hills: Sage Publications, 1983); Robert Hartmann, ed., *Poverty and Economic Justice: A Philosophical Approach* (Ramsey, N.J.: Paulist Press, 1984); Raphael Samuel and Gareth Jones, eds., *Culture, Ideology, and Politics: Essays for Eric Hobsbawm* (London: Routledge & Kegan Paul, 1982).

7. See Nona Glazer and Carol Creedon, eds., *Children and Poverty: Some Sociological and Psychological Perspectives* (Chicago: Rand McNally, 1970), 105.

8. Volker Hunecke, "Überlegungen zur Geschichte der Armut im vorindustriellen Europa," *Geschichte und Gesellschaft* 9 (1983), 480–512. Bronislaw Geremek, *La potence ou la pitié* (Paris: Gallimard, 1987).

9. Brian Tierney, *Medieval Poor Law: A Sketch of Canonical Theory and Its Application in England* (Berkeley & Los Angeles: Univ. of California Press, 1959), 132, 11f. Cf. Gertrude Himmelfarb, *The Idea of Poverty: England in the Early Industrial Age* (New York: Knopf, 1984), 25, 536 n. 5.

10. Christoph Sachsse and Florian Tennstedt, eds., *Geschichte der Armenfürsorge in Deutschland: Vom Spätmittelalter bis zum 1. Weltkrieg* (Stuttgart: Kohlhammer, 1980), 13.

11. Thomas Fischer, *Städtische Armut und Armenfürsorge im 15. und 16. Jahrhundert* (Göttingen: Schwartz, 1979), 9ff. A similar comment about the lack of systematic comparative studies of urban poor relief is given by Robert Jütte, *Obrigkeitliche Armenfürsorge in Deutschen Reichsstädten der frühen Neuzeit* (Cologne: Böhlau, 1986), 2–3.

integrated research programme. . . . A study of Early Modern poverty dealing with *all* its major aspects would not only be fashionable, but justified,
if it combined the results already achieved with new knowledge based
on original research.[12]

I have quoted Riis not to suggest that this book will provide the "fashionable"
and "justified" study he calls for, but to emphasize the general lack of such
studies altogether.

The purpose of this study is to explore the church's contributions to the
late medieval–early modern origins of modern understandings of poverty and
welfare. I am particularly concerned with focusing on the contribution of
church and theology to this comprehensive effort, and with providing students
of the subject with resources for further study. Thus this work is divided into
two parts. The first is an attempt to provide a comprehensive and systematic
presentation of the church's contributions to the development of social welfare
in the early modern period. Part Two consists of selected primary texts that
illustrate Part One.

Goals

The narrative of Part One has a number of goals. The first is to incorporate
the material from the vast amount of individual studies on early modern poor
relief into a systematic historical account with specific reference to the church
and theology[13] from an orientation of historical theology. However, my interest
in the influence of ideas and attitudes upon the late medieval and Reformation
development of poor relief is not to be understood as a suggestion that social,
economic, and political factors and events were not also important. Clearly
it is one thing to theologize about charity or poor relief, and quite another
thing to be confronted by a diseased beggar in time of plague or an angry
group of unemployed laborers. While ideals and ideas may bend or even
topple before the winds of events, however, ideas have their own power to
influence events. This is important to state at the outset because the recent
stimulating preoccupation of the historical profession with social history has
led some historians to denigrate theology and intellectual history in the
understanding of the Reformation in particular and church history in general.
"Perhaps Reformation theology was really less the cause than the consequence

12. Riis I, vii.
13. "The study of charity is a case in which the effect of normative religious teaching
and its internalisation can be examined. The activity spurred by the resounding teaching on charity can be a measure not only of the nature and forms of understanding
and interpretation of religious ideas, but of the ability exhibited by the laity to integrate
changing circumstances of life with the prevalent moral and religious norms." Miri
Rubin, *Charity and Community in Medieval Cambridge* (Cambridge: Cambridge Univ. Press,
1987), 3.

of social change: A Christian answer to the pressing questions of the time or the legitimation of long overdue social change, the ideology of an 'early bourgeois revolution'? . . . Luther shapes the Reformation and society, but is on his part shaped by society."[14] The social historian rightly points out that the simple assumption that theological treatises, sermons, and legislation reflect what actually occurred in peoples' daily lives is a "flight from history."

"On the other hand, ideas do have consequences, and in the sixteenth century the ideas that preoccupied Europeans were in large measure religious ideas."[15] As Robert Jütte points out, it was the theologians above all who were consulted on the question of reform of poor relief in order, in the words of R. H. Tawney, "to lend a moral sanction to secular policy."[16] I would go beyond these words of Tawney to argue that in the Reformation theologians not only provided moral sanctions for secular policies, their theological imaginations helped to create and shape these policies.[17] Thus, according to Benjamin Nelson, Luther and Calvin "gave everything a new axis and a new center," thereby fundamentally affecting the structures, "decision matrices," and "very rationales" of the culture. "What matters is that Luther and Calvin cleared the way for a new *conscience*, a conscience beyond the casuistries of the *moral* conscience of the Middle Ages. . . . The result was the advance of a series of new images and institutions of individual and collective responsibility, new perceptions and types of consensual structures."[18] Similarly, the sociologist Robert Wuthnow argues that Luther "created, as it were, a *discursive field* in which to bring together in imaginative ways the practical realities of institutional life on the one hand and the ideals evident in Scripture on the other."[19]

Although my approach is not that of a social historian, the presentation in this book of the motives and theories related to late medieval and Ref-

14. Wolfgang Reinhard, "Möglichkeiten und Grenzen der Verbindung von Kirchengeschichte mit Sozial- und Wirtschaftsgeschichte," in Gerte Klingenstein & Heinrich Lutz, eds., *Spezialforschung und "Gesamtgeschichte"* (Munich: Oldenbourg, 1982), 275.
15. David Steinmetz, *Luther in Context* (Bloomington: Indiana Univ. Press, 1986), ix. Cf. also Alister McGrath, *The Intellectual Origins of the European Reformation* (Oxford: Basil Blackwell, 1987), 2; Steven Ozment's criticism of those social historians who give religious history short shrift in his "Pamphlets as a Source: Comments on Bernd Moeller's 'Stadt und Buch,' " in W. Mommson, ed., *Stadtbürgertum und Adel in der Reformation* (Stuttgart: Klett-Cotta, 1979), 47; and Steven Ozment, "The Social History of the Reformation: What Can We Learn from the Pamphlets?" in Hans-Joachim Köhler, ed., *Flugschriften als Massenmedium der Reformationszeit* (Stuttgart: Klett-Cotta, 1981), 171ff.
16. Robert Jütte, *Obrigkeitliche Armenfursorge*, 356, with reference to R. H. Tawney, *Religion and the Rise of Capitalism* (Harmondsworth, England: Pelikan, 1977), 169.
17. Himmelfarb, *Idea of Poverty*, 19, speaks of the " 'moral imagination' . . . that makes sense of reality, not by being imposed on reality (as ideology is) but by so thoroughly penetrating it that the reality has no form or shape apart from it."
18. Benjamin Nelson, *The Idea of Usury: From Tribal Brotherhood to Universal Otherhood*, 2d ed. (Chicago: Univ. of Chicago Press, 1969), 240, 242.
19. Robert Wuthnow, *Communities of Discourse: Ideology and Social Structure in the Reformation, the Enlightenment, and European Socialism* (Cambridge: Harvard Univ. Press, 1989), 134.

ormation poor relief will be supplemented by accounts of their legislative and administrative praxis. By including these legislative and administrative materials as well as their own context in pre-Reformation ideas on poverty and poor relief, I hope to approach a second goal of this study. This goal is not only to advance beyond the so-called confessional studies of the nineteenth century (which more or less focused on theological motivation of poor relief in order to prove or disprove a cause-effect relationship between the Reformation and social welfare reform), but more important, to suggest and document how faith became active in the development of political, economic, and social structures to serve the neighbor. Unless the history of the church's contributions to social welfare may be perceived in legislation and administration as well as in theological and ethical theory, those contributions will be too easily read as only an ideological superstructure employed by the powerful to justify the "really real" economic social order. Such an ideological reading would interpret the history of the church's contribution to social welfare as either illusory or as a chronology of oppressive motivations and actions contingent upon the pressure of external forces such as the fear of disease, rebellion, and loss of a cheap labor market.[20]

A third goal of this study is to provide resources for contemporary theology and the churches in the present struggle with poverty and social justice. Requests for such resources are increasingly surfacing in ecumenical conferences and publications.

> The history of the Church is the Gospel actually experienced. The experience of poor and oppressed people is especially important. Since it was to them that Jesus himself turned especially, we have here in a real sense the key to the correct interpretation of church history. *The task of the historian is to trace out the history of the Gospel in relation to the poor and oppressed.*[21]

Historical distance can be a surprising component of contemporary comprehension. Fernand Braudel, the renowned French historian, has pointed

20. "Conventional social theory errs in supposing that historical change is caused by changes in basic social, economic, and political conditions alone. There is, in fact, no such thing as social, economic, and political conditions (or forces) alone; they are always part of a context of perception and feeling. Nor are there values, ideas, beliefs—alone; as a social matter, they are always interconnected with 'material interests.' Power is also an idea; justice is also a force. Neither *causes* the other, in the physical-science sense of that word." Harold J. Berman, *Law and Revolution: The Formation of the Western Legal Tradition* (Cambridge: Harvard Univ. Press, 1983), 403.
21. Lukas Vischer, ed., *Church History in Ecumenical Perspective* (Papers and Reports of an International Ecumenical Consultation held in Basel October 12–17, 1981) (Bern: Evangelische Arbeitsstelle Oekumene Schweiz, 1982), 107; emphasis added. Cf. also Ivan Varga's point that it must be determined whether the church's efforts for the reconstruction of society are "historically grounded," in his "Capitalism and the Return to Religion," *Ecumenist* 18/4 (1980), 59.

out that if you live in a foreign city for a year you will not learn a great deal about that city. When you return home, however, you will be surprised by your increased comprehension of some of the most profound and individual characteristics of your homeland. You did not previously understand these characteristics because you were too close to them; you knew them too well. Likewise, a visit to the past provides distance and a vantage point for comprehending the present.[22] Or, in the words of another scholar, "far away facts—in history as in navigation—are more effective than near ones in giving us true bearings."[23]

To develop a sense for the tradition of the church can be both liberating and energizing. It is instructive to rediscover that many of the major theologians and church traditions we appeal to today include perspectives that are all too often found offensive when voiced by contemporary liberation theologians. Many late medieval canonists and theologians as well as the sixteenth-century Reformers clearly saw the gospel in this-worldly terms as prophetic protest against the rich and powerful and as a mandate for structural social changes that were to serve the neighbor in terms of social justice. This is not to suggest that "blame the victim" ideology did not exist in the late medieval and Reformation era, but to point out that the insight also existed that redistribution of wealth was of little use without changing the institutional structures that create poverty. Quietism, individualism, and privatism are modern distortions of the gospel, in spite of popular misinformation.

Limitations

The time parameters for this study are roughly 1300 to 1600. Although the sixteenth century will be the main focus, it will be useful to include the medieval context for Reformation attitudes, theories, and programs. These three centuries are of particular interest because, especially in the latter part of the Middle Ages, the traditional relationships between the poor and the nonpoor underwent drastic changes with regard to theories, attitudes, and the communalizing of poor relief.

Although I have made an effort to include results of secondary studies of the conditions and reactions of the poor themselves, the primary focus will be on the theoretical, legislative, and administrative perspectives of the nonpoor toward the poor.[24] One reason for this limitation is aptly summarized

22. Fernand Braudel, "History and the Social Science," in Peter Burke, ed., *Economy and Society in Early Modern Europe* (New York: Harper & Row, 1972), 24.
23. Alexander Murray, "Religion among the Poor in Thirteenth-Century France: The Testimony of Humbert de Romans," *Traditio* 30 (1974), 285.
24. The value of this orientation is discussed in Peter Matheson, "Adam's Burden: Diagnoses of Poverty in Post-Medieval Europe and the Third World Now," *Tijdschrift voor Geschiedenis* 89/2 (1976). For a recent study of the reactions of the poor to poverty, cf. Riis II.

by the Italian historian A. Sapori: "Everything concerning the poor disappears with their death, the darkness of their life finds its equivalent in oblivion."[25] Or, as stated by the renowned French scholar of poverty, Michel Mollat, "The poor have never had a say; they have always played a minor role; they have left no records."[26]

It will be helpful to refer from time to time to medieval and Reformation theories of property and to developing reactions to early capitalism, or "usury" as it was then frequently called. It is also tempting to discuss the Reformation understandings of the diaconate. But while appropriate references will be made to these aspects of the subject, they will not be my primary focus.

Sources

The primary sources include late medieval writings about poverty and the poor, pre-Reformation begging orders and legislation, the writings of Reformers and humanists, poor-relief legislation stemming from Reformers and town councils, administrative records, and the observations of eyewitnesses. Some social historians may find this "history from above" suspect. This criticism is well taken but should not be used to belittle the sources available, especially since the voices of the poor themselves continue to be so mute. The words of Gertrude Himmelfarb regarding eighteenth- and nineteenth-century sources may be applied to our concern for the medieval and early modern sources:

> The fact is that during all of the eighteenth century and well into the nineteenth, an important part of the history of the poor was in fact made by the "higher orders," by landlords and employers most obviously, but also by reformers, philanthropists, politicians, government officials, writers, economists, social critics, clergymen, doctors, magistrates, justices of the peace, and guardians of the poor. All of these impinged in myriad and momentous ways upon the lives of the poor. . . . It is surely important

25. A. Sapori, *Studi di storia economica* (*secoli XIII–XIV–XV*), vol. 1 (Firenze: Sansoni, 1955), 165, quoted by Erich Maschke in his "Die Unterschichten der mittelalterlichen Städten Deutschlands," in Erich Maschke & Jürgen Sydow, eds., *Gesellschaftlichen Unterschichten in den südwestdeutschen Städten* (Stuttgart: Kohlhammer, 1967), 4. Cf. also Wolfram Fischer, *Armut in der Geschichte* (Göttingen: Vandenhoeck & Ruprecht, 1982), 7f.
26. Michel Mollat, "The Poor in the Middle Ages: The Experience of a Research Project," in Riis I, 29. Cf. also Murray, "Religion among the Poor," 285. The lack of historical records regarding the poor persists into the nineteenth century and, some would argue, even up to the present. Hearing the voice of the poor is further complicated even today by the fact that it is not a univocal voice. Cf. Himmelfarb, *Idea of Poverty*, 14f. Even in modern times the voice of the laity is not very well heard. Cf. Clyde Griffen, "Rich Laymen and Early Social Christianity," *Church History* 36 (1967). On the other hand, scholars have attempted to reconstruct conditions by painstaking examinations of tax registers, hospital records, and demographic and dietary data.

to know what conceptions of poverty inspired their efforts and what perceptions of the poor made them think that the poor (or particular groups of the poor) could or should be reformed.[27]

Part Two of this volume consists of a selected annotated anthology of these primary sources. The purpose of the anthology is to provide a usable collection of primary sources that are otherwise widely scattered and inaccessible to English-speaking students. I hope this collection will also stimulate further interest and research.

Perspectives

Historians, theologians, and social scientists have long recognized that the sixteenth century was the watershed of poor relief. Their interest in this root of modern social welfare has led to a large number of secondary studies, many of which I utilize and refer to in this work. At the risk of oversimplification, it is useful at this point to sketch with a few examples the major orientations of the literature on this subject.

The older literature has frequently been classified as confessional because of its efforts to establish either an exclusively Protestant or Catholic origin for early modern poor relief. This confessional orientation is not necessarily limited to works from the nineteenth century.[28] A second major orientation traces poor relief to Renaissance humanism. The most recent work is that of the social historians who focus on social control as the motivation for early modern poor relief.[29]

Confessional Studies

In the late nineteenth century a wealth of studies were made on the history of poor relief. The studies explored local histories in detail and strove to be

27. Himmelfarb, Idea of Poverty, 16.
28. See, for example, Harold Grimm, "Luther's Contributions to Sixteenth Century Organization of Poor Relief," ARG 81 (1970). W. K. Jordan attributed modern welfare to English Calvinism. See his trilogy: Philanthropy in England, 1480-1660 (London: Allen & Unwin, 1959); The Charities of London, 1480–1660 (London: Allen & Unwin, 1960); and The Charities of Rural England, 1480-1660 (London: Russell Sage Foundation, 1961).
29. For useful overviews of the secondary literature, see Thomas Fischer, Städtische Armut, 261–65; Jütte, Obrigkeitliche Armenfürsorge, 31–45; Sachsse & Tennstedt, Geschichte der Armenfürsorge, 80–83; Frank Lane, "Poverty and Poor Relief in the German Church Orders of Johann Bugenhagen, 1485–1558," Ph.D. diss., Ohio State University (1973), 96–108; Elsie McKee, "John Calvin on the Diaconate and Liturgical Almsgiving," Ph.D. diss., Princeton University (1982), 112–27, since published by Librairie Droz, Geneva (1984); Lee Palmer Wandel, "Images of the Poor in Reformation Zurich," Ph.D. diss., University of Michigan (1985), 1–28, since published as Always among Us: Images of the Poor in Zwingli's Zurich (Cambridge: Cambridge Univ. Press, 1990).

comprehensive. Most of these were written by church historians who were also clergy, scholars who were motivated to present the story of the churches' care for the poor by their own contexts of developing social welfare programs. A good example of this is Uhlhorn's fundamental and still very useful study, *Die christliche Liebesthätigkeit*. Especially in France, Germany, and Italy, the churches' struggles with social problems necessarily involved relating to new social, economic, and political developments. This struggle over the character of civilization, or *Kulturkampf* as it was termed in Germany, undoubtedly confessionally colored the historical studies of poor relief. Protestant scholars viewed Luther and the Reformation as the beginning of the modern era. The tendency was thus to locate new theories and policies for social welfare in the Reformation and to disparage or deny Catholic contributions. Conversely, Catholic scholars argued for the contributions of medieval and sixteenth-century Catholics and denied the importance of the evangelical Reformers.[30] It is not surprising, then, that most of these studies tend to focus on confessionally specific theological theories for poor relief.

Protestant scholars such as Uhlhorn argued that Luther's rejection of the salvatory merit of good works cut the nerve of indiscriminate medieval almsgiving designed to spiritually benefit the giver, and thereby made possible the development of rational, communal welfare policies that were far more effective in serving the poor.[31] The Catholic scholars Georg Ratzinger and Franz Ehrle, S.J., argued to the contrary that the Reformation was the continuation of a late medieval ethical decline and that the development of urban community poor relief stemmed from ancient Catholic theology, canon law, and thirteenth-century poor orders rather than from Luther.[32] These confessional polemics not only created a good deal of heat, they also shed light on the subject of poor relief itself; in order to substantiate their respective confessional claims, the scholars had to explore the questions of influences and chronology.

Protestant scholars located the origins of early modern poor relief in German cities, especially the Lutheran Nuremberg. Catholic scholars argued for the seminal influence of the Low Countries, especially the poor-relief order

---

30. This Protestant-Catholic debate goes back at least to the seventeenth century. See Edward P. de G. Chaney, " 'Philanthropy in Italy': English Observations on Italian Hospitals, 1545–1789," in Riis I, 185, 210 n. 2.
31. Gerhard Uhlhorn, *Die christliche Liebesthätigkeit*, 3 vols. in 1, 2d ed. (Stuttgart: Gundert, 1895), 515ff.
32. Georg Ratzinger's *Geschichte der kirchlichen Armenpflege* (Freiburg im Breisgau: 1868, 1884) won the Munich Theology Faculty prize for a history of Christian poor relief. Franz Ehrle, *Beiträge zur Geschichte und Reform der Armenpflege* (Freiburg im Breisgau: 1881), and "Die Armenordnungen von Nürnberg (1522) und von Ypern I (1525)," *Historisches Jahrbuch der Görres-Gesellschaft* 9 (1888). For an overview of these and other confessionally oriented studies, see Felix Pischel, "Die ersten Armenordnungen der Reformationszeit," *Deutsches Geschichtsblätter* 17 (1916), 317–29, and Otto Winckelmann, *Das Fürsorgewesen der Stadt Strassburg vor und nach der Reformation bis zum Ausgang des sechzehnten Jahrhunderts* (Leipzig: 1922), 200ff.

of the city of Ypres, which they claimed was motivated by the work of the Catholic humanist Juan Vives, De subventione pauperum (1526). The contemporary scholarly consensus is that the spread of poor-relief reform across Europe originated in southern Germany. The reference to Ypres introduces into the discussion the question of the role of Renaissance humanism.

Renaissance Humanism

Following the earlier lead of the great Belgian historian Henri Pirenne, scholars such as Natalie Davis and Brian Pullan have emphasized the pivotal role of Erasmian humanists, lawyers, and capitalists in the reform of poor relief.[33] What was important in the early modern development of poor relief, these scholars argue, was not confessional allegiance but the urban responses to poverty informed by the humanists' sense of civic community and their rational refinements of institutions, business practices, and education.

Social History

In agreement with those scholars who focus on the contributions of Renaissance humanism to the development of civic poor relief, the social historians believe that the Reformation was at best tangential to new forms of social welfare. The social historians add the distinctive perspective that the critical factor in urban welfare programs was the increasingly perceived need to control the poor.[34]

The aim of social control is to create a deep-rooted consensus within civil society, which leads to the acceptance of the social and political

33. Henri Pirenne, Histoire de Belgique, vol. 3 (Brussels: Lamertin, 1907); Natalie Zemon Davis, "Poor Relief, Humanism, and Heresy: The Case of Lyons," Studies in Medieval and Renaissance History, vol. 5, ed. W. H. Bowsky, (Lincoln: Univ. of Nebraska Press, 1968); Brian Pullan, Rich and Poor in Renaissance Venice: The Social Institutions of a Catholic State to 1620 (Cambridge: Harvard Univ. Press, 1971); and "Catholics and the Poor in Early Modern Europe," Transactions of the Royal Historical Society, 5th Series, 26 (1976). The contemporary studies that dismiss theological influences rest their case primarily upon the studies of Davis and Pullan. Cautionary warnings have been raised against this "aconfessional" type of interpretation that downplays or brackets the role of religion. Cf. Hunecke, "Überlegungen zur Geschichte der Armut," 493; Reinhold C. Mueller, "Charitable Institutions, the Jewish Community, and Venetian Society: A Discussion of the Recent Volume by Brian Pullan," Studi Veneziani 14 (1972), 75ff.; Anton Schindling, "Die Reformation in den Reichsstädten und die Kirchengüter," in Jürgen Sydow, ed., Bürgerschaft und Kirche (Sigmarinen: Thorbecke, 1980), 87 n. 74.
34. Along with the studies of Thomas Fischer and Robert Jütte noted above, see Jütte's essay "Poor Relief and Social Discipline in Sixteenth Century Europe," European Studies Review 11 (1981), 25–52, and Thomas Brady's review of Jütte's book, in which he says, "it is surely time to lay to rest the old debate about poor relief and the Lutheran Reformation," SCJ 17/3 (1986), 391. Cf. also Uta Lindgren, "Europas Armut: Probleme, Methoden, Ergebnisse einer Untersuchungsserie," Saeculum 28 (1977), 396–418, 399–400.

order as legitimate and purposive. This was especially necessary in the sixteenth century, since the coercive means at the disposal of rulers were limited and weak.[35]

The poor and the marginalized people of the time were seen as threats to civic stability, industry, and progress. For these reasons the sixteenth-century cities developed paternalistic welfare legislation and bureaucracies to determine the residency, need, and worth of the poor. In short, the key to the fundamental change in the relationship between the poor and nonpoor was social control and discipline.[36]

In its crass presentation this social control perspective "is a peculiarly modern way of thinking, patently at variance with the beliefs most people lived with for most of history.[37]

The analysis of religious movements exclusively in and through their social contexts distorts late medieval religion. . . . The notion of religious change as merely a response to social change also handicaps the historian by foreclosing the possibility that changes in society may be adjustments to new ideas and values, that religion and ideology shape as well as reflect social experience.[38]

As manipulative as religion may seem to some later historians, contemporaries not only saw nothing amiss but actually expected the church and faith to speak and act constructively for the betterment of the community.

35. R. W. Scribner, *Popular Culture and Popular Movements in Reformation Germany* (London & Ronceverte: Hambledon Press, 1987), 177.
36. Kamen asserts that fear was the root motivation for social welfare reform. "At the roots of the new concern over poor relief lay a profound fear of the proletariat. In every case without exception, therefore, the initial steps taken by the authorities were disciplinary rather than ameliorative." Henry Kamen, *The Iron Century: Social Change in Europe 1550–1660* (New York: Praeger, 1971), 405. Lis and Soly give a more nuanced version of the same argument: "The argument that the growing efficiency of social policy was the result of religious or moral motivations is unsound. It is not that sixteenth-century reformers and eighteenth-century philosophers exercised no influence upon poor relief; but in most cases, their ideas were only put into practice when they could be 'translated' into economic or political terms, that is, when the trinity of charity–control–labor regulation coincided with the real or imagined interests of employers and authorities." Catherina Lis and Hugo Soly, *Poverty and Capitalism in Pre-Industrial Europe* (Atlantic Highlands, N.J.: Humanities Press, 1979), 221–22; cf. also 92–94.
37. Himmelfarb, *Idea of Poverty*, 23–24; cf. also 29, 32–33.
38. Steven Ozment, "Social History of the Reformation," 175. Cf. also Wolfgang Rochler, *Martin Luther und die Reformation als Laienbewegung* (Wiesbaden: Steiner, 1981), 70. A recent strong assertion of the role of religion in shaping social and economic history is Boyd Hilton, *The Age of Atonement: The Influence of Evangelicalism on Social and Economic Thought, 1795–1865* (New York: Clarendon Press, 1988).

Whether one endorses or takes issue with any of these interpretive perspectives, it is important to realize that there are no presuppositionless approaches to this material. The scholar who believes religion is an epiphenomenon to social and economic phenomena will read the data differently than will one who believes religious commitment may motivate and create social change.[39] My own orientation supports the importance of religion for social change. Thus it should not be surprising if I find the interpretations of some social historians to be unnecessarily reductionistic. I am convinced that theology does have social implications—not all of which may be socially constructive, I hasten to add. Therefore, I hope to demonstrate the coherence of social reform with theology.[40] I will strive to allow the sixteenth-century documents to speak for themselves. This is another reason many of them are included in Part Two of this volume.

39. A classic divergence on this point with regard to the rise of capitalism in the sixteenth century is that of Marx and Weber. See, for example, H. R. Trevor-Roper, *Religion, the Reformation, and Social Change* (London: Macmillan, 1967), 4f.; Ephraim Fischoff, "The Protestant Ethic and the Spirit of Capitalism: The History of a Controversy," and Sidney Burrell, "Calvinism, Capitalism, and the Middle Classes: Some Afterthoughts on an Old Problem," in S. N. Eisenstadt, ed., *The Protestant Ethic and Modernization: A Comparative View* (New York: Basic Books, 1968).
40. This felicitous phrasing comes from McKee, "John Calvin on the Diaconate," 126. Eisenstadt, *Protestant Ethic*, 3–45, speaks of the "transformative effect" of theology.

Part One

Reformation Initiatives
for the
POOR

Chapter 1

Poverty and Charity in the Middle Ages

EVERY ATTEMPT to present a comprehensive or encyclopedic description of medieval conceptions, attitudes, and realities of property and poverty faces a number of frustrations.[1] The sources allow only a sporadic and disconnected insight into the social, economic, and legal problematic of the historical development of the acquisition, use, and passing on of property. General assessments and evaluations cannot comfortably account for regional differences. The great variations of poverty and its perceptions throughout Europe sometimes complement each other and sometimes conflict to the point of cognitive dissonance. The Middle Ages is also a long time period, and it is not always possible to support developmental perspectives by intensive studies of a particular locale and time.[2] In short, the origins and development of medieval conceptions and perceptions of poverty and the poor were and continue to be such controversial as well as complex subjects that univocal statements and judgments must be treated with caution.

It is not my intention in the following chapter to present a comprehensive overview of poverty and property in the Middle Ages. The purpose of this chapter is rather to provide the context for the focus on early modern contributions to poor relief and social welfare. With this purpose in mind, I have

1. Cf. the comments by Hans-Jürgen Goertz, "Eigentum: Mittelalter," in TRE 9 (Berlin: de Gruyter, 1982), 417.
2. The only modern comprehensive study of poverty and the poor in the Middle Ages is Michel Mollat's *Les pauvres au Moyen Age* (Paris: Hachette, 1978), which synthesizes fourteen years of local studies and researches done in connection with his Sorbonne seminar.

sought to sort out the following particular facets of the medieval complex of concepts, realities, and perceptions of poverty and the poor: (1) the concept of poverty as expressed in medieval vocabulary; (2) the theology or ideology of poverty; (3) descriptions of the levels and extent of poverty; (4) poverty and urban development; and (5) medieval attitudes and responses to the poor.

The Concept of Poverty

The terms "poor" and "poverty" are notoriously elastic words. In fact, these terms are very difficult to define. Wealth is measurable but poverty is intangible. Although wealth and poverty are relative to each other, it is much easier to comprehend the former than the latter. The poor person is not only the individual bereft of the means of existence, but also the weakest person in a group or society, whether it be in terms of money, privilege, or prestige.[3] Throughout the Middle Ages the terms "poor" and "poverty" were stretched to encompass a multitude of virtues as well as vices. Without some working definitions of these terms it will be difficult to sort out the various theological, spiritual, social, economic, and political associations that cluster around them.

Early modern concepts of poverty and attitudes toward the poor were strongly influenced by the received tradition of the Middle Ages. This received tradition was itself profoundly influenced by the Bible. The Middle Ages were not only informed by the Bible but accepted it as the norm, law, and regulation of human life. "When confronted by a phenomenon, medieval men would seek its model in the Bible."[4] The "red thread of the Bible" not only bound and united the various social structures into a unity but gave them permanence and stability.[5] Such unity was not uniformity. The medieval period included a number of concepts of poverty and the poor. These varying concepts were specific as to time and context but were not limited to particular situations. Thus a concept or attitude might fade into the background only to reemerge later. What is important for our purposes is not the biblical text itself but the medieval reading of that text. The Middle Ages provided the conceptual capital for the Reformation struggles to understand and respond

3. Bronislaw Geremek, "Renfermement des pauvres en Italie (XIV–XVIIᵉ siècle): Remarques préliminaires," *Histoire économique du monde méditerranéen 1450–1650* (Toulouse: Privat, 1973), 205.

4. Jacques Le Goff, *Your Money or Your Life: Economy and Religion in the Middle Ages* (New York: Zone Books, 1988), 21.

5. Maria Lodovica Arduini, "Biblische Kategorien und mittelalterliche Gesellschaft: 'Potens' und 'Pauper' bei Rupert von Deutz und Hildegard von Bingen (XI bzw. XII Jh.)," in Albert Zimmermann, ed., *Soziale Ordnungen im Selbstverständnis des Mittelalters*, MM 12/2 (Berlin: de Gruyter, 1980), 469. Cf. the classic work by Beryl Smalley, *The Study of the Bible in the Middle Ages* (Notre Dame: Univ. of Notre Dame Press, 1964).

to poverty and the poor. Mollat refers to this as the permanence at the most profound level of a "collective *mentalité*."[6]

The conceptual components of this collective *mentalité* created a large vocabulary that included a wealth of terms referring to spiritual, moral, and social conditions.[7] The qualifying function of these words preceded their substantive use. At first poverty designated the quality and then the condition of a person, without regard to social estate. Thus a man, a woman, a priest, a knight, or a peasant could be spoken of as poor when perceived to be suffering something with regard to the normal condition of his or her respective social position. But the relativity of poverty—one is always more or less poor than another—led to increasing ambiguity in the use of the word.

When an adjective assumes the status of a noun, the usage corresponds to the establishment of a category, an abstraction. The "poor" evoked images of affliction, the state of that affliction, feelings of compassion or horror, and eventually fear of social disturbance, even revolt.[8] The development of the vocabulary for poverty and the poor reflects the historical development of poverty itself. For destitution in general Latin includes the words *egens*, *egenus* (needy, destitute), *indigens* (in want), *inops* (helpless through poverty), *insufficiens*, *mendicus* (beggar), and *miser* (unfortunate and needy); for lack of food, *esuriens* (a craving hunger), *famelicus* (famished person); for lack of clothing, *nudus*, *pannosus* (ragged, tattered); other vocabulary covers physical, mental, familial, and social adversities. Terms meaning "pitiable" or "wretched" (*miserabilis*, *miserabilis persona*) initially had a nuance of compassion.

German as well as the Romance languages had versions of the Latin *pauper verecundus*,[9] the shamefaced poor who were too timid or ashamed to beg in public; these people received a certain admiration for their discretion. This category illustrates the relativity of late medieval and early modern poverty, as well as the potential for anachronism in contemporary historical study. For example, the *poveri vergognosi* of fourteenth- and fifteenth-century Italy were "poor" because they had suffered a loss of status, not because they were indigent or existentially poor.

> Poverty did not mean misery, the lawyers said, "but a necessity of those things required to live rightly." Even with alimentation, "unless he has

6. Michel Mollat, "La notion de pauvreté au Moyen Age: position de problèmes," *Revue d'histoire de l'Eglise de France* 70 (1966), 23. For a brief discussion of the origin and problems of this term, collective *mentalité*, see Himmelfarb, *Idea of Poverty*, 11.

7. A list of the key Latin words and their opposites is given in appendix 3 of Mollat, vol. 2, 841–42. For much of the following I am using Mollat's "Introduction" to his *Pauvres au Moyen Age*, 9–21.

8. On the poor and social rebellion, see Michel Mollat & Philippe Wolff, *The Popular Revolutions of the Late Middle Ages* (London: Allen & Unwin, 1973); Norman Cohn, *The Pursuit of the Millennium* (New York: Harper & Row, 1961).

9. German: *verschämten Armen*; Italian: *poveri vergognosi*; French: *le pauvre honteux*. Such persons were also known as "house poor" and "deserving poor."

enough to live well and blessedly, he is called poor." There was a difference between indigence (*egestas*) and poverty. The first lacked food, the second that necessary to live correctly. "He who has no goods at all is said to be in the most extreme poverty." With this legal terminology in mind, we can grasp the significance of references in testaments and communal laws to persons "not so much in poverty but in the greatest misery," "not so much poor as in extreme necessity," for what they are: not rhetoric, but important operative distinctions in everyday life.[10]

Such an operative distinction was, however, a distinction between the "worthy" and the "unworthy" poor. Besides the urban elites who had fallen on hard times, the great majority of the "worthy" poor were those in the classic categories delineated in the Bible: widows, orphans, and the sick. The "unworthy" poor, the "useless" poor, were those perceived as vagabonds and healthy beggars unwilling to work. These latter persons became the subject of late medieval beggar literature.[11]

Various sets of antonyms expressed the social situation of the poor person. The general but pervasive opposition was, of course, rich-poor (*dives-pauper*). The more specific oppositions indicated varying social and economic conditions. Powerful-poor (*potens-pauper*), forceful-poor (*miles-pauper*), and citizen-poor (*civis-pauper*) correspond to social, military, and urban weakness—that is, inability to attain the respective rights, values, and positions that give a person status in society.

"Pauper" in the above antinomies does not have the contemporary sense of material destitution, but rather indicates an inferior position. In the early Middle Ages, the poor were those who needed the defense of the powerful. Although it is anachronistic, the term "lower class" could be used here, especially when *pauperes* is modified by *omnes*. In other words, the poor were those exposed to the clutches of the powerful. In later medieval developments, the poor were those who were defenseless before the military and those who lacked the rights of citizens.[12]

10. Richard C. Trexler, "Charity and the Defense of Urban Elites in the Italian Communes," in Frederic C. Jaher, ed., *The Rich, the Well Born, and the Powerful: Elites and Upper Classes in History* (Urbana: Univ. of Illinois Press, 1973), 72. This view of poverty is common among the theologians as well as the canon lawyers. Cf., for example, the excerpts from Francisco de Vitoria's (c. 1480–1546) discussion on almsgiving from his commentary on Thomas's *Summa* in Walter Shewring, ed., *Rich and Poor in Christian Tradition* (London: Barnes, Oates & Washbourne, 1948), 171–78.
11. See Hunecke, "Überlegungen zur Geschichte," 494–97.
12. For a description and discussion of the complexities of these social relationships, consult the articles by Karl Bosl: "Potens und Pauper: Begriffsgeschichtliche Studien zur gesellschaftlichen Differenzierung im frühen Mittelalter zum 'Pauperismus' des Hochmittelalters," in his *Frühformen der Gesellschaft im mittelalterlichen Europa* (Munich: Oldenbourg, 1964); "Gesellschaftsentwicklung 500–900," and "Gesellschaftsentwicklung 900–1350," in *Handbuch der deutschen Wirtschafts- und Sozialgeschichte*, vol. 1. (Stuttgart: Union Verlag, 1971).

The above vocabulary is descriptive of those who were involuntarily poor. The discussion of the concepts and descriptions of poverty in the Middle Ages is complicated by the application of biblical vocabulary to those in certain conditions of weakness (such as widows and orphans) as well as to those who voluntarily chose poverty (such as monastics and mendicants). Further, a growing class of outcast beggars and "dishonorable" people arose in the later Middle Ages.[13]

Voluntary poverty is synonymous with humility and renunciation, and thus accompanies charity to the top of the virtues.[14] The title of *pauper Christi*, the poor of Christ, was originally related to the monks who had voluntarily chosen poverty for the love of God, but it also came to be applied to the involuntary poor as an expression of respect for the image of the humiliated Christ present in their lives. The concept of condescendence thus has theological as well as social connotations. But the condescendence suggested by the diminutive forms of *pauperculus* and *paupertinus* could also lead to the condescension of disdain. It was then only a matter of degree to move from disdain to scorn to repulsion.

The humility of the poor was thus not consistently related to the humility seen by the theologians as a biblical virtue, as, for example, expressed in the Magnificat. The weakness of the poor was seen as approximate to the vulgarity of the peasant, the *ignobilis* of lowly origin; the *vilis* of commonness became vileness. In fact, "pauper" at times became a synonym for *agricola* or *laborator*, those who wrested their living from the soil or day by day by their labor. The term "poor laborer" summed up the condition of those who struggled for their daily bread, uncertain of the future and vulnerable to calamity. The poor—dirty, ill-smelling, and in rags—became repugnant (*abjectus*). By the twelfth century such miserable persons were called the *pauperes*, distinguished from the *egeni*, the traditional biblical poor consisting of widows, orphans, and pilgrims. The poor in this sense were those suffering from a variety of miseries for whom material aid was identified with the demands of justice. Those termed *indigentes*, in contrast, were regarded as having a deficiency of character.

The Latin formulations and their translations continued to retain at least some expression of the fundamental notion and spirit of charity. "Pauper" and "poor" continued through the Middle Ages to have a religious connotation, but by the fourteenth century the growing vernacular vocabulary for the disinherited was characterized by a degradation of this sense. Terms designating the beggar were now charged with the presumption of laziness

13. See Franz Irsigler, "Bettler und Dirnen in der städtischen Gesellschaft des 14.–16. Jahrhunderts," in Riis II; and Franz Irsigler & Arnold Lassotta, *Bettler und Gaukler, Dirnen und Henker: Randgruppen und Aussenseiter in Köln 1300–1600* (Cologne: Graven Verlag, 1984).
14. Marie-Louise Théral, "Caritas et paupertas dans l'iconographie médiévale inspirée de la psychomachie," in Mollat, vol. 1, 295–317.

and idleness. Increasing efforts were made to distinguish the able-bodied beggar from the truly needy, the "unworthy" poor from the "worthy" poor. The suspicion of delinquency and criminality that weighed on the socially marginal multiplied the categories of vagabonds and wandering beggars.

"A poor man is a person who, on a permanent or temporary basis, lives in a state of weakness, dependency and humiliation, characterized by being deprived of the means (variable according to period and society) of power and respect: money, relations, knowledge, physical strength, intellectual ability, freedom and personal dignity. He is a man who lives from day to day, unable to improve his condition by himself." This definition can include all those who have been cheated of their rights, social rejects, misfits and outcasts. Nor does it exclude those who, from ascetic or mystical ideals, wanted to isolate themselves, and out of devotion chose to live in poverty among the poor.[15]

Thus the term "poverty" lacks precision, and now as before it is a fluid and ambiguous term; it is, among other things, a judgment formed by the spirit of the observer. In the absence of universal objective criteria, many different situations may be comprehended as poverty: begging, indigence, impoverishment, social subordination, political or military impotence. But the most fundamental reality of poverty, that which has awakened most consciences across the centuries and which can be defined with the most precision, is indigence. The etymology of the term "indigence" denotes the lack of necessities for survival, the inability to obtain minimal nourishment, clothing, and lodging.[16]

Theology and Poverty

One of the theological problems that arose in the sociology of the early church was not poverty but wealth. As middle- and upper-class people entered the early Christian community, the obvious bias of the gospel toward the poor raised the question, so succinctly expressed by the famous sermon of Clement of Alexandria: "How is the rich man to be saved?"[17] The answer was: by giving alms to the needy. This seemingly simple response drew upon a selection of biblical passages that contributed to an ideology of poverty with social as well as theological significance for the Middle Ages.

15. Mollat, "The Poor in the Middle Ages," in Riis I, 31–32.
16. Charles-M. de la Roncière, "Pauvres et pauvreté à Florence au XIVᵉ siècle," in Mollat, vol. 2, 662.
17. Clement of Alexandria (c. 150–c. 215), "Who Is the Rich Man That Shall Be Saved?" in *Ante-Nicene Fathers*, vol. 2 (Grand Rapids, Mich.: Eerdmans, 1956).

I use the term "ideology" to indicate that by the early medieval period the Christian faith had come to serve as a "cognitive and moral map of the universe."[18] This development is not unique to Christianity, for religion has traditionally functioned this way. The sociologist Peter Berger claims that every human society is involved in an ongoing task of structuring a meaningful world for itself. Faced by the constant possibility of personal and cultural collapse into chaos, humankind has perpetually grounded social theories and structures in the cosmos, thereby giving ontological status to its institutions. "Put differently, religion is the audacious attempt to conceive of the universe as being humanly significant."[19] In the Middle Ages this audacity was realized by the church, which as "an international society with an international center of government"[20] legitimated and sanctified life and society through theology and sacraments. This relationship of the heavenly city to the earthly city is the expression of "the urgent medieval belief that there must be some agency through which the divine order is brought into the human order, by which the divine law becomes positive legal codes."[21]

The architect of the theological perspective dominant through the Middle Ages was Saint Augustine (354-430). His doctrine of charity became the heart of medieval Christianity. Charity or love directed toward God is the "motion of the soul to enjoy God for his own sake and one's self and the neighbor for the sake of God." Cupidity, that is, love directed away from God, is the "motion of the soul bent upon enjoying one's self, the neighbor, and creatures without reference to God."[22] For Augustine, love not only makes the world go 'round; love sustains the entire cosmos. It is even the essential ingredient in sin, which is misdirected love. Thus he defines the two cities, the heavenly and the earthly: "Two cities have been formed by two loves: the earthly by the love of self, even to the contempt of God; the heavenly by the love of God, even to the contempt of self."[23]

At the risk of oversimplification, the complex theology of Augustine may

18. *International Encyclopedia of the Social Sciences* (New York: Macmillan, 1968), vol. 7, 69.
19. Peter Berger, *The Sacred Canopy: Elements of a Sociological Theory of Religion* (New York: Anchor Books, 1969), 28.
20. Brian Tierney, *Medieval Poor Law: A Sketch of Canonical Theory and Its Application in England* (Berkeley & Los Angeles: Univ. of California Press, 1959), 3.
21. Michael Wilks, *The Problem of Sovereignty in the Later Middle Ages* (London: Cambridge Univ. Press, 1963), 163–64, 469–70. See also Heiko A. Oberman, "The Shape of Late Medieval Thought: The Birthpangs of the Modern Era," ARG 64 (1973), 27.
22. Augustine, *De doctrina Christiana*, PL 34:72. "In an age when culture was thought of exclusively in terms of the understanding of a classical text, the Bible was nothing less than the basis of a 'Christian culture,' a *doctrina Christiana*." Peter Brown, *Augustine of Hippo* (Berkeley: Univ. of California Press, 1969), 263.
23. Augustine, *The City of God* (New York: Modern Library, 1950), 477. Cf. D. W. Robertson, "The Doctrine of Charity in Medieval Literary Gardens," *Speculum* 26 (1951), 24: "These two loves, Charity and cupidity, are the two poles of the medieval Christian scale of values. For Saint Augustine and for his successors among medieval exegetes, the whole aim of Scripture is to promote Charity and to condemn cupidity."

be thought of diagrammatically in terms of ascent.[24] Augustine believed in a hierarchy of being, the apex of which is God, the highest good, being itself. This metaphysic conceives of God as the eternal, absolute, immutable being, and thereby conceives of all beings below God as relative, temporal, transient, and incomplete. Thus Augustine begins his autobiography with the confession: "Thou madest us for Thyself, and our heart is restless, until it repose in Thee."[25] This theology of ascent is graphically expressed in his image of the traveler, journeying to his or her homeland, who is in danger of enjoying the journey itself and thereby forgetting the destination. In other words, we may use the world as an aid on the way of love up to God; but if we enjoy the world, misdirected love (*cupiditas*) drives us downward away from God to the earth.[26] The earthly city is a foreign land; here we are pilgrims, travelers on our way to the heavenly city, our homeland. In this theology, in capsule form, the great medieval themes of pilgrimage, renunciation, alienation, and asceticism are incorporated into the heart of medieval Christian theology— love. Thus alienation and order are intimately related in the fundamental theology of the West. In a real sense, the story of medieval development may be described as the history of efforts to realize in society the right relationship of alienation and order.[27]

Love of the earthly city leads to disaffection from the heavenly city; and love of the heavenly city frees one from the earthly city. Here the biblical suspicion of riches[28] receives systematic theological articulation. Pride and covetousness are the major vices; humility and almsgiving are the major virtues. "It is enough," says Augustine, "if riches do not destroy their possessors; it is enough if they do them no harm; help them they cannot."[29] While this is a modification of the earlier claim of Tertullian (d.c. 225) that God always justifies the poor and damns the rich,[30] this statement nevertheless is an endorsement of poverty as the favored status for the Christian life. This concept found its most startling expression in Francis of Assisi (c. 1181–

24. For a classic exposition of Augustine with this orientation, see Anders Nygren, *Agape and Eros*, (Philadelphia: Westminster Press, 1953).

25. Augustine, *The Confessions of Saint Augustine* (New York: Collier Books, 1966), 11.

26. Augustine, *De doctrina Christiana*, PL 34:20–21 (bk. 1, chap. 4).

27. "The concepts of *via, viator* [way, wayfarer], the related ones of *peregrinus, peregrinatio* [pilgrim, pilgrimage], and of *alienus, alienatio* [foreign, alienation] on the one hand, and of *ordo, ordinare* [order, to set in order] on the other, are quite essential ingredients of early Christian and medieval thought and life." Gerhart B. Ladner, "Homo Viator: Medieval Ideas on Alienation and Order," *Speculum* 42 (1967), 233.

28. For example, Mark 10:25; Matt. 19:24; Luke 18:25; Luke 6:20; Matt. 5:3; James 5:1-3.

29. Augustine, *Enarrationes in Psalmos* 85:3, PL 36–37:1083. See Shewring, *Rich and Poor in Christian Tradition*, 20.

30. See F. Graus, "The Late Medieval Poor in Town and Countryside," in Sylvia Thrupp, ed., *Change in Medieval Society* (New York: Appleton-Century-Crofts, 1964), 315.

1226), whose life was not an imitation of the real poor of his time but rather his own stylization of this apostolic model.[31]

The monastic movement both interiorized and projected upon society the human condition of pilgrim and wayfarer. The genius of the Benedictine Rule was its emphasis upon stability. In its ascetic withdrawal from this world, the monastic community provided a glimpse of divine order through its highly ordered life and liturgy. Yet every pilgrim who appears at the door of the monastery must be received as though he or she were Christ himself.[32] "Early medieval saints' lives show very clearly that genuine monastic, and generally speaking, ascetic *peregrinatio* [pilgrimage] was highly esteemed as a radically Christian way of life, which possessed its own *stabilitas* [stability]."[33] There is a danger inherent in a social ideology that prizes alienation even when it is contained in religious and ethical structures; what is a virtue for the orthodox may easily become a vice (or worse) for the disillusioned, demoralized, and rebellious. "Any view of the culture and the social psychology of preindustrial Europe cannot neglect the tensions which Christianity itself engendered in instructing the faithful that this present world and the ideal Christian society were out of joint, and that men were created for something far, far better."[34]

The monastic efforts to respond to these inherent social tensions highlighted by the gospel varied in response to actual social developments. The Benedictine response was oriented to tension between the powerful and the weak, a social phenomenon predominant in preurban agricultural and feudal society. The major vice was perceived to be pride, often associated with power and status. The Benedictine order, most of whose members came from the nobility, sought protection against the sin of pride by abandoning worldly power. Their voluntary poverty was thus not material but rather spiritual in nature; in fact, Benedictine monasteries were frequently comfortable and occasionally magnificent. This material comfort was not seen as a contradiction to their vows, because the monks' function was prayerful struggle against the violent forces of their age. Knightly violence was ritualized and thus restrained by the monastic liturgy that spiritually sanctioned Christian warfare.

With the economic and social changes accelerating in the eleventh century, however, came concomitant changes in the Christian ideals and vices. The major vice was seen now as avarice rather than pride; consequently, material poverty was more highly regarded than spiritual poverty. The mendicant movements associated with men like Waldo and Francis emphasized the abandonment of material wealth and literal rather than spiritual pilgrimage and wandering. As the Benedictines sought protection for themselves

31. See Uta Lindgren, "Europas Armut: Probleme, Methoden, Engebnisse einer Untersuchingsserie," *Saeculum* 28 (1977): 397.
32. See Mollat, "The Poor in the Middle Ages," in Riis I, 46.
33. Ladner, "*Homo Viator*," 242.
34. David Herlihy, "Alienation in Medieval Culture and Society," in Frank Johnson, ed., *Alienation: Concept, Term, and Meanings* (New York: Seminar Press, 1973), 126–27.

and their society from pride, so the mendicants sought protection for themselves and their society from avarice. As the Benedictines sought within a feudal context to develop a moral theology in response to power and violence, so the Franciscans and mendicants sought within an urban context to develop a moral theology in response to the developing money economy and to aid townsmen toward a vision of Christian citizenship. The commercial revolution of 1000 to 1350 effected a theological development in the understanding of poverty and its religious significance.[35]

This revolutionary potential lay dormant for the first millennium of the Middle Ages, probably because the society was predominantly rural and agricultural, and thanks to an ideology of poverty that provided a place in society for the involuntary poor. But the urban commercial revolution created great spiritual anxiety and guilt among the new self-assertive urban merchants and laity now involved in the cash economy that endangered their souls. The dictum of canon law that "a merchant is rarely or never able to please God"[36] was clearly not an endorsement of the new social realities. It was to the spiritual needs of the wealthy bourgeois and struggling artisans, not to the poor, that the Dominicans and Franciscans, respectively, addressed their preaching and theology. The mendicants developed a theology of poverty that allowed "considerable maneuverability for the laity, who in their daily lives constantly move back and forth between spiritual aspiration and urban-commercial involvement."[37] Thus it may be ironical but it is not accidental that not long after his death, Saint Francis was perceived as the patron and protector of merchants.[38] "The new preaching was an attempt to provide an ... urban laity with the tools to work for their own salvation."[39]

The ideology of poverty was a theological construct that made charity a condition of salvation. Later scholasticism gave this epigrammatic formulation in the phrase, "faith formed by charity." Even before such theological precision, the early church was developing a theological and social perspective that included a symbiotic relationship between rich and poor. This symbiosis was vividly expressed in the second-century similitude of the vine and the sturdy elm tree. The huge elm itself bears no fruit. The vine, growing along

35. See Lester K. Little's writings on this important monastic shift: "Pride Goes Before Avarice: Social Change and the Vices in Latin Christendom," *American Historical Review* 76/1 (1971); "L'utilité sociale de la pauvreté volontaire," in Mollat, vol. 1; "Evangelical Poverty, the New Money Economy and Violence," in David Flood, ed., *Poverty in the Middle Ages* (Werl: Dietrich-Coelde, 1975); and *Religious Poverty and the Profit Economy in Medieval Europe* (Ithaca, N.Y.: Cornell Univ. Press, 1976); see also Bernd Moeller, "The Town in Church History," in Derek Baker, ed., *The Church in Town and Countryside* (Oxford, England: Blackwell, 1979), 261ff.
36. Little, *Religious Poverty*, 38.
37. Daniel Lesnick, *Preaching in Medieval Florence: The Social World of Franciscan and Dominican Spirituality* (Athens: Univ. of Georgia Press, 1989), 149; cf. also 41, 130, 174–78.
38. Little, *Religious Poverty*, 217.
39. Lesnick, *Preaching in Medieval Florence*, 37.

the ground, bears only poor fruit that is easily crushed underfoot. But when the elm supports the vine, the vine is able to bear rich fruit.[40]

Biblical passages, especially from such popular apocryphal writings as Tobit and Sirach, provided warrants for the redemptive significance of charity. In these passages almsgiving and charity are presented as not only a kind of investment in heaven but even a remedy for sin. Tobit advocates almsgiving as a way of "laying up a good treasure for yourself against the day of necessity. For charity delivers from death and keeps you from entering the darkness; and for all who practice it charity is an excellent offering in the presence of the Most High" (4:9-11). "For almsgiving delivers from death, and it will purge away every sin" (12:9). Sirach, which by the third century was so esteemed by the Latin church that it came to be known as Ecclesiasticus, provided what must certainly be one of the more memorable passages: "Water extinguishes a blazing fire: so almsgiving atones for sin" (3:30). Ecclesiasticus further warns against withholding from the poor because God hears the prayers and curses of the poor (4:1-6). The religious significance of poverty is also succinctly expressed in the verse, "A man may be prevented from sinning by his poverty, so when he rests he feels no remorse" (20:21).[41]

The power these verses exerted on the medieval mind was enhanced by the New Testament condemnations of the wealthy and the exhortations to discipleship that urge giving up everything to follow Jesus. The saying attributed to Jesus that "it is easier for a camel to go through the eye of a needle than for someone who is rich to enter the kingdom of God," is, of course, well known (Matt. 19:24; Mark 10:25; Luke 18:25). Another famous Gospel story, overworked by the medieval clergy, tells of the rich young man who asks Jesus what he must do to be saved. Jesus tells him to sell all he has, give the proceeds to the poor, and follow Jesus (Mark 10:17-21). Of course, Jesus' mandates were not always well received in the Middle Ages, but since the medieval person was ultimately concerned about salvation, these and similar passages were taken quite seriously.

The symbiotic relationship between rich and poor that developed from various biblical passages and from the writings of the church fathers included the following components: The poor are favored in God's sight, for God has specially chosen the poor for his own people. Indeed, God himself is among the poor, for God humbled himself in the incarnation to become a fellow pilgrim and wayfarer. Wealth is a danger to salvation, but this danger is

40. "The Shepherd," *Ante-Nicene Fathers*, vol. 2 (Grand Rapids, Mich.: Eerdmans, 1956), 32.
41. These verses are representative of a wider literature concerned with poverty and almsgiving. The quotations are from *The Oxford Annotated Bible with the Apocrypha*, RSV (New York: Oxford Univ. Press, 1962). Renaissance humanists found in these verses a means for reconciling the Christian faith with classical antiquity, and a support for their argument that poverty is necessary for civic virtue. See Hans Baron, "Franciscan Poverty and Civic Wealth as Factors in the Rise of Humanistic Thought," *Speculum* 13/1 (1938).

effectively overcome through almsgiving. By giving alms to the poor, the rich atone for their sins and receive in return the intercessory prayers of the poor.

Almsgiving may atone for other sins beyond the burden of wealth, as the following medieval sermon illustration (reputed to be based on an account from Gregory the Great) suggests. An unchaste man was generous to the poor. Upon his death, he, like all adulterers, was compelled to cross a slippery bridge suspended over a bottomless sea of sulphur and pitch in which the devil swam like a frog in a filthy pond. Like everyone else in this class of sinners, the man slipped and fell. Two angels grasped him by the hands that had given alms, and drew him upward. The devil, however, grabbed him elsewhere and attempted to drag him down. The story, pointedly, does not tell who won the struggle.[42]

This theology of poverty to a certain extent associated its victims with a sort of spiritual order that is inconceivable apart from an economy of salvation in the community of saints. Through its function of suffering, poverty acquired a social dimension otherwise reserved for the rich. This is the key to the thoughts and attitudes of the twelfth century with regard to poverty and the poor. Most of the authors of the time appear to consider the poor to be in service to the rich, created for their salvific function. Many tracts, letters, and sermons speak of works of mercy under the generic name of "alms." The role of the poor is to receive because the gift is an obligation.

Thus the poor person is a privileged creditor. Each person must give according to his or her means and estate. The poor become an object of love, of charity. The rich, whether their wealth be in the form of money, office, power, or knowledge, are to serve the poor. The humiliation of poverty is a sign representing the humiliation of Christ. A familiar theme becomes that of the poor as representatives of God as Judge. So Peter Lombard insisted on the satisfaction role of charity, which extinguishes sin.[43] The poor person is considered a born intercessor with God, a sort of concierge of paradise. Christ was incarnated anew in the poor. The popularity of Saint Martin of Tours, whose iconography was widespread, reflects this theme. Bishop Thierry of Amiens, in consecrating the church of Saint Martin aux Jumeaux, recalled the saint who had clothed Christ under the guise of a poor person. The poor person is not only the image of Christ the Judge and of Christ the Redeemer,

---

42. H. Hering, "Die Liebesthätigkeit der deutschen Reformation," *Theologische Studien und Kritiken* 56 (1883), 680–81.

43. Thomas dealt with almsgiving in his section on charity, but later theologians and ethicists included it under the topics of the virtues and penance. Cf. Thomas Aquinas, *Summa Theologiae* (New York: McGraw-Hill; London: Eyre & Spottiswoode, 1975), vol. 34; and Gerhard Uhlhorn, "Vorstudien zu einer Geschichte der Liebesthätigkeit im Mittelalter," *Zeitschrift für Kirchengeschichte* 4 (1881), 67–69. Uhlhorn related the view of the meritoriousness of alms to a false concept of property (p. 52), whereas Hering saw the ascetic orientation of medieval ethics as the root of that concept of property (Hering, "Die Liebesthätigkeit," 678).

but also of the living and present Christ. This conviction is what informs the formula of the Hospitalers, "the poor are our Lords."

The vocation of the poor is summarized in a sermon by Alain of Lille in 1198: Christ cannot live among the prelates who dwell in simony. He is refused refuge among the knights who shelter plunder. There is no lodging for him among the citizens who practice usury. He is rejected by the merchants who are dishonest. There is no place for him in the community because it is ruled by thievery. Where then shall Christ dwell? Only among the poor of Christ, of whom it is said: Blessed are the poor in spirit.[44]

The medieval preachers and theologians did not hesitate to refer to this relationship of the rich to the poor as a commercial transaction—the poor carry the riches of the wealthy on their backs to heaven. The theologian of the medieval church, Augustine, had stated:

> If our possessions are to be carried away, let us transfer them to a place where we shall not lose them. The poor to whom we give alms! With regard to us, what else are they but porters through whom we transfer our goods from earth to heaven? Give away your treasure. Give it to a porter. He will bear to heaven what you give him on earth.[45]

The motivating power of this "higher hedonism" was not lost on the countless preachers and theologians of succeeding generations who were concerned to promote almsgiving. So, for example, Giulio Folco, a sixteenth-century member of a Roman confraternity, exhorted his confreres to remember their own souls by giving alms. "*Elemosina* [almsgiving] was an easy way to salvation; our treasures can be placed in heaven through the hands of the poor, and we can leave to our children a great patrimony—the piety and merit of alms-giving."[46]

> If giving alms helped to wash away sin, then helping the poor was a way for the wealthy to gain salvation. Just as the confraternity was a mutual aid organization that provided insurance against a sudden plunge from affluence to poverty, so it was also, through the opportunity to give to the poor, a means of acquiring insurance for the life eternal.... [It] promised to that member who did his or her best to follow its statutes the blessing of God in this world and everlasting life in the next. Under

44. Mollat, *Pauvres au Moyen Age*, 140–41. But as the thirteenth-century Dominican Humbert de Romans came to realize, poverty broke more spirits than it blessed, and led people to blaspheme God. Murray, "Religion among the Poor," 307f.
45. *The Fathers of the Catholic Church*, vol. 11 (Washington, D.C.: Catholic Univ. Press, 1963), 268.
46. Christopher Black, *Italian Confraternities in the Sixteenth Century* (Cambridge: Cambridge Univ. Press, 1989), 171.

the circumstances that was a handsome return upon a modest invest-ment.[47]

This contractual understanding of charity is explicitly presented in the sermons of the Italian Dominican Giordano da Pisa: the beggar who receives aid is obliged to pray for his benefactor. "God has ordered that there be rich and poor so that the rich may be served by the poor and the poor may be taken care of by the rich. And this is a common organization among peoples. Why are the poor given their station? So that the rich might earn eternal life through them."[48] This medieval preaching not only provided the psychological motivation for the act of charity; it also provided the poor with a consciousness of their utility.[49]

This ideology continued to exert its influence for centuries. The seventeenth-century abbé J. B. Thiers "pointed out the legitimacy of ine-quality—and so of poverty—in a status society; but also, following the most traditional of teaching, that the rich are the true poor in the midst of their riches. All that counted in winning salvation by works was the transformation of wealth into charity. . . . The poor were necessary to both salvation and to production."[50]

The idea of the poor carrying the wealth of the rich to heaven was graphically expressed in funeral rituals in which the deceased left funds to clothe a number of poor and provide for their participation in the funeral procession.[51] "The will became a religious means, almost sacramental, of associating one's wealth with the working of one's personal salvation."[52] In a prototypical fund-raising letter of the thirteenth century, Pope Gregory IX closely followed Augustine's perspective:

Since as the Apostle says, we shall all stand before the tribunal of Christ to be received according as we have borne ourselves in the body, whether

47. Lester K. Little, *Liberty, Charity, Fraternity: Lay Religious Confraternities at Bergamo in the Age of the Commune* (Northampton, Mass.: Smith College, 1988), 97.
48. Sermon of 1303/4 cited by Lesnick, *Preaching in Medieval Florence*, 126. See also 151: "The Franciscan encouraged charity for the benefits it brought to the giver." The Catholic renewal movement of the sixteenth and seventeenth centuries did not sig-nificantly alter this motivation for charity. "It was not the poor person himself who counted but the act accomplished in the sight of God or for the good of the church." Louis Chatellier, *The Europe of the Devout: The Catholic Reformation and the Formation of a New Society* (Cambridge: Cambridge Univ. Press; Paris: Editions de la Maison des Sciences de l'Homme, 1989), 133.
49. Bronislaw Geremek, *La potence ou la pitié* (Paris: Gallimard, 1987), 50, 65–66.
50. Daniel Roche, "A Pauper Capital: Some Reflections on the Parisian Poor in the Seventeenth and Eighteenth Centuries," *French History* 1/2 (1987), 186f. See also Eman-uel Chill, "Religion and Mendicity in Seventeenth-Century France," *International Review of Social History* 7 (1962), 423.
51. For examples, see Joel Rosenthal, *The Purchase of Paradise: Gift Giving and the Aristocracy, 1307–1485* (London: Routledge & Kegan Paul; Toronto: Univ. of Toronto Press, 1972), 103–9.
52. Philippe Aries, "Richesse et pauvreté devant la mort," in Mollat, vol. 2, 533.

good or ill, it behooves us to anticipate the day of harvest with works of great mercy, and, for the sake of things eternal, to sow on earth what we should gather in heaven, the Lord returning it with increased fruit.[53]

Two important implications should not be overlooked here. One is that the medieval understanding of poverty and the poor is related to ecclesiology. The other is that the poor had an important function, an estate if you will, in the medieval Christian society.[54] Ecclesiology played both overt and subtle roles. Overtly it is clear that poor relief was to pass through the church. Certainly individuals in the Middle Ages never lacked opportunity to exercise one or more of the mandates of Matthew 25 by giving food, drink, and clothing to the poor, visiting the sick and prisoners, and welcoming strangers.[55] But it was the church that was the major social conduit for charity and relief of the poor. Thus the church was both the recipient and the dispenser of alms. The wealthy did not deal directly with the poor in any substantial sense; the church was the middleman. The traditional warrant for this was that everything of the church belonged to the poor. The theological warrant was based on two premises: first, the poor referred to in the Lukan list of those to be invited to the banquet was taken to include the clergy, the voluntary poor.[56] Second, theologians and ethicists held that it was best to give alms to those worthy of them, the virtuous poor—the clergy. "Consequently when wealth was left in general 'for the poor' and 'for pious causes' and was motivated by the love of God, executors often distributed it to the clergy."[57]

By the late fourteenth century, critics of the church began to ask why the church did not straightaway give its endowment to the poor because by rights it belonged to them. Wycliffe (c. 1330–1384) was one of the most notorious of these critics. On the basis of church tradition that alms should not be given to the able-bodied poor, Wycliffe and others attacked the mendicant friars for despoiling the true poor. The Wycliffite Bible translates the banquet

53. "Letter of Authorisation for Collections for Charitable Institutions," Fourth Lateran Council, 1215. Tierney, *Medieval Poor Law*, 46. Also discussed by Miri Rubin, *Charity and Community in Medieval Cambridge* (Cambridge: Cambridge Univ. Press, 1987), 184f.
54. Tierney, *Medieval Poor Law*, 44ff.
55. I.e., the "seven works of mercy." The seventh work was burying the dead (Tobit 1:20f.; 2:1ff.). See M.-H. Vicaire, "La place des oeuvres de miséricorde dans la pastorale en pays d'oc," in *Assistance et charité*, Cahiers de Fanjeaux 13 (Fanjeaux: Privat, 1978); and Curt Schweicher, "Werke der Barmherzigkeit," in Englebert Kirschbaum, ed., *Lexikon der christlichen Ikonographie*, vol. 1 (Rome: Herder, 1968). For extensive discussions of the confraternal development of the seven works of mercy, see Black, *Italian Confraternities*, chaps. 9–10, and Maureen Flynn, *Sacred Charity: Confraternities and Social Welfare in Spain, 1400–1700* (Ithaca, N.Y.: Cornell Univ. Press, 1989), chap. 2.
56. Luke 14:13-14: "But when you give a banquet, invite the poor, the crippled, the lame and the blind. And you will be blessed because they cannot repay you, for you will be repaid at the resurrection of the righteous." Cf. also Luke 14:21.
57. Trexler, "Charity and the Defense of Urban Elites," 67. Cf. also Uhlhorn, "Vorstudien," 69.

parable of Luke 14 so that a scriptural warrant for mendicant begging is removed by reading "poor" not as a noun but as an adjective for the crippled, lame, and blind.[58] But even such sharp social critics as Langland did not advocate fundamental reform of theology and ethics but rather their renewal. The critics did not reject evangelical poverty but called for its purification. Langland insists "that the poor man should be worthy of his calling because that calling is so high. Poverty is kin to God himself and so to his saints."[59] An important point, sometimes missed by modern scholars, is that medieval thinking did not distinguish between gifts to the church for spiritual goods (such as prayer services) and gifts to what we would tend to regard as secular charity (such as alms to the poor). "The medieval mind (and social conscience) made no distinction between an eventual sacerdotal and a social end of charity."[60]

The development of the doctrines of purgatory and indulgences further enhanced the crucial role of ecclesiology in benevolence. Alms, as mentioned above, had a penitential role not only for the militant church on earth but also mitigated the purgatorial torment of the suffering church. Already in the twelfth century, testaments and charters were marked by what became part of a legal formula: "For the salvation of my soul and the souls of my ancestors and successors."[61]

This ecclesiological understanding of poverty and the poor thus provided not only a function to the poor but even an estate. That is, the poor had a status in the divine order of the world. Having a status meant having a role in society. That role was in the symbiosis of rich and poor expressed in terms of alms and intercessory prayer. In this context, begging was a recognized way of life in Christian society.[62]

Thus, from within the perceived immutability of the feudal structure, the powerful ninth-century Archbishop of Reims, Hincmar, subscribed to the formula recounted in the "Life of Saint Eloi": "God could have made all persons rich but he willed that there be poor in the world so that the rich

---

58. Margaret Aston, " 'Caim's Castles': Poverty, Politics, and Disendowment," in Barrie Dobson, ed., *The Church, Politics, and Patronage in the Fifteenth Century* (New York: St. Martin's Press, 1984), 45–81.
59. Helen C. White, *Social Criticism in Popular Religious Literature of the Sixteenth Century* (New York: Octagon Books, 1973), 7, and chap. 1, "The Piers Plowman Tradition," passim.
60. Rosenthal, *Purchase of Paradise*, 9–10.
61. Rubin, *Charity and Community*, 185. Rosenthal, *Purchase of Paradise*, 11ff.; Uhlhorn, "Vorstudien," 70–72.
62. Cf. Irsigler & Lassotta, *Bettler und Gaukler*, 20; Rolf Kiessling, *Bürgerliche Gesellschaft und Kirche in Augsburg im Spätmittelalter* (Augsburg: Mühlberger, 1971), 219; and Maria Moisa, "Fourteenth-Century Preachers' Views of the Poor: Class or Status Group?" in Raphael Samuel & Gareth Jones, *Culture, Ideology, and Politics: Essays for Eric Hobsbawn* (London: Routledge & Kegan Paul, 1982), 165f.

would have an opportunity to atone for their sins."[63] Such perspectives created an obstacle to realistic understanding of poverty and its sources. In the concise words of André Vauchez: "The religious conception of poverty which was the foundation of the works of charity created a sort of screen which obscured a true perception of the realities of wretchedness."[64] Lis and Soly suggest that this attitude toward poverty more than obscured the realities of misery; it perpetuated them and maintained both a labor market and social equilibrium.

> The sanctification of poverty justified the *status quo*: the poor were nailed to a cross at the bottom of society. Since they brought about the necessary mediation between this world and the other, their place on earth seemed indispensable. . . . In short, the 'social contract' of the High Middle Ages came to this: since to be saved the rich needed the poor, the poor had the duty to remain poor, while the rights attached to their status implied the duty of submission to the rich. Did not Christ, the apostles, and St. Francis cheerfully endure their poverty? Hence widows, the sick and lame, and beggars who accepted their lot were seen as the chosen of God, and the poverty of underpaid wage labourers was noted with approval (if at all).[65]

The Exigencies of Poverty

Obviously poverty in the Middle Ages was not merely a phenomenon of the collective mentality informed by the dominant theology. Excluding those who chose voluntary poverty for its religious and spiritual compensations, life for the majority of the medieval population was precarious at best. Mollat's graphic description of conditions by the twelfth century serves as an introduction to a synthesis of research on the extent and levels of poverty in the Middle Ages:

> Incompetent (in the full legal sense), the poor man has no ties whatsoever. No feudal superior, no ancestors, "neither hearth nor home," "no fixed

---

63. PL 87:533. Cited by Mollat, *Pauvres au Moyen Age*, 61. "It was this that made Guzmán de Alfarache cynically defend the impostures of false beggars. Since charity was given, he argued, less for the material benefit of the recipient than for the spiritual benefit of the donor, it might as well be given to the false poor as to the real. This perverse view is a good reflection of the weakness in the old medieval attitude to poverty." Henry Kamen, *The Iron Century: Social Change in Europe 1550–1560* (New York: Praeger, 1971), 403.
64. André Vauchez, "Le peuple au Moyen Age: du 'Populus Christianus' aux classes dangereuses," in Riis II, 16. Also, Geremek, *Potence ou la pitié*, 30: "The praise of alms provided the rich the possibility of obtaining their salvation, sanctioned wealth, and justified it ideologically."
65. Catherine Lis & Hugo Soly, *Poverty and Capitalism in Pre-Industrial Europe* (Atlantic Highlands, N. J.: Humanities Press, 1979), 22.

abode"; essentially the poor man lives on the sidelines—faithless and lawless. Has the vagrant even any connection with the Church? Has he been baptized, married? Rejected, attacked and bitten by dogs that bark when they pick up his scent, he is not even granted Christian burial after his death. His isolation is seen from his external "habitus" [dress], his behaviour and his occupations, his language, where he lives and even where he begs: the poor man remains at the door—the monastery gates, the church porch, the doorstep of a house are all "as it were borders that separate the world of penury and plenty." His isolation reaches its most extreme and abject point when the attempt to rehabilitate him, obvious but well-meaning, in fact tends to depersonalize him. By acting as the occasion for the rich man's saving alms, he certainly acquires a role, a spiritual "status," but he is still a dependent; as the image of the suffering Christ the poor man disappears in Him, losing all identity. Feelings of humiliation and humility become totally assimilated, if not confused, and yet an ambiguity remains.[66]

The abysmal quality of Mollat's poor person's life is, if possible, even more terrible when we learn of the large number of compatriots sharing the suffering. The difficulty in estimating the number of poor in the late Middle Ages is related both to the relativity of poverty itself and the lack of adequate records from the time. Estimates of the proportion of poor among the population of Europe range from 20 percent up to 80 percent depending upon how poverty is defined. "Indeed, the number of those living at subsistence minima can almost always be estimated at 40 or 50 per cent of local, regional, or national population. These figures, however, tell us nothing of the ways in which poverty manifested itself."[67] "Poverty was widespread in pre-industrial Europe, and one can venture to say that three-fourths to four-fifths of the population suffered from severe nutritional deficiencies, poor clothing, and miserable housing facilities."[68]

The Extent and Levels of Poverty

Quantitative statistics on the extent and levels of poverty in the late Middle Ages are difficult to determine. The social and economic investigation of the

66. Mollat, "The Poor in the Middle Ages," in Riis I, 33.
67. Lis & Soly, *Poverty and Capitalism*, 219. "Any attempt to put the problem of poverty and vagrancy into perspective must begin with a reminder of the dimensions of that problem. It is undeniable that the numbers of the poor, as such, were large. Between them, they comprised anything from 50 to 60 per cent of the population of any area of reasonable size, and on occasion their numbers were higher still." John Pound, *Poverty and Vagrancy in Tudor England* (London: Longman, 1971), 79. Cf. also Hunecke, "Überlegungen zur Geschichte," 489.
68. Carlo M. Cipolla, "Economic Fluctuations, the Poor, and Public Policy (Italy, 16th and 17th Centuries)," in Riis I, 65. Cf. Geremek, *Potence ou la pitié*, 77f.

lower class in medieval and early modern European cities is now being intensively pursued, but it is a very recent endeavor. The sources available for this work include not only the writings of participants in the society but also such social documents as tax registers, local ordinances and legislation, political documents, hospital and foundation records, and data that indicate wages and minimal standards for living.[69] These documents are difficult to work with. Tax registers, for example, are concerned mostly with property taxes and thus obviously exclude those without property.[70] Also important but difficult to interpret are the numerous testaments made to foundations serving the poor and those unable to work. Qualitative sources include documents from urban councils and guilds, letters, judiciary records, and urban chronicles. These are important sources, but it must be kept in mind that social history is stubborn stuff.[71] This caveat is illustrated closer to home by a recent article in the *Boston Globe* that reported on the difficulty of efforts to count the homeless in Boston, not to mention the news reports of politically influenced and controversial statistics that give vastly different estimates of the number of poor in America.[72] What is clear, however, for the medieval city is that poverty was a social constant, and that the data available do not reflect the real numbers and needs of the poor population.[73]

One of the more recent developments in historical research for estimating the extent of poverty is computing "the minimal human requirement for food, satisfied in the cheapest possible manner."[74] In this method the nutritional needs of persons are calculated on the basis of contemporary data with regard to age and nature of work and are then read back into historical contexts. These nutritional needs involve not only the number of daily calories but

69. For a discussion of the problems with sources and their use, see Ulf Dirlmeier, *Untersuchungen zu Einkommensverhältnissen und Lebenshaltungskosten in oberdeutschen Städten des Spätmittelalters (Mitte 14. bis Anfang 16. Jahrhundert)* (Heidelberg: Carl Winter Universitätsverlag, 1978), 10–19; and Erich Maschke, "Unterschichten der mittelalterlichen Städte Deutschlands," in Erich Maschke & Jürgen Sydow, eds., *Gesellschaftlichen Unterschichten in den südwestdeutschen Städten* (Stuttgart: Kohlhammer, 1967), 4–5.
70. Dirlmeier, *Untersuchungen*, 493; Maschke, "Unterschichten," 17; Erik Fügedi, "Steuerlisten, Vermögen und soziale Gruppen in mittelalterlichen Städten," in Ingrid Bátori, ed., *Städtische Gesellschaft und Reformation* (Stuttgart: Klett-Cotta, 1980).
71. For an alternative methodological and conceptual reading of the sources, a reading that challenges the assumption of massive poverty, see Thorold J. Tronrud, "Dispelling the Gloom. The Extent of Poverty in Tudor and Early Stuart Towns: Some Kentish Evidence," *Canadian Journal of History* 20 (1985). Tronrud argues that some scholars have mistaken contemporaries' measurement of social inequity for a subsistence poverty line.
72. "Boston undertakes census of its homeless residents," *Boston Globe*, 2 October 1986, 1.
73. Maschke, "Unterschichten," 71; Dirlmeier, *Untersuchungen*, 529–31; and W. P. Blockmans and W. Prevenier, "Poverty in Flanders and Brabant from the Fourteenth to the Mid-Sixteenth Century: Sources and Problems," *Acta Historiae Neerlandicae*, vol. 10 (The Hague: Nijhoff, 1978), 33.
74. Blockmans and Prevenier, "Poverty in Flanders," 21.

also the various required sources of energy, such as proteins, fats, minerals, and vitamins. This means that the poverty line cannot be determined on the basis of only the cheapest source of calories—bread—because this food does not satisfy all dietary needs. The known dietary regulations of philanthropic, monastic, and military institutions make it possible to calculate the cost of living and the diet's food value for different times and places. Riis gives an example of this method from the known daily rations on the Venetian galleys of about 1310.

> The composition of the diet was as follows: ship's biscuit 68.4% of total calories, wine 9.6%, cheese 4.0%, salt pork 9.4%, beans 8.6%, giving a total of 3,915 calories a day, of which 71.3% came from carbohydrates (wine excluded), 14.3% from fats and 14.4% from protein. With the pork and the beans a stew was made, but instead of beans some other vegetable, presumably "dry vegetables" like dried peas, lentils etc., might be used. The number of calories, almost 4,000, contained in this diet is considerable. Further, of the 114.4 g protein, only 13.2 g were of animal origin (pork and cheese), which is too little. The quantity of fats (55.5 g) was also too slight, the Florentine mason needed 65–70 g a day.[75]

When the researcher proceeds to calculate the percentage of income needed for a minimum subsistence, say in bread, the result is an approximation of the poverty level for a particular context. Blockmans and Prevenier estimate that 63 percent of a journeyman's annual wage was expended on bread in Bruges in 1482–83. La Ronciere estimates that in early fourteenth-century Florence many wage-earners received a wage equivalent to less than 2,000 grain calories per day although 3,000 calories were necessary for a desirable minimum diet.[76]

As useful as such studies are, a number of criticisms have been raised with regard to their accuracy. As contemporary experience shows, the poor may lack sufficient information about a healthy diet to enable them to choose the necessary nutrients. Furthermore, the poor may follow taste and convention in dietary choices rather than health considerations. The determination of what constitutes a minimum nutritive diet is not as objective and scientific as it may at first seem. The fact that a nutritious diet requires balance is also important. While the minimum calorie intake might be met by bread, a person who ate only bread could be malnourished for lack of protein and fat. The idea that it is possible in the study of contemporary less-developed countries or of historical periods to establish "a scientific, 'absolute' poverty line" is "highly debatable and fraught with difficulties."[77]

75. Thomas Riis, "Poverty and Urban Development in Early Modern Europe (15th–18th/19th Centuries): A General View," in Riis I, 2.
76. Blockmans and Prevenier, "Poverty in Flanders," 27–28; de la Ronciere, "Pauvres et pauvreté à Florence," 661–745. Cf. also Lis and Soly, *Poverty and Capitalism*, 17–20.
77. Wilfred Beckerman, "The Measurement of Poverty," in Riis I, 62. For a strong

Although the approach of defining poverty in terms of the minimal level of subsistence may leave something to be desired in terms of precision, it does provide a means of estimating the large percentage of income the poor had to expend just to survive. This estimation in turn graphically illustrates that many people lived day to day without any reserves and could be pushed into severe difficulty by any number of crises. "In normal times the beggars accounted in the cities for some ten per cent of the population. But a figure of this kind, even if correct, is misleading in so far as it conceals one of the main characteristics of the phenomenon of poverty, that is its recurrent wide fluctuations in magnitude."[78] The crises that pushed people, especially the many underemployed, into poverty included war, epidemic, crop failure, monetary manipulation, and falling levels of investment.

Wars created widespread economic distress, primarily from the devastation to the countryside caused by roving armies; in the process, the armies also spread infectious diseases. The devastation of epidemics was related, especially for the poor, to famines caused by crop failures, whether these failures were due to natural phenomena or to human causes such as war. Crop failures were frequent and severe in the Middle Ages, and their severity was increased by the lack of adequate marketing and transportation facilities. "Graphs showing the movement of the prices of grains in any area of pre-industrial Europe are the best commentary on a situation of extreme instability."[79] Famine, of course, struck the poor the hardest and also left them the most vulnerable to epidemics. The circulation of disease-carrying rats, fleas, and lice increased when depleted granaries drove the pests into the streets, when imports of grains increased, and when bands of beggars migrated from the country into the city. It was also not unusual for trade with an infected city to be blockaded; thus an area of epidemic would be driven into even worse straits.

The most significant epidemic of the Middle Ages was the plague that struck Europe in the mid-fourteenth century. Hunecke states unequivocally that the first major turn in the history of poverty occurs in the years after 1348. "They form the dividing line between the medieval and Early Modern history of poverty."[80] Friedrich Lütge argues that the human devastation wrought by the plague was so great that it substantially affected all subsequent social and economic developments: "That seething torrent which has been the modern history of our continent has its source in the middle of the

---

argument against the subsistence definition of poverty, see Martin Rein, "Problems in the Definition and Measurement of Poverty," in Peter Townsend, ed., *The Concept of Poverty: Working Papers on Methods of Investigation and Life-Styles of the Poor in Different Countries* (New York: American Elsevier, 1970).
78. Cipolla, "Economic Fluctuations," 65.
79. Ibid., 67.
80. Hunecke, "Überlegungen zur Geschichte," 491.

fourteenth century.[81] Lütge also argues that the tremendous depopulation of Europe caused by the plague is the key to understanding the extended agricultural crisis that followed in its wake.[82] Not only did grain prices fall steeply because of the drop in population, but wealth became concentrated among those lucky enough to survive; wages rose because of the lack of laborers, and prices for manufactured goods rose.

> Looked at in this light, the problem of the origin of "early capitalism" will have to be answered differently, not only by placing the beginnings into the second half of the fourteenth century but also by giving the matter a new twist and recognizing that a decisive factor was the concentration of estates in the hands of survivors, often in the form of ruthless occupation of property become ownerless.[83]

One of the major consequences of the plague, then, was that employers in nearly every European country were confronted by a structural shortage of labor and the demand for higher wages. The repeated response of authorities was to enact legislation to ensure an adequate work force at preplague wages. Migration of workers was restricted, all able-bodied persons under sixty without means of support were to accept employment at the earlier wage rates, and charity to sturdy beggars was forbidden. These "Statutes of Laborers"

> attempted to crush the hopes of the poor for better living conditions and to remove the sole benefit bequeathed by the millions of cottars, servants, and day labourers mowed down by the epidemics. Princes, who had never before been concerned with such matters, coordinated a system of social control designed to protect the interests of a rich minority. The ban on migration, the obligation to accept the old wage levels, the expulsion of sturdy beggars from the towns, and their exclusion from alms all aimed to regulate the rural labour market and thus to support seigneurial reaction. Town magistracies, on their side, fixed maximum wages yet made no effort to halt the influx of unskilled labourers, because they considered demographic recovery to be the best way to depress wages. The sole problem posed by migration for the towns was the potential threat to

---

81. Friedrich Lütge, "The Fourteenth and Fifteenth Centuries in Social and Economic History," in Gerald Strauss, ed., *Pre-Reformation Germany* (New York: Harper & Row, 1972), 367.
82. The classic argument that the crisis was due to population change rather than market conditions is Wilhelm Abel's *Agrarkrisen und Agrarkonjunktur in Mitteleuropa vom 13. bis zum 19. Jahrhundert* (Berlin, 1935). Cf. also W. Abel, *Massenarmut und Hungerkrisen im vorindustriellen Deutschland*, 3d ed. (Göttingen: Vandenhoeck & Ruprecht, 1986). Lis and Soly refer to Abel as "an eloquent proponent of neo-malthusian models" (*Poverty and Capitalism*, 224).
83. Lütge, "Fourteenth and Fifteenth Centuries," 344.

their security. Hence many local authorities took steps to control begging more efficiently after the Black Death.[84]

These many ordinances were unable to achieve their supposed intended control of the labor market, but they do indicate a significant shift in attitudes. The poor were now being evaluated as to whether they were worthy of aid; there was growing concern about begging; and a new ethic of work was arising. It is in this period of the late fourteenth century that the terms "poor" and "laborer" become interchangeable. Poverty was becoming the way of life for the urban majority.

Poverty and Urban Development

The rural poor perceived the late medieval city as a place of refuge and opportunity. It is likely that, just as earlier generations in bondage to lords sought freedom in the city ("*Stadtluft macht frei nach Jahr und Tag*"—city air makes one free after a year and a day), so the later generations in bondage to poverty sought freedom from want in the cities. The terrible discovery of most of these migrants was that the city in fact generated poverty. The city was, in Mollat's words, "the cross-roads of destitution."[85] This destitution was spiritual as well as physical; the urban dweller's melancholy, as depression was called in the Middle Ages, grew from the consciousness of having lost social and familial roots and bonds.[86]

A fundamental reason for the misery experienced by the majority of the population of the late medieval city was the shift that had been occurring for some time from a gift economy to a profit or money economy. Already by the eleventh century, money had developed into a tool to be used for the creation of more money and goods rather than just a treasure to be displayed. This change affected every aspect and corner of society. "Thus life in the new profit economy raised acute problems involving impersonalism, money, and moral uncertainty."[87]

The impersonalism was related directly to the growth of the cities. The quality of interpersonal relationships experienced in the small village, where common tasks and dialect undergirded identity and solidarity, was diminished markedly as a town grew in size and as the number of specializations related to a market economy increased. Anonymity may be heady at first, but the

84. Lis & Soly, *Poverty and Capitalism*, 50. Cf. Bronislaw Geremek, *The Margins of Society in Late Medieval Paris*, trans. Jean Birrell (Cambridge: Cambridge Univ. Press, 1987), 31.
85. Mollat, *Pauvres au Moyen Age*, 293. Geremek, "Renfermement," 206: "The town is the natural setting of pauperism." And Geremek, *Margins of Society*, 342. Cf. also Lis and Soly, *Poverty and Capitalism*, 63.
86. Jacques Chiffoleau, *La comptabilité de l'au-delà* (Rome: École Française de Rome, 1980), 205ff., 430.
87. Little, *Religious Poverty*, 19; for much of what follows, see chap. 2, "Adapting to the Profit Economy," 19–41.

initial euphoria quickly evaporates when one needs personal and material support.

Anonymity was a function not only of the size of towns and cities but also of the use of money, an impersonal medium of exchange. Lester K. Little relates the rise of both formal education and formal prostitution in the cities to this anonymous, impersonal medium of money by "young people separated from family, household, priest, or village." Since up to half of any given urban population consisted of immigrants from the countryside, "the individual experience of encountering and then having to cope with urban complexity and impersonalism was a continually recurring phenomenon." The loosening of social ties and the relaxation of traditional systems of constraint and supervision in the towns and cities contributed to their becoming a natural setting for pauperism.[88]

The corrosive power of money quickly led to the substitution of avarice for pride as the most deadly sin. The word "money" replaced the name of Christ in the traditional acclamation, "Christ conquers, Christ reigns, Christ rules the world." The received tradition with its rejection of usury perpetuated by the dictum of canon law that "a merchant is rarely or never able to please God" left the new merchant and entrepreneurial classes without ethical support. Ethicists and canonists now set about to develop a social and economic morality for mercantile activity.[89]

In the city as in the country, those vulnerable to poverty included the sick, handicapped, aged, single women, widows, and orphans. A new characteristic of the city was the occurrence of the working poor. The laborer was particularly vulnerable to the fluctuations of an uncontrolled market economy.

> Uprooted inhabitants of the countryside, having sought refuge in the towns, were confronted with a society in which socio-economic contrasts were much more pronounced. In 1549, a Councillor of Jachymov declared bluntly, "One pays, the other labours." Nowhere was the distinction between capital and labour expressed so sharply as in the metropoles. The gulf between rich and poor grew wider than ever before, widening both absolutely and relatively, due to the intensity of concomitant enrichment and impoverishment processes.[90]

The day laborer was always on the threshold of poverty, literally living hand to mouth.

The medieval urban lower class included all those who were vocationally dependent, not just day laborers. These people—journeymen, apprentices,

88. Geremek, "Renfermement," 206.
89. Harold J. Berman, Law and Revolution: The Formulation of the Western Legal Tradition (Cambridge: Harvard Univ. Press, 1983), 336–39, 618 nn. 5ff.
90. Lis & Soly, Poverty and Capitalism, 75. Cf. also Geremek's description of urban misery in Potence ou la pitié, 82–96.

servants, independent women, and beggars—comprised the weakest part of the urban population. In general, they lacked civic rights and respect. This is clear from what we know of their housing situations. In Nuremberg at the beginning of the fifteenth century only citizens with property worth at least 200 gulden[91] were allowed to live in the inner city; the rest of the population could settle in the areas between the first and second walls. In Bautzen around 1400 the poorest guilds, especially the weavers, lived in the outer part of the city. Furthermore, the housing conditions were crowded and unhealthy; many of the poor lived in cellars.[92] Housing segregation of the poor eventually became a self-conscious aspect of city planning as well as a natural economic development.[93]

The laboring poor, known (for whatever comfort it may have provided them) as the "honest poor," practiced independent vocations that left them highly dependent upon wages. Even under normal conditions they lived close to the edge of subsistence; unfavorable individual or collective conditions would at the least make their lot difficult if not seriously endanger their lives. Some of the working poor therefore received outside assistance. The border between independence and dependence was quite fluid. The technical tax concept for the lowest economic groups gives some indication of the number of these people. Known as the *Habnits* (have nots) or *nihil habens* in the Latin sources outside Germany, they were not completely without property but were certainly economically marginal. About two-thirds of the 1475 surtax list for Augsburg consisted of these "have-nothings."[94]

The tax lists do not give an adequate sense of the numbers of urban poor because they do not include the poorest inhabitants. This type of source can be supplemented by testaments, as the following extreme example illustrates. In 1350 the Lübeck citizen Radekin vam See bequeathed 80 Lübeck marks for the poor, with the stipulation that each poor person receive one penny and that surplus funds be used to buy shoes and clothes for the poor. In 1355 he raised the bequest to 100 Lübeck marks. On the basis of 192 pennies to one mark, this would mean that vam See calculated distribution

---

91. "In terms of buying power in 1525 one gulden bought ten geese, or a pair of riding boots, or five bushels of rye, or about thirty-five gallons of common wine. Persons with taxable wealth in excess of 100 gulden were usually householders of moderate means. Families earning less than 50 gulden a year (and having no reserves) were living in poverty." Peter Blickle, *The Revolution of 1525: The German Peasants' War from a New Perspective*, trans. T. Brady & H. C. E. Midelfort (Baltimore: Johns Hopkins Univ. Press, 1985), ix.
92. Maschke, "Unterschichten," 20–22.
93. See Irsigler & Lassotta, *Bettler und Gaukler*, 32–44. See also Geremek, *Margins of Society*, 81: "The very poor also lived in huts and shanties on the town moat, near the marsh, in the fields, and on the outskirts of the town, in the shanty-towns of the Middle Ages. . . . These slums certainly constituted a large part of the urban landscape in the poor districts."
94. Maschke, "Unterschichten," 18; and la Ronciere, "Pauvres et pauvreté à Florence," 662–69.

to 15,360 poor persons in 1350 and 19,200 poor persons in 1355. It is estimated that at this time Lübeck included at most 24,000 inhabitants. Thus, if these calculations are taken literally, 64 percent and 80 percent of the population in 1350 and 1355 respectively were in poverty. These are fantastic figures even taking into account the effects of the plague and the probable swelling of the population by immigration.[95]

An investigation of the records of the major alms distributions in Göttingen at Invocavit, Laetare, and Corpus Christi indicates that in the mid-fifteenth century approximately a third of the population were considered eligible for alms. These were people whose existence did not literally depend upon charity but who belonged to the urban population with the least income and property and therefore were the most prone to crises. The criteria for the determination of need are not known, but wage-earners with low income, little property, and many children were included. Laborers were paid in the morning so that their wives could fetch the wage and buy food for the evening meal—a suggestion of the extent to which these people lived from day to day.[96]

Groups other than day laborers also lived on the edge of subsistence. One group was known as the house poor. Generally from the milieu of the guilds and urban elites, these were "honorable" persons who through various circumstances beyond their control had been thrust into conditions of poverty. For whatever personal and public reasons, they were reluctant to beg on the streets. Thus they were known as the house poor or as the "deserving poor" because they were not supported publicly as beggars but rather lived in their own dwellings. (Occasionally they received their board in well-to-do homes.) The term "house poor" first appears at the end of the thirteenth century and is expressly distinguished from public beggars. The numerous foundations for the house poor based on testaments[97] may indicate that this was a large group, but it may indicate as well that this was a preferred group.[98]

An example of such a foundation is that by the Frankfurt physician Johann Wiesebeder in 1428, which established a perpetual alms for

persons who suffer affliction at home who nevertheless have passed their days with honor; housepoor who nourished themselves by their faithful work and yet have no adequate earnings; such persons who earlier have earned their needs but who now on account of age or sickness are no longer able to do so; further pious housepoor who are overburdened with

95. Maschke, "Unterschichten," 54–55.
96. Ibid., 57–59.
97. On the early law of charitable trusts, see Berman, *Law and Revolution*, 230–37.
98. See Trexler, "Charity and the Defense of Urban Elites"; Amleto Spicciani, "The 'Poveri Vergognosi' in Fifteenth-Century Florence," in Riis I; Irsigler & Lassotta, *Bettler und Gaukler*, 24f.

children and cannot feed them; and finally, pious housepoor women in childbed or expecting.[99]

The fluctuating class of the poor also included beggars. Begging was considered a vocation, even an estate, and thus was a recognized way of earning a living. The resident local beggar therefore had a place in medieval urban society. The Augsburg surtax of 1475 mentioned above also lists 107 beggars. Like a day worker, the beggar paid a weekly tax of four pennies. Thus a beggar must have earned an amount comparable to the wages of a day worker—about twelve pennies a day (one-third of a day's wages was the weekly head tax). The person who made begging a vocation was not excluded from property formation. In Basel in 1453–54, three beggars and three blind men paid taxes based on property in the category of 0–10 gulden.[100]

The lower class of the medieval city was homogeneous in terms of economic weakness and lack of civic rights, but it was heterogeneous in its differentiation into groups with distinct social and economic characteristics: the laboring poor, the house poor, and the beggars. Consequently the medieval urban responses to poverty among these groups also varied.

Medieval Urban Reactions to Poverty

It is difficult to analyze how the poor themselves responded to their plight. They do not seem to have thought of themselves as divorced from the total Christian society.[101] Indeed, until the late Middle Ages, the poor were not perceived as morally different from anyone else; it was the rich who were morally suspect.

Resources for social welfare in the Middle Ages included devotional confraternities and guilds. In Venice, lay religious societies termed *Scuole* were also philanthropic organizations. Their almsgiving and charitable activities not only accumulated merit for their members but also expressed a sense of brotherhood and mutual responsibility to their class. In the fourteenth century, "the practice of charity harmonized with the general enterprise of saving souls through the accumulation of merit."[102] A guild was a sworn union that obligated its members to mutual protection and assistance. Its two constitutive elements were the guild oath and the guild meal. Although frequently thought of today as a monopolistic economic association, which indeed it was, the guild was also a religious and charitable association. The guilds provided for

---

99. Maschke, "Unterschichten," 63.
100. Ibid., 68–69.
101. See Paul Slack, "The Reactions of the Poor to Poverty in England c. 1500–1750," in Riis II, 19, 21–22; and Mollat, "Les réactions des pauvres à la pauvreté en France au bas Moyen Age," in Riis II.
102. Brian Pullan, *Rich and Poor in Renaissance Venice: The Social Institutions of a Catholic State to* 1620 (Cambridge: Harvard Univ. Press, 1971), 65.

their sick, disabled, and poor members during their lifetimes, and then buried them and gave offerings for their souls.[103]

In the late Middle Ages it became increasingly difficult and in many cases impossible for journeymen to gain access to guilds and thereby also to civic rights and vocational independence. The guilds restricted entrance, and thereby competition, by raising the standards of the required "master work" and the entrance fee to levels unattainable by nonmembers. Specific conditions varied from city to city and from guild to guild, so it is difficult to make general statements. However, by the late Middle Ages it was very difficult for any person to enter a guild unless his father had belonged to it. In the north German cities in the fifteenth century, the only way for a poor journeyman to acquire citizenship and a craft was to marry a master's widow or daughter.[104]

One of the responses of the poor journeymen to this increasingly restrictive social and economic situation was to form associations and brotherhoods of their own. These associations, closely connected to ecclesial obligations, were efforts to create a form of social as well as religious security for the workers.[105] Stressing honor and morality, the brotherhoods controlled the relationships of members. The brotherhoods provided funds to support the sick and those out of work. They provided for burial of those who died. The brotherhoods thus were reflections of the guilds to which the masters belonged. These associations and brotherhoods were significant forces in the fashioning of the collective consciousness of the poor journeymen.[106]

The handicapped and beggars also formed brotherhoods. In Frankfurt in 1480 a brotherhood of the blind and lame was in existence, and in Strasbourg in 1411 a group of twenty-five poor, blind persons formed a brotherhood that after 1433 developed into the *Fraternitas pauperum mendicantium Argentinensis* (Strasbourg Brotherhood of the begging poor). In 1454 in Zülpich a brotherhood existed of crippled, blind, and other poor who lived by alms; members' contributions provided a fund for sick relief. In Basel, a brotherhood of vagrants and other dishonorable persons was legally incorporated.[107] From the end of the fourteenth century, a veritable colony of thousands of these outcasts (cesspool cleaners, executioners, grave diggers, and so on) and beggars lived

---

103. Cf. Berman, *Law and Revolution*, 390–92; and Otto G. Oexle, "Die mittelalterlichen Gilden: Ihre Selbstdeutung und ihr Beitrag zur Formung sozialen Strukturen," in Zimmermann, ed., *Soziale Ordnungen*, 203–26.
104. Maschke, "Unterschichten," 14–16, 38–42.
105. See "Bruderschaften," TRE, vol. 7 (Berlin/New York: de Gruyter, 1981); and André Vauchez, "Confraternities and Guilds in the Middle Ages," in Carter Lindberg and Emily Albu Hanawalt, eds., *Through the Eye of a Needle: Judeo-Christian Roots of Social Welfare* (Kirksville, Mo.: Thomas Jefferson Univ. Press, forthcoming).
106. See Gerhard Uhlhorn, *Die christliche Liebesthätigkeit*, 3 vols. in 1, 2d ed. (Stuttgart: Gundert, 1895), 485–90.
107. Maschke, "Unterschichten," 70; cf. Otto Winckelmann, *Das Fürsorgewesen der Stadt Strassburg und nach der Reformation bis zum Ausgang des Sechzehnten Jahrhunderts* (Leipzig: 1922), 68f., 78ff. Nr. 36. It was, however, rare for beggars to develop organized self-help alliances. See Irsigler & Lassotta, *Bettler und Gaukler*, 58–60.

on the outskirts of the city in an area called Kohlenberg (the ash pile). The Basel citizens probably lived in fear of them.[108]

The Basel example is unusual. Urban society was fairly successful in marginalizing the dishonorable poor. In the face of this marginalization, and with the difficulties poor journeymen encountered in getting established, the poor wandered from city to city during the fifteenth century and later. In prior times an immigrant might adapt slowly to urban life and be able to develop a new craft or trade as an apprentice, enjoying the support of at least familial structures. With changes in the modes of production and the massive migrations following the demographic upsurge and the process of rural impoverishment, the traditional mechanisms of progressive assimilation of newcomers practically ceased to exist.[109] Thus migration of the poor became part of a vicious circle of increased costs for citizenship and guild membership designed to keep out the poor. The poor, who could not afford citizenship in the city, strove to acquire it in the smaller towns and suburbs around the city in hopes of acquiring a claim on the city's alms.

The growing presence of the wandering poor and foreign beggars contributed to a shift in perception of the poor in the cities. The poor aroused anxiety and fear not only as potential bearers of criminality and disease, but also as sources of revolt. Suspicion grew that many of the poor were beggars because they were too lazy to work.[110] Governments throughout Europe began to develop legislation designed to control the poor, and also to make distinctions among the poor in order to determine which ones deserved support.

In England the famous Statutes of Laborers had their beginnings in the 1349 Ordinance of Laborers enacted by the Council of Edward III; this law established the duty of all able-bodied men to work. Additional provisions by Parliament in subsequent years mandated that men and women under the age of sixty who were without means of support had to accept employment at wages current before the plague. Workers were not to abandon their employers; vagrancy was to be severely punished; and employers were not to pay wages higher than those already determined. Furthermore, it was forbidden to give charity and alms to able-bodied beggars who "do refuse to labour, giving themselves to idleness and vice, and so that they may be, through want, compelled to labour for their necessary living."[111]

In Spain, the Cortes of Aragon in 1350 set the legal maximum wage and threatened banishment not only for those who asked for more but also for those who paid more. In Castile in 1351 a severe ordinance against begging

108. Heiner Boehncke & Rolf Johannsmeier, *Das Buch der Vaganten, Spieler, Huren, Leutbetrüger* (Cologne: Prometh Verlag, 1987), 53.
109. Geremek, *Potence ou la pitié*, 160.
110. In the medieval list of sins, sloth or *accidia* also refers to the despair and bitterness that result from too many misfortunes and too few resources. Alexander Murray, "Religion among the Poor in Thirteenth-Century France: The Testimony of Humbert de Romans," *Traditio* 30 (1974), 311–13.
111. Cited by Lis & Soly, *Poverty and Capitalism*, 49.

mandated that all able-bodied men over the age of twelve were to work for fixed wages. In 1381 Juan I legitimated forced labor without wages for captured wandering beggars. The Portuguese crown between 1349 and 1401 proclaimed a series of laws on labor and wages; these included a passport system to hinder migration and begging. In France in 1351, King John the Good limited alms to only the sick, lame, and aged, mandating that sturdy beggars be expelled from Paris in three days if they did not find work.[112]

The Nuremberg Begging Order of 1370 is frequently referred to as one of the first urban efforts to restrict begging by administrative measures. Only natives were allowed to beg, and then only after producing two or three credible witnesses to the authorities that they were dependent upon alms. Such beggars were then given badges identifying them as legitimate beggars. The practice of identifying the poor by badges and then later by particular uniforms continued into the early twentieth century.[113] Vagrants and the able-bodied were denied permission to beg, and foreign beggars were allowed to beg for only three days and then were not to return to the city for a year. In 1478 the order was renewed. Those who sought permission to beg now also were examined to determine whether they could recite the Lord's Prayer, Hail Mary, the Creed, and the Ten Commandments.[114] This 1478 Begging Order was probably the model for the similar one established by the Town Council of Würzburg in 1490.

The oldest begging order in Cologne, which is probably from 1435, states:

> Our town councillors further understand that many people, men and women, pursue their begging here in the city although they are strong and healthy, and could well earn their own bread. . . . Therefore our lords command that all these healthy people shall work and serve for their livelihood, and whoever will not work shall most quickly be expelled from the city. He who does not act according to this command and remains and begs in Cologne, shall be arrested by the judge and placed in one

112. These examples are given in Lis & Soly, *Poverty and Capitalism*, 48–50. Cf. also Bronislaw Geremek, *Truands et misérables dans l'Europe moderne*, 1350–1600 (Paris: Gallimard, 1980), 71–87. Geremek posits that the repressive legislation against vagabondage had the ideological goal of maintaining manual labor as the proper obligation of the lower class, and the economic goal of maintaining a labor pool to provide workers at low wages.

113. See P. Cunnington & C. Lucas, *Charity Costumes of Children, Scholars, Almsfolk, Pensioners* (London: A. & C. Black, 1978). For printed sources for Nuremberg from 1370–1699, see Willi Rüger, *Mittelalterliches Almosen wesen: Die Almosen Ordnungen der Reichsstadt Nürnberg* (Nuremberg: Nürnberger Beiträge zu den Wirtschafts- und Sozialwissenschaften, 31, 1932). For examples of the time from Constance, see Otto Feger, ed., *Vom Richterbrief zum Roten Buch: Die älterer Konstanzer Ratsgesetzgebung* (Constance, 1955), 3, 8, 11, 14, 20, 30, 52.

114. Irsigler & Lassotta, *Bettler und Gaukler*, 25–26.

of the city towers for a year where he will receive only bread and water; thereafter he shall be driven out of the city.[115]

Lis and Soly evaluate these begging orders to be "of great significance" for later European social development.

> For the first time a sharp and explicit distinction was made between paupers, who had a right to assistance because of their physical weakness, and sturdy beggars, to whom alms might in no circumstances be given. This discrimination implied a break with earlier attitudes; collective glorification of poverty as such belonged *de facto* to the past. The duty to work was the harbinger of a new ethic: the exaltation of self-employment directed towards the production of material goods. Moreover, for the first time secular authorities were concerned about begging. Thus the basis was laid for the appearance of a coordinated system of social control directed by public authorities in place of private persons. Since the clergy, traditional refuge of the poor, raised no protest, the way lay free and open for a gradual secularization of charity.[116]

In attempting to control vagrancy and begging, authorities made the distinction between the unworthy and the worthy poor, the able-bodied beggar and the incapacitated. This distinction, already present in canon law, became a legal concept when the fourteenth-century English Parliament made it an offense to be a masterless man, a vagabond.[117] Sources from the Middle Ages make clear that those who made their living by begging were not a homogeneous group. The poor were differentiated not only on the formal level by groupings such as the house poor and hospital inmates but also according to the type of begging "trades" they practiced. For example, a 1304 record from the Cologne Holy Spirit Hospital lists the following begging trades: lepers; students; Beguines and mendicants; pilgrims to holy places; cripples; the sick; orphan children; discharged mercenaries; victims of war, famine, and natural catastrophes; those unable to work; those unwilling to work; and those without work.[118]

The methods and techniques of the professional beggars varied. Some solicited on the streets, some went from door to door, others stood in front of churches and cloisters. Some even went into churches and accosted worshipers during services. This latter practice had been expressly forbidden (to no avail, it seems)[119] in Cologne in 1330 by an edict of Archbishop Henry II.

115. Karl Trüdinger, *Stadt und Kirche im spätmittelalterlichen Würzburg* (Stuttgart: Klett-Cotta, 1978), 26; cf. also 116–17.
116. Lis & Soly, *Poverty and Capitalism*, 51.
117. A. L. Beier, *Masterless Men: The Vagrancy Problem in England 1560–1640* (London/New York: Methuen, 1985), 9–10.
118. Irsigler & Lassotta, *Bettler und Gaukler*, 44–45.
119. Geremek, *Truands et misérables*, 120, gives an example of a fifteenth-century effort to control such begging by the chapter of Notre Dame in Paris.

Begging techniques were illustrated in the art of the time and in a wealth of literature intended to alert people to fraudulent begging practices. In his writing on Christian pilgrimage, Geiler of Kaisersberg,[120] the famous Strasbourg Cathedral preacher, described the empty-handed pilgrim who goes into a large city, where he meets some merciful people who contribute enough for him to continue his pilgrimage. Instead of resuming his journey, however, the pilgrim realizes he has a good thing going and continues to beg in the streets. Soon he apprentices himself to a wise local beggar and learns the best places to beg.

The goal of sermons by preachers like Geiler and the literature on beggars that was flourishing by the fifteenth century was to warn against false beggars and swindlers. The almsgiver was to be alert to deceitful methods and techniques. An early example is the 1420 poem "Des Teufels Netz" (The Devil's Net),[121] in which the devil describes how he nets representatives of all estates, including "worldly" beggars. These are healthy people who through dissolute and lazy lives have sunk to poverty and begging. They resort to a variety of tricks to get alms, sometimes distorting their bodies as if they are crippled, sick, and lame. In his famous "Ship of Fools" (1494), Sebastian Brant set such tricks to verse:

> Bold begging charms full many a fool,
> For begging has become the rule
> And ranks among our best professions:
> Church orders teem with rich possessions
> And yet lament their pauper state.
> Poor cadgers, ah, the pity's great!
> •   •   •   •   •   •   •   •
> To beg some men will always choose,
> Though they could work if but they would,
> They're young and strong, their health is good,
> Save that their back they'll not incline,
> These sluggards have a corpse's spine.
> Their children in their youth they train
> To profit well by beggar's gain,
> •   •   •   •   •   •   •
> Beggardom every country spatters.

120. Re: Geiler's attack on false beggars and the "bad poor," see Francis Rapp, "L'Église et les pauvres à la fin du Moyen Age," *Revue d'histoire de l'Église de France* 52 (1966), 42; and Rolf Johannsmeier, "Die Angst vor den Armen: Bettlerszenen vom Oberrhein," in Boehncke & Johannsmeier, *Das Buch der Vaganten.*

121. See Bruno Boesch, "Zu Sprache und Wortschatz der alemannischen Dichtung 'Von des tüfels segi' (Teufels Netz)," *Alemannisches Jahrbuch* (1971/72); and Ruth Mohl, *The Three Estates in Medieval and Renaissance Literature* (New York: Columbia Univ. Press, 1933), 88ff.

• • • • • • • •

He uses crutches when he's out,
But not when no one is about;
He throws a fit before a crowd
So everyone will shout aloud;
He borrows children by the score
So he'll have mouths to feed galore,

• • • • • • • • • •

He limps, he's hunched and very sick,
He ties his leg to crutch or stick
Or hides a bone 'neath garments thick.
Should anyone inspect his wound
He'd find it very shrewdly bound.
Beggars I grant a deal of space,
They're plentiful in every race
And evermore their numbers grow,
For begging's pleasant, that they know,
Except for those who have no choice,
The rest in cadgers' weeds rejoice.[122]

The most significant work historically of this genre is the *Liber Vagatorum* (*The Book of Vagabonds*) of 1510 attributed to Mathias Hütlin, master of the hospital at Pforzheim.[123] The work is divided into three parts. The first part describes twenty-eight different types of beggars and swindlers. The second part gives a comprehensive review of the most important methods used to trick people into giving alms. The third part provides a list of Rotwelsch-German words, the particular argot of these beggars.[124] The main concern of the author is to unmask false beggars and their deceptive practices. This work

122. Edwin H. Zeydel, trans. & ed., *The Ship of Fools by Sebastian Brant* (New York: Dover, 1962), 208–11.
123. See P. Assion, "Matthias Hütlin und sein Gaunerbuchlein, 'de Liber Vagatorum,'" *Alemannisches Jahrbuch* (1971/72), and Piero Camporesi, *Il libro dei vagabondi* (Turin: Einandi, 1973). For the text itself with an English translation by J. C. Hotten and revised by D. B. Thomas, see *Liber Vagatorum: The Book of Vagabonds* (London: Penguin, 1932). A modern German edition is in Boehncke & Johannsmeier, *Buch der Vaganten*, 79–101. The best recent study of this prototype of the "anatomy of roguery" literature is Robert Jütte, *Abbild und soziale Wirklichkeit des Bettler- und Gaunertums zu Beginn der Neuzeit: Sozial-, Mentalitäts-, und Sprachgeschichtliche Studien zum Liber Vagatorum* (1510) (Cologne & Vienna: Böhlau, 1988). Cf. also John Van Cleve, *The Problem of Wealth in the Literature of Luther's Germany* (Columbia, S.C.: Camden House, 1991).
124. See Jütte, *Abbild*. In England the language of rogues and vagabonds was called "cant" and "Pedlar's French." "It is doubtful whether Pedlar's French represented an alternative ideology. It provided a means of communication but its parameters were quite narrow." Beier, *Masterless Men*, 126. For discussion and examples of French rogue literature, see Geremek, *Margins of Society*, 210–22, 306ff.

proved to be very popular and was reprinted in a number of editions and languages, including one with an introduction by Luther.[125]

The descriptions of the various tricks practiced to arouse sympathy usually include rather colorful stories. The chapter on "cripples" tells of a beggar in Selestat who had cut the leg off a thief who had been hanged. He would sit and beg in front of the churches with his own leg tucked under him and this decayed limb in front of him. Another beggar, perhaps jealous of this man's trick, went to the town authorities, who then came to investigate. The trickster ran off so fast that "a horse could not have caught him." Later he was caught in Achern and hanged, and the dried leg was hanged along with him.

A more humorous account of divine justice being meted out to beggars is from a collection of sermon illustrations by Jacques de Vitry (c. 1160–1240). In this story two wandering beggars, one blind and the other lame, are caught up in a crowd awaiting a procession bearing the miracle-working body of Saint Martin. The beggars strive to get out of the crowd for fear that if the miraculous body passes them "we shall be healed immediately, and no one in the future will give us any alms, but we shall have to work and labor with our own hands." In spite of their efforts to escape, the procession overtook them and "they were healed against their will."[126] A less humorous outcome is reported in the story of a sturdy beggar who appeared in Augsburg in 1434. His trick was to collapse on the street and appear to die. After he received last rites and money was collected for his burial, he suddenly arose and made off with the money. Caught repeating this act in other cities, he was hanged.[127]

Common to much of the literature about false beggars are descriptions of such tricks as chewing soap to produce a foamy mouth, wrapping oneself in bloody rags, tying up limbs to appear crippled, wearing broken chains as if escaped from prison or slavery, and carrying infants—especially maimed and screaming ones—for sympathy. One account tells of a man who wandered the countryside with the head of a cadaver. He told people that it was the head of his son, who had died on a pilgrimage to Saint James of Compostela. The man then begged for funds so he could take the head to Rome and have his son's sainthood confirmed. When the man was arrested, it was discovered that he had accumulated the enormous sum of 20 florins by this ploy.[128]

Authorities and later reformers used such stories in their efforts to distinguish legitimate beggars from false. The motivation for making this distinction was primarily theological, not social. Properly directed alms created an interest-bearing treasure in heaven; alms given to frauds went to the kingdom of the devil rather than the kingdom of God. Thus the beggar literature served to assist the charitable citizen concerned about the correct investment

---

125. WA 26:634–54. See Part Two, section 5.6, of this volume.
126. Marshall Baldwin, ed., *Christianity through the Thirteenth Century* (New York: Harper & Row, 1970), 396. See Part Two, section 5.2, of this volume.
127. Maschke, "Unterschichten," 69.
128. Geremek, *Truands et misérables*, 190.

of alms and the avoidance of the false beggars' "embezzlement of heaven."[129] The *Liber Vagatorum* and similar literature were decisively influenced by the medieval doctrine of almsgiving as developed by Thomas Aquinas.[130]

The sensationalism of these stories undoubtedly focused disproportionate attention on the perceived criminal element among the poor. The moralizing analysis of false begging placed responsibility for the poverty of the beggar upon the person's own laziness, immorality, and/or lack of faith. The documents do not mention the possible economic and social mechanisms that could have caused the person's impoverishment; they do not consider begging as a means of self-help. The impoverished in many cases had few possibilities beyond living by their wits.[131] Some recent studies suggest that the stereotypes presented in the rogue literature of the sixteenth and seventeenth centuries rarely corresponded with reality.

> Vagrants were criticised by pamphleteers because they appeared to conform to no social norm: they did not have wives, families, homes or religion. But in so far as these accusations were true, they were a consequence, not a cause, of life on the roads. As far as we can tell, the poor tried to maintain their respectability and their adherence to social conventions for as long as possible. . . . It would therefore seem to be a mistake to think of "the poor" as having distinct social attitudes. Social distinctions were imposed on them from above.[132]

These social distinctions imposed from above not only reflected the perceived reality of the time, they also helped to create it. The Europe-wide stigmatization of beggars and the repressive measures that led to the criminalization of begging were expressions of the fear of the social instability present in the masses of beggars and vagrants. The anxiety that the poor were subversive and intent upon turning the world upside down stimulated the development of a subculture of the marginalized. This subculture's secret language, Rotwelsch, enabled "safe" communication among its participants; its diverse roots indicate the heterogeneous composition of medieval vagrancy.[133]

129. Boehncke & Johannsmeier, *Buch der Vaganten*, 44–45.
130. Assion, "Matthias Hütlin," 87f.; Hans Scherpner, *Theorie der Fürsorge* (Göttingen: 1962), 50, 203f.; Jütte, *Abbild*, 43. For a positive treatment of Thomas, see Stephen Pope, "Aquinas on Almsgiving, Justice, and Charity: An Interpretation and Reassessment," *Heythrop Journal* 32 (1991).
131. Irsigler & Lassotta, *Bettler und Gaukler*, 56–57.
132. Slack, "Reactions of the Poor," 24.
133. See Jütte, *Abbild*, chaps. 3–4. For an example of late medieval fear and scapegoating of vagrants, see R. W. Scribner, "The *Mordbrenner* Fear in Sixteenth-Century Germany: Political Paranoia or the Revenge of the Outcast?" in Richard J. Evans, ed., *The German Underworld: Deviants and Outcasts in German History* (London & New York: Routledge, 1988).

The Secularization of Charity

The poor were by no means only loathed, feared, or treated oppressively by others. The practice of charity was viewed during this time as a means of ensuring salvation; it fulfilled the religious injunction (summarized in Matthew 25) to feed, clothe, and support the poor. To modern sensibilities, it may seem that the medieval attitude toward the poor was a utilitarian one. However, it is likely that many persons felt sincere concern for neighbors in need, although such concern may not be documentable for the historian.

What is of interest in the late medieval period is that all the motivations and concerns regarding the poor begin to find expression in new ways. Modern historians refer to these developments as the rationalization and secularization of charity. This should not be understood in a post-Enlightenment sense of civil autonomy from the church. I intend the phrase "secularization of charity" to serve as shorthand for the late medieval efforts by civil authorities to increase their role or even gain control in the administration of ecclesial resources for charity. The secularization process that took place in various areas of charity is also referred to as a communalization process. The communalizing of poor relief included the initiatives of groups of citizens and later the support and involvement of public authorities, such as town councils functioning as trustees and guardians of charitable foundations.[134]

These terms, "rationalization" and "secularization," are useful descriptors, but it is important to not read into them the post-Enlightenment values that separate reason and the secular from theology, worship, and the church. The medieval mind did not conceive of reason as autonomous nor of civic life separate from religious life. Even the complex relationships of ecclesial and civil authority, laws, economics, and politics, with all the attendant particular problems present in a medieval episcopal city like Augsburg, were seen by contemporaries as a whole.[135] So, for example, the Brückner foundation in Würzburg with its citizen membership and town guardianship designated bread and a half measure of wine for all the poor who attended the Lord's Supper, but only bread for those who did not.[136]

The beginnings of the rationalization and secularization of charity may be seen in the development of the means of distribution of charity through the tables of the poor (Latin: *mensa Sancti Spiritus*; German: *heilige Geisttafel*; French: *Tables des pauvres*; Spanish: *Plats dels Pobres*), the use of charity tokens,

---

134. In his study on the city of Augsburg in the late Middle Ages, Rolf Kiessling traces the development of poor relief from an ideology of almsgiving closely linked to the church, to its gradual movement away from ecclesial institutional bonds in the fourteenth and fifteenth centuries, toward the beginnings of a more rationalized, centralized urban welfare program. Kiessling, *Bürgerliche Gesellschaft*, 219, 239. Trüdinger, *Stadt und Kirche*, 114–15.

135. Kiessling, *Bürgerliche Gesellschaft*, 358.

136. Trüdinger, *Stadt und Kirche*, 116.

pawnshops (Latin: *Mons pietatis*; French: *Mont-de-piété*; Italian: *Monti di Pietà*), confraternities, and hospitals. All of these developments indicate the growing awareness of the magnitude of poverty as a social problem and the recognition that its solution required a reasoned application of the resources of the community.

As a consequence of these insights, public authorities were increasingly involved in relief measures and in intermittent efforts to prevent conditions conducive to poverty. The rationalizing and secularizing processes went hand in hand, but they proceeded at varying rates throughout Europe. A common characteristic everywhere, however, was the urban context for these developments.

The pressure for poor relief was, of course, greater in the cities than in the countryside. The communalization of poor relief began in the cities when citizens without the direct influence of the church began to assist the house poor. In the early stages of this development, the urban administration was also not involved; thus it may not properly be called communal poor relief. It had rather a social character related to the community itself and mutual benefit associations.

To appreciate the contributions of the early modern city to the development of social welfare, it is necessary to recall that unlike today's secular city, the early modern city had a communitarian character of covenantal, participatory, and class dimensions. Like the medieval guilds, the cities and towns were based on a covenant, a solemn collective oath (or series of oaths) to a publicly expressed charter. This was not so much a social contract as "a kind of sacrament; it both symbolized and effectuated the formation of the community and the establishment of the community's law."[137] The participatory aspects of this covenantal community included mutual assistance and protection with regard to all aspects of the community's social, economic, and political life. This should not be confused with contemporary concepts of democracy, because the community was founded not on individuals per se but on subordinate communities.[138] Belonging to one of these subcommunities was crucial for an individual's legal as well as social existence. Some persons, such as vagabonds, wandering beggars, and those in certain professions, were marginalized to the extent of being outsiders. Finally, it is important to recall that while the cities understood themselves to be divinely instituted—the foundation oath, after all, was "a kind of sacrament"—their self-understood mission was not that of the church to maintain worship and doctrine. The role of the city was primarily "to control violence and to regulate political and economic relations—that is, to keep peace and to do justice."[139]

137. Berman, *Law and Revolution*, 393.
138. "French social historians have given the name *société des ordres* ('society of orders') and German social historians have given the name *Ständestaat* ('state of estates') to this type of social structure. . . ." Ibid., 394.
139. Ibid., 395.

Thus, for example, in Braunschweig the two major annual distributions of goods to the poor were arranged according to the municipal areas of the town. The so-called *Hagelspende* (hail-alms) took place on the Friday before Saint Margaret's Day so "that God would give grace for the harvest." The other distribution was on the Friday before the Exaltation of the Cross. The great bell of St. Martin would sound and then the watchman would call through the streets, "Bread! Bread!" Donations would then be distributed in front of the town hall.

Cologne provides a more characteristic example. The population of the city was made up of nine communities, each of which had its own citizen judge who could exercise decisions on minor cases. Each section of the city conducted its own poor relief. The town districts or wards generally corresponded with the parishes, but the poor relief was not conducted by the parish. While this system is the forerunner of communal poor relief, it is not yet developed beyond the contributions of groups of citizens. The ward elder administered the goods for the poor that were at hand and collected and distributed gifts. The distribution took place in front of the church doors, not in the church. There a table was set up to hold the gifts brought by the members of the community. The poor came to the table to pick up their assistance. Because the tables were often set up before churches named Sanctus Spiritus, this form of poor relief came to be known as the Holy Spirit Table (*heilige Geisttafel*).[140] "The term *mensa Sancti Spiritus* [Latin: Holy Spirit table] was used to describe the fund or portion of revenues set aside for the poor, regardless of the specific means of distribution. Donations and bequests were made in favor of the 'table of the Holy Spirit,' so that in time this form of charity came to rely upon a broad and sometimes substantial economic base."[141]

This form of local aid was also well developed in the Low Countries. Distributions, made on certain days of the week and on feast days, consisted of clothing, shoes, bread, meat, dried herring, peas, oil, wine or beer, and firewood. Reserves were stocked in the cellars and attics of the "guest houses," which also included kitchens, refectories, and distribution rooms. During periods of crisis such as famine or economic disturbances in employment

<hr />

140. Uhlhorn, *Christliche Liebesthätigkeit*, 506–7. Many hospitals and foundations for the poor were dedicated to the Holy Spirit as the comforter of the poor and sick. See F. J. Mone, "Armen- und Krankenpflege vom 13. bis 16. Jahrhundert," *Zeitschrift für die Geschichte des Oberrheins* 12 (1861), 10f. and the source documents 142–94. The frequent appellation of Holy Spirit to hospitals and other institutions of charity reflects the theological identity of love, *caritas*, and the Holy Spirit expressed in Peter Lombard's *Sentences*. See Hering, "Liebesthätigkeit," 664. The name may also be traced back to the hospital-founding Order of the Brothers of the Holy Spirit, endorsed by Innocent III in 1198. See Axel Murken, "Von den ersten Hospitälern bis zum modernen Krankenhaus," in Carl Meckseper, ed., *Stadt im Wandel: Kunst und Kultur des Bürgertums in Norddeutschland 1150–1650* (Stuttgart-Bad Canstatt: Edition Cantz, 1984), vol. 3, 192.
141. William J. Courtenay, "Token Coinage and the Administration of Poor Relief during the Late Middle Ages," *Traditio* 3/2 (1972), 285.

and buying power, these tables for the poor were unable to meet the sharply increased needs.[142]

In Catalonia, examples of these tables for the poor are well documented. Here, too, the tables were founded by laity and administered by *probi homines* (honest persons) who were elected annually. The resources of the tables came from foundations made by the laity and from offerings of the faithful. Royal and papal authorities did not intervene other than to confirm the privileges of these foundations. The form of relief practiced was similar to that in the north of Europe: distribution of provisions, clothes, shoes, sometimes money, communal meals, and assistance at home. At Santa Maria del Mar, a system of loans with very low interest was instituted. These tables were for the benefit not only of the habitually indigent but also the laboring poor, who frequently needed temporary help. Assistance was reserved for the needy of the parish; public beggars were excluded. The administrators determined the criteria for need. During the time of prosperity in Barcelona in the fourteenth century the tables were sufficiently endowed, but by the end of the century an economic decline had set in and the number of poor increased. Even so, this form of poor relief was not negligible. For example, the Plat of Santa Maria del Pi provided for 791 men and 758 women in 1423, and 935 men and 375 women in 1428. In nearly all cases the men were heads of households.[143]

The occasional distribution of money and the provision for low-interest loans foreshadows or parallels the development of poor-relief tokens and pawnshops for the poor. The development of charity tokens—a kind of early food stamp—may have come as early as the mid-thirteenth century. Their purpose was to facilitate the administration of charity, but they also played a role as token coinage. In connection with Italian confraternities, the tokens were given to the poor before the annual chapter meeting and feast in order to ensure that only the "deserving" poor would receive charity. These tokens, usually of lead, may also have arisen in the context of the king's entertaining the poor on Maundy Thursday in commemoration of Jesus' washing of his disciples' feet. While royal Maundy money initially consisted of coins of intrinsic value, tokens may have been introduced as a means of keeping accounts and distributing charity. It is argued that the application of these tokens to poor-relief distributions constituted a significant transformation of charity that included "the laicization of poor relief" and "a rationalization of the process of giving to the needy."[144]

As noted earlier, the rise of the money economy had negative social effects upon medieval society. In a sense, general potential for depersonalization and alienation that comes with money transactions also carried over into the use of money and token coinage for charity. The giver-receiver relationship shifted from the interpersonal ideal of the biblical stories that

142. Mollat, *Pauvres au Moyen Age*, 332–34.
143. Ibid., 331–32.
144. Courtenay, "Token Coinage," 284–85.

exercised so much power on the medieval mind, to a more commercial relationship. There was, so to speak, another side to this coin: charity tokens and money alms decreased the patronizing aspects of charity in kind, such as gifts of food and clothes. At the same time this approach also allowed the poor some freedom of choice over their lives.[145]

The most important contribution of token coinage for charity, however, was in rationalizing poor relief and thus also enhancing the already initiated process of laicization (secularization) and centralization of poor relief. In his article on token coinage, William Courtenay lists a number of reasons why tokens were significant for the development of relief. The token system allowed the issuing agency, a confraternity or municipal institution, for example, to better control who received aid and to reduce indiscriminate charity. The tokens, even those marked with a specific item such as bread, functioned as a supplemental currency. In effect this meant a larger amount of available small change for charity, which was important in the absence of legitimate money in small denominations. Furthermore, this substitute money allowed charitable institutions to defer expending their resources—not all tokens would be redeemed for goods at any one time. "Ultimately, such a system meant that an institution could coin more tokens (more substitute currency or claims on goods) than it had resources to cover, thus giving more aid to the poor at less cost to the institution."[146] Also, the token that had stamped upon it the particular gift intended—for example, bread—made it more difficult for the recipient to use it for other purposes, such as getting drunk on wine.[147] Finally, although the tokens probably did not retain for long a fixed value as coinage, they did provide the recipient some assurance of obtaining the item in spite of price fluctuations.

The rationalizing of efforts to relieve the poor is also manifest in the development of the *montes pietatis*. These ecclesial charitable institutions, loosely translated as ecclesial pawnshops or forerunners of credit unions, are usually attributed to the efforts of fifteenth-century Franciscans in Italy.[148] The

145. Ibid., 295.
146. Ibid., 289–92. The inherent weakness, of course, was that of creating more tokens than the institutional resources could cover. Before this type of collapse, however, the token coinage system was attacked by an urban population that objected to its limited negotiability and by political authorities who saw it undermining their control of the monetary system.
147. According to Humbert de Romans, many wage-earners spent their money in pubs and thus left their wives and children impoverished. Murray, "Religion among the Poor," 294, 313f.
148. This is the argument especially of Pullan, who is interested in defending medieval Catholic poor relief against charges that it was indiscriminate, unorganized, and ineffective. Pullan also claims that the Monti di Pietà anticipate "by some seventy years the many attempts in Germany, France and the Low Countries in the 1520s and '30s to pool resources in a common chest or all-embracing almonry." Pullan, "Catholics and the Poor," 22. See also Pullan's *Rich and Poor*, 431–625. Lindgren, "Europas Armut," 414, points to earlier fifteenth-century Spanish examples.

earliest example, however, is that of the bishop of London, who in 1361 bequeathed one thousand marks for founding an account to provide interest-free loans valid for a year's use. The amount of the loan rose according to the status of the borrower: ten pounds for a commoner, twenty for a citizen, and fifty for a bishop. The purpose of the *montes* was to collect funds that could then be loaned to the honorable poor and thereby protect them from the avarice of usurers. Those who donated funds to these banks received no interest other than spiritual rewards.

The humanistic argument for the development of the *montes* was that loans were preferable to charity because they would have a preventive rather than a remedial function. The point was that it was easier to prevent degradation than to overcome it after the fact. Furthermore, loans were perceived not only as a means of stimulating recovery but also as an instrument more in conformity with human dignity than charity was. In some cases the funds were eventually supplied by the king or state bank, and thus the state became involved in providing loans at low or no interest. These institutions were most widespread in Italy and Spain.[149]

Brian Pullan has argued that the *Monti di Pietà* are significant evidence for the development of medieval Catholic institutional poor relief in the form of providing inexpensive credit to the poor. The Observant Franciscan preachers who promulgated them "were undoubtedly exercising their traditional function of defending the poor against real or supposed oppressors."[150] In his review article on Pullan's study, Reinhold Mueller points out that these "oppressors of the poor" were perceived primarily to be Jewish bankers.

Agitation against Jews culminated in a movement to eliminate the evils of usury by instituting Christian Monti di Pietà throughout Italy.... As is well known, Franciscan preachers ... were most active in furthering the cause of the Monti di Pietà. These men preached against the Jews, using such themes as the "ritual murder of Christian youths" to incite the populace and thereby gain acceptance of their plans for the establishment of Monti di Pietà.[151]

"Charity became, at best, a secondary and occasional function."[152] Richard Trexler, in an article published three years before Pullan's, suggests that these

149. Cf. Mollat, *Pauvres au Moyen Age*, 335–38; John Gilchrist, *The Church and Economic Activity in the Middle Ages* (London: Macmillan, 1969), 115, 121.
150. Pullan, "Catholics and the Poor," 22.
151. Reinhold C. Mueller, "Charitable Institutions, the Jewish Community, and Venetian Society: A Discussion of the Recent Volume by Brian Pullan," *Studi Veneziani* 14 (1972), 64–65. Cf. also Black, *Italian Confraternities*, 228–29, 230: "Frustratingly little is known about many of these Monti, their organisation, the degree of assistance they gave to the poor (or not so poor) borrowers, and the involvement of confraternities with their organisation and development."
152. Mueller, "Charitable Institutions," 72.

institutions did not benefit the actual poor but rather the elite who were suffering from the credit crisis of the times. "The *Monti di Pietà* did not in fact aid the salaried working class, the *popolo minuto*, but the majority of the pos-sessing class. Poverty must be understood in its contemporary context; hence the problem of the fallen rich must be considered as part of the general credit crisis of the quattrocento."[153] The point of these loans and the charitable activities of similar confraternities was not to assist the indigent but to maintain the status of middle- and upper-class citizens.

> Medieval and early modern charity was not only a tool to control the *popolo minuto* through ameliorative charity; nor can its intent be conceived of as simple Christian love for the less fortunate. It was also an instrument to preserve political and social authority by maintaining the honor of the elite that governed and administered.[154]

The Hospital Movement

The urban laity that was directing its religious energy into the confraternity movements of the thirteenth and fourteenth centuries also found another outlet directly beneficial to community welfare: the hospital movement.[155] Here, too, the process of rationalization and laicization is evident in the growing specialization, administration, research, and therapeutic concerns of the numerous hospitals founded before the mid-fifteenth century. Italian hospitals were particularly renowned; for example, the famous Florentine hospital S. Maria Nuova became the model for London's Savoy hospital as well as hospitals in Germany.[156]

In the West the clergy, especially the regular or monastic clergy, had long practiced medical charity. The famous chapter 36 of the sixth-century *Rule of Saint Benedict* is often cited as evidence for monastic responsibility to care for the sick:

> Before all things and above all things care must be taken of the sick, so that they may be served in very deed as Christ himself; for he said: "I was sick and ye visited me"; and "what you did to one of these least ones, ye did unto me." But let the sick on their part consider that they are being served for the honour of God, and not provoke their brethren who are serving them by their unreasonable demands. Yet they should be patiently borne with, because from such as these is gained a more abundant reward. Therefore let the abbot take the greatest care that they

153. Trexler, "Charity and the Defense of Urban Elites," 84.
154. Ibid., 104. Cf. also Mueller, "Charitable Institutions," 57–59, 80–81.
155. On the Eastern origins of hospitals, see Timothy Miller, *The Birth of the Hospital in the Byzantine Empire* (Baltimore: Johns Hopkins Univ. Press, 1985).
156. See Edward P. de G. Chaney, " 'Philanthropy in Italy,': English Observations on Italian Hospitals, 1545–1789," in Riis I, 189; and Uhlhorn, *Christliche Liebesthätigkeit*, 371.

suffer no neglect. For these sick brethren let there be assigned a special room and an attendant who is God-fearing, diligent, and careful. . . .

The emphasis of this passage is on the care of sick monks, not the care of the laity. Chapter 31, however, offers encouragement to care for those outside the monastic community, although this injunction seems limited to the traditional biblical poor: "take the greatest care of the sick, of children, of guests, and of the poor, knowing without doubt that he [the cellarer] will have to render an account for all these on the Day of Judgement."[157] This continued to be the basic orientation for medieval hospitals. So, for example, the purpose of the Holy Spirit Hospital in Pfüllendorf is set forth as follows:

> This house is dedicated to the exercise of the works of mercy for the salvation of the faithful. These works shall be performed day and night. Namely: the naked shall be clothed, the hungry fed, the weak refreshed, women cared for in the six weeks before childbirth, widows, orphans, and pilgrims who come from every direction shall not be denied food and shelter.[158]

Monasteries were the refuge of the poor. This role extended to concern for the sick poor and included development of simple and inexpensive remedies. A famous example of medical treatises intended to benefit the poor is the *Thesaurus pauperum*, "which listed simple but salubrious herbs that could be gathered in the fields."[159] It is appropriate at this point to respond to the pervasive view that medieval hospitals were hardly more than hospices that focused on care rather than cure. This perspective gained wide currency through Rotha Clay's description of the medieval hospital as an institution primarily ecclesial rather than medical. "It was for care rather than cure: for the relief of the body, when possible, but pre-eminently for the refreshment of the soul. By manifold religious observances, the staff sought to elevate and discipline character. They endeavoured, as the body decayed, to strengthen the soul and prepare it for the future life."[160] Certainly the medieval hospital

157. Darrel W. Amundsen and Gary B. Ferngren, "Medicine and Religion: Early Christianity through the Middle Ages," in Martin E. Marty & Kenneth L. Vaux, eds., *Health/Medicine and the Faith Traditions: An Inquiry into Religion and Medicine* (Philadelphia: Fortress Press, 1982), 115–16. On the development of Benedictine cloister hospitals, see Siegfried Reicke, *Das deutsche Spital und sein Recht im Mittelalter* (Stuttgart: Enke, 1932), vol. 1, 13–25; and Dieter Jetter, *Geschichte des Hospitals*, vol. 1: *Westdeutschland von den Anfängen bis 1850* (Wiesbaden: Steiner, 1966), 11–21.
158. Uhlhorn, *Christliche Liebesthätigkeit*, 372. See Mone, "Armen-und Krankenpflege," 142f., for the documents.
159. Amundsen & Ferngren, "Medicine and Religion," 117. The author of this thirteenth-century treatise may have been Peter Hispanus, who became Pope John XXI in 1276.
160. Rotha M. Clay, *The Hospitals of Medieval England* (London, 1909), xvii–xviii. Similarly, Elizabeth Speakman wrote: "A regular surgical and medical service was not, as a rule, found in the hospitals before the sixteenth century. What the medieval hospitals

would not have conceived of divorcing care and cure; "a hospital without arrangements for worship was unknown to the Middle Ages."[161] But it is equally important to note the medieval view that the art of medicine is God's gift for human benefit, and that many large secular hospitals retained physicians as staff members.[162]

Perhaps some of the confusion over the function of medieval hospitals has arisen from the profusion of names and types of hospitals in the sources. Medieval terminology is not uniform; hospitals included institutions with specific functions of asylum and separation of lepers and the mentally disturbed from the society at large, as well as more general functions of curing those ailments amenable to the medical knowledge of the time. The latter hospital functions also included provision of rest and nourishment for the sick, malnourished, and run-down poor, rest homes for the aged, foundling homes, and orphanages.[163] Furthermore, a hospital could enjoy the status of a religious institution and thus, according to later medieval canonists, have ecclesial privileges such as exemption from tithes.

An eyewitness account of the early development of hospitals throughout Europe is provided by the thirteenth-century ecclesiastic and historian Jacques de Vitry, who devoted a chapter of his *History of the West* to hospitals for the poor and homes for lepers. Those ministering to the poor and lepers are described as "ministers of Christ" who are "deeply compassionate and feeling with respect to the poor and the sick." "Moreover for Christ's sake, very many of them suffer the filth of the sick and nearly intolerable annoyances, thereby inflicting outrages upon themselves which no other kind of penitance may be . . . compare[d]." In short, Vitry graphically adds, the spirits of those serving the sick poor are fertilized by the filthy excrement in which they work.[164] This ascetic and transcendental motivation continued to be a major

provided was nursing, food, rest, and religious consolation." "Mediaeval Hospitals," *Dublin Review* 133 (1903), 290. Lis & Soly, *Poverty and Capitalism*, 23–24, make this same point in a somewhat modified way: "Health care was of secondary significance. . . . Emphasis lay on *hospitalitas*, especially for the needy." Pullan also follows Clay on this point; see his *Rich and Poor*, 205 n. 23.

161. Reicke, *Deutsche Spital*, vol. 1, 198. See also Kiessling, *Bürgerliche Gesellschaft*, 238: "Care of the sick without the care of the church was inconceivable in this period."

162. See Rubin, *Charity and Community*, 150f.; and Katherine Park, *Doctors and Medicine in Early Renaissance Florence* (Princeton: Princeton Univ. Press, 1985); Carlo M. Cipolla, *Public Health and the Medical Profession in the Renaissance* (Cambridge: Cambridge Univ. Press, 1976); Mone, "Armen-und Krankenpflege," 14–23. Cologne established a position of town physician in 1457. Uhlhorn, *Christliche Liebesthätigkeit*, 375–76.

163. Cf. John Durkin, "Care of the Poor: Pre-Reformation Hospitals," in David Roberts, ed., *Essays on the Scottish Reformation 1513–1625* (Glasgow: Burns, 1962); Uhlhorn *Christliche Liebesthätigkeit*, 372–74; Geremek, *Margins of Society*, 170–80.

164. John F. Hinnebusch, *The Historia Occidentalis of Jacques De Vitry: A Critical Edition* (Fribourg: University Press, 1972), 146–51. See also Appendix C, 276–84, for a detailed list of early hospitals, their histories, and secondary sources about them. See also Michel Mollat, "Hospitalité et assistance au début du XIIIᵉ siècle," in David Flood, ed., *Poverty in the Middle Ages* (Werl: Coelde, 1975).

component in Catholic hospital work in the following centuries. As Vincent de Paul expressed in the mid-seventeenth century: "The Daughters of the Hôtel Dieu have as their end first their own perfection and then the relief of the sick."[165]

A hospital could be a lay institution primarily intended for providing physical relief. "A hospital, a house of relief for the poor, sick, and aged, could be founded by anyone, just as a man could open his door to a needy person."[166] Throughout the late Middle Ages individuals continued to found hospitals for the sake of their own souls as well as the physical well-being of those admitted. "But by far the most significant and enduring influence upon the medieval hospital came from the development of the city into a political corporation. With this development a completely new element was introduced into the hitherto ecclesially determined poor relief: an organized citizenry."[167] The older ecclesial institutions were unable to meet the increased demands upon them created by both the growing number of urban immigrants without means, and by the striving of the wealthy citizenry for security in sickness and in old age. Thus in 1256 the citizens of Hannover "enkindled by zeal for the good and motivated by the Holy Spirit," founded a hospital "in which pilgrims and other poor wanderers shall be given shelter, and the blind, lame, and those laden with other illnesses shall be taken in and cared for."[168]

The citizens themselves now began to take over welfare responsibilities. With their provision of the means for these activities, whether by individual or corporate enterprise, the citizenry also laid claims upon the authority and right to the direction or at least the control of the hospitals. A political motive was at work as well, in the extension of the city's legal power into areas that up to this point had been the reserve of other powers, above all that of the church; this power became established within the limits of the control of the citizens' commonweal.[169]

165. Pullan, "Catholics and the Poor," 31; cf. also Pullan, *Rich and Poor*, 266, and Cassie C. Fairchilds, *Poverty and Charity in Aix-en-Provence* 1640–1789 (Baltimore: Johns Hopkins Univ. Press, 1976).

166. Rubin, *Charity and Community*, 103. Rubin's reference is to the *glossa ordinaria* in the "Constitutiones Clementis papae quinti" II, col. 297 in c. Quia Contingit Clem., III, II, 2. See also John H. Mundy, "Hospitals and Leprosaries in Twelfth- and Early Thirteenth-Century Toulouse," in J. H. Mundy, R. Emery, & B. N. Nelson, eds., *Essays in Medieval Life and Thought* (New York: Columbia Univ. Press, 1955), 192, 198ff. The hospitals constituted as a whole the principal domain of charitable activity. It was here that the church carried out its mission of assisting the needy. But it is also necessary to note the enormous role played in this area by individual initiative. Geremek, *Margins of Society*, 197.

167. Reicke, *Deutsche Spital*, vol. 1, 196.

168. Uhlhorn, *Christliche Liebesthätigkeit*, 363.

169. Behind all the ideas for reform of beggary was the idea of the *bonum commune* (the common good). R. Jütte, "Vagantentum und Bettlerwesen bei Hans Jakob Christoffel von Grimmelshausen," *Daphnis* 9 (1980), 130. On the history of the understanding of the commonweal, see Ernst-Wilhelm Kohls, *Die Schule bei Martin Bucer in ihrem Verhältnis*

On the basis of these urban expansionist tendencies, the citizenry established itself in relationship to the welfare institutions ruled by the church. Citizens sought to remove from ecclesial supervision the institutions that they founded and regarded as their own. Up to this time the institutions of welfare and poor relief had existed expressly in the hands of ecclesial powers and carried the forms of the church.

Although isolated incidences of this new development occurred in the second half of the twelfth century, it really came into play in the thirteenth century.[170] Confraternities became more influential, and monastic hospitals acknowledged civic authorities. A good number of new foundations by citizens date from this period. The domination in them of the laity prepared the way for the communalizing of the welfare institutions in the fourteenth century. Again, however, it should be noted that this communalizing process was not a secularization in the modern sense of the term. Indeed, the very juridical concept of a foundation was a contribution by the canonists. The "foundation" or "corporation of goods" (*Stiftung* in German; *fondation* in French) was a legal device that governed the use of a donation for the sake of the beneficiaries stipulated by the donor.

> It consisted of a personification of the purposes to which property, money, land, and incorporeal rights had been dedicated. Thus an ecclesiastical benefice itself—the property rights and duties connected with a clerical office, the income from economic activities adhering to the office, and all other perquisites of it—was treated as a legal person, with power through its officers to conduct its own economic and legal affairs as a single entity. A hospital or poorhouse or educational institution, or a bishopric or abbey, could be viewed not only as a corporation of persons but also as a corporation of goods.[171]

The change was not in the essence of the institution but in its direction and management; that is, a shift from ecclesial to lay administration.

The origin of this secularization of charity foundations is related to the emancipation of citizenry in the area of financial legislation. The developing amortization legislation of the late Middle Ages provided an opportunity for the cities to defend themselves against the increasing accumulation of assets in the hands of the church. Tax-free charity foundations became secularized as their assets and administration passed to the founders and to their heirs; this change was made possible by the shifting of the foundations from the sphere of the "law of things or property" (*Sachenrecht*) to that of the "law of

---

zu Kirche und Obrigkeit (Heidelberg: Quelle & Meyer, 1963), 121–29: "Exkurs II: Zur Bedeutung und Geschichte des Begriffes 'gemein nutz'."

170. Many guilds had their own hospitals. For a list of examples see Uhlhorn, *Christliche Liebesthätigkeit*, 364, and F. J. Mone, "Ueber die Armenpflege vom 13. bis 16. Jahrhunderts," *Zeitschrift für die Geschichte des Oberrheins* 1 (1850).

171. Berman, *Law and Revolution*, 239–40. Cf. also Reicke, *Deutsche Spital*, vol. 2, 286–88.

inheritance." While previously a foundation was a donation to a saint as a legal person, it now became a legal institution of the common civil law.[172]

The church's influence was more and more narrowed to the spiritual sphere. Nevertheless, the hospital priest continued to be as necessary as the hospital administrator. By the beginning of the fourteenth century, the communalized hospital was the norm. The jurisdiction of the church was now limited to pastoral care, even though the lay movement did not assail the character of the hospital as an ecclesial institution. However, by the end of the fifteenth century town councils began to affix the city's coat of arms to the hospitals within the city.[173]

The urban authorities began to bring under their jurisdiction those hospitals that were under the oversight of the bishop and cloisters. One of the earliest examples of this occurred in the city of Strasbourg in 1263. The 1321 Oathbook of the city of Cologne determined that the city council should choose four provisors of the Holy Spirit House who would be responsible to the council for preserving the goods of the House. Later the council took over all hospitals whose foundations did not determine the naming of masters. In 1510 the council determined that it would oversee all the hospitals within the city and that the city shield should be mounted on all of them. This action did not represent opposition to nor rivalry with the church, but rather a strong move toward centralization under the aegis of the city's responsibility for the well-being of its citizens.[174]

A further impetus in the direction of town control of hospitals may have been the association of poverty and disease. Plague and poverty went hand in hand; in time of epidemic, the wealthy fled to safety. Mid-fifteenth-century Florentine legislators created plague-isolation hospitals. Such unhealthy confinement of the sick poor only confirmed the urban bias that "plague and poverty were close companions"—the conditions in these pesthouses led to increased mortality.[175]

Monetary Testaments to Charitable Orders

Substantial financial resources for medieval charitable foundations came from the legacies of persons concerned to fulfill the "seven works of mercy" and to preserve their souls in eternity with God. From the religious point of view

172. Marion Tietz-Strödel, *Die Fuggerei in Augsburg: Studien zur Entwicklung des sozialen Stiftungsbaus im 15. und 16. Jahrhundert* (Tübingen: Mohr, 1982), 8–9; with references to Hans Liermann, *Handbuch des Stiftungsrechtes* (Tübingen, 1963), vol. 1, 159, 164; and Rüger, *Mittelalterliches Almosenwesen*, 51, 53ff.

173. The above description is dependent on Reicke, *Deutsche Spital*, vol. 1, 196–98, 207–8, 251ff., 276–77; vol. 2, 56–70; and Jetter, *Geschichte des Hospitals*, 21–38. See also Hering, "Liebesthätigkeit," 697ff.

174. Uhlhorn, *Christliche Liebesthätigkeit*, 366–67.

175. Ann G. Carmichael, *Plague and the Poor in Renaissance Florence* (Cambridge: Cambridge Univ. Press, 1986), 126ff. See also Geremek, *Potence ou la pitié*, 177–79.

these pious works were a means of expiation for sin. After the testator's death, the legacy funded masses for his or her soul as well as charitable works.[176] The medieval person was not only acutely aware that life is short and the hour of death uncertain, but also vividly sensitive to standing before God the Judge at death. The poor are an object of charity because they are intercessors before God on behalf of the almsgivers. As one scholar cryptically notes: "In the confrontation of the townsman with God, the poor have their role to play."[177] Thus, *pro remedio animae* (for the remedy of my soul) is a frequent phrase in wills, for their essential religious purpose is securing salvation.

This concern for salvation was heightened among the late medieval townsmen and merchants, whose activities were increasingly in conflict with medieval ecclesial morality. Testaments were perceived as a means to extinguish sin and to procure eternal treasure "which neither rust nor moth may consume, nor thieves steal."[178] Legacies were a major support for confraternities. "The rule of the Misericordia of Nembro expressed the hope that any member who left a will would recall the mercy granted by the membership and thus leave some thing to the consortium in remission of his or her sins. 'For as water extinguishes fire,' the rule reminds members, 'alms extinguish sin.' "[179] In short, there was, in Chiffoleau's phrase, a "mathematics of salvation."

Of course, the desire to save one's soul was not the only motivation behind charitable legacies. Other motives included the desire for reconciliation with God and for a quiet and peaceful conscience; attachment to a particular saint; personal predilection for a particular ecclesial corporation or one of its members, penance for a particular sin. Whatever the personal motivations behind the testaments, it is important to remember their primarily religious-cultic character and to resist the anachronous temptation to

176. Medieval monastic expressions of this practice are discussed in Joachim Wallasch, "Konventsstärke und Armenfürsorge in mittelalterlichen Klöstern, Zeugnisse und Fragen," *Saeculum* 39 (1988), 184–99, 193ff.

177. Françoise Leclère, "Recherches sur la charité des bourgeois envers les pauvres au XIVe siècle à Douai," *Revue du Nord* 48 (1966), 144, 154. For further references and bibliography, see Gerhard Jaritz, "Seelenheil und Sachkultur," in *Europäisches Sachkultur des Mittelalters* (Vienna: Verlag der Österreichischen Akademie der Wissenschaften, 1980), 59–60; Gerhard Jaritz, "Die Realienkundliche Aussage der sogenannten 'Wiener Testamentsbücher,' " in *Das Leben in der Stadt des Spätmittelalters* (Vienna: Verlag der Österreichischen Akademie der Wissenschaften, 1977), 185ff.; Gertrud Rücklin-Teuscher, *Religiöses Volksleben des ausgehenden Mittelalters in den Reichsstädten Hall und Heilbronn* (Berlin: Ebering, 1933), 106–10; Ahasver von Brandt, *Regesten der Lübecker Bürgertestamente des Mittelalters* (Lübeck: Schmidt-Römhild, 1964); Ahasver von Brandt, "Mittelalterliches Bürgertestamente," in *Stiftungsberichte der Heidelberger Akademie der Wissenschaften. Philosophische-historische Klasse* 3 (1973); Hans Lentze, "Das Seelgerät im mittelalterlichen Wien," *Zeitschrift der Savigny-Stiftung für Rechtsgeschichte. Kanonistische Abteilung* 44 (1958); M.-S. de Nucé de Lamothe, "Piété et charité publique à Toulouse de la fin du XIIIe siècle d'apres les testaments," *Annales du Midi* 76 (1964); Chiffoleau, *Comptabilité, passim*; Geremek, *Margins of Society*, 183–92; R. Po-Chia Hsia, "Civic Wills as Sources for the Study of Piety in Muenster, 1530–1618," *SCJ* 14/3 (1983).

178. Rücklin-Teuscher, *Religiöses Volksleben*, 87, 106.

179. Little, *Liberty, Charity, Fraternity*, 74–75.

displace religious concerns with social ones.[180] Thus, as Chiffoleau points out, the profound shift in the hierarchy of salvatory works in the late Middle Ages from charitable bequests to the endowment of masses is due to the increased value attributed to the multiplication of intercessions for the dead at that time. Between 1360 and the beginning of the sixteenth century, the mass becomes the essential preparation for the journey, the price of passage from this world to the next. The works of mercy and charitable gestures regain their importance after the Council of Trent, when it is necessary to reaffirm, in the face of the doctrine of justification by grace, that works contribute to salvation.[181]

The object of the testaments was to cope with death and provide for the hereafter. "Most forms of charity had an impact on this world's social fabric, but they were intended to secure a place for the donor in the next one."[182] The expressions of testaments took many forms: money, foods (sometimes complete meals), clothes, and provisions for baths (the *Seelbad*). Money was frequently given out during funeral ceremonies in order to attract as many poor people as possible and induce their prayers for the testator. Foundations were also established in this connection to provide annual distributions to the poor, usually during Advent, Lent, and the anniversary of the testator's death. When the legacy was to a house for the poor, the executor could exercise control over the inhabitants. Because the poor could not afford the entrance fee for the town bathhouses, a favorite medieval charitable act was to provide baths for the poor, frequently followed by meals. Rich townsmen also favored giving clothes or cloth to the poor because this contributed to an ostentatious display at their funeral procession as well as intercessory prayers.

Testaments for hospitals included houses for lepers, strangers, and pilgrims. Hospitals were a favored focus for charity because their many inmates meant that the benefactor would receive many prayers of intercession, and these prayers were guaranteed by the ordinance of the foundation. The medieval hospital was in many ways a parallel to the beneficed cloister. As citizen testaments to hospitals grew in number, the hospitals took on an increasingly citizen character. Poor and sick persons continued to be taken into the hospitals, but personal citizen involvement led to a growing rationalization of the hospital foundation and administration. Benefactors often entered the hospitals to live out their old age on their own benefice.

Testaments were also directed to the poor in the broadest sense—to the church in general, which used the resources for various ecclesial corporations.

180. Cf. Lentze, "Seelgerät," 81. Geremek, *Margins of Society*, 183: "Charitable bequests are easily explained. They are a means of atoning for sins, of restoring goods improperly acquired, and a convenient way of settling accounts with life." Cf. also John H. Mundy, "Charity and Social Work in Toulouse, 1100–1250," *Traditio* 22 (1966).
181. Chiffoleau, *Comptabilité*, 323ff., 353–56.
182. Steven Epstein, *Wills and Wealth in Medieval Genoa*, 1150–1250 (Cambridge: Harvard Univ. Press, 1984), 170; see also v–vi, 6–7, 159–62, 167–200.

Even public works were the object of testaments. The construction of a bridge or improvement of a road was understood as assistance to pilgrims, mendicant monks, and traveling preachers, and thus vicarious participation in their good works.

The Church—Helper and Hinderer of the Poor

The origins of early modern social welfare and the church's involvement in these origins is, even in overview, a complicated story. Clearly, the church in its theology and praxis both intended to protect and serve the poor and actually accomplished this in many ways. The church was instrumental in the collection and distribution of vast amounts of material aid to the needy by means of alms, hospitals, foundations, confraternities, and low-interest loans. At its best, the church also lived out its gospel in solidarity with the poor and in the confidence and eschatological hope inspired by the biblical story of Lazarus.

As the Middle Ages grew in complexity, however, the medieval church and its theology increasingly became less effective in and even a hindrance to the poor's welfare. The theological and ethical structures of the church were not equal to the massive pauperism arising from the social, demographic, economic, political, and natural conjunctures of the late Middle Ages. The theological understanding of poverty as a virtue—an understanding developed in a profoundly ecclesial as well as agricultural and gift-giving society—was challenged by the development of an urban society that prized wealth over poverty. Certainly the church in its canonical and theological expression had long distinguished between the "worthy" and "unworthy" poor, but it was unprepared for and unequal to the strain that would be put on such a distinction by the pauperization attendant upon urban development, and the distrust, anxiety, and censure engendered in the cities by the poor. A church and theology that sanctified poverty as the favored path to salvation, and that created thousands of able-bodied beggars in the monastic and mendicant orders, was hard-pressed by a developing urban and proto-capitalist society that strove to sanctify labor and condemn idleness.

At the same time, this developing urban society was thoroughly imbued with the church's values even as it struggled to apply them to a new context. Thus the Begging Orders in various cities were not designed to combat pauperism but to control some of its expressions by protecting the public from swindlers, foreign beggars, and able-bodied idlers. These Begging Orders were the forerunners of sixteenth-century Poor Orders, but they predate the Reformation motto "that there should be no beggars among Christians" and the idea that all incapable of work should be supported by the community. The ideal Christian life was still seen in terms of monasticism; voluntary poverty and begging were still seen as holy; and salvation was still sought in alms and charity foundations, the motto for which was *ac remedium animae—*

"for the sake of salvation." Medieval charity helped the poor by supporting them in their poverty.

The lack of a social ethic in medieval charity was a hindrance to the development of prophylactic measures against the growth of pauperism. But if the social ethics of the medieval church are judged wanting from a later perspective, some elements of its personal ethic warrant reiteration in our day. "We would do well to live by the medieval canon law which said that 'poverty is not a kind of crime,' that 'in case of doubt it is better to do too much than do nothing at all,' and that above all the intrinsic human dignity of the poor is to be respected by all who seek to help."[183]

183. Carter Lindberg, "Through a Glass Darkly: A History of the Church's Vision of the Poor and Poverty," *Ecumenical Review* 33 (1981), 51–52; citations from Tierney, *Medieval Poor Law*, 133.

Chapter 2

Urban Realities
and Reformation Ideals

RELIEF OF THE POOR in the late Middle Ages rested upon hospitals
and alms. Alms was the form of charity that individuals dispersed
personally or, as was mainly the case for larger sums, gave to the churches
and cloisters for distribution. A fundamental religious motivation for such
charity was personal salvation. This is evident in the charters of charitable
foundations right up to the eve of the Reformation. A representative example
is the alms foundation created by the Freiburg guild master Peter Sprung on
8 April 1510. The preface of the charter reads:

> . . . we understand the instructions and counsel in the Holy Scriptures
> that alms for the relief and feeding of the neediest poor are good deeds
> most pleasing to God, for he himself has said that what anyone does for
> the least among his own, he does for God himself. So also blessed Tobiah
> exhorts his son to give his temporal goods for alms and not turn his face
> away from the poor for . . . alms redeem from sin and death and preserve
> the soul of the merciful from damnation.[1]

The primary concern here is not the economic situation of the poor, nor even
the potential social significance of alms, but rather the biblical injunction to

---

1. StA Freiburg XVII Stiftungen, Sprung 1510 April 8. Cited by Thomas Fischer, "Der
Beginn frühmoderner Sozialpolitik in deutschen Städten des 16. Jahrhunderts," in
*Arbeitspapiere des Forschungsschwerpunktes Reproduktionsrisiken, soziale Bewegungen und Sozial-
politik,* Nr. 3. Universität Bremen (1980), 13.

give alms and their perceived utilitarian value for the donor in terms of forgiveness of sins and acquisition of merit for salvation.

Late medieval mendicant preaching exhorted the rich to sacrifice their earthly goods for the sake of heavenly rewards. The focal point of this preaching was not social change or even amelioration of the conditions of the poor recipient, but rather the spiritual health of the donor. This preaching "was an attempt to provide an increasingly spiritually anxious and self-assertive urban laity with the tools to work for their own salvation."[2] This universal orientation was anchored in the sacrament of penance and served as the essential motivation for the creation of charitable foundations. As effective as this motivation was in the proliferation of charitable foundations, it was limited in the actual relief of the poor. A large number of foundations had a weak financial basis. The distribution of alms was not primarily concerned with the improvement of the social and economic situation of the poor, but with the salvation of the donor. Most of the foundations lacked clear directions for their constructive use beyond the common directive that the recipient was to pray for the soul of the benefactor.

The churches and cloisters that administered charitable foundations lacked specific criteria for support of the needy. Alms distributions occurred on various days throughout the year, such as saints' days and anniversaries of the founders' deaths. At those times, irrespective of the relative social needs and the specific needs of individual beggars, a fixed amount of money or food was distributed. The ecclesial foundations did not coordinate their efforts in planning distributions, nor in determining the extent of needs in the area. Further, only a fuzzy distinction was drawn between the needy and others. The system tended to promote the expansion of beggary into a regular trade.

The late medieval reactions to this situation included the development of begging ordinances designed to curb false begging; literary attacks upon beggars such as the *Liber vagatorum*; and growing urban concern to move from arbitrary alms distributions to communal welfare programs. The latter strove to realize a more rational process for support of the needy, a process that entailed centralizing the welfare resources in the community itself. In this confluence of accentuated social problems and the tensions and antagonisms between urban magistrates and the clerical guardians of ecclesial foundations over how to address these problems, the new doctrines of the Reformers made a major contribution to social welfare policy and legislation. Just as the medieval religious understanding subordinated social welfare to the poverty-alms-salvation complex, so the Reformation religious understanding of salvation liberated energies and resources for social change. This observation is not meant to minimize the motivating forces of fear and reasons of state in early modern urban efforts to seek new solutions to dramatically increased

2. David Lesnick, *Preaching in Medieval Florence: The Social World of Franciscan and Dominican Spirituality* (Athens: Univ. of Georgia Press, 1989), 37; cf. also 131, 174.

urban poverty. It is intended rather to give due to Luther and those who followed him for their creation of a new field of discourse concerning Christian responsibility.

In these days of the ascendancy of social history, the claim that religion can function as an agent of social change is no longer in style and is indeed often vigorously attacked.[3] Therefore it is important to reiterate the transformative effects of religion. In a recent article Steven Ozment wrote:

> It has recently been argued that the chief obstacle to a comprehensive history of the Reformation is a "persistent reluctance on the part of Western historians to concede that the Reformation, a 'religious event,' may have been shaped by social influences." Such belief has inspired a new historiography in which "social context" has become a kind of magical key to human behaviour. The reverse of the above proposition may, however, be closer to the truth: the obstacle to a comprehensive history of the Reformation may lie rather in the reluctance of modern historians to ask how a 'religious event' functioned as an agent of social change in what all agree was a uniquely religious age. How did the widespread displacement of traditional religious beliefs, practices, and institutions reshape man and society in the sixteenth century? That is the crucial question of Reformation historiography.[4]

Certainly it is not my intention to suggest that the Reformation can be reduced to theology, but to restore the roles of ideas and human motivations to our understanding of social change. In fact, it is when we understand the ideas and motivations of the Reformers within their historical, social context that their unique contributions stand out. Two elements, in particular, of this context stand out with regard to the development of early modern social welfare: humanism and the late medieval urban development.

My decision to discuss humanist and urban contributions to the development of poor relief at this point does not indicate that I regard these phenomena as prior in chronology and/or importance to the contributions

3. "The best recent research suggests ... that it is difficult to correlate any significant social change in sixteenth-century Europe with the introduction of Protestant religion." Thomas Brady, *Ruling Class, Regime and Reformation at Strasbourg* 1520–1555 (Leiden: Brill, 1978), 11 n. 39.
4. Steven Ozment, "The Social History of the Reformation: What Can We Learn from the Pamphlets?" in Hans-Joachim Köhler, ed., *Flugschriften als Massenmedium der Reformationzeit* (Stuttgart: Klett-Cotta, 1981), 176–77. Wolfgang Rochler makes a similar point when he states that in contrast to social history, "the historical event of the Reformation becomes transparent in the light of its theological motivations." *Martin Luther und die Reformation als Laienbewegung* (Weisbaden: Steiner, 1981), 70. Cf. also Abel A. Alves, "The Christian Social Organism and Social Welfare: The Case of Vives, Calvin, and Loyola," SCJ 20 (1989), 13f.: "Social control and social responsibility were interwoven, and recognition of a mixture of spiritual and material motives seems far more accurate than arguments that systems of poor relief arose purely from the latter."

of the Reformers. This discussion is placed here in order to simplify a great deal of complex material. I note this because some scholars would argue the priority of humanist contributions over those of the Reformers, while others would do likewise for the importance of urban development. Certainly there is sound insight in the catchphrases "no Renaissance, no Reformation," and "no town, no Reformation"; however, Martin Luther was neither a humanist nor urban, but a monk in a backwater town. Some humanists made their intellectual contributions to welfare policies before Luther made his, and others made theirs after the Reformation was under way; furthermore, some humanists were also Reformers and vice versa. The clue to the impact of these proposals, however, lies less in their chronology than in their substance.

Humanist Contributions and Ideas

It is fitting to begin this overview of humanist contributions with that most renowned scholar of the sixteenth century, Desiderius Erasmus (c. 1469–1536). One of his most widely read works—indeed, one of the most widely read books of the age—was *Enchiridion Militis Christiani* ("Handbook of the Militant Christian"). This was Erasmus's most popular effort to provide the laity with a simple manual on what it means to live the Christian life in the world. It was first published in 1503 and went through eight more Latin editions between 1514 and 1518. The following translations indicate its acceptance throughout Europe: English, 1518; Czech, 1519; German, 1520; Dutch, 1523; Spanish, 1526; French, 1529; Portuguese, 1541; Italian, 1542; Polish, 1582.[5] Erasmus's ideal of a Christian lay theology was well established in the imperial cities and found expression in the phrase of Joachim Vadian (1485–1551), a proponent of Zwinglian reform in St. Gall: "monasticism in the world."[6]

Desiderius Erasmus's Good Christian

In a manner reminiscent of Saint Francis, Erasmus radicalizes the tradition about poverty. "You believed that only to monks was property forbidden and poverty imposed? You have erred, for it pertains to all Christians. The civil law punishes you if you take to yourself what belongs to another. It does not punish you if you refuse your possessions to a needy brother. Yet even so

---

5. John P. Dolan, trans., *Erasmus: Handbook of the Militant Christian* (Notre Dame, Ind.: Fides Publishers, 1962), 58. Cf. Robert Stupperich, "Das Enchiridion militis christiani des Erasmus von Rotterdam nach seiner Enstehung, seinem Sinn und Charakter," ARG 69 (1978).

6. Ernst-Wilhelm Kohls, "Evangelische Bewegung und Kirchenordnung in oberdeutsch-en Reichsstädten," *Zeitschrift der Savigny-Stiftung für Rechtsgeschichte, Kanonistische Abteilung* 53 (1967), 115f.

Christ will punish you."[7] Like the church fathers[8] whom Erasmus studied so diligently, he sharply criticized his contemporaries' commitment to profit. "A person who spends his whole life gathering wealth might be a good businessman but he can hardly be a good Christian. . . . You can neither keep nor get great riches without sin."[9]

The purpose of charity, Erasmus argued, is not the "higher hedonism" of accumulating merits for salvation, but the service of one's neighbor. Erasmus's personal ethics is expressed in his reference to Saint Paul, who

> bids us all to bear one another's burdens, since we are all members of one another. See, therefore, whether they belong to this body, whom now and again you hear speaking in this way: "My property came to me by inheritance; I do not possess it by fraud. Why should I not enjoy it according to my own inclination, and abuse it? Why should I give anything to them to whom I owe nothing? I squander it, I lose it, yet what is lost is mine. It makes no difference to others." Your fellow member opens wide his mouth with fasting, while you reek with the flesh of partridge. Your unclothed brother horrifies you, yet your clothing is rotting with moths and decay. You gamble away a thousand pieces of gold in one night, while some poor girl, in dire need, prostitutes her body and loses her soul, for which Christ poured out His soul. You say: "What has that to do with me? My own concerns take up all my thoughts." Do you see yourself a Christian with this mind, fit not even for a man?[10]

Erasmus was not concerned only about the misuse of wealth by the rich. With many of his contemporaries, he also attacked the professional beggars who used tricks to bilk the naive. In his colloquy "Beggar Talk" (first printed in 1524), he exposes some of the ways beggars fool the "suckers" they meet. The colloquy concludes with one of the beggars extolling the freedom and good life of begging:

> This freedom, than which nothing is sweeter, belongs to no king more than it does to us. I don't doubt there are many kings who envy us. Whether there's war or peace, we're safe. We're not taxed when the public is plundered by levies. No one investigates our lives. . . . Neither in peace nor war may kings enjoy themselves, and the mightier they are the more

7. Dolan, *Erasmus*, 133.
8. The church fathers were a resource for humanist reflections on poor relief. See Natalie Zemon Davis, "Gregory Nazianzen in the Service of Humanist Social Reform," *Renaissance Quarterly* 20/4 (1967).
9. Dolan, *Erasmus*, 151, 152.
10. Ibid., 131–32.

men they fear. The common people have a superstitious dread of harming us, as though we were under God's protection.[11]

The other beggar in the dialogue is not so sure, however, that this idyllic life will continue. He has heard that "citizens are already muttering that beggars shouldn't be allowed to roam about at will, but that each city should support its own beggars and all the able-bodied ones forced to work."[12] Luther had indeed proposed just such measures four years earlier in his writing *To the Christian Nobility of the German Nation Concerning the Reform of the Christian Estate* (1520), and numerous German cities had already enacted legislation to prohibit begging entirely and to provide social welfare for their poor citizens.

Although Erasmus indicates awareness of these laws against begging, his social concern is primarily expressed in terms of a renewed personal ethic, such as that so forcefully stated in his *Handbook*. More comprehensive expressions and even programs for social reform and welfare were articulated by his friends and fellow humanists, Thomas More and Juan Luis Vives. They all share the elements of rational social and moral construction of the future ideal city and state that distinguish early modern utopias from their medieval predecessors that idealized the "good old days" of harmony, and plenty under a just king.[13]

Thomas More's Ideals

Thomas More (1478–1535) is well known for his *Utopia* (1516), a kind of alter ego to Machiavelli's *Prince*, which appeared about the same time.[14] In his work, More sharply criticizes the political and social abuses of the day. The English land enclosures, he argues, will only lead to more poverty; the laws against vagabonds are misdirected; the mendicant friars are worse than beggars; the rich live at the expense of the poor; and money and property have become the measure of all things. The second book of his *Utopia* describes a land ruled by reason and righteousness. Because everything is held in common and no private property exists to stimulate greed, there are no poor people or beggars. Religion in this Utopia is primarily a system of ethics that instills

11. Craig R. Thompson, ed. & trans., *The Colloquies of Erasmus* (Chicago: Univ. of Chicago Press, 1965), 253. (See Part Two, section 6.1 of this volume.) It is of interest that this clever attack on the poor by depicting them as glorious vagabonds of the open road continues in our own day. Cf. the editorial column by David Wilson titled ". . . and want no part of the rat race" in the *Boston Sunday Globe*, 28 February 1988.
12. Thompson, *Colloquies*, 254.
13. See F. Graus, "Social Utopias in the Middle Ages," *Past and Present* 38 (1967), 3–19.
14. These two works are characterized by a turn to reason and experience as the bases for the state, and a turn away from the medieval Augustinian model of the city of God. See Thomas Nipperdey, "Die Utopia des Thomas Morus und der Beginn der Neuzeit," in his *Reformation, Revolution, Utopie* (Göttingen: Vandenhoeck & Ruprecht, 1975), 132.

discipline, regard for others, and a work ethic that precludes idleness, for "he who does not work, does not eat" (2 Thess. 3:10). The ideals of this "nowhere" community are discipline and the dignity of manual labor, giving it the flavor of a kind of reformed monasticism.[15] More's social criticism is couched in the protective device of irony, while at the same time he effectively uses satire to point out the discrepancy between what is and what ought to be. Thus it seems clear that *Utopia* was written "to promote humanistic, Erasmian social reform."[16] The fact that More expressly refused translation of this Latin tract (it first appeared in English in 1551) further indicates a particular audience of learned readers.[17] More's creation has continued to stimulate diverse interpretations. *Utopia* has been interpreted as the forerunner of socialism and communism, the model of a civil democratic state, a description of the contemporary English tensions between feudalism and capitalism, a practical political tract in the line of English imperialism, and an ideology for an English welfare state.[18]

More's later writings would seem to confirm the view that he did not intend his *Utopia* as a model for a Christian state. In his *Dialogue of Comfort against Tribulation*, written during his imprisonment before execution, he discusses whether persons may properly possess riches in light of the masses of the poor. He justifies wealth on the basis that goods are necessary in order to help the poor, and that to abolish wealth would only create more poor people and beggars. At the same time he argues that people always live in community, and that an individual's wealth should benefit that community. "For surely the riche mannes substance is the welspring of the poore mannes living."[19] More also affirmed that a Christian may be wealthy without being damned. The rich are not justified before God by giving up their wealth. Rather, the rich are to so administer their goods that they support the poor. More's demand is not for the abolition of property but the divinely willed use and administration of it. So in his *Confutation of Tyndale* he characterizes as heretical the teaching that all should be held in common.[20] As was true of Erasmus, More's convictions and social criticism, as insightful as they were, were not translated into social legislation.

15. See Robert M. Adams, trans. & ed., Sir Thomas More, *Utopia: A New Translation, Backgrounds, Criticism* (New York: W. W. Norton & Co., 1975), 157.
16. Adams, *Utopia*, 164.
17. Hans Süssmuth, *Studien zur Utopia des Thomas Morus* (Münster: Aschendorff, 1967), 33–34.
18. Ibid., 1–9; Adams, *Utopia*, 139f.; Nipperdey, "Utopia," 115.
19. Cited by Süssmuth, *Studien*, 124.
20. Ibid., 125. This was the "heretical" view of Thomas Müntzer and some of the Anabaptist communities. The critique of More's *Utopia* is also anticapitalist and anti-individualist. See Nipperdey, "Utopia," 131. Property and wealth were, as noted above, the factors of spiritual anxiety and stress in the late medieval city.

Johann Eberlin's Historical Demands

More's *Utopia* was a Catholic, humanist, and pre-Reformation expression of social criticism. The first Protestant utopia was published by Johann Eberlin von Günzburg (c. 1460–1533) in 1521.[21] Known as *Wolfaria*—that is, the place where people "fare well"—it consists of pamphlets ten and eleven of his series known as the *Fünfzehn Bundesgenossen*.[22] There is no evidence that Eberlin had read More's *Utopia*, but the wide dissemination in Europe of More's work[23] and the many parallels between the two utopias invite comparison. Like More's fictional traveler Hythlodaeus who brought the story of the island Utopia, Eberlin's traveler Psitacus brought the statutes for a new welfare state from the land of Wolfaria. Both writers are concerned with rectifying unjust social conditions and developing educational and welfare programs. Eberlin's focus is the reform agenda of the early Reformation, which he learned from Luther. Unlike More, who went to his death for his Catholic faith, Eberlin expressed throughout his work a vigorous, even violent, anticlericalism, especially against the mendicant cloisters. The impact of the Reformation upon Eberlin also gives his work more of a historical demand for the reform of society, in contrast to the ahistorical orientation of most utopias.[24] Thus with regard to beggars and the poor, Eberlin wrote:

There shall be no beggars in our land. However, the poor people shall be provided for every holiday through the goods given by God's prompting to the churches. If more is needed it shall be supplied from the city's common purse. The authorities shall have great diligence for the poor. The poor shall not be commended to the priests because they are unfaithful to the poor and lie for their own advantage. That is how the monks and priests gained all their wealth. The poor had been entrusted

21. For an extended discussion of Eberlin's contribution to reform in general and of his *Wolfaria* in particular, see Steven Ozment, *The Reformation in the Cities* (New Haven: Yale Univ. Press, 1975), 90–108.
22. Critical editions of these pamphlets are in Adolf Laube, ed., *Flugschriften der frühen Reformationsbewegung* (1518–1524), 2 vols. (Berlin: Akademie Verlag, 1983), vol. 2, 1038–50, 721–30. An English translation of the eleventh pamphlet is in Jacob Shapiro, *Social Reform and the Reformation* (New York: AMS Press, 1970) (reprint of 1909), 118–25. See also Gottfried Geiger, "Die reformatorischen Initia Johann Eberlins von Günzburg nach seinen Flugschriften," in Horst Rabe, H. Molitor, & H.-C. Rublack, eds., *Festgabe für Ernst Walter Zeeden* (Münster: Aschendorff, 1976).
23. The second part of More's *Utopia* was translated into German soon after its publication in 1516. See Günter Vogler, "Reformation als 'frühbürgerliche Revolution': Eine Konzeption in Meinungstreit," in Peter Blickle, ed., *Zwingli und Europa* (Zurich: Vandenhoeck & Ruprecht, 1985), 56.
24. See Susan Bell, "Johann Eberlin von Günzburg's Wolfaria: The First Protestant Utopia," *Church History* 36 (1967), 129; and Günter Vogler, "Von Eberlin zu Stiblinus—Utopisches Denken zwischen 1521 und 1555," in Siegfried Hoyer, ed., *Reform, Reformation, Revolution* (Leipzig: Karl Marx Universität, 1980), 144f.

to them who should have been their shepherds. All the poor who need charity shall carry identification.[25]

In Eberlin's new state, agricultural and manual labor are elevated and business is discouraged. Usury is abolished; game, fish, and timber are public property. Care of the sick, including the provision of physicians, is at public expense. These are all aspects of the social program advocated by the early Reformers. Yet *Wolfaria* is also marked by a humanist moralizing strain that has confidence in the power of education to bring about social change.[26] This is, however, "a humanism with a difference, a humanism trying to reach the people, not sequestered in the rarified atmosphere of a Platonic Academy or a Senior Common Room."[27]

An Anonymous Apocalyptic

It was not until after the Peasant's War was suppressed in 1525 that another major utopian writing appeared, the anonymous *Von der newen Wandlungen eynes christlichen Lebens* (On the New Transformations of a Christian Life) (1526 or 1527).[28] The tone and content of this writing reflect the postwar situation. The looked-for transformation of Christian life is not presented in some island utopia or country like Wolfaria but is expected to be worldwide. God will equalize all human estates, and people will no longer say, "This is mine." People will all work together for the honor of God and the commonweal. No one will have anything better than another, and taxes will be abolished. While this social program still echoes some of the early Reformation concerns as well as those of the peasants' movement, its utopianism places these concerns outside of space and time.[29]

The inspiration for this pamphlet was primarily the New Testament, in particular those verses from the Magnificat already taken up by others such as Thomas Müntzer as the "gospel for the poor": "He has shown strength with his arm; he has scattered the proud in the thoughts of their hearts. He has brought down the powerful from their thrones, and lifted up the lowly; he has filled the hungry with good things, and sent the rich away empty"

---

25. Laube, *Flugschriften,* 724.
26. More and Erasmus revived a bold Stoic optimism that conceived the human being "as a perfectible creature whose supreme distinction is his natural gift of reason and his capacity for a rational, unified social life." Robert Adams, "Designs by More and Erasmus for a New Social Order," *Studies in Philology* 42 (1945), 136. To More, a just, reasonable, and good social order will create just, reasonable, and good individuals. Nipperdey, "Utopia," 116.
27. Bell, "Johann Eberlin," 125; see also Laube, *Flugschriften,* 623.
28. *Hans Hergot und die Flugschrift "Von der newen Wandlungen eynes christlichen Lebens"* (Leipzig: VEB Fachbuchverlag, 1977) provides a facsimile edition with a transcription and introduction by Max Steinmetz.
29. Vogler, "Von Eberlin," 146ff.

(Luke 1:51-53). The author expresses the conviction that the prefeudal, pre-capitalistic, primitive Christian community was better than any succeeding society, and he yearns for its restitution. The utopia presented here is a medieval monastic model of a Christian-agrarian communism, anti-urban and anti-bourgeois, emphasizing a rural life of peasants and craftsmen who will live in equality and hold all goods in common.

Kaspar Stüblin's Power of Education

The publication of Basel humanist Kaspar Stüblin's *De Eudaemonensium Republica* in 1555 took place in different circumstances than did Eberlin's work or the *Newen Wandlungen*. The peasant's movement was no longer active; revolutionary unrest had ebbed; the feudal order was stabilized; the ruling class was secure under the Peace of Augsburg; and the Counter-Reformation was effectively under way. Stüblin was not interested in speaking to the common people, in contrast to Eberlin and the author of *Newen Wandlungen*—his tract is in Latin, not German.

Stüblin's work is close to More's. He even called his island Macaria, a name More applied to an isle near his Utopia. Stüblin's hope for the moral renewal of society rests on the power of education to create an ideal state. Stüblin's work, however, differs from earlier utopian writings in several respects. For Stüblin, economic problems play only a subordinate—indeed a superficial—role. Whereas More saw private property as the source of evil, Stüblin sees luxury as a source of jealousy. In contrast to the others' valuation of manual labor, Stüblin denigrates it, thereby perpetuating an old humanist aristocratic bias. Oriented toward the classics and humanism, he accepted the contemporary social status quo.[30]

Juan Luis Vives's Prophetic Pragmatism

A humanist who has received inordinate credit for his reflections on assisting the poor is the Spanish Catholic friend of More, Juan Luis Vives (1492–1540). His treatise, *De subventione pauperum* (1526), dedicated to his adopted city of Bruges, has been credited with influencing reform of poor relief in the Netherlands and in the Empire. Born in Valencia of Jewish heritage, Vives grew up experiencing no other mode of efficient poor relief than the secular one that had existed in his well-administered city for centuries. In the words of Alice Tobriner:

> Each of his procedures—the basic analysis of poverty, the census of the poor, the control of moneys in order to offset pilfering, the right of the poor to work and the correlative duty of the state to provide employment, the development of public works through a judicious use of the otherwise

unemployed, the sensitivity that administrators must express in their personal relationships with the impoverished—all these indicate a distinctive personalism and individualism which is Vives's mentality, stemming as it does from a unique Spanish-Moorish-Jewish origin.[31]

Vives left his native Valencia permanently at the age of seventeen because he feared the Spanish Inquisition, so it is more probable that the immediate influences upon his program for poor relief came from his circle of humanist friends and his later experience. It was Erasmus himself who encouraged Vives to compose an elaborate commentary on Saint Augustine's *City of God*. Vives dedicated it to the English king Henry VIII. Soon after its publication in 1522, Cardinal Wolsey invited Vives to lecture at Oxford. The invitation had been prompted by Thomas More, whom Vives had met three years earlier in Bruges. Vives lived at the More home during April of 1525.

Surely More and Vives must have spent no little time on the practicalities of poverty; the need to outlaw begging in fact as well as in letters; the means of determining who were the poor in order to distribute the goods of the city with greater justice; and the urgency of education for the children of the poor because without education the future itself boded ill for the state. While he did not actually write his essay on poor relief while in England, it demands too much of the imagination—and of a sensitivity about both More and Vives—to assume that they had never discussed the concept at some length. (Tobriner, p. 17)

In fact, Vives's treatise has been compared to More's *Utopia* with the claim that it "surpasses the *Utopia* in the prophetic pragmatism of its programs."[32] Vives embodied the Renaissance aspirations for intellectual, moral, and re-

31. Alice Tobriner, A *Sixteenth-Century Urban Report* (Chicago: Univ. of Chicago Press, 1971), 22. The second part of Tobriner's book is an English translation of Book 2 of Vives's *De subventione pauperum*. A 1526 edition is in Harvard University's Houghton Library. On the importance of Vives's heritage, cf. Uta Lindgren, "Avicenna und die Grundprinzipien des Gemeinwesens in Francesc Eiximenis 'Regiment de la Cosa Pública' (Valencia 1383)," in Albert Zimmermann, ed., *Soziale Ordnungen im Selbstverständnis des Mittelalters*, MM 12/2 (Berlin: de Gruyter, 1980), 449–59. Lindgren points out that the Franciscan monk Eiximenis dedicated his writings to the city council of Valencia. Furthermore, in Eiximenis's writing he cites numerous times the Arabic philosopher Avicenna. In fact, it appears that Vives had little influence upon his homeland. "Nothing was more impious to Spaniards than the government management of poor relief that was occurring in northern Europe." Maureen Flynn, "Charitable Ritual in Late Medieval and Early Modern Spain," SCJ 16/3 (1985), 335–48, 348.
32. Carlos G. Noreña, *Juan Luis Vives* (The Hague: Nijhoff, 1970), 96. "Vives' idea on welfare, not as an ecclesiastical work of charity but as a publicly financed assistance, reveals a secular conception of social ethics totally foreign to the Christian feelings of that age." Noreña, *Juan Luis Vives*, 21. I shall argue below that such a "foreign" social ethics had already been advanced by Luther and his colleagues.

ligious reform. The Stoic and Socratic conception of virtue informed his confidence that individuals could be educated into a morality capable of reorienting institutions to the ethical service of humankind.[33] At the same time, Vives also breathes the puritan and industrious spirit of the merchant bourgeoisie of Bruges itself. He was in tune with the nascent capitalism that could not develop without manual labor and that perceived work as the key to prosperity.[34]

The specific inspiration or request for formulating his humanistic ideas with reference to poor relief came from the mayor of Bruges, Louis de Praet, who was in London at the same time as Vives. In his dedicatory letter to the Senate and Town Council of Bruges in 1526, Vives wrote: "Actually, I had been asked to do this some time ago, when I was in England, by Lord Praet, your burgomaster, who deliberates deeply and often—as, indeed, he ought—concerning the public welfare of the city (Tobriner, p. 33).

De subventione pauperum is divided into two books. Book I discusses the individual's responsibility to give to the poor in terms of a traditional understanding of charity as a constituent part of Christian piety. Vives shares the medieval view that poverty is a divine means against self-presumption because it makes the person dependent upon the community. He refers to the medieval theologians' favorite biblical passages from Tobit and Sirach to support the claim that both poverty and the charity it incites are pleasing to God. Charity, he states, merits divine rewards and remits sins. Yet while Vives stands in the midst of the medieval tradition with these arguments, he also goes beyond it by arguing that poverty is devastating to the poor and to the common good of the community. Theoretically he praises poverty as an aid to the religion and morality of both the poor and those who aid them; practically, however, he speaks against poverty and urges that it be overcome. "He himself sensed this split and sought to mediate between these divergent perspectives by characterizing his proposals for helping the poor as necessary only because of the decline of piety."[35] Because private charity is not sufficient to meet the needs of the poor, organized charity is necessary. This is the subject of his famous Book II.

Vives begins Book II by reminding the city authorities that they are responsible for the well-being of the whole community. Neglect of both the reality and the causes of poverty is irrational and detrimental to this responsibility because poverty fosters crime, civil insurrection, immorality, irreligion, and disease. He vividly describes the connection between the prevalence of begging and the plague:

33. Ibid., 178. See also Alain Guy, *Vives ou l'Humanisme engagé* (Paris: Seghers, 1972), 123ff.

34. Marcel Bataillon, "J. L. Vivès: Réformateur de la bienfaisance," *Bibliothèque d'humanisme et Renaissance* 14 (1952), 141–59, 142–43.

35. Wilhelm Weitzmann, *Die soziale Bedeutung des Humanisten Vives* (Borna-Leipzig, 1905), 6.

A mutual danger imperils the commonwealth from the contagion of disease. It happens too often that one man has brought into the community some serious and dreadful disease, such as the plague, or syphilis, or the like, causing others to perish. What sort of situation is this, when in every church—especially at the solemn and most heavily attended feasts—one is obliged to enter the church proper between two rows or squadrons of the sick, the vomiting, the ulcerous, the diseased with ills whose very names cannot be mentioned. And more, this is the only entrance for boys and girls, the aged and the pregnant! Do you think these are made of such iron that fasting as they are, they are not revolted by this spectacle—especially since ulcers of this sort are not only forced upon the eyes but upon the nose as well, the mouth, and almost on the hands and body as they pass through? How shameless such begging! I will not even discuss the fact that some who have just left the side of one dead of the plague mingle with the crowd. (Tobriner, p. 36)

Because the church has failed to exercise meaningful charity,[36] it is up to the magistrates to emulate the examples of the ancient Romans, Athenians, and Jews by forbidding begging, providing welfare for the poor, and producing good citizens. The authorities are therefore responsible for both overseeing the lives of the poor and providing financial support for those in need because of either unemployment or underemployment.

Investigators into the needs of the poor should perform their task humanely and kindly. While nothing should be given if the judgment on their needs is unfavorable, still intimidation should never be applied unless deemed necessary in dealing with the refractory or the rebels against public authority. (Tobriner, p. 42)

At the same time, there should be no idle poor except those unable to work due to old age and ill health. After favorably quoting Paul's injunction to the Thessalonians that "if anyone will not work, then let him not eat," Vives stated: "Therefore, no one must be permitted to live indolently in the state; rather, as in a well-ordered home, everyone has his own role and its related tasks to perform. As the saying goes, 'By doing nothing, men learn to do evil' " (Tobriner, p. 39).

Vives called for sufficient hospitals to care for all the sick, blind, aged, and insane. Vives was far ahead of his time in advocating compassionate care of the mentally ill. "He who has suffered so should be treated with such care and delicacy that the cure will not enlarge or increase the condition. . . . Above all, as far as it is possible, tranquillity must be introduced into their minds, for it is through this that reason and mental health return" (Tobriner,

36. Similar to other contemporary critics of the church, Vives indicts the clergy for living off the poor. See Tobriner, *Sixteenth-Century Urban Report*, 44–45.

pp. 41–42). However, the hospitals are to serve the true poor, not the lazy, who are to be expelled by the civic authorities. Likewise, foreign beggars are to be provided with the minimal means to return to their own cities. Native beggars who refuse to work are to be expelled.

Vives was optimistic about resources for funding his civic welfare proposal. He believed that proper administration of hospital endowments, including redistribution of surplus funds, would be more than sufficient. This funding would be augmented by whatever work those living in the hospitals were able to do. "I am told that the wealth of hospitals in any town you can name is so great that, if it were properly administered, there would be more than enough for supplying all the ordinary as well as unforeseen and extraordinary needs of the citizens" (Tobriner, pp. 45–46). Citizens should be encouraged to leave money in their wills for welfare, including the old custom of providing food for the poor at the funeral. Since only the really needy will be helped, funds will be sufficient. However, if funds are lacking, then voluntary contributions are to be solicited in the principal churches. These occasional supplemental funds would be overseen by "two honest and trustworthy men . . . chosen by the Senate not so much for wealth as for a mind free from greed and selfishness." A last resort would be to have the overseers ask wealthy men "to aid the poor whom God has committed to the latter's zealous care. At least the hospital could borrow what is needed; if the wealthy insist on it, this loan could be repaid later in good faith when alms are more plentiful" (Tobriner, pp. 46, 47). In extreme necessity, the state can intervene with public funds.

What is of interest here, especially in light of later commentators' praise of Vives as an innovator in welfare reform, is his inability to move far beyond the medieval understanding of charity. Although he clearly argues that responsibility for welfare should rest with the state, he is unable to advance a rationale for reliable funding. His humanistic concern for self-improvement in knowledge and morality, and, I suggest, the weight of the medieval ideology of almsgiving, prevent him for envisioning a thorough reform of poor relief. He appears more concerned with the benefits that accrue to the giver than the recipient.

> Almsgiving should always be voluntary, as Paul said, "Each man . . . according as he has decided in his heart, not grudgingly or from obligation." No one should be forced to do good, otherwise the very concept of doing good is lost. . . . [God] will bless righteous undertakings, increasing for the rich the sources of their charity, as well as the alms of the poor who modestly ask, gratefully receive, and prudently spend. . . .
>
> As for the unemployed poor themselves, they should learn not to make provisions for the distant future, for this increases their sense of human security and lessens their dependence on God. They should rely not on human assistance but on Christ alone, Who has exhorted us to relinquish all concerns for our sustenance to Him and His Father. . . . The

poor should lead an angelic life, so to speak, intent on prayer first for themselves and then for the weal of those by whom they have been assisted, so that the Lord Jesus might consider them worthy to receive recompense a hundredfold in everlasting blessings. (Tobriner, pp. 47–48)

Vives's ideal of charity has a puritan conception of a certain economic marginality that was to preclude the spiritual danger of material comfort. The universal mandate of work was complemented by the rule of austerity. Those in the hospital were to live a pure and sober life. Two town censors, chosen annually, were entrusted with the surveillance of the morals of the poor. Vives further suggested that the morals of the rich youth be monitored as well. This concern for moral reform under the initiative and guidance of the municipality suggests that moral austerity was not the monopoly of Protestant towns such as Zurich and Geneva.[37]

Vives concludes his treatise with a list of the material and spiritual advantages that will result from his welfare plan. His last sentence reads: "Hereafter, we shall obtain that celestial reward which we have shown is prepared for the man of charity" (Tobriner, p. 57).

Humanism's Influence on Poor-Relief Reform

In spite of the fact that the city of Bruges[38] did not accept Vives's plan until 1556—thirty years after Vives dedicated it to the city—many contemporary scholars continue to credit Vives with personally instituting a modern concept of civic welfare. In her introduction to Vives's treatise, Tobriner wrote:

Vives designed his pattern for poor relief in Bruges specifically for his own city, yet he included the principle of municipal administration applicable anywhere. Apparently the city of Lille adopted his plan of action in 1527, Ypres (with modifications) in 1529, and Mons, Oudendarde, and Valenciennes in 1531. His principles appear in the Imperial Decree of Charles V for the Empire in 1531 and, according to the thesis of this paper, in the first systematic poor law of England promulgated by Henry VIII in 1531. (pp. 14–15)

Earlier, the German historian Feuchtwanger gave exuberant praise to Vives. "This new order was neither the work of Protestantism nor Catholicism, but rather a work of the intellectual and economic Renaissance." Vives's writing "signifies not only in theory but also in its thoroughly practical goal and effect

37. Bataillon, "J. L. Vivès," 155.
38. The town secretary of Leiden, Jan van Hout, recommended Vives's program in 1577 but was unsuccessful in convincing the Leiden magistrates. See Robert Muchembled's review of P. Brachin, trans. & ed., *Van Hout et Coornhert: Bienfaisance et répression au XVIe siècle* (Paris: Vrin, 1984), in *Revue du Nord* 69 (1987).

a new era of social politics and charitable activity."[39] At the same time, the famous French historian Henri Pirenne wrote of Vives: "It was through the efforts of a friend of Erasmus that it came about in Belgium. There it was neither Protestant nor Catholic; it was in the full force of the word, a work of the Renaissance."[40] An influential essay by the American historian Natalie Zemon Davis forcefully attributed welfare reform to humanist influence "following an Erasmian program for reform."[41] More recently, Margo Todd has so enthusiastically argued this thesis that she mistakenly attributes earlier German developments to the later work of Vives.[42] Furthermore, numerous contemporary history texts attribute the well-known and important poor-relief order of the Catholic city of Ypres to the influence of Vives.[43] Linda Martz is a notable exception when she writes: "Vives should not be credited with prompting the welfare reforms of Bruges since his treatise was published after the city had taken this step, and the magistrates may have been influenced by the reforms already carried out in Mons, Ypres, Strasbourg and Nuremberg."[44]

The Ypres poor-relief order first appeared six months before Vives's tract, and Vives did his best to conceal his work from even his closest associates until its publication.[45] Bataillon states that the claim of Vives's influence on Ypres and the whole movement of poor-relief reform is an error that can no longer be perpetuated.[46] Furthermore, Bataillon suggests that Vives was influenced by the poor-relief innovations of the German Reformation via the

39. L. Feuchtwanger, "Geschichte der sozialen Politik und des Armenwesens im Zeitalter der Reformation," *Jahrbuch für Gesetzgebung, Verwaltung und Volkswirtschaft im Deutschen Reich* 32 (1908), 187, 193.

40. Henri Pirenne, *Histoire de Belgique*, vol. 3 (Brussells: Lamertin, 1907), 280.

41. Natalie Zemon Davis, "Poor Relief, Humanism, and Heresy," chap. 2 in her *Society and Culture in Early Modern France* (Stanford: Stanford Univ. Press, 1975), 59ff. Paul Fideler makes a similar argument for Tudor England in his "Christian Humanism and Poor Law Reform in Early Tudor England," *Societas—A Review of Social History* 4 (1974). A more nuanced discussion of humanists and reformers is James Kittelson, "Humanism and the Reformation in Germany," *Central European History* 9 (1976): 303–22.

42. Margo Todd, *Christian Humanism and the Puritan Social Order* (Cambridge: Cambridge Univ. Press, 1987). For her thesis of the priority of Christian humanism, see 17, 19; for her mistaken chronology, see 144f.

43. For example, the recent and well-received interpretation of the history of Christianity by John Bossy, *Christianity in the West 1400–1700* (Oxford: Oxford Univ. Press, 1985), 145f.

44. Linda Martz, *Poverty and Welfare in Hapsburg Spain: The Example of Toledo* (Cambridge: Cambridge Univ. Press, 1983), 11.

45. Tobriner, *Sixteenth-Century Urban Report*, 15ff.; Noreña, *Juan Luis Vives*, 2, 96, 98, 146, 177, 196f. On the origins of the Ypres order, see Carter Lindberg, "La théologie et l'assistance publique, le cas d'Ypres (1525–1531)," *Revue d'histoire et de philosophie religieuses* 61 (1981).

46. Bataillon, "J. L. Vives," 141. See also Robert Stupperich, "Das Problem der Armenfürsorge bei Juan Luis Vives," in August Buck, ed., *Juan Luis Vives* (Hamburg: Hauswedell, 1981). Bronislaw Geremek, *La potence ou la pitié* (Paris: Gallimard, 1987),

positive impressions of them he received from his Dutch friend Gérard Gel-denhouwer. Some months before the publication of *De subventione pauperum*, Geldenhouwer related to Vives his enthusiasm for what he had witnessed in a recent visit to Strasbourg. In this reformed city

> no one begs; the itinerant poor are lodged a day and a night at the expense of the city; then unless prevented by illness, they are constrained to leave with a travelling expense. The poor of the city receive just what they need to live decently according to the situation of each; and all this is administered in good faith from the public funds. Blaspheming, cursing, carousing, drunkenness, and gambling are prohibited by edict.[47]

Whether Geldenhouwer also informed Vives about the Lutheran poor-relief theory and praxis that he undoubtedly encountered during his visits to Wittenberg and Bremen is a matter of speculation.[48]

This development of urban poor relief so intimately connected with the earliest stages of the Lutheran Reformation, to which Erasmus already referred in his 1524 colloquy "Beggar Talk," may well have been the reason for Roman Catholic polemics against Vives and the first Poor Relief Order of Ypres, a polemic that Vives himself anticipated (Tobriner, pp. 50–53). Both Vives and the Bruges Order were attacked by the Augustinian monk Villavicencio as heretical for alienating the essential prerogatives of the church; and Philip II revoked the edict his father, Charles V, had issued against begging. The charge of Lutheran heresy may be a recognition of the connection between changing social structures and the new theology of the Reformation.[49] It may well be that reform of poor relief in the Low Countries was a "curious and doubtless generally unconscious introduction of Lutheran principles into the legislation of Catholic cities and countries."[50]

244, also posits the developments in Nuremberg, Strasbourg, and Ypres as sources for Vives's book.

47. Henry de Vocht, ed., *Literae virorum eruditorum ad Franciscum Cranveldium* (1522–1528), Louvain, 1928), 515; cited by Bataillon, "J. L. Vivès," 144.

48. See the entry on Geldenhouwer in *Neue Deutsche Biographie* 6 (Berlin, 1964), 170. In 1525 Geldenhouwer published his account of his travels, including a visit to Wittenberg, where he met Luther. In Bremen he was received by Jakob Propst, who had studied at Wittenberg and who had developed a social welfare program modeled after that in Wittenberg. Cf. Ortwin Rudloff, *Bonae Litterae et Lutherus: Texte und Untersuchungen zu den Anfängen der Theologie des Bremers Reformators Jakob Propst* (Bremen: Hauschild, 1985), 145, 156–57, 203, 215.

49. Lindberg, "La théologie," 35.

50. Paul Bonenfant, "Les origines et le caractère de la Réforme de la bienfaisance publique aux Pays-Bas sous le règne de Charles-Quint," *Revue belge de philosophie et d'histoire* 6 (1927), 230.

Late Medieval Urban Developments

The stage upon which the humanists played out their conviction that education can change character, and their desire—in Erasmian terms—to create the perfect urban monastery, was the stage of urban crisis. According to Davis, "The context for welfare reform, it seems to me, was urban crisis, brought about by a conjuncture of older problems of poverty with population growth and economic expansion."[51] In recent years Reformation scholarship has been fascinated by the late medieval city and its role in the reception and advance of the Reformation. This fascination is summarized by the oft-quoted sentence written by the English scholar, A. G. Dickens: "Again, after all we have written in previous chapters, we need but briefly to recall that the German Reformation was an urban event at once literary, technological and oratorical."[52] The stimulus for this assertion and the wealth of international research it reflects was the 1962 study by Bernd Moeller, *Reichsstadt und Reformation*.[53]

This intensive and increasingly extensive research on the relationship of the Reformation to the late medieval city relates theology and social history. The cities were disposed favorably toward the Reformation because the Reformation facilitated their approach to social problems such as financing poor relief and emancipation from church courts.[54] Town magistrates had long desired control of church properties as a means to support the financial responsibilities of the whole community. The Reformation contributed a new element to this long-standing community concern: the removal of ecclesi-

51. Davis, "Poor Relief," 59. Geremek, *Potence ou la pitié*, 101, makes the same point: "The expansion of the merchant economy and urbanization were of major consequence. They are the factors that set in motion and accelerated the process of differentiation in the heart of the particular groups of medieval society, and are responsible for a massive pauperization."
52. A. G. Dickens, *The German Nation and Martin Luther* (London: Arnold, 1974), 182. Two German scholars in particular begin their own essays with reference to this statement. See Hans-Christoph Rublack, "Forschungsbericht Stadt und Reformation," in Bernd Moeller, ed., *Stadt und Kirche im 16. Jahrhundert* (Gütersloh: Mohn, 1978), 9; Hans-Christoph Rublack, "Reformatorische Bewegung und städtische Kirchenpolitik in Esslingen," in Ingrid Bátori, ed., *Städtische Gesellschaften und Reformation* (Stuttgart: Klett-Cotta, 1980), 193; and Bernd Moeller, "The Town in Church History," 257.
53. An expanded version appeared in French in 1966 and in English in 1972. A reprint with an extensive afterword surveying research to date appeared in 1987: Bernd Moeller, *Reichsstadt und Reformation*, rev. ed. (Berlin: Evangelische Verlagsanstalt). Useful reviews of research include Rublack, "Forschungsbericht"; Kaspar von Greyerz, "Stadt und Reformation: Stand und Aufgaben der Forschung," ARG 76 (1985); and Heinrich Schmidt, *Reichsstädten, Reich und Reformation* (Stuttgart: Steiner, 1986), 1–16. See also Anton Schindling, "Kirche, Gesellschaft, Politik, und Bildung in Strasbourg," in Grete Klingenstein & Heinrich Lutz, eds., *Spezialforschung und "Gesamtgeschichte"* (Munich: Oldenbourg, 1982), 185–88.
54. Hans-Christoph Rublack, "Reformation and Society," in Manfred Hoffman, ed., *Martin Luther and the Modern Mind* (New York: Mellen Press, 1985), 257.

astical property from the legal system of the universal church and the assignment to the local secular authority of the right and responsibility to control it according to an evangelical exercise of religion and the assumed purpose of the foundation.[55] Hans-Christoph Rublack has used the catchwords *emancipation, participation,* and *frustration* to summarize the ways in which various scholars have related theological convictions and social aspirations.[56]

The emancipation thesis, associated with Bernd Moeller's work, "sees the main appeal of the Reformation to lie in its providing a new line of defense for late medieval communal values (*Genossenschaft*) in the face of mounting centralizing tendencies (*Herrschaft*)."[57] Taking his cue from the sociologist Max Weber's ideal types, Moeller describes the town as a sacral community. "Towns were sacral communities and they were conscious—emphatically so—of being distinct as such not only from the world around them, but also from the generally current forms of religious life."[58] This civic aspiration to the Augustinian City of God and thus "a miniature *corpus christianum*" (Christian commonwealth)[59] may be seen as a link to the humanist utopian vision described above.[60] If townsfolk could be taught that they participate in a sacral corporation, then the sharing of social obligations should be a logical consequence.

The thesis of emancipation is developed on the basis of the struggle of the late medieval urban magistrates to take over the administration of ecclesial institutions such as poor relief. Over the course of centuries, the urban parish had become encrusted with revenues, foundations, legacies, benefices, laws, and services. This seemingly impenetrable web of ecclesial, theological, legal, and social responsibility hindered efficient utilization of the church's resources. It "had to be an outrage to every rational minded person."[61] Therefore the Reformation is seen as the continuation of an urban rationalization and secularization process. The Reformation is thus a communalization of institutions that, while integral to the city, had long remained outside its control because directed by a hierarchical clergy ultimately responsible to Rome. From this perspective the Reformation appears implicitly as a town council Reformation (*Ratsreformation*), for it "overcame hindrances which up

---

55. Anton Schindling, "Die Reformation in den Reichsstädten und die Kirchengüter," in Jürgen Sydow, ed., *Bürgerschaft und Kirche* (Sigmarinen: Thorbecke, 1980), 77.
56. Rublack, "Reformatorische Bewegung," 194ff.
57. Ozment, *Reformation in the Cities,* 6.
58. Moeller, "Town in Church History," 259.
59. Bernd Moeller, *Imperial Cities and the Reformation* (Philadelphia: Fortress Press, 1972), 49. Luther may be unique among the Reformers for rejecting the possibility and desirability of establishing the medieval ideal of the *corpus christianum.* See Lindberg, "Theology and Politics: Luther the Radical and Müntzer the Reactionary," *Encounter* 37 (1976).
60. An early description of Zwingli's theology includes also Plato's *Republic.* See Heiko A. Oberman, *The Dawn of the Reformation* (Edinburgh: T. & T. Clark, 1986), 49.
61. Karlheinz Blaschke, "Die Auswirkung der Reformation auf die städtischen Kirchenverfassung in Sachsen," in Moeller, *Stadt und Kirche,* 166.

to then had stood in the way of the full development of urban policy interests."[62]

The participation thesis sees the Reformation as a movement from below,
that is, by the populace (*Volksbewegung*). Here the ideas of the Reformation—
for example, Luther's dictum of the universal priesthood of the baptized—
are means for its supporters to achieve their goal of increased participation
in urban governance.[63] In this sense, the Reformation serves as an ideology.
In a broader sense this is the thesis of the Marxist theory of the Reformation
as an early bourgeois revolution. Whether this theory is presented in terms
of a schema of underlying class conflict or a schema of social conflict, it
expresses the view that the essential characteristic of the Reformation ideology for the people was opposition to the growing centralization of urban
government. Over against the efforts to conceptualize the Reformation only
as an ideology legitimating social movement, Moeller emphasizes the con-
gruence of Reformation ideas with the late medieval ideas of a cooperative
society (*Genossenschaft*). Participation is realized not in conflict but in the
revitalization of an urban confederation wherein the authorities are responsible for the temporal as well as the spiritual well-being of the citizens. Thus
in Nuremberg as well as in other upper German cities, the first unequivocal
reform measure was the pronouncement of an alms order.[64]

The frustration thesis is represented by the American historian Steven
Ozment, who emphasizes that the ideas of the Reformation were of interest
to the urban population because they released the citizens from the frustrations of the complicated and oppressive late medieval ecclesiastical system
for securing salvation.[65] In opposition to Moeller, Ozment's point is that the
Reformation did not support the medieval goal of sanctifying the city but
rather desanctified it. This desacralization reduced the multifarious, pluralistic, ecclesial, and clerical system of the late Middle Ages to a materially
and psychologically bearable certainty of salvation focused in Word and sacrament, expressed in Reformation preaching and the Lord's Supper. The concomitant reduction of the multitudinous special institutions of cloisters,
brotherhoods, foundations, and clerical hierarchies also brought financial
release and the possibility for constructively reformulating social welfare.

As historians have recently pointed out, the urban reception of the Reformation was not a simple event easily explicated in categories of universal

62. Ibid., 162.
63. For one example among many, see Uwe Plath, "Der Durchbruch der Reformation
in Lüneburg," in G. Korner et al., eds., *Reformation vor 450 Jahren* (Lüneburg, 1980), 50.
64. Gottfried Seebass, "Stadt und Kirche in Nürnberg im Zeitalter der Reformation,"
in Moeller, *Stadt und Kirche*, 69.
65. Ozment, *Reformation in the Cities*. Basil Hall, "The Reformation City," *Bulletin of the
John Rylands Library* 54 (1971/72), 118, also speaks of "a frustrated desire for change in
the cities." The theme of release from religious burdens and the consequent liberation
for a new secular piety is also argued by Scott Hendrix, "Luther's Impact on the
Sixteenth Century," *SCJ* 16 (1985), 3–14.

or metahistory. The Reformation message was subject to the conditions of urban policy and society and conflicts of interest, many of which varied from one locale to another. Hans-Christoph Rublack, for example, addresses this complexity of reception in terms of an interim phase of development between the incubation of reformatory ideas and their institutionalization.[66]

The various efforts of historians to develop a typology for the urban reception of the Reformation have been summarized by Kaspar von Greyerz.[67] One group of typologies is oriented to understanding the urban Reformation in terms of political movements centering in the people (*Volksreformation*), the town council (*Ratsreformation*), aristocracy (*Fürstenreformation*), or the community (*Gemeindereformation*). Greyerz argues that the view of the Reformation as a movement from below toward the top only holds good for the first half of the sixteenth century; conversely, the view of the Reformation as a conservative revolution from the top down is only possible when the movement character of the urban Reformation is ignored.

A second kind of typology presents the urban Reformation in terms of phases of development. "Preachers and laymen learned in Scripture provided the initial stimulus; ideologically and socially mobile burghers, primarily from the (larger) lower and middle strata, created a driving wedge of popular support: and government consolidated and moderated the new institutional changes."[68] Thus already in 1522, the Nuremberg town council, following the example of Wittenberg, created a new poor-relief order that as a whole may be regarded as a fruit of evangelical preaching, even if the extent of the preacher participation in its completion is not exactly known.[69] In his study of the Reformation in Nuremberg, Günter Vogler distinguishes five stages of chronological development: the policy of the pre-Reformation church; the introduction of the Reformation process in 1517; its continuation in the years 1521–25; its intensification under the pressure of revolutionary movement in the city and the countryside in 1524–25; and, from 1525, the takeover of leadership in most cases by the city councils.[70]

A third variant of the effort to provide a typology of the urban Reformation is the description of the sequence of events associated with the reform among the Hanseatic cities. Here, as in the other efforts, the problem remains of incorporating local differences in the proposed models.[71]

---

66. Rublack, "Reformatorische Bewegung," 195f.
67. Greyerz, "Stadt und Reformation."
68. Ozment, *Reformation in the Cities*, 131. Also Kohls, "Evangelische Bewegung," 117: "The evangelical movement was above all a preaching movement which took up Luther's concerns."
69. Gottfried Seebass, *Das reformatorische Werk des Andreas Osiander* (Nuremberg: Verein für Bayerische Kirchengeschichte, 1967), 181.
70. Günter Vogler, *Nürnberg, 1524/25: Studien zur Geschichte der reformatorischen und sozialen Bewegung in der Reichsstadt* (Berlin, 1982), cited by Greyerz, "Stadt und Reformation," 47.
71. Greyerz, "Stadt und Reformation," 48.

The intense preoccupation of Reformation scholars with the relationship between the city and the Reformation has raised three topics of particular interest for the study of the development of poor relief: (1) social control; (2) the importance of pamphlet literature in the spread of the Reformation; and (3) the related discussion of the distinction between lay culture and learned culture with regard to the process of communicating the Reformation.

The social control theme is presented in works such as that by Lis and Soly. The assumption behind this theme is the introduction or, better, the intensifying of urban conflict by the Reformation. This theme is closely related to the increased interest among historians in social history, and their concomitant interest in moving beyond the older question of how the Reformation transformed society to the question of how the Reformation was also shaped by the social context in which it arose. The concept of social control stems from the field of sociology, but sociologists differ on the content of this concept. However, Robert Scribner has provided a working definition of social control as "the forces which maintain the existing order, enable the continuation of political power, and permit political influence upon social forms."[72]

Scribner discusses four forms of social control, which he does not conceive of as mutually exclusive but rather as a comprehensive spectrum of a total phenomenon. The first is the exercise of coercion either directly by the application of power or indirectly by law. This includes police measures to maintain law and order, such as a curfew, as well as political controls such as the prohibition of inflammatory speeches or assemblies.[73] The second form is political regulations covering civic order, ranging from city constitutions and administration to particulars such as guild statutes. The third form of social control is the legitimation of the existing order; that is, the principles justifying the continuation of such medieval urban responsibilities as the duty of the government to further the commonweal and care for rich and poor alike. The fourth all-encompassing principle, ideology, justifies the existing order not just in terms of its goals, as above, but also in terms of its values. This principle can be expressed in worldly terms (government is necessary because all people are born unequal); or in theological terms (all authority is ordained by God). "The goal of social control is to engender in the civic society a deeply rooted consensus which accepts the social and political order as legitimate and useful."[74]

The question of how this social control was engendered is closely tied to the question of how the Reformation was communicated. In this regard interest in Reformation pamphlet literature has grown to the point where it

---

72. Robert Scribner, "Sozialkontrolle und die Möglichkeit einer städtische Reformation," in Moeller, *Stadt und Kirche*, 58.
73. On the disciplinarian elements in poor-relief legislation, see Robert Jütte, "Poor Relief and Social Discipline in Sixteenth-Century Europe," *European Studies Review* 11 (1981), 25–52.
74. Scribner, "Sozialkontrolle," 59.

is practically a field of research in its own right. The criticism from a social-historical perspective of the importance of pamphlets is that the ecclesial and theological frame of reference of the pamphlet's author is not necessarily that of the reader. Thus the reader's grasp of the content may diverge from the author's intent.[75] Furthermore, it has been argued that given the extremely low literacy of the time, only a small minority had direct access to these writings.

Mark Edwards has cogently argued that the whole issue of literacy in the sixteenth century needs to be rethought. He makes the point that such valid admonitions should not be exaggerated.

> The sheer mass of the printing effort and its wide geographic distribution—and the amount of trade that this production and distribution represents—allows us to draw with some assurance inferences about the popularity of certain beliefs and convictions. If we assume conservatively that each printing of a work by Luther numbered from two hundred to one thousand copies, we are talking about an output for Luther alone of 620,000 to 3,100,000 copies during the period 1516–1546! And this total does not include the numerous whole and partial editions of Luther's Bible translation. To sell this many treatises and pamphlets, significant numbers of people had to be spending significant sums of money to read Martin Luther. . . . In light of publication statistics such as these, it seems far more plausible to assume a certain meeting of the minds between author and audience than to deny it.[76]

Furthermore, access to the vernacular treatises written for a popular audience was enhanced by the "multiplier effect" of the reader sharing the ideas with the illiterate. When the reader was a preacher, the ideas of a treatise could be multiplied thousands of times.

"Certainly the significance of preaching can hardly be overestimated."[77] Here, too, the preached sermon may have been heard differently than intended, but it has been well argued that preaching was the decisive presupposition for the introduction of the Reformation. This argument leads back to the significance of theology to both the Reformation and its attendant social change. A leading American social historian, Thomas Brady, wrote: "The leading ideas of Reformation Germany were chiefly theological ideas, without a firm grasp of which the culture and self-consciousness of the age simply cannot be understood." Brady's concern with social history led him to continue: "That they play a relatively minor role in this study is due rather to

---

75. See, for example, Miriam Usher Chrisman, *Lay Culture, Learned Culture: Books and Social Change in Strasbourg, 1480–1599* (New Haven: Yale Univ. Press, 1982).

76. Mark U. Edwards, Jr., "Statistics on Sixteenth-Century Printing," in Phillip Bebb & Sherrin Marshall, eds., *The Process of Change in Early Modern Europe: Essays in Honor of Miriam Usher Chrisman* (Athens: Ohio Univ. Press, 1988), 161.

77. Greyerz, "Stadt und Reformation," 28.

the specific aims of the work than to an ignorance of their significance."[78] I am reversing Brady's point for the purposes of this study: The Reformation contributions to the development of early modern poor relief cannot be understood without a firm grasp of their social and historical context. That these social and historical factors are subordinated to the ideas of the Reformers "is due rather to the specific aims of the work than to an ignorance of their significance."

The Urban Reception of the Reformation

Germany on the eve of the Reformation was a land of cities.[79] Although the great majority of the some three thousand municipal areas at this time were small towns of less than 2,000 in population, a few surpassed 20,000 inhabitants. The characteristics of these towns included:

1. Internal freedom from feudal conditions. Within the city walls, citizens had in principle a legal equality among themselves.

2. A certain political autonomy. The organization of the towns' administrations in town councils followed a certain rationality. The center of the town was not a castle but the town hall.[80] The Reformers had access to this center not just by their writings and sermons but also by personal relationships through their colleagues, students, and followers.

3. An economic center. In the larger towns, specific urban vocations of crafts and commerce were jealously protected. The money economy that facilitated commerce also stimulated new forms of administration. This urban life required of its citizens a certain work ethos of rationality and accountability.

4. A social system of mutuality and reciprocity. The ideal of public interest before private need (*Gemeinnutz geht vor Eigennutz*) was theologically as well as politically grounded.[81] That urban reality (namely, the marginalization of the poor and other class conflicts) did not mirror this ideal of community does not gainsay its grip upon the theological, political, and intellectual imaginations of the time.

---

78. Brady, *Ruling Class*, 46.
79. For much of what follows I am indebted to Bernd Moeller's article, "Luther und die Städte," in *Aus der Lutherforschung: Drei Vorträge* (Opladen: Westdeutschen Verlag, 1983).
80. Hans-Christoph Rublack, "Grundwerte in der Reichsstadt im Spätmittelalter und in der frühen Neuzeit," in Horst Brunner, ed., *Literatur in der Stadt* (Göttingen: Kümmerle, 1982), 15.
81. Ibid., 26. See also Winfried Schulze, "Vom Gemeinnutz zum Eigennutz: Über den Normenwandel in der ständischen Gesellschaft der frühen Neuzeit," *Historische Zeitschrift* 243 (1986); and Günter Vogler, "Gemeinnutz und Eigennutz bei Thomas Müntzer," in Siegfried Bräuer & Helmar Junghans, eds., *Der Theologe Thomas Müntzer* (Berlin: Evangelische Verlagsanstalt, 1989), 179–83.

5. Increasing literacy. In general, outside of the city few beyond the clergy could read and write, but the cities were becoming places of literacy where books were made, sold, read, and collected. Correspondingly, the cities were the social setting for new ideas and ways of thinking. Movements such as humanism had their focal points in urban society, and citizens were receptive to new ideas through books.[82]

6. An exploding and explosive religiosity. The church tower was the central symbol of the personal and collective security system,[83] but religious imagery was not limited to the church spire. The production and reception of ecclesial art was an urban phenomenon. On the eve of the Reformation, the volume of works created and given for ecclesial purposes reached an unprecedented level. Many churches were stuffed with images and altars.

Of all these characteristics of the late medieval city, it is the religiosity that provided the most fertile soil for the seed of the Reformation. The living world of piety and foundations was financed by the citizens. Foundation masses and brotherhoods proliferated with the citizens' intensifying concern for salvation. Brotherhoods formed cartel arrangements so that the benefits of membership in one would be multiplied by ties to the others. Even so, the example of the Bremen citizen who died in 1511 with membership in no less than twenty-one brotherhoods is not exceptional. The piety of the time was marked by a striving for achievement. This emphasis on achievement was, in the words of Bernd Moeller, "perhaps the most important mark of pre-Reformation urban piety."[84]

Testaments frequently expressed this widespread mentality, marked by fear of divine judgment and the drive to confirm salvation by religious performance and achievement. Those who occupied a civic world of producing and acquiring goods were fascinated by the idea that earthly treasure could in the end yield heavenly treasure. Contemporaries were engaged in behavior Chiffoleau characterizes as literally an "economy of salvation" that calculated the "price of passage" from this life to the next in a kind of grand "bookkeeping of the beyond."[85] In this regard, religion reflected the culture; in religion as in early capitalism, contracted work merited reward. But as Luther himself paradigmatically discovered, spiritual anxiety and insecurity are not

---

82. See Bernd Moeller, "Stadt und Buch: Bemerkungen zur Struktur der reformatorischen Bewegung in Deutschland," in Wolfgang Mommsen et al., eds., *Stadtbürgertum und Adel in der Reformation* (Stuttgart, 1979).

83. Rublack, "Grundwerte," 16.

84. Bernd Moeller, "Korreferat zu Wolfgang Reinhard: Luther und die Städte," in Erwin Iserloh & Gerhard Müller, eds., *Luther und die politische Welt* (Stuttgart: Steiner, 1984), 119; Moeller, "Luther und die Städte," 15f.

85. Jacques Chiffoleau, *La comptabilité de l'au-delà* (Rome: École Française de Rome, 1980), 214ff., 302, 305: The legacy to the poor was not a small part of the "price of passage," but "beyond being the occasion of 'good works' [the poor] remained a symbolic intercessor." Cf. Jürgen Sydow, *Bürgerschaft und Kirche* (Sigmarinen: Thorbecke, 1980), 17: God held a place in the business books of the medieval merchant.

overcome by calculation and installment plans. Since every self-achievement can be surpassed, the certainty of salvation remains just beyond secure grasp.

This insecurity helps to explain why urban dwellers were attracted to Luther's Reformation message and why it was not confined to a particular sector of society. Luther's message was attractive because its primary concern was not social but existential; it focused upon the human condition itself in terms of death and life, sin and forgiveness, bondage and freedom. This message "had the unique power to touch all the social tensions of the time, to draw them into its orbit, to transform them."[86] It was precisely this existential focus of the Reformation that powered behavioral change. "In short, it can be said that altogether in the Upper German Imperial cities at the beginning of the sixteenth century the instruments and the players were, so to speak, ready for Luther with his theology to provide the notes."[87]

One of the notes Luther provided was the link between the religious and economic mentalities of achievement.

> You see, the greedy man deprives himself of eternal life, because his heart is swollen with many concerns. Because he has all these worries, he is forced to fear the dangers of fire and water. As many worries threaten him as there are grains of sand on the seashore. Thus he destroys this life as well as that which is to come, just as "godliness has the promise" (cf. 1 Tim. 4:8). Greed is the worship of idols. You see, greed worships money, but godliness worships God. The greedy man is uncertain and is deprived both of this life and that which is to come. (LW 28:372)

The medieval effort to acquire salvation and the avarice for personal gain are reflected in the late medieval "numerical delirium" that calculated investments in masses and charitable works and the resulting dividends of reduced time in Purgatory. Salvation was subjected to measurement. Theology was penetrated by the cumulative logic and calculations of marketing accountancy.[88] Luther's reversal of the medieval theology of achievement by a biblical theology of grace caught the attention of an anxious citizenry. "There is no doubt that the doctrine of justification struck a broad response. It formed the basis and the starting point of ecclesial and social criticism in all the places investigated."[89]

This urban attraction to Luther's message stimulated its urban communication. The city was the place of the book, and Luther was an incredibly

---

86. Moeller, "Town in Church History," 265. See also Volker Press, "Martin Luther und die sozialen Kräfte seiner Zeit," in Iserloh & Müller, *Luther und die politische Welt*, 215; Volker Press, "Reformatorische Bewegung und Reichsverfassung," in Volker Press & Dieter Stievermann, eds., *Martin Luther: Probleme seiner Zeit* (Stuttgart: Klett-Cotta, 1986); Heinrich Schmidt, *Reichsstädten, Reich, und Reformation*, 330, 332f.
87. Kohls, "Evangelische Bewegung," 116.
88. Chiffoleau, *Comptabilité*, 355–56, 390, 425, 429–35.
89. Schmidt, *Reichsstädte, Reich und Reformation*, 335.

prolific writer. By 1520 he had already produced 82 writings that appeared in no less than 607 editions; assuming a run of a thousand copies each, this meant more than 500,000 pieces.[90] This was only the beginning of the flood of printed writings that allowed Luther and then the other Reformers to transmit their messages to the literate citizen. These writings were not in scholarly Latin but in German. For the pious citizen as for Luther himself, the fundamental question concerning salvation was how to assure oneself of a gracious God—through the accumulated but never sufficiently complete performance of good works, or through faith in Christ. The people were receptive to Luther's message because it answered their question.[91]

Luther's answer—justification by grace alone through faith alone—brought with it a new ethos of community. That love of one's neighbor not only followed from faith but belonged to the essence of being Christian was nowhere easier to understand or more pressing to realize than in the delicate social situation of the city. This is seen in the lapidary sentence of Luther's Erfurt friend, Johann Lang: "Where one seeks the common good, there dwells God; but where one seeks his own, there dwells the devil." Ulrich Zwingli, Luther's contemporary and the reformer of Zurich, expressed this more sharply when he asserted that the decision for the gospel is also a decision for the public good (*gemeinen Nutzen*), because life in the bonds of "human teaching" only produces greed (*Eigennutz*).[92] Martin Bucer, the reformer of Strasbourg, summarized this late medieval theme in his 1523 tract, "That No One Should Live for Himself, But Rather for Others."[93] This theme corresponds to the necessities of urban life, and is further complemented by the doctrine of the priesthood of all believers. In the evangelical cities this theology was worked out in various ways, including making poor relief and social welfare a public duty of the entire community. In place of the medieval institutional diaconate of the church, the Reformation advocated a community diaconate.[94] The many foundations and testaments of churchly organizations were now redirected through community legislation toward charitable goals.[95]

90. Moeller, "Luther und die Städte," 18.
91. Ibid., 23.
92. Peter Blickle, *Gemeindereformation: Die Menschen des 16. Jahrhunderts auf dem Weg zum Heil* (Munich: Oldenbourg, 1987), 151.
93. Martin Bucer, *Deutsches Schriften*, vol. 1 (Gütersloh, 1960), 29ff. Cf. Ernst-Wilhelm Kohls, *Die Schule bei Martin Bucer in ihrem Verhältnis zu Kirche und Obrigkeit* (Heidelberg: Quelle & Meyer, 1963), 121–29.
94. Gerta Scharffenorth, *Den Glauben ins Leben ziehen . . . Studien zu Luthers Theologie* (Munich: Kaiser, 1982), 116. Cf. Peter Gierra, "Luthers reformatorische Erkenntnis als Anstoss zum Aufbau der Armenfürsorge," in Peter Gierra, ed., *Impulse zur Diakonie in der Lutherstadt Wittenberg* (Berlin: Evangelische Verlagsanstalt, 1983).
95. Scharffenorth, *Den Glauben*, 24–25.

Luther's Theology and Social Welfare

Perhaps Luther's pastoral sense led him to put his finger so decisively on the pulse of late medieval anxiety and insecurity. That pulse beat most strongly in the veins of medieval efforts to secure an insecure existence: the sacrifice of the mass. The numerous foundations, testaments, and brotherhoods all had as their goal the securing of prayers and intercessions for the dead.

> The splendor of medieval worship with its candles, chants, vigils, ringing of bells, splendid implements and magnificent vestments, the riches of innumerable cloisters and foundations, the support of thousands of simple priests for saying mass who lived primarily from the stipends and money given for masses, all this stemmed to a very great extent from endeavors to aid souls in purgatory. Before the Reformation there was hardly a testament which did not include considerable sums for the holding of masses and other services for the dead.[96]

This achievement-oriented piety and account-book mentality, so succinctly expressed in the phrase "the mathematics of salvation," received theological articulation as a covenant with God and neighbor. One of the key scholastic phrases for this covenant theology and its concomitant social and spiritual insecurity was *facere quod in se est*—do what lies within you. That is, if you strive to love God and your neighbor to the best of your ability, weak as that may be, God will reward your efforts with the grace to do even better. God, the medieval theologian claimed, has made a covenant to be our contractual partner in creation and salvation.

The social, economic, and political developments of the late medieval world are reflected in this theology, which presumes the responsibility of individuals for their own life, society, and world on the basis and within the limits of the covenant stipulated by God. The concern of the theologians was to provide an avenue of security through human participation in the process of salvation. This was their response to the crises of the late medieval period. The result of this theology, however, was to enhance the crises by throwing people back upon their own resources. The remarkable religious intensity of this time was fueled by "an oppressive uncertainty about salvation together with the longing for it."[97] Ecclesial theology consciously stimulated the uncertainty of knowing whether one had done one's best by its translation and emphasis upon Eccles. 9:1: "No one knows whether he is worthy of God's love or hate" (cf. LW 15:144).

---

96. Hans Bernhard Meyer, S.J., *Luther und die Messe* (Paderborn: Bonifacius, 1965), 131.
97. Bernd Moeller, "Piety in Germany around 1500," in Steven Ozment, ed., *The Reformation in Medieval Perspective* (Chicago: Quadrangle Books, 1971), 55. Cf. Carter Lindberg, "Luther and the Crises of the Late Medieval Era: An Historical Interpretation," *African Theological Journal* 13/2 (1984).

Luther's response to this uncertainty of salvation began with the recognition that the religious solution of trying to merit God's favor only compounds the problem. Indeed, Luther was convinced that whenever salvation is conceived in covenantal terms, prerequisites for salvation will be imposed. No matter how minimal such prerequisites may be, they always shift the burden of proof for salvation from God to the individual.

Thus Luther generally regarded all covenants with God negatively. In contrast, Luther emphasized God's testament to sinners as the secure basis for certainty of salvation.

> A testament, as everyone knows, is a promise made by one about to die, in which he designates his bequest and appoints his heirs. A testament, therefore, involves, first, the death of the testator, and second, the promise of an inheritance and the naming of the heir. Thus Paul discusses at length the nature of testament in Rom. 4, Gal. 3 and 4, and Heb. 9. We see the same thing clearly also in these words of Christ. Christ testifies concerning his death when he says: "This is my body, which is given, this is my blood which is poured out" (Luke 22:19-20). He names and designates heirs when He says "For you" (Luke 22:19-20; 1 Cor. 11:24) "and for many" (Matt. 26:28; Mark 14:24), that is, for those who accept and believe the promise of the testator. For here it is faith that makes men heirs, as we shall see. (LW 36:38)

To emphasize his point, Luther says:

> Let someone else pray, fast, go to confession, prepare himself for mass and the sacrament as he chooses. You do the same, but remember this is all pure foolishness and self-deception, if you do not set before you the words of the testament and arouse yourself to believe and desire them. You would have to spend a long time polishing your shoes, preening and primping to attain an inheritance if you had no letter and seal with which you could prove your right to it. But if you have a letter and seal, and believe, desire, and seek it, it must be given to you, even though you were scaly, scabby, stinking and most filthy. (LW 35:88)

This image of God's testament not only clearly illustrates Luther's radical theology of justification by grace alone apart from good works; it also suggests the secular utility[98] implicit in his theology. The sinner can bring nothing to

---

98. Dickens, *The German Nation*, 66: "Too often the element of secular utility in Luther's thought has been underestimated by his pious biographers, yet they would surely be justified in regarding his secular structures as arising from religious and theological foundations." From the same work, p. 64: "Several of his writings envisage realistic programmes of social reform worthy to be placed alongside the most striking of those enunciated by humanists. In particular his *Christian Nobility*, while devoting minimal attention to theological foundations or cultural ideals, says more about actual prob-

God in order to attain forgiveness except his or her sin. Here Luther turned the medieval logic of salvation upside down. Fellowship with God is not achieved through improving and perfecting oneself through good works. Rather, fellowship with God is the gift of God apart from works. Luther never tired of vigorously proclaiming that the burden of proof for salvation rests not upon one's deeds but upon God's action. It is difficult to fully appreciate the depth of gratitude felt among all social strata of Luther's contemporaries for this Reformation message.[99]

The secular utility of Luther's theological reorientation with respect to social welfare is both destructive and constructive. Justification by grace alone sharply undercuts the medieval understanding of testaments as human contributions to the divine account books of salvation.

> Not what Christ has commanded, but what men have invented, is called "giving for God's sake"; not what one gives to the needy, the living members of Christ, but what one gives to stone, wood, and paint, is called "alms."[100] And this giving has become so precious and noble that God himself is not enough to recompense it, but has to have the help of others, bulls, parchments, lead, plate, cords large and small, and wax in green, yellow, and white. If it makes no show, it has no value. It is all bought from Rome at great cost "for God's sake," and such great works are rewarded with indulgences here and there, over and above God's reward. But that miserable work of giving to the poor and needy according to God's commandment must be robbed of such splendid reward, and be content simply with the reward that God gives. The latter work is therefore pushed to the rear and the former is placed out in front, and the two when compared shine with unequal light. (LW 45:284)

Because salvation is now perceived as the foundation of life rather than the goal and achievement of life, the energy and resources poured into acquiring other-worldly capital can be redirected to this-worldly activities. For Luther and his colleagues this meant that faith is to be active in service to the neighbor. To live otherwise is to invite divine judgment.

---

lems and possible solutions than his contemporaries said in far greater space." Blickle concludes that the peasants and citizens paraphrased Reformation doctrine in terms of the communalization of the church and the instrumentalization of the gospel, expressed in brotherly love and the common good. Peter Blickle, "Die soziale Dialektik der reformatorischen Bewegung," in Peter Blickle, ed., *Zwingli und Europa*, 88.

99. Gottfried Seebass, "The Reformation in Nürnberg," in Lawrence Buck & Jonathon Zophy, eds., *The Social History of the Reformation* (Columbus: Ohio State Univ. Press, 1972), 38; Ozment, *Reformation in the Cities*, 8–9.

100. This point will be emphasized by other early Reformers such as Karlstadt, Bucer, and Zwingli, and becomes a source for their linking of iconoclasm and poor relief. Cf. Carlos M. N. Eire, *War against the Idols: The Reformation of Worship from Erasmus to Calvin* (Cambridge: Cambridge Univ. Press, 1986), 90; and Lee Palmer Wandel, *Always among Us: Images of the Poor in Zwingli's Zurich* (Cambridge: Cambridge Univ. Press, 1990).

Beware, therefore, O man! God will not ask you at your death and at the Last Day how much you have left in your will, whether you have given so and so much to churches—although I do not condemn this—but he will say to you, "I was hungry, and you gave me no food; I was naked, and you did not clothe me" [Matt. 25:42-43]. Take these words to heart, dear man! The important thing is whether you have given to your neighbor and treated him well. Beware of show and glitter and color that draw you away from this! (LW 45:286; WA 6:45, 12–18)

Other theological motifs correlative to justification by grace alone also motivated and informed this service to the neighbor. Among the watchwords commonly associated with the early Reformation, as well as "grace alone" and "faith alone," were "scripture alone" (*sola scriptura*), "the freedom of the Christian," and "the priesthood of all believers."

The first official response to Luther in 1518 already correctly saw the critical implications of *sola scriptura* for the authority of the church.[101] In *The Babylonian Captivity of the Church* (1520), Luther asserted that the church is always servant to scripture. "It is the promises of God that make the church, and not the church that makes the promise of God. For the Word of God is incomparably superior to the church, and in this Word the church, being a creature, has nothing to decree, ordain, or make, but only to be decreed, ordained, and made. For who begets his own parent?" (LW 36:107). There is nothing esoteric about this. "The words of God . . . are to be retained in their simplest meaning as far as possible. Unless the context manifestly compels it, they are not to be understood apart from their grammatical and proper sense, lest we give our adversaries occasion to make a mockery of all the Scriptures" (LW 36:30).

In freeing the Word of God from, in Luther's view, the tyrannical control of the clergy, Luther also freed words from the control of all elites. Together with the media explosion caused by the development of printing, this freeing of the Word had a profound effect upon the communication of new ideas. Luther's emphasis upon the Word also relativized all human structures, thereby freeing them from ideology for service to the neighbor. Thus, the gospel is professed "with hand and mouth" (LW 53:64).[102] With regard to social change, "Protestant doctrine provided the sturdy tools requisite for a de jure dismantling of the old ecclesiastical system and the world that it had for so long controlled. . . . It was especially the Scripture test of Protestants that provided magistrates and city councils a quasi-legal basis for expelling the old church."[103]

101. See Carter Lindberg, "Prierias and his Significance for Luther's Development," SCJ 3/2 (1972).
102. Cf. Carter Lindberg, "Conflicting Models of Ministry—Luther, Karlstadt, and Muentzer," *Concordia Theological Quarterly* 41/4 (1977), 46.
103. Ozment, *Reformation in the Cities*, 117.

Luther further criticized the authority of the medieval church over secular life on the basis of Christian freedom and the priesthood of all believers. In his 1520 treatise "The Freedom of a Christian," Luther succinctly related the social ethics of the Reformation to his doctrine of justification: "A Christian is a perfectly free lord of all, subject to none. A Christian is a perfectly dutiful servant of all, subject to all" (LW 31:344). By virtue of baptism Christians are "the freest of kings" and "priests forever." The Christian "is by faith so exalted over all things that, by virtue of a spiritual power, he is lord of all things without exception, so that nothing can do him any harm." Furthermore, "as priests we are worthy to appear before God to pray for others and to teach one another divine things" (LW 31:354–55).

In Luther's theology the church is no longer a hierarchical institution but a community of believers in which "no one is for himself, but extends himself among others in love" (WA 12:48). Thus Luther translated ecclesia not as "church" but as "community" (*Gemeinde*), "congregation" (*Gemeine*), and "assembly" (*Versammlung*).[104] Indeed, as part of his assistance to the town of Leisnig in establishing a poor-relief order, Luther developed his early model of congregationalism, "That a Christian Assembly or Congregation Has the Right and Power to Judge All Teaching and to Call, Appoint, and Dismiss Teachers, Established and Proven by Scripture" (LW 39:301–14). To be sure, Luther's theological and social thought "owes debts to numerous predecessors, yet in the last resort it arises from his own doctrine of the Church, a largely original line of thought which can be traced back to his early writings."[105] "*Late medieval developments were a threshold as well as a foothold.*"[106]

Luther crossed this threshold already in the "Ninety-five Theses" when he wrote: "Christians are to be taught that he who gives to the poor or lends to the needy does a better deed than he who buys indulgences" (LW 31:29, Thesis 43). Conversely, "he who sees a needy man and passes him by, yet gives his money for indulgences, does not buy papal indulgences but God's wrath" (LW 31:29, Thesis 45). Furthermore, Luther was already rejecting the tradition that the poor are the treasure of the church, the means of good works through almsgiving. "St. Laurence said that the poor of the church were the treasures of the church, but he spoke according to the usage of the words in his own time" (LW 31:30–31, Thesis 59). Luther's reference to Saint Laurence is of interest because the older tradition stemming from the writings of Ambrose presented Laurence as the exemplar for selling the liturgical art and treasure of the church in order to provide for the poor. Laurence, a third-century Roman deacon, was confronted by Roman officials who demanded he turn over the church's treasure. Laurence showed the officials the assembled poor of the city, and explained that the poor were the true treasure of

104. Dickens, *The German Nation*, 67.
105. Ibid.
106. Ozment, *Reformation in the Cities*, 118. Emphasis added.

the church.[107] Ironically, Luther's Thesis 51 echoes the classic sense of the Saint Laurence story: "Christians are to be taught that the pope would and should wish to give of his own money, even though he had to sell the basilica of St. Peter, to many of those from whom certain hawkers of indulgences cajole money (LW 31:30).

Faith as Foundation of Work

Luther's convictions were soon elaborated by the criticisms and constructive suggestions in his treatises "The Blessed Sacrament of the Holy and True Body of Christ, and the Brotherhoods" (1519) and "To the Christian Nobility of the German Nation" (1520).

The former treatise is of special interest not only because it contains in a nutshell the foundations for Luther's theological and legislative contributions to social welfare, but also because it illustrates Luther's conviction that worship is the foundation for service. Thus in his 1523 "Preface" to the Leisnig ordinance for community welfare, Luther wrote: "Now there is no greater service of God [gottis dienst, i.e., worship] than Christian love which helps and serves the needy, as Christ himself will judge and testify at the Last Day, Matthew 25[:31-46]. This is why the possessions of the church were formerly called bona ecclesiae, that is, common property, a common chest, as it were, for all who were needy among the Christians" (LW 45:172–73; WA 12, 13, 26ff).[108] Thus Luther's social ethics in general and his social welfare activity in particular may be understood as a work of the people flowing from worship. For Luther, worship thrusts the Christian into the world to serve the neighbor. Indeed, Luther can characterize the daily life of the Christian as worship (Gottesdienst) because to serve the neighbor and thus obey God's commandment is worship. Conversely, Luther characterized monastic contempt for daily life as idolatrous. Thus vocation may be defined as "Gottesdienst in the worldly realm."[109] In short, the reform of worship entailed the renewal of social life.[110]

107. For the story of Saint Laurence and its use by Ambrose and successors to justify the sale of liturgical art for support of the poor, see Conrad Rudolph, The "Things of Greater Importance": Bernard of Clairvaux's "Apologia" and the Medieval Attitude toward Art (Philadelphia: Univ. of Pennsylvania Press, 1990), 80–82.
108. Cf. Helmar Junghans, "Sozialethisches Denken und Handeln bei Martin Luther," Evangelische Monatsschrift Standpunkt 70/3 (1989), 67–71, 70; and Gerhard Müller, "Zu Luthers Sozialethik," in Helmut Hesse & Gerhard Müller, eds., Über Martin Luthers "Von Kauffshandlung und Wucher" (Frankfürt am Main: Verlag Wirtschaft und Finanzen, 1987), 59–79, 64f.
109. Vilmos Vajta, Die Theologie des Gottesdienstes bei Luther (Stockholm: Svenska Kyrkans Diakonistyrelses Bokförlag, 1952), 314; also 21–23, 305–6, 309–14. See also Theodor Strohm, "Martin Luthers Sozialethik und ihre Bedeutung für die Gegenwart," in Hans Süssmuth, ed., Das Luther-Erbe in Deutschland: Vermittlung zwischen Wissenschaft und Öffentlichkeit (Düsseldorf: Droste Verlag, 1985), 83.
110. See Theodor Strohm, "'Theologie der Diakonie' in der Perspektive der Reformation," in Paul Philippi & Theodor Strohm, eds., Theologie der Diakonie (Heidelberg: Heidelberger Verlagsanstalt, 1989), 183.

It is this liturgical-sacramental foundation of social ethics that distinguishes Luther from both the humanists' program and medieval Catholic ethics. Whereas the humanists tied social reform to education and a concomitant optimism about the human will, the medieval church's sacramental theology of transubstantiation slipped over to an *ex opera operato* (in virtue of the action) sense of the works of charity. "It was not the poor person himself who counted but the act accomplished in the sight of God or for the good of the Church."[111] Maureen Flynn makes a similar observation: "Like charity, memorial drama conferred grace *ex opera operantis*, by reason of the good pious sentiments of those who performed it." Although strictly speaking theologically, "sacramentals differ from the sacraments in that they do not produce grace *ex opera operato*, . . . there appeared to have been little doubt [among the laity] that the rites were efficacious bearers of grace."[112]

In his treatise "The Blessed Sacrament of the Holy and True Body of Christ, and the Brotherhoods," Luther vigorously attacked the late medieval relationship of brotherhoods, testaments, and the achievement-piety of the mass. In contrast to the egocentricity of the late medieval testamentary striving for salvation, Luther emphasizes community rooted in God's testament for humankind. To Luther, the brotherhoods are a case study of group selfishness, the reverse of the communion of saints. This treatise presents the first suggestions of a communal use of resources for the poor, the common chest. It is of particular interest in light of the modern tendency to divorce theology from social change that this tract is addressed "to the laity."[113] This tract is also intimately linked to Luther's theology of the Eucharist. By 1525 a total of fourteen German editions and one Latin translation of this treatise had been published (LW 35:48).

That Luther was at home with the urban milieu[114] is evident in his discussion of the "fellowship of all the saints" (*communio*) by analogy with the inhabitants of a city. Again, Luther specifically relates reform of the mass to social ethics.

> The *significance* or effect of this sacrament is fellowship of all the saints. . . .
> Hence it is that Christ and all saints are one spiritual body, just as the
> inhabitants of a city are one community and body, each citizen being a

111. Louis Chatellier, *The Europe of the Devout: The Catholic Reformation and the Formation of a New Society* (Cambridge: Cambridge Univ. Press; Paris: Editions de la Maison des Sciences de l'Homme, 1989), 133.

112. Maureen Flynn, *Sacred Charity: Confraternities and Social Welfare in Spain, 1400–1700* (Ithaca, N. Y.: Cornell Univ. Press, 1989), 142, 180 n.93.

113. "Für die Leyen," WA 2:739; StA 1:271. Luther's concern to provide theological and ethical guidance to the laity pervades his writings; see in this regard his exposition of the fourth petition of the Lord's Prayer and the seventh commandment: Scharffenorth, *Den Glauben*, 317; and Albrecht Peters, *Kommentar zu Luthers Katechismen: Die Zehn Gebote* (Göttingen: Vandenhoeck & Ruprecht, 1990), 255–78.

114. Reinhard, "Luther und die Städte," 88; Moeller, "Korreferat," 113f.

member of the other and of the entire city. All the saints, therefore, are members of Christ and of the church, which is a spiritual and eternal city of God. And whoever is taken into this city is said to be received into the community of saints and to be incorporated into Christ's spiritual body and made a member of him. . . . To carry out our homely figure, it [Christian fellowship] is like a city where every citizen shares with all others the city's name, honor, freedom, trade, customs, usages, help, support, protection, and the like, while at the same time he shares all the dangers of fire and flood, enemies and death, losses, taxes, and the like. . . . Here we see that whoever injures one citizen injures an entire city and all its citizens; whoever benefits one [citizen] deserves favor and thanks from all the others. So also in our natural body, as St. Paul says in 1 Corinthians 12[:25-26], where he gives this sacrament a spiritual explanation, "The members have [the same] care for one another; if one member suffers, all suffer together; if one member is honored, all rejoice together." This is obvious: if anyone's foot hurts him, yes, even the little toe, the eye at once looks at it, the fingers grasp it, the face puckers, the whole body bends over to it, and all are concerned with this small member; again, once it is cared for all the other members are benefitted. This comparison must be noted well if one wishes to understand this sacrament, for Scripture uses it for the sake of the unlearned. (LW 35:50–52; StA 1:273f.)

"Just as we could not put up with a citizen who wanted to be helped, protected, and made free by the community, and yet in his turn would do nothing for it nor serve it," we should not put up with those in the church who "will not help the poor, put up with sinners, care for the sorrowing, suffer with the suffering, intercede for others, defend the truth, and at the risk of [their own] life, property, and honor seek the betterment of the church and of all Christians" (LW 35:57; StA 1:278). "Just as a citizen whose property has suffered damage or misfortune at the hands of his enemies makes complaint to his town council and fellow citizens and asks them for help," the Christian goes to the sacrament "to receive a sign from God that I have on my side Christ's righteousness, life, and sufferings, with all holy angels and the blessed in heaven and all pious men on earth" (LW 35:53f.; StA 1:275f.).

Just as the sacrament is understood to be a communion and fellowship with God and the saints, so its consequences are understood to be fellowship with others. For Luther the sacrament applies not only to one's personal affliction but also to the affliction of all the needy everywhere.[115] "As love and support are given you, you in turn must render love and support to Christ in his needy ones. . . . Here the saying of Paul is fulfilled, 'Bear one another's burdens, and so fulfil the law of Christ' [Gal. 6:2]. See, as you uphold all of

115. Ursala Stock, *Die Bedeutung der Sakramente in Luthers Sermonen von 1519* (Leiden: Brill, 1982), 248f.

them, so they in turn uphold you; and all things are in common, both good and evil" (LW 35:54; StA 1:276). Indeed, on the basis of the sacrament, the Christian "must fight, work, pray" for the needy (LW 35:54).

For Luther, social ethics is integral to the sacrament.[116] From his perspective the late medieval church had broken this connection between worship and welfare, to the detriment of each. "So we at present see to our sorrow that many masses are held and yet Christian fellowship which should be preached, practiced, and kept before us by Christ's example has virtually perished" (LW 35:56). Referring to the early church, Luther continues:

> But in times past this sacrament was so properly used, and the people were taught to understand this fellowship so well, that they even gathered food and material goods in the church, and there—as St. Paul writes in 1 Corinthians 11—distributed among those who were in need. We have a vestige of this [practice] in the little word "collect" in the mass, which means a general collection, just as a common fund is gathered to be given to the poor.... This has all disappeared, and now there remain only the many masses and the many who receive this sacrament without in the least understanding or practicing what it signifies. (LW 35:57; StA 1:277f.)[117]

In interpreting the origin of the "collect" as a general collection and fund gathered to be given to the poor, Luther may have been aware of patristic sources that linked worship and welfare. If so, these sources may have served as rudimentary models for his development of the common chest concept of social welfare.[118]

The loss of communal fellowship is evident in the brotherhoods; these, Luther charges, have become so self-serving that "temporal lords and cities

---

116. See Michael Beyer, "Die Neuordnung des Kirchenguts," in Helmar Junghans, ed., *Das Jahrhundert der Reformation in Sachsen* (Berlin: Evangelisches Verlagsanstalt, 1989), 96; and Annaliese Sprengler-Ruppenthal, *Mysterium und Riten: Nach der Londoner Kirchenordnung der Niederländer* (ca. 1550 bis 1566) (Cologne: Böhlau, 1967), 181, 206.

117. In his 1520 "Treatise on the New Testament, that is, the Holy Mass," Luther explains the "collects" as offerings of food and goods that are "blessed for distribution to all the needy" (LW 35:95; StA 1:300).

118. Cf. Justin Martyr's "First Apology" in Cyril Richardson, ed., *Early Christian Fathers* (Philadelphia: Westminster Press, 1953), 287: "What is collected is deposited with the president, and he takes care of orphans and widows, and those who are in want on account of sickness or any other cause, and those who are in bonds, and the strangers who are sojourners among [us], and briefly, he is the protector of all those in need." Similarly, Tertullian's "Apology" in *Ante-Nicene Fathers* 3 (1953), 46. The renaissance of patristic studies at Wittenberg was heralded by Melanchthon's 1518 inaugural lecture, "On the Reform of Studies." On Luther's early acquaintance with patristics and humanist contributions to it, see Helmar Junghans, *Der junge Luther und die Humanisten* (Weimar: Böhlau, 1984); and Maria Grossmann, *Humanism in Wittenberg 1485–1517* (Nieuwkoop: de Graaf, 1975).

should unite with clergy in abolishing" this misconduct, which is so bad a sow would not consent to be their patron saint (LW 35:68; StA 1:284f.).[119] Real brotherhood would be to "gather provisions and feed and serve a tableful or two of poor people, for the sake of God. . . . Or they should gather the money which they intend to squander for drink, and collect it into a common treasury. . . . Then in cases of hardship, needy fellow workmen might be helped to get started, and be lent money, or a young couple of the same craft might be fitted out respectably from this common treasury (LW 35:68–69; StA 1:285). True brotherhood is that which does not seek its own benefit but that of others, "above all that of the community" (LW 35:72; StA 1:287).

Luther's suggestions for the reform of church and society in this and other writings now pouring off the presses[120] were well received by influential, concerned citizens. These "unidentified members of the Saxon court, jurists, Wittenberg professors, and other widely respected men" (LW 44:119–20; StA 2:90ff.) encouraged what is widely regarded as "one of the most significant documents produced by the Protestant Reformation" (LW 44:117; StA 2:93ff.), "To the Christian Nobility of the German Nation Concerning the Reform of the Christian Estate." Here, too, Luther had a broad audience in mind and not just the nobility. Written in German, the tract makes appeals throughout to emperor, princes, lords, and cities. In less than a month, the first edition of four thousand copies was sold out.

As significant as Luther's proposals for reform of society were, "the greatest significance of this book lies in its theological basis."[121] In shorthand form, this theological basis for secular initiative in reform of church and society is Luther's thesis that all the baptized are priests. The universal priesthood of all the baptized (or all believers, as it is frequently but misleadingly expressed) undercut the medieval distinction of clergy and laity upon which all of Western social, political, legal, and religious thought was based. In his formulation of the priesthood of all the baptized, "Luther gave the existence of the city an entirely new and more profound significance; the fundamental law of the community by which all members were equal in principle and enjoyed the same rights was from then on anchored in theology. . . . The integration into the urban community of ecclesiastical persons and institutions was now theologically legitimate."[122] Luther's theology was directly applicable and liberating for urban people long engaged in a struggle

---

119. Luther contrasts the brotherhoods' self-love (*eigennützigen Liebe*) with the sacrament-inspired love for all persons (*gemeinnützigen Liebe*). Cf. Stock, *Bedeutung der Sakramente*, 201, 218f., 272f., 276, 310.

120. In his 1520 "Treatise on Good Works," Luther called upon government to control the conspicuous consumption and "usury" that was impoverishing people (LW 44:95–96; StA 2:74). In a period of less than six months after the Leipzig Debate, Luther published sixteen treatises. See LW 44:117.

121. Bernhard Lohse, *Martin Luther: An Introduction to His Life and Work* (Philadelphia: Fortress Press, 1986), 127. Cf. LW 45:95, 97.

122. Moeller, *Imperial Cities*, 71–72.

with the church over responsibility for the community. In an image that spoke directly to this context, Luther declared: "Would it not be unnatural behavior, if a fire is raging through the town, for someone to stand back quietly and let it burn more and more wherever it would, only because he does not have the power of mayor? . . . Is not every burgher here obliged to sound the alarm and call the others?" (LW 44:137).

On this basis that the temporal power to punish the wicked and protect the good is God-ordained (LW 44:130), Luther advocated that the civil authorities proceed to abolish all begging and that every city develop social welfare programs to care for its poor. Luther's position is stated in the following extensive quotation from "To the Christian Nobility":

One of the greatest necessities is the abolition of all begging throughout Christendom. Nobody ought to go begging among Christians.[123] It would even be a very simple matter to make a law to the effect that every city should look after its own poor, if only we had the courage and the intention to do so. No beggar from outside should be allowed into the city whether he might call himself pilgrim or mendicant monk. Every city should support its own poor, and if it was too small, the people in the surrounding villages should also be urged to contribute, since in any case they have to feed so many vagabonds and evil rogues who call themselves mendicants. In this way, too, it could be known who was really poor, and who was not.

There would have to be an overseer or warden who knows all the poor and informs the city council or the clergy what they needed. Or some other better arrangement might be made. As I see it, there is no other business in which so much skullduggery and deceit are practiced as in begging, and yet it could all be easily abolished. Moreover, this unrestricted universal begging is harmful to the common people. I have figured out that each of the five or six mendicant orders [Franciscans, Dominicans, Augustinians, Carmelites, Servites] visits the same place more than six or seven times every year. In addition to these there are the usual beggars, the "ambassador" beggars [those claiming to represent particular saints], and the panhandlers. This adds up to sixty times a year that a town is laid under tribute! This is over and above what the secular authorities demand in the way of taxes and assessments. All this the Romanist See steals in return for its wares and consumes for no purpose.

123. Two years later, Luther's colleague Andreas Bodenstein von Karlstadt published a treatise against begging and for poor relief with this same title. The biblical warrant was Deut. 15:4, which had already been used by Luther in his "Long Sermon on Usury" (LW 45:281). See Carter Lindberg, " 'There Should Be No Beggars Among Christians': An Early Reformation Tract on Social Welfare by Andreas Karlstadt," in Carter Lindberg, ed., *Piety, Politics, and Ethics: Reformation Studies in Honor of George Wolfgang Forell* (Kirksville, Mo.: Sixteenth Century Journal Publishers, 1984).

To me it is one of God's greatest miracles that we can still go on existing and find the wherewithal to support ourselves!

To be sure, some think that if these proposals were adopted the poor would not be so well provided for, that fewer great stone houses and monasteries would be built, and fewer so well furnished. I can well believe all this. But none of it is necessary. He who has chosen poverty ought not to be rich. If he wants to be rich, let him put his hand to the plow and seek his fortune from the land. It is enough if the poor are decently cared for so they do not die of hunger or cold. It is not fitting that one man should live in idleness on another's labor, or be rich and live comfortably at the cost of another's hardship, as it is according to the presently perverted custom. St. Paul says, "Whoever will not work shall not eat" [2 Thess. 3:10].[124]

In contrast to the pre-Reformation efforts to control begging through late medieval legislation and the discouragement of begging in the writings of the various humanist social reformers, Luther advocated the abolition of *all* begging: "Nobody ought to go begging among Christians." Luther's position on begging is not merely a consequence of his awareness of the deleterious effects of widespread begging in the cities and countryside; it is primarily a consequence of his theology of justification by grace alone, which precludes any salvific benefits to poverty and to alms. "Poverty and suffering make no one acceptable to God."[125] Luther's attack on begging was directed not merely to abuses but to the heart of the medieval theological and ecclesiological system. This fact did not escape the notice of the papacy; in Leo X's bull warning of excommunication, "Exsurge Domine," this was one of the articles for which Luther was condemned.[126]

Some scholars claim that Luther's conception of begging, willingness to work, and unemployment can be viewed as typical of early modern, bourgeois attitudes—nearly liberal, in fact, because it seeks causes within the individual and does not consider the profound social and economic changes of the time.[127] This viewpoint does not sufficiently consider the ecclesial and faith

124. LW 44:189–91; StA 2:146–47. The attack on "voluntary poverty" is, of course, directed against the monks and clergy. Luther also advocated government social assistance in his "Large Sermon on Usury" (1520); see LW 45:281f., 287.

125. J. G. Walch, ed., *Dr. Martin Luthers sämmtliche Schriften* (St. Louis: Concordia, 1880–1910), vol. 11, 1199; WA 10, III, 176–200.

126. D.-S. H. Denzinger & A. Schönmetzer, eds., *Enchiridion symbolorum, definitionum et declarationum de rebus fidei et morum* (Barcelona/Freiburg/Rome: 1963), 1491, Article 41: "Praelati ecclesiastici et principes saeculares non male facerent, si omnes saccos mendicitatis delerent." The condemned statement is taken from Luther's "Long Sermon on Usury" (LW 45:282f.): "I hold that the spiritual and temporal authorities would be discharging their duty properly if they did away with all beggars sacks."

127. See Karlheinz Blaschke's comments in note 409, StA 2:146. Bonnie Lee Brummel's Ph.D. dissertation, "Luther on Poverty and the Poor" (Columbia University, 1979), and article, "Luther and the Biblical Language of Poverty," *Ecumenical Review* 32 (1980), argue

foci of Luther's position. Luther's most vigorous attack on begging is directed not against the unemployed and underemployed but against the clergy who make a vow of poverty and live high off everyone else's hog.

> Is this not a brazen mockery of God and men to pretend the vow of poverty, and yet by so doing to seek in idleness sure plenty and excess, produced and provided by others.... By general assent, by common usage, and in everyday language material poverty means to be in want, in need of food and clothing. Who ever heard tell of a poverty which possessed nothing of its own but everything of everyone else? O fools and deceivers, who through covetousness will exploit the people with feigned words, as Peter prophesied [2 Pet. 2:3]. (LW 44:358)[128]

Luther had already excoriated clerical indulgence sellers in his "Long Sermon on Usury" (1520):

> Following studiously after their faithful shepherd [the pope], his lambs strayed about in the land with indulgences; wherever there is a parish festival or an annual fair these beggars gather like flies in summer and all preach the same song, "Give to the new building, that God and the holy lord St. Nicholas may reward you." Afterward they go to their beer or wine, also "for God's sake," and the commissioners are made rich from the indulgences, also "for God's sake." But neither commissioners nor legates are necessary to tell us that we should give to the needy according to God's commandment. (LW 45:285)

Luther asserts that these mendicant monks should be put to work if they want to eat, for not only are the mendicants themselves a major financial drain on resources that should go to the poor, their mendicancy is a handy disguise for other scoundrels (LW 44:110).[129] "For one day the wickedness of vagrants and imposters will compel the godly to limit the liberality and the benefactions they confer on the needy, since very many hypocrites accustomed to mendicancy, under the name and appearance of poor exiles, snatch away blessings from those who are truly paupers" (LW 7:337).

Furthermore, Luther viewed work from the perspective of his understanding of the gospel and faith. He thus understood work as a divine commission embedded in the creation itself. "As birds are born to fly, so persons are born to work" (WA 1:505). Work was not the consequence of the fall nor a means

---

that during the critical years of the 1520s Luther spiritualized his understanding of poverty. I do not share this evaluation.

128. In 1524 Luther wrote, "Isn't it a crying shame? Up to now, a town with four or five hundred population could turn over to the mendicant monks alone the equivalent of five, six, or seven hundred gulden" (LW 45:318).

129. Bronislaw Geremek, *The Margins of Society in Late Medieval Paris*, trans. Jean Birrel (Cambridge: Cambridge Univ. Press, 1987), 136ff., 145, makes this same point.

to achieve either salvation or any kind of puritanical self-control (WA 7:31; LW 31:360). Luther clearly rejected any and all forms of asceticism. While it is necessary to work in order to eat, it is also necessary to eat in order to work (WA 36:216, 21ff.).

Work is to be understood in terms of faith rather than in a context of anxiety and care (*Sorge*). At best, care is related to respect of one's neighbor in the form of assistance (*Für-Sorge*). Monks and nuns, concerned only with "religious" works, are plagued by insecurity and anxiety about whether their works please God. In contrast, those who follow the commandments of God may have confidence they are doing God's will. Daily work is a form of worship within the world (*weltlicher Gottesdienst*) through service to the neighbor.[130] Thus, the working Christian is characterized by faith and hope in God. It is significant that Luther did not tuck these perspectives away in learned treatises but proclaimed them in sermons and in his Large Catechism.[131] The Christian is to work as if everything depends upon him or her, but in faith the Christian is certain that the results depend upon God. Work is really nothing other than a mask (*larva*) under which God himself works.

> What else is all our work to God—whether in the fields, in the garden, in the city, in the house, in war, or in government—but just such a child's performance, by which He wants to give His gifts in the fields, at home, and everywhere else? These are the masks of God, behind which He wants to remain concealed and do all things. . . . We have the saying: 'God gives every good thing, but not just by waving a wand.' God gives all good gifts; but you must lend a hand and take the bull by the horns; that is, you must work and thus give God good cause and a mask. (LW 14:114-15; WA 31:I, 436, 7ff)

This perspective is basic to Luther's ethics of work and economics. His understanding of faith here is not that of a faith in providence that "expects a roasted chicken to fly into one's mouth" (WA 16:263, 6).[132] His view of work understands its outcome as personal, but still receives it as something given. The outcome of the work is left to the disposition of God, and therefore, Luther argues, one can work in confidence. It is exactly in the understanding of work as the commission or command of God that inner confidence and

---

130. Helmut Hesse, "Über Luthers 'Von Kauffshandlung und Wucher,'" in Helmut Hesse & Gerhard Müller, eds., *Über Luthers "Von Kauffshandlung und Wucher"* (Frankfurt am Main: Verlag Wirtschaft und Finanzen, 1987), 26; Müller, "Zu Luthers Sozialethik," 64–65: All honorable work is related to God, is *Gottesdienst*.

131. Cf. *The Book of Concord: The Confessions of the Evangelical Lutheran Church*, trans. & ed. Theodore G. Tappert (Philadelphia: Fortress Press, 1959), 381.

132. This is the imagery of "Schlaraffenland" or the "Land of Cockaigne," an earthly paradise that fosters laziness. See Ross H. Frank, "An Interpretation of *Land of Cockaigne* (1567) by Pieter Breugel the Elder," SCJ 22 (1991), 302–3.

certainty is strengthened. Luther's sharpest expression of this conviction was in his reformed understanding of vocation.

Luther's understanding of vocation, intimately related to his teaching of the priesthood of all believers, was a complete transvaluation of the medieval values associated with work. Luther rejected the medieval ecclesial dichotomy between the active life and the contemplative life, and thus lifted secular life out of the inferiority assigned it by the medieval church. This radical shift is rightly seen as a "Copernican revolution."[133] The medieval church devalued the laity's work in the world by regarding it as a means to a goal without intrinsic creative and ethical value, in comparison to the ideal monastic life and the contemplative life. At best, the medieval church valued work for penitential and ascetic purposes.[134] This perspective placed personal good work over social change. Luther's point is that to personally wash the feet of a poor person is praiseworthy, but the little-noted effort to create social justice and assistance for the poor is far more virtuous.

> But if a prince or a princess were to go to a hospital sometime and there wait on the poor and wash their feet—as we read that St. Elizabeth did, and as some great folk in foreign lands still do, that would be a great thing! That glitters! It opens people's eyes and gives them a greater reputation than all the virtues give! And it is true! We have to praise it and we ought to praise it as a great and beautiful, though human, act of virtue. But what is it compared with the divine act of virtue a prince performs when he continually does this greater service [creation of social equity and assistance] to all who are poor or who would otherwise become poor? No one praises this, for no one knows it or considers it. (LW 13:54)

Luther turned on its head the ecclesial and especially monastic exaltation of the contemplative life as the only real work and vocation. He praised work as joyous service to God and the neighbor. The Christian is not called out of the world but into it. Christian vocation, hitherto limited to the religious, was now extended to all believers. Every Christian is called to fulfill a divinely ordained place in the world. To reject work, then, is to reject one's divine calling to serve others, and by this rejection one becomes a burden to others. Indeed, Luther perceived laziness as a form of thievery, for it is living off the labor of another. This renunciation of the medieval ideal of the contemplative and the mendicant life as well as of every form of quietism is exemplified in the treatise of Luther's friend and co-worker, Wenzeslaus Linck, *Von Arbeit und*

---

133. Moeller, *Reichsstadt und Reformation*, rev. ed., 33; Seebass, "Reformation in Nürnberg," 34.
134. Hildeberg Geist, "Arbeit: Die Entscheidung eines Wortwertes durch Luther," *Luther-Jahrbuch* 13 (1931), 91ff. Cf. Christofer Frey, "Die Reformation Luthers in ihrer Bedeutung für die moderne Arbeits- und Berufswelt," in Hartmut Löwe & Claus-Jürgen Roepke, eds., *Luther und die Folge* (Munich: Kaiser, 1983).

Betteln (On Work and Begging) (1523), which expresses the idea of work in terms of a comprehensive ethos of activity and the commonweal.[135]

Work and Economics

Luther's understanding of work was particularly significant for his two-fronted struggle for justice for the poor against the medieval economic system on the one hand and the developing money economy of early capitalism on the other hand.[136] In opposition to the scholastic hierarchy of work with its devaluation of manual labor and its limitation of vocation to ecclesial professions, Luther proclaimed the ethical value of all work that serves others. Work is the mask behind which the hidden God himself continues the creation and opposes evil and thereby gives every person what is necessary for life. In his concept of vocation, Luther combined the biblical concepts of calling (*klasis*) and daily work (*ergon*). Work is a service to God and to the neighbor. The goal of Luther's ethic of vocation therefore is not self-sanctification as in almsgiving, but rather service to the neighbor and the securing of his or her basic needs. The clues to this service are right at hand.

> The Bible has been put into your workshop, into your hand, into your heart. It teaches and preaches how you should treat your neighbor. Just look at your tools—at your needle or thimble, your beer barrel, your goods, your scales or yardstick or measure—and you will read this statement inscribed on them.... All this is continually crying out to you: "Friend, use me in your relations with your neighbor just as you would want your neighbor to use his property in his relations with you." (LW 21:237)

In Luther's thought, the relative equality of all kinds of work is based not upon productivity, profits, achievements, and acquisitions but upon work's character as service for the common good, for the necessary means of survival,

135. Printed in Laube, *Flugschriften*, 2, 1086–1108. Cf. Charles E. Daniels, Jr., "Hard Work, Good Work, and School Work: An Analysis of Wenzeslaus Linck's Conception of Civic Responsibility," in Buck & Zophy, *Social History of the Reformation*, 41–51; Ozment, "Social History of the Reformation," 183–87; Jürgen Lortz, *Die reformatorische Wirken Dr. Wenzeslaus Lincks in Altenburg und Nürnberg* (Nuremberg: Korn & Berg, 1978).

136. See Theodor Strohm, "Luthers Wirtschafts- und Sozialethik," in Helmer Junghans, ed., *Leben und Werk Martin Luthers von 1526 bis 1546* (Berlin: Evangelische Verlagsanstalt, 1983). Gustav Schmoller, one of the architects of Prussian social legislation under Bismarck, regarded Luther's writings on economics as "very significant and discerning" and of interest for political economics with regard to both their economic and ethical perspectives. Since Schmoller, however, little attention has been paid to this aspect of Luther's theology. See Leopold von Caprivi, "Mit scharfen ökonomischen Blick: Luthers Schrift vom Kaufhandel und Wucher bleibt aktuell," *Lutherische Monatshefte* 21 (1982), 383. Scharffenorth, *Den Glauben*, 316, also notes that it is surprising how little attention has been paid in research to Luther's writings on economic questions.

and its relation to the ecology of God's creation. Here Christian love is oriented to creaturely order.

This social-ethical perspective is the key to Luther's understanding of property. Property is a gift of God to be used for the neighbor. Thus Luther unequivocally rejected as a deception the medieval poverty movement epitomized by Saint Francis.[137] On Francis, Luther commented: "I do not think that Francis was an evil man; but the facts prove that he was naive or, to state it more truthfully, foolish" (LW 2:327). His foolishness was in supposing money was evil in itself, and in displacing the free forgiveness of sins through Christ by a new law of renunciation.

> If silver and gold are things evil in themselves, then those who keep away from them deserve to be praised. But if they are good creatures of God, which we can use both for the needs of our neighbor and for the glory of God, is not a person silly, yes, even unthankful to God, if he refrains from them as though they were evil? For they are not evil, even though they have been subjected to vanity and evil.... If God has given you wealth, give thanks to God, and see that you make right use of it. (LW 2:331)

The problem is not money but its use. The greedy misuse the world by striving to acquire it; the monastics, by struggling to renounce it (LW 28:370–72; LW 30:248).[138] The end result for both is personal insecurity because trust is placed in self-achievement rather than in God. Meanwhile, the neighbor is neglected.

The medieval ideology of poverty had been entrenched for centuries, but the acceptance of the idea that money can make money was relatively new in Luther's day. The canonists and theologians of the sixteenth century discussed these new financial practices largely in terms of the medieval condemnation of usury—a condemnation reaffirmed as late as the Fifth Lateran Council of 1515.[139] Although Luther, too, uses the medieval term of "usury,"

137. LW 22:50: "Many people, of both high and low estate, yes, all the world, were deceived by this pretense. They were taken in by it, thinking: 'Ah, this is something extraordinary! The dear fathers lead such an ascetic life; ...' Indeed, if you want to dupe people, you must play the eccentric."
138. Cf. Oswald Bayer, "Luther's Ethics as Pastoral Care," *Lutheran Quarterly* (1990).
139. One of Luther's major theological opponents, Johann Eck, was notorious for his defense, allegedly in collusion with the Fugger banking house, of interest-bearing loans. See Heiko A. Oberman, *Werden und Wertung der Reformation* (Tübingen: Mohr, 1977), 161–87; Steven Rowan, *Ulrich Zasius: A Jurist in the German Renaissance, 1461–1535* (Frankfurt: Klostermann, 1987); John T. Noonan, *The Scholastic Analysis of Usury* (Cambridge: Harvard Univ. Press, 1957); Benjamin Nelson, *The Idea of Usury: From Tribal Brotherhood to Universal Otherhood*, 2d ed. (Chicago: Univ. of Chicago Press, 1969); and Jacques Le Goff, *Your Money or Your Life: Economy and Religion in the Middle Ages* (New York: Zone Books, 1988).

his attack is directed against the financial practices of early capitalism. By all accounts, the entrepreneurial spirit was well-established by this time.

To Luther the calculating entrepreneur was extremely distasteful. He was convinced that the capitalist spirit divorced money from use for human needs and necessitated an economy of acquisition. From his "Brief Sermon on Usury" (1519) to his "Admonition to the Clergy to Preach against Usury" (1540), Luther consistently preached and wrote against the expanding money and credit economy as a great sin.

> After the devil there is no greater human enemy on earth than a miser and usurer for he desires to be above everyone. Turks, soldiers, and tyrants are also evil men, yet they must allow the people to live ... indeed, they must now and then be somewhat merciful. But a usurer and miser-belly desires that the entire world be ruined in order that there be hunger, thirst, misery, and need, so that he can have everything and so that everyone must depend upon him and be his slave as if he were God. (WA 51:396, 12)

In Luther's eyes, the international cartels, the multinational corporations of his day, were continually burdening and defrauding the poor. "Everyone misuses the market in his own willful, conceited, arrogant way, as if it were his right and privilege to sell his goods as dearly as he pleases without a word of criticism."[140]

This "lust for profits," Luther observed, had many clever expressions: selling on time and credit, manipulating the market by withholding or dumping goods, developing cartels and monopolies, falsifying bankruptcies, trading in futures, and just plain misrepresenting goods (LW 45:261–73). Such usury, Luther argued, affects everyone. "The usury which occurs in Leipzig, Augsburg, Frankfurt, and other comparable cities is felt in our market and our kitchen. The usurers are eating our food and drinking our drink." Even worse, however, by manipulating prices, "usury lives off the bodies of the poor" (WA 51:417, 11–17). In his own inimitable style, Luther exploded: "The world is one big whorehouse, completely submerged in greed" where the "big thieves hang the little thieves" (LW 21:180, 221; WA 51:362; LW 25:172; LW 13:60; WA 31:I, 206, 31f.) and the big fish eat the little fish.[141] Thus he exhorted pastors to condemn usury as stealing and murder, and to refuse the sacrament to usurers unless they repent (WA 51:367, 10-368, 16).[142]

140. *Book of Concord*, 397.
141. The monopolistic trading companies "oppress and ruin all the small businessmen, like the pike the little fish in the water, just as if they were lords over God's creatures and immune from all the laws of faith and love" (LW 45:270).
142. The pre-Reformation preacher of Strasbourg, Geiler of Kaysersberg, had earlier expressed a similar conviction. See Thomas Brady, *Turning Swiss: Cities and Empire*, 1450–1550 (Cambridge: Cambridge Univ. Press, 1985), 121.

It is important to note that Luther was concerned not merely about an individual's use of money, but also about the structural social damage inherent in the idolatry of the "laws" of the market. Ideas of an impersonal market and autonomous laws of economics were abhorrent to Luther because he saw them as both idolatrous and socially destructive. He saw the entire community endangered by the financial power of a few great economic centers. The rising world economy was already beginning to suck up urban and local economics, and to threaten to create an as yet unheard-of opposition between rich and poor. He saw an economic coercion immune to normal jurisdiction that would destroy the ethos of the community.

Luther was not isolated among his contemporaries in calling for government control of the new economics. This subject had been debated at the Imperial Diets since 1512, but the influence of the monopolies effectively curtailed demands for controls.[143] In this context Luther was urged, perhaps by princes as well as jurists and theologians, to expose "these financial evils . . . so that, even though the majority may not wish to do right, at least some people—however few they are—may be delivered from the gaping jaws of avarice" (LW 45:245; WA 15:293). Luther believed that the church was called to reject publicly and unequivocally these economic developments and to develop a constructive social ethic that would include public accountability of large businesses through government regulation.[144] Only through government regulation was justice possible for the poor. Luther's departure from his scholastic forerunners on economic questions was to remove the church from the role of economic regulation. "The radical aspect of Luther's advice, then, was that he gave all of this authority over socioeconomic matters to the territorial state."[145]

A prince is to help the poor, the orphans, and the widows to justice, and to further their cause. . . . For this virtue includes all the works of righteousness: as when a prince or a lord or city has good laws and customs; when everything is regulated in an orderly way; and when order is kept by people in all ranks, occupations, trades, businesses, services, and works, so that it is not said: "The people are without laws." For where

143. One of the motives for Luther's 1524 treatise "Trade and Usury" was the failure of the Nuremberg Diets of 1522 and 1524 to take any effective action against monopolies. See LW 45:241–43; and Hermann Kunst, *Evangelischer Glaube und politischer Verantwortung* (Stuttgart: Evangelisches Verlagswerk, 1976), 363. The political discussions of the monopoly issue at the Imperial Diets are reviewed in Clemens Bauer, "Conrad Peutingers Gutachten zur Monopolfrage: Eine Untersuchung zur Wandlungen der Wirtschaftsanschauungen im Zeitalter der Reformation," ARG 45 (1954). For a recent discussion of monopolies, see Brady, *Turning Swiss*, 119–30.
144. See Igor Kiss, "Luthers Bemühungen um eine sozial gerechtere Welt," *Zeichen der Zeit* (1985).
145. William J. Wright, *Capitalism, the State, and the Lutheran Reformation: Sixteenth Century Hesse* (Athens: Ohio State Univ. Press, 1988), 21.

there are no laws, the poor, the widows, and the orphans are oppressed. Then there is no peasant so low that he cannot practice extortion. And this is equally true of buying, selling, inheriting, lending, paying, borrowing, and the like. It is only a matter of one getting the better of another, robbing him, stealing from him, and cheating him. This happens most of all to the poor, the widows, and the orphans. (LW 13:53)

In the end, Luther considered early capitalism to constitute a *status confessionis* (a condition requiring a particular confessing of Christian faith) for the church, in spite of the fact that many of his contemporaries began to think he was tilting at windmills.[146]

Luther's exhortations to government regulation of large business gained little effective support. As Luther himself commented in his 1524 treatise: "Kings and princes ought to look into this matter and forbid them by strict laws. But I hear that they have a finger in it themselves (LW 45:271).[147] It is hardly surprising that at a time when interest rates could soar to 50 percent, bankers turned a deaf ear to his call for a 5 percent ceiling on interest. Thus Luther found that it was easier to motivate assistance to individuals than it was to curb the economic practices that created poverty. Poverty's squalor calls for redress, whereas the attractive trappings of business muffle criticism.

Yet the effects of early capitalism could be felt. In Wittenberg between 1520 and 1538, prices doubled but wages remained the same. Luther called this disguised robbery and greed.[148] "How skillfully Sir Greed can dress up to look like a pious man if that seems to be what the occasion requires, while

---

146. Strohm, "Luthers Wirtschafts- und Sozialethik," 219. Cf. Hermann Barge, *Luther und der Frühkapitalismus* (Gütersloh: Bertelsmann, 1951); Werner Elert, *Morphologie des Luthertums* (Munich: Beck, 1958), vol. 2, 477–83. Karl Marx's admiration of Luther as "the first German political economist" stems not only from Luther's excoriation of early capitalism, but also from Luther's sense of the essence of capitalism and its inner drive to buy labor and reproduce itself. Cf. Hermann Lehmann, "Luthers Platz in der Geschichte der politischen Ökonomie," in Günter Vogler et al., *Martin Luther: Leben–Werke–Wirkung*, 2d ed. (Berlin: Akademie Verlag, 1986), 279–94; and Gisela Kahl, "Martin Luther, 'der älteste deutsche Nationalökonom,' " in *Martin Luther: Leistungen und Wirkungen Wissenschaftliche Zeitschrift* (Gesellschaftswissenschaftliche Reihe. Friedrich-Schiller-Universität Jena) 33/3 (1984), 315–26. On the still influential interpretations of Luther by Troeltsch, Weber, and Niebuhr, cf. Nelson, *Idea of Usury*; Strohm, "Luthers Wirtschafts- und Sozialethik," 206, 209; and Carter Lindberg, "Reformation Initiatives for Social Welfare," in D. M. Yeager, ed., *Annual of the Society of Christian Ethics 1987*, 79–99. For a discussion of the contemporary Lutheran debate on *status confessionis*, cf. Eckehart Lorenz, ed., *The Debate on "Status Confessionis": Studies in Christian Political Theology* (Geneva: Lutheran World Federation, 1983).
147. On the other hand, response to his earlier writings on economics was sufficient to spur him to publish his 1524 treatise "Trade and Usury." "I have been asked and urged to touch upon these financial evils" (LW 45:245).
148. Barge, *Luther und der Frühkapitalismus*, 35. For the views of Luther's contemporaries on wealth, see John Van Cleve, *The Problem of Wealth in the Literature of Luther's Germany* (Columbia, S.C.: Camden House, 1991).

he is actually a double scoundrel and a liar" (LW 21:183). In 1538 and 1539, grain speculation in the wake of a bad harvest forced up prices and motivated Luther to exhort both the Wittenberg town council and the Elector to take vigorous countermeasures. Unsatisfied by their response, Luther vented his indignation in sermons and then in his treatise to the pastors to preach against usury. "God opposes usury and greed yet no one realizes this because it is not simple murder and robbery.... Thus everyone should see to his worldly and spiritual office as commanded to punish the wicked and protect the pious" (WA 51:422, 15-523, 2).

Luther's 1519 and 1520 sermons on usury inspired his more radical followers to surpass his condemnation of usurers and to condemn those who pay interest as sharing in the usurer's sin. The most notorious instance was that of Jakob Strauss, the evangelical preacher at Eisenach.[149] Eisenach and its environs included an unusually large number of churches, cloisters, and ecclesial corporations, to which much of the population owed interest payments. The financially exploitative practices of these ecclesial institutions, not surprisingly, had created a strong current of resentment in the people. In this situation, Strauss issued fifty-one theses against usury, "Haupstücke and Artikel christlicher Lehre wider den unchristlichen Wucher" (The Principal Items and Articles of Christian Teaching against the Unchristian Usury).[150] Strauss proclaimed that charging even one penny of interest constitutes usury (Thesis 5), and also that the paying of interest is equally against the gospel of Jesus Christ (Thesis 24). To the great consternation of the ecclesial institutions that had invested much of their funds in annuities, many peasants and citizens took Strauss to mean they no longer had to pay charges to their creditors. Appeals were made to the Elector, who appointed his son Johann Friedrich to investigate the situation. Luther's opinion was requested through Chancellor Brück. Luther made it clear that though he too was against usurious interest, it was untenable to claim that persons paying interest were guilty of usury. Furthermore, it was not in the power of the debtor to declare interest invalid; the matter was for the authorities, not the individual, to decide. In any case an individual should not be his or her own judge.[151]

---

149. Strauss (c. 1480–c. 1532), a native of Basel, became an evangelical preacher in Eisenach toward the end of 1522. See Hermann Barge, *Jakob Strauss: ein Kämpfer für das Evangelium in Tirol, Thüringen, und Süddeutschland* (Leipzig: Heinsius, 1937). Nelson, *Idea of Usury*, 36–45, contains a useful account of the controversy, with references. See also Kunst, *Evangelischer Glaube*, 80–83, and Ozment, "Social History of the Reformation," 187–88. Some years later, the Anabaptist community in Münster radicalized Strauss's position. Not only was interest not to be paid, but the money economy was to be replaced by a barter economy. Similar to Saint Francis, the Münster Anabaptists proclaimed that money was unclean for Christians. See James Stayer, "Christianity in One City: Anabaptist Münster, 1534–1535," in Hans J. Hillerbrand, ed., *Radical Tendencies in the Reformation: Divergent Perspectives* (Kirksville, Mo.: Sixteenth Century Journal Publishers, 1988), 128–30.
150. Laube, *Flugschriften*, vol. 2, 1073–76.
151. See Gottfried Maron, " 'Niemand soll sein eigner Richter sein': Eine Bemerkung zu Luthers Haltung im Bauernkrieg," *Luther* 46 (1975).

At the suggestion of the Elector, Strauss sought to clarify his position through a supplementary treatise that appeared in early 1524: "Das Wucher zu nehmen und zu geben unserem christlichen Glauben und brüderlichen Liebe zuwider ist" (To Take and to Give Interest Is Contrary to Our Christian Faith and Brotherly Love). The very title of this treatise reasserted Strauss's conviction that the giving of interest is as opposed to Christian faith and brotherly love as is the taking of interest. The issue now, however, was not just that of interest but of the elevation of the Bible, especially the Mosaic laws of sabbatical and Jubilee releases, to a pattern for society. In other words, Strauss, like other radicals such as Karlstadt and Müntzer, was advocating the gospel as a new law for society.

To Luther this position was a confusion of law and gospel, a confusion of social ethics and theology; in short, a reintroduction of the Christian legalism Luther opposed in the medieval church. Luther's criticism of Karlstadt, Müntzer, and Strauss was that they tied civil renewal and reform to conversion: "For because they do not distinguish between the kingdom of Christ and the kingdoms of the world, they make Christianity a matter of changing certain externals" (LW 12:42). Along with his personal responses to Prince Johann Friedrich, Chancellor Brück, and Strauss (WA Br 3:176–79, 274–78, 305–8), Luther publicly expressed his position in his "Trade and Usury":

> I have often taught thus, that the world ought not and cannot be ruled according to the gospel and Christian love, but by strict laws and with sword and force, because the world is evil. It accepts neither gospel nor love, but lives and acts according to its own will unless compelled by force. Otherwise, if only love were applied, everyone would eat, drink, and live at ease at someone else's expense, and no one would work. Indeed, everyone would take from another what was his, and we would have such a state of affairs that no one could live because of the others. (LW 45:264)

Theologically, to Luther, a Christian society is a contradiction in terms because it would make God's free grace into social legislation. Practically, to Luther, a Christian society is impossible because "Christians are rare people on earth. This is why the world needs a strict, harsh temporal government which will compel and constrain the wicked to refrain from theft and robbery, and to return what they borrow" (LW 45:258).

Luther's position by no means precludes the responsibility of Christians to advise and exhort governmental authorities. Luther himself wrote essays urging Christian princes not just to build a hospital for the poor but to make their whole land into a kind of hospital in terms of aid to the truly needy. This would preserve "rich or poor, his living and his goods for everyone, so that he does not have to become a beggar or a poor man" (LW 13:53). In particular, Luther convinced the Elector Johann to give a Franciscan monastery, which he had planned to use as his princely sepulcher, to the town of Wittenberg for use as a hospital for the poor (WA Br 4:248–49).

In his 1525 response to the Danzig town council request for advice on reform, Luther reaffirmed his conviction that society cannot be ruled by the gospel, because the gospel requires willing hearts moved by God's Spirit. The gospel is for despairing consciences, but hard and stubborn minds need reason and the law. "Christians are not needed for secular authority. It is not necessary for the emperor to be a saint [in order to have decent government]. It is sufficient for the emperor to possess reason" (WA 27:417–18).

> For we zealously admonish, write, proclaim, cry aloud, that man should use wisdom, power, and other creatures of God in this life for managing and settling present business. There is the place where our reason works, provides, and runs as if on its own race track as much as it can. But in the presence of God all these things are nothing, nor do they count for anything, for here a better righteousness and a greater power than ours is required. (LW 12:21)[152]

Reason replaced ecclesial legitimation in politics. This concept is easily misunderstood today if we think of reason in post-Enlightenment terms as autonomous reason. It is also misunderstood by one-sided interpretations of Luther's writings on the Peasants' War that presume that the sword is the only means Luther conceived of for political rule.[153] For Luther, the essential characteristic for worldly rule is reason informed by wisdom and equity.[154] In "A Sermon on Keeping Children in School" (1530), Luther wrote:

> All experience proves this ["Wisdom is better than might"] and in all the histories we find that force, without reason or wisdom has never accomplished anything. . . . Briefly, then, it is not the law of the fist but the law of the head that must rule—not force but wisdom or reason—among the wicked as well as among the good. (LW 46:238–39)

The matter of interest or usury should be approached on the basis of reason and natural law so that it, along with all human laws, should be pressed to conform to equity (*epieikeia* or *aequitas*).[155] A sudden abolition of interest would be unjust to lenders. An equitable solution would be to set an annual interest rate of 5 percent, which would be tied to a particular

152. See also WA 40: II, 207, 30.
153. Junghans, "Sozialethisches Denken," warns against this error.
154. H. G. Haile, *Luther: An Experiment in Biography* (Princeton: Princeton Univ. Press, 1983), 345–49; Ulrich Duchrow, *Christenheit und Weltverantwortung* (Stuttgart: Klett-Cotta, 1970), 495–500; Scharffenorth, *Den Glauben*, 259, 236ff.
155. See WA 25:58–60; LW 29:74–77.

mortgage so that the lender would share in the risks as well as the returns. If the return is less than 5 percent, the interest should be adjusted accordingly, "just as natural law teaches." Equity should also be related to the individual's circumstances. The well-to-do lender could be induced to waive a part of the interest, whereas an old person without means should retain it (WA Br 3:484–86).

The influence of these views upon legislation was minimal. Duke George of Saxony, cousin of Luther's protector Elector Johann but staunch opponent of Luther, introduced legislation in Dresden in 1529 that prohibited the usual 15 to 20 percent interest rates in favor of a 5 percent annual rate. This in turn influenced the reform of the Zwickau city laws in 1539. The Dresden legislation, however, was frequently violated.

That these examples may indicate more failure than success is confirmed by the 1564–65 controversy in Rudolstadt. The Lutheran pastor there refused to commune two parishioners who lived by "usury." The theological faculties of Wittenberg, Jena, and Leipzig were requested to give their opinions. They concluded against the pastor, who then had to leave town. The theologians did not recognize Luther as an authority on this issue. A similar crisis in Regensburg in 1587 led to the expulsion of a group of five preachers. After this, no serious efforts were made to acknowledge Luther's position on usury. Luther's followers first ignored and then forgot his position against early capitalism.[156]

The powerful of his day countered Luther's efforts to "put a bit in the mouth of the Fuggers and similar companies" (LW 44:213) by advocating government regulation of business and the remission of burdensome debts on the poor. Luther was not the only one to meet resistance from the business establishment. When Emperor Charles V made motions in the direction of stricter business controls, the Fugger banking house reminded him of his outstanding debts, and the mining monopolies claimed the right to act as they pleased.[157] In his criticism of chaotic currency systems and their vulnerability to debasement, of supply and price manipulations, and with his call for government control of prices and supervision of credit, Luther put his finger on the symptoms of the economic relations of his time.[158] Luther was not utopian in these matters. He commented that the world cannot be without usury anymore than it can be without sin, but woe to the person by whom it comes (WA 51:354, 1–12). At the end of his treatise on trade he wrote: "Now I know full well that this book of mine will be taken amiss; perhaps they will toss it to the winds and remain as they are. But it will not be my fault, for I have done my part to show how richly we have deserved it if God should come with his rod (LW 45:272).

---

156. Barge, *Luther und der Frühkapitalismus*, 40–44; Nelson, *Idea of Usury*, 92–94.
157. Elert, *Morphologie*, 476–77; Brady, *Turning Swiss*, 130.
158. Strohm, "Luthers Wirtschafts- und Sozialethik," 218. Cf. Andreas Pawlas, "Zur Kalkulation einer 'gerechten' Preis bei Luther," *Luther* 60 (1989).

From Charity to Social Assistance

On the personal level, Luther was ever ready to serve the poor and oppressed who constantly presented themselves to him. His letters reveal his concern for the poor and his esteem for service to others as the norm for Christian life. Through Spalatin he pled for the poor with the Elector, whom he called a *patronus pauperum* (patron of the poor). In one lengthy and finally unsuccessful case, he interceded for a widow who wished to cancel her bequest of her house to the canons because she needed to help her sister. Luther pursued this case for two years. Convinced that "God is the judge for the poor and the needy (WA 6:7, 4–5), Luther was involved in numerous appeals on behalf of widows, the poor, invalids, and prisoners. He was especially active on behalf of poor pastors and monks and nuns who had left their cloisters. His notorious generosity with his own income was at times a matter of concern to his wife. But, as he commented, that person fasts the best who is so absorbed in his work that he does not know he is fasting.[159]

Although Luther's predilection for being personally indiscriminate in charity is rather well known,[160] his advice for responding to poverty is to develop rational, urban, social welfare legislation. Convinced that everyone has the right to the basic necessities of life, Luther was concerned to develop prophylactic as well as remedial social assistance. "For so to help a man that he does not need to become a beggar is just as much of a good work and a virtue and an alms as to give to a man and to help a man who has already become a beggar" (LW 13:54).

Following close upon the publication of his treatise "To the Christian Nobility," which elaborated the calls for governmental assistance to the poor already sounded in his 1519 and 1520 sermons on usury, the Wittenberg town council with Luther's assistance formulated an ordinance to ensure the regulation of public assistance to the city's house poor and to make begging unnecessary.[161] This was the first effort to translate Luther's theological ethics into social legislation. This "Order of the Communal Purse" provided for funds to be collected weekly and deposited in a chest with three separate locks. The four stewards of the purse, one from each quarter of the town, were to be elected on the basis of their knowledge of the citizenry and their needs.

159. H. Hering, "Die Liebestätigkeit der deutschen Reformation," *Theologische Studien und Kritiken* 56 (1883), 57, 262ff.; and Eberhard Schendel, "Martin Luther und die Armen," *Lutherischen Kirche in der Welt* 36 (1989), 113–14.
160. In his foreword to his edition of the *Liber Vagatorum*, Luther admits, "I myself in recent years have been fooled by these vagabonds and blabbermouths more than I wish to confess" (WA 26:639). See also E. G. Schwiebert, *Luther and His Times* (St. Louis: Concordia, 1950), 266, 597; and LW 3:183.
161. Ernst Koch, "Zusatz zur Wittenberg Beutelordnung: 1520 oder 1521," WA 59:62–65, with bibliography. For a discussion of the controversy over authorship, see Carter Lindberg, "Karlstadt, Luther, and the Origins of Protestant Poor Relief," *Church History* 46 (1977), 324ff.

The only criterion for distribution of loans or outright gifts was to be the need of the recipient. Mendicant monks were to be banned from the town. Provisions were made for care of the sick and mentally ill. The first town doctor responsible for the poor was installed in 1527.[162]

Luther's direct influence upon the immediately subsequent developments of social welfare in Wittenberg was curtailed by the Diet of Worms and the following months he spent in protective custody in the Wartburg Castle (April 1521 to March 1522). During this time his colleague Karlstadt assisted the city council with further legislation, *Ain lobliche Ordnung der Fürstlichen Stat Wittenberg* (A Praiseworthy Ordinance of the Princely City of Wittenberg) (January 1522), and contributed his own treatise on begging and poor relief, "There Shall Be No Beggars among Christians."[163]

Although Karlstadt later charted an alternative to Luther's understanding of Reformation,[164] this tract reflects Karlstadt's dependence upon Luther's earlier expressions of theological and programmatic concern for the poor that culminated in the *Beutelordnung* and then the Wittenberg Order of 1522. It is the second half of a larger treatise concerned with the abolition of images, the full title of which is *Von Abtuhung der Bylder und das keyn Bedtler unther den Christen seyn sollen* (On the Abolition of Images and That There Shall Be No Beggars among Christians). This title reminds us once again of the connection between idolatry and neglect of the neighbor initially stated by Luther that led to iconoclasm with Karlstadt and Zwingli.

In this writing Karlstadt emphasizes that preventive action against the causes of poverty is crucial even as remedial work continues to address the particular needs of people in distress. Civic authority is to play a major role, and vocational training is to provide access to employment beyond menial labor. The work of social welfare is an expression of the Christian response to God's law and saving activity. Although Karlstadt stresses God's support for the poor and oppressed, he neither romantically identifies the poor with

162. Wolfgang Böhmer & Friedrich Kirsten, "Der gemeine Kasten und seine Bedeutung für das kommunale Gesundheitswesen Wittenbergs," *Wissenschaftliche Zeitschrift: Martin-Luther-Universität: Mathematisches Naturwissenschaftliches Reihe* 34/2 (1985), 50–51.
163. The Wittenberg order is in Sehling, vol. 1, 696ff., and Hans Lietzmann, ed., *Die Wittenberger und Leisniger Kastenordnung* (Kleine Texte 21) (Berlin, 1935). For Karlstadt's tract see Hans Lietzmann, ed., *Von Abtuhung der Bilder und das keyn Bedtler unther den Christen seyn sollen* (Kleine Texte 74) (Bonn, 1911), and Lindberg, "There Should Be No Beggars among Christians." See also Part Two, sections 6.2 and 7.1, of this volume.
164. See Hermann Barge, *Andreas Bodenstein von Karlstadt*, 2 vols. (Leipzig, 1905, reprint 1968); Ronald J. Sider, *Andreas Bodenstein von Karlstadt* (Leiden: Brill, 1974); Ulrich Bubenheimer, "Andreas Rudolff Bodenstein von Karlstadt," in Wolfgang Merklein, ed., *Andreas Bodenstein von Karlstadt, 1480–1541* (Karlstadt, 1980); Calvin Pater, *Karlstadt as the Father of the Baptist Movements* (Toronto: Univ. of Toronto Press, 1983); Carter Lindberg, "Karlstadt's 'Dialogue' on the Lord's Supper," *Mennonite Quarterly Review* 53 (1979); and Carter Lindberg, "The Conception of the Eucharist According to Erasmus and Karlstadt," in Marc Lienhard, ed., *Les dissidents du XVIᵉ siècle entre l'Humanisme et le Catholicisme* (Baden-Baden: Koerner, 1983).

the Kingdom of God nor paternalistically regards them as objects for church service or good works. Within a couple of years after writing this treatise, Karlstadt manifested his solidarity with the poor by renouncing academe and becoming a farmer. The events that followed, including his expulsion from Electoral Saxony, prevented him from making further effective contributions to social welfare.

Like Luther and so many of his contemporaries, Karlstadt graphically depicted begging as omnipresent. "Beggars are running all about after bread, begging for bread in the streets, before the houses, or sitting before the churches. We should not tolerate but rather banish such people"[165] There is no excuse for the mendicants just because they are willing beggars.

> Their desire and action is unchristian, fraudulent, and noxious, for they have no pretext for their begging in Holy Scripture. They repeatedly deceive the poor and the rich about them, and they injure the poor with their demands for cheese, corn, bread, beer, wine, and testament, and all sorts of things.[166]

It is a Christian social responsibility, Karlstadt argued, to abolish such false begging and to assist the honest poor. The latter course involves developing policies and means to prevent poverty as well as to meet immediate needs. Karlstadt exhorts the civil authorities to enforce a ban on begging and to be diligent in helping the poor. He presents a vision of civic reform by "Christian magistrates," who are called upon not just to maintain the status quo among the poor, but to support the poor in the development of vocational skills. "Whether one desires to be a printer, goldsmith, baker, tailor, shoemaker, or learn a similar craft, or to begin to employ and promote, they shall help everyone according to his requirements. For they shall lend their brethren what they need."[167] The money lent for this purpose was to be repaid to the common chest if possible, but if reimbursement were to impose a hardship, it would not be demanded or expected. The means for this program were already at hand in the common chest. The funding for the common chest included the income from the brotherhoods and parish endowments available through the death or renunciation of the priest.[168]

The scriptural basis for Karlstadt's perspectives on poor relief includes few references to those favorite texts of Christian ethicists: Ps. 41:1 ("Happy are those who consider the poor") and Matt. 25:40 ("as you did it to one of the least of these who are members of my family, you did it to me"). Instead,

165. Lietzmann, Abtuhung, 23; Lindberg, "There Should Be No Beggars," 160.
166. Lietzmann, Abtuhung, 28; Lindberg, "There Should Be No Beggars," 164.
167. Lietzmann, Abtuhung, 25; Lindberg, "There Should Be No Beggars," 161.
168. Luther was concerned that government appropriation of monastic property should provide for the cloister inmates whether or not they chose to leave, and that needy heirs of the founders receive "at least a large portion of it." See LW 45:171ff.

Karlstadt launched into an extended and often strained exegesis of Deuter-onomy 15, a chapter concerned with the sabbatical year release of slaves and debts. This orientation to the Old Testament is a clue to the impending divergence from Luther's understanding of reform by Karlstadt and the more radical reformers to follow him. Luther and the radical reformers fundamen-tally disagreed not only on the significance of Deuteronomic precedents as the basis for Christian social organization, but on the question of whether a "Christian" commonwealth or even a "Christian" city was a theological and social possibility.[169] In an earlier study I suggested nondoctrinal as well as theological factors behind Karlstadt's preoccupation with Deuteronomy, but I would now emphasize that for Karlstadt the law of Moses and the law of Christ are continuous and provide the pattern for the social life of the re-generate.[170] In the early 1520s, however, this basic theological difference from Luther's dialectic of law and gospel had not yet led to a parting of the ways between the two reformers.

In any case, Karlstadt developed the idea in his treatise that for a Christian every day is the same as the Jubilee year for the ancient Israelite. Thus the Christian is bound at all times to release debts and provide the poor with what they need. Even though God created the poor so that the rich can help them, and even though the poor will always be with us, we nevertheless shall have no beggars.[171]

Deut. 15:12 directs that every Hebrew slave was to receive freedom in the seventh year. Karlstadt therefore maintained that no one should be forced into servitude. Rather than applying this argument to the plight of contem-porary day laborers, Karlstadt applied it to monks and nuns.

> The highest civil authority should release and free such monks and nuns now in the Seventh Year. They should be provided with aid and help towards a legitimate life and temporal support according to their ability. For they are held and termed servants and maids, and have their Seventh Year daily.[172]

The tract ends with an expression of fear of failure: "I fear that even in this necessary and Christian article, that what is agreed and should happen will not happen, so we will be called and be other than Christians."[173]

---

169. Nelson, *Idea of Usury*, 39–40: "Karlstadt's *Abtuhung der Bilder* and Strauss's *Das Wucher zu nehmen* were two of the earliest treatises clearly to focus on a problem which was to be of paramount importance in every major crisis of Protestantism in the early modern epoch: What was the proper interpretation and embodiment of the Judeo-Christian ideal of brotherhood? Or, to put the question in the terms used in the Age of the Reformation, to what extent was Christian Europe bound to emulate the fraternalistic institutions of the Hebrew Commonwealth?"
170. Lindberg, "Karlstadt, Luther, and the Origins," 324; and Carter Lindberg, *The Third Reformation?* (Macon, Ga.: Mercer Univ. Press, 1983), 68ff.
171. Lietzmann, *Abtuhung*, 25; Lindberg, "There Should Be No Beggars," 162.
172. Lietzmann, *Abtuhung*, 28; Lindberg, "There Should Be No Beggars," 164.
173. Lietzmann, *Abtuhung*, 29; Lindberg, "There Should Be No Beggars," 165.

Luther shared Karlstadt's pessimism from time to time, but the ideas regarding social assistance broached in his writings of 1519–20 were widely appropriated. Towns and cities began to approach Luther for assistance in drafting new legislation for church and society. One of the first to do so was the town of Leisnig.

The Leisnig Ordinance[174] is important for a number of reasons. First, Luther was personally involved in its creation and thus it essentially corresponded to his conception.[175] Second, it was fraternal in that it represented agreement among the city, the local nobility, and the surrounding villages of the parish.[176] Third, it provided a model for other towns to follow and a source of inspiration for pamphleteers, such as Wenzeslaus Linck.[177]

The right of the parish assembly to establish a common chest is based on the doctrine of the priesthood of all the baptized. It is noteworthy that Luther's assistance to Leisnig stimulated his early model of congregationalism. Luther's term for church, both universal and local, is *Gemeinde* (assembly or community). He regarded the civil community and the church community as coextensive, forming a single unit in which state and church were not easily distinguishable. Furthermore, the idea that religion is a private matter was totally foreign to the sixteenth century. Thus it is understandable that the newly awakened striving for ecclesial self-responsibility at the same time produced new thinking about civil community relationships and the administration of its properties. Lacking a modern sharp distinction between church and state, the Reformers willed that the total community be restructured according to Reformation principles. However, when, as in the case of Leisnig, conflict arose between the city council and the parish, Luther stood on the side of the parish.[178]

Leisnig was a small town situated on the Mulde river, south of Wittenberg and east of Leipzig, with a population in 1523 of about fifteen hundred. The

174. "Fraternal Agreement on the Common Chest of the Entire Assembly at Leisnig," LW 45:159–94 with Luther's preface; WA 12:1–30. Cf. Lindberg, "Reformation Initiatives"; and Grimm, "Luther's Contributions," 226–29.

175. Karl Dummler, "Die Leisniger Kastenordnung von 1523," *Zeitschrift für evangelisches Kirchenrecht* 29 (1984), 338. Kawarau's point that this is the first town to receive Luther's assistance does not take into account Wittenberg's *Beutelordnung*. G. Kawarau, "Zur Leisniger Kastenordnung," *Neues Archiv für sächsische Geschichte und Altertumskunde* 3 (1880).

176. Laube, *Flugschriften*, 1072, stresses the significance of this order transcending class and local distinctions.

177. The original printing was at the end of May 1523. A copy marked with the date of purchase as 6 July 1523 has survived. A Low German and six High German editions soon followed. It also appeared in a collection published in Strasbourg in 1523. See WA 12:8–9, 703; Laube, *Flugschriften*, 1071.

178. WA 12:1ff. Cf. Martin Brecht, "Luthertum als politische und soziale Kraft in den Städten," in Franz Petri, ed., *Kirche und gesellschaftlicher Wandel in deutschen und niederländischen Städten der werdenden Neuzeit* (Cologne: Böhlau, 1980), 7; Heinrich Bornkamm, *Luther in Mid-Career, 1521–1530* (Philadelphia: Fortress Press, 1983), 121ff.; and Gerhard Uhlhorn, *Die christliche Liebesthätigkeit*, 3 vols. in 1, 2d ed. (Stuttgart: Gundert, 1895), 555.

Leisnig parish also included eleven surrounding villages. According to contemporary law, Leisnig was both a religious and a political community because of the ecclesial jurisdiction over the city granted in 1191 to the abbot of Buch, a nearby Cistercian monastery. This jurisdiction was repeatedly confirmed into the fifteenth century. Hence the evangelical movement in Leisnig, stimulated by that in Wittenberg, was involved in continual conflict with the monastery until the visitation commission confirmed the town's independence in 1529. In September 1522, Luther had responded to the appeal of the town and had spent a week in Leisnig assisting the parish in developing a comprehensive church order that included a common chest for poor relief. In January of 1523 the town council and the congregation sent two representatives to Wittenberg with a formal letter requesting Luther's further advice on their proposed ordinance (WA Br 3:21–23; WA 12:3ff.; LW 45:163ff).

The letter notes the establishment of a common chest "to the honor of God and for the love of fellow Christians" and also requests Luther to provide the community with a biblical rationale for the calling of evangelical pastors and an evangelical order of worship. Luther responded to the town council on 29 January 1523 with a letter expressing his great joy over their ordinance and hoping that it "shall both honor God and present a good example of Christian faith and love to many people" (WA Br 3:23).[179] By early summer Luther had responded in print to the town council's requests for biblical warrants for its action with the following treatises: "Ordinance of a Common Chest: Preface. Suggestions on How to Deal with Ecclesiastical Property," "That a Christian Assembly or Congregation Has the Right and Power to Judge All Teaching and to Call, Appoint, and Dismiss Teachers, Established and Proven by Scripture," and "Concerning the Order of Public Worship" (LW 45:161–76; 39:303–14; 53:7–14). Once again, it is evident that for Luther worship and social ethics are inseparable.

On the basis of Luther's earlier visit and consultation, and now his enthusiastic support, the Leisnig assembly set up a common chest and reformed the order of worship. The organization and the principles of the Leisnig Order include the election of ten directors or trustees by the community every year on the first Sunday after 13 January: "two from the nobility, two from the incumbent city council, three from among the common citizens of the town, and three from the rural peasantry." Three detailed record books were to be kept in the chest, which was protected by four different locks and kept in a secure place in the church. Keys to the four locks were assigned to the representatives of the different groups involved. This precaution not only protected against theft but probably also against gossip. Being an administrator of the common chest was a responsibility that required many hours

---

179. Brecht, "Luthertum," 10: "In spite of Luther's disclaimer of vigorous ecclesial organization, the fact certainly may not be overlooked that his, Bugenhagen's and Nuremberg's church orders were widely effective as models."

every week. The directors were to give triennial reports to the entire community. The funds from the common chest were also to be used for maintenance of buildings, pastors' salaries, and the schools—including a special
school for girls. This inclusiveness of responsibilities proved to be a problem.
A few years later the great Wittenberg formulator of church orders, Johann
Bugenhagen, separated the funds for poor relief from the funds for maintenance of the church and education.[180]

All begging was prohibited in Leisnig. This prohibition was a major departure from the late medieval begging ordinances whose purpose was to
control, not eliminate, begging. Uhlhorn makes the point that these medieval
ordinances were motivated by political economics rather than by the religious
ethics of the Reformation orders.

> None of these [medieval] ordinances pursued the goal to do away with
> begging by an ordered poor relief program providing for the needy. . . .
> These orders were thus able to provide little help for they had the effect
> of, so to speak, legalizing and organizing begging, thereby strengthening
> it more than combatting it. The complaint became universal that begging
> was increasing in spite of the ordinances.[181]

Reformation poor-relief orders mandated that only the truly needy should
be supported; all others must either leave or work. This theme was repeated
in countless later pamphlets under the overworked motto, "He who does not
work shall not eat."

A distinctly new feature of the Leisnig Order compared to its forerunners
in Wittenberg was the provision of taxation for its maintenance. The initial
funding for the common chest came from expropriated church properties, foundations, and testaments that the medieval church had cultivated as works
contributing to salvation. Luther hoped that the Leisnig example would result
in "a great decline in the existing foundations, monastic houses, chapels, and
those horrible dregs which have until now fattened on the wealth of the whole
world under the pretense of serving God" (LW 45:169f.). At the same time, Luther
was concerned about the possibility of plundering the church: "There is need
of great care lest there be a mad scramble for the assets of such vacated
foundations and everyone makes off with whatever he can lay his hands on"
(LW 45:170).[182] Luther advised that the ecclesial assets should be placed in the
common chest after those who wished to remain in the cloisters were provided
for, those who wished to leave the monastic life were given transitional support,
and funds were restored to the needy families of donors. The remaining capital

---

180. Strohm, "Luthers Wirtschafts- und Sozialethik," 221.
181. Uhlhorn, *Christliche Liebesthätigkeit*, 543. The repetition of these ordinances suggests
their ineffectiveness.
182. In his advice to the town council of Plauen regarding appropriation of the local
Dominican cloister, Luther refers to Leisnig as a model (WA Br 3:592–93).

was still a major financial resource. With foresight for potential insufficiency in the future, however, it was decreed

> that every noble, townsman, and peasant living in the parish shall according to his ability and means, remit in taxes for himself, his wife, and his children a certain sum of money to the chest each year, in order that the total amount can be arrived at and procured which the deliberations and decisions of the general assembly ... have determined to be necessary and sufficient. (LW 45:192)

The Leisnig common chest was responsible for a variety of services, including maintenance and construction of common buildings such as the church, school, and hospital as well as storing grain and peas for use during lean times and for regulating prices during emergencies. "In this way the people of the whole parish everywhere in the city and villages may by the grace of God have recourse to these stores for bodily sustenance in times of imminent scarcity, through purchase, loans, or grants as the directors may deem fitting and appropriate" (LW 45:191).[183] In terms of direct relief to the poor, the order regulated disbursements of loans and gifts to newcomers to help them get settled; to the house poor to help them become established in a trade or occupation; and to orphans, dependents, the infirm, and the aged for daily support. It has been said that a key to the character of a society is how it treats its youth and its elderly, and so it may be of interest to glimpse what Leisnig intended for its most vulnerable inhabitants.

> Poor and neglected orphans within the city and villages of our entire parish shall, as occasion arises, be provided with training and physical necessities by the directors out of the common chest until such time as they can work and earn their bread. If there be found among such orphans, or the children of impoverished parents, young boys with an aptitude for schooling and a capacity for arts and letters, the directors should support and provide for them. ... The girls among the neglected orphans, and likewise the daughters of impoverished parents, shall be provided by the directors out of the common chest with a suitable dowry for marriage. (LW 45:190)
>
> Those individuals in our parish and assembly who are impoverished by force of circumstance and left without assistance by their relatives ... and those who are unable to work because of illness or old age and are so poor as to suffer real need, shall receive each week on Sunday, and at other times as occasion demands, maintenance and support from our common chest through the ten directors. This is to be done out of Christian love, to the honor and praise of God, so that their lives and health may be

---

183. Some towns had taken this measure as early as the thirteenth century. Ulf Dirlmeier, "Lebensmittel- und Versorgungspolitik mittelalterliche Städte als demographisch relevantor Faktor?" *Saeculum* 39 (1988).

preserved from further deterioration, enfeeblement, and foreshortening through lack of shelter, clothing, nourishment, and care, and so that no impoverished person in our assembly need ever publicly cry out, lament, or beg for such items of daily necessity. (LW 45:189)

The ordinance concludes by declaring that all its articles and provisions "shall at all times be applied, used, and administered faithfully and without fraud by the parish here in Leisnig for no other purpose than the honor of God, the love of our fellow Christians, and hence for the common good" (LW 45:194).

Enforcement of the Leisnig ordinance got off to a rocky start. The town council balked at levying taxes for poor relief and refused to relinquish to the administrators of the common chest its own claim to dispose of church property. Luther bitterly complained to the Elector and to others over this development. Finally, in 1529, through the work of the visitation committee, he had the satisfaction of experiencing the confirmation of the common chest as he himself had originally envisioned it.[184]

This latter experience with the town council highlights the tension that was developing at this time between the Christian community and the civil community, between the jurisdiction of the town council with its responsibility for civil order, and the responsibility of the parish with its ethical obligations. Luther and his comrades-in-arms had first to organize the Christian community. It is noteworthy that the Leisnig ordinance bore the title of a "fraternal agreement." To Luther's mind it properly belonged in the parish as an ethical association. To Luther, the distribution of competencies between spiritual and temporal responsibilities was a fluid one, involving the reciprocal penetration of worldly experience, responsibility, organization, and the Christian ethos of community. If social welfare, hospitals for the sick and for plague victims, and homes for widows and orphans bore sometimes a more civic and sometimes a more ecclesial character, this was an openness Luther had already expressed in his writing to the Christian nobility.

Therefore, just as those who are now called "spiritual," . . . are neither different from other Christians nor superior to them, . . . so it is with the temporal authorities. . . . Everyone must benefit and serve every other by means of his own work or office so that in this way many kinds of work may be done for the bodily and spiritual welfare of the community, just as all the members of the body serve one another [1 Cor. 12:14-26]. (LW 44:130, 189ff.)

When successful, this openness led to the coordination of free ecclesial initiatives with public initiatives and thus to efficacious social welfare policies.[185]

184. See Bornkamm, *Luther in Mid-Career*, 125; Strohm, "Luthers Wirtschafts- und Sozialethik," 221; Karl Trüdinger, *Luthers Briefe und Gutachten an weltliche Obrigkeiten* (Münster: Aschendorff, 1975), 60ff.
185. Strohm, "Luthers Wirtschafts- und Sozialethik," 221.

Chapter 3

Reforming Responses and Roman-Radical Reactions

 IN 1523 LUTHER had expressed his hope that the Leisnig ordinance would "present a good example of Christian faith and love to many people" (WA Br 3:23). Responses to his hope were immediate and varied. Town after town, both evangelical and Catholic, began to incorporate his ideas for social welfare into legislation. So widespread was the response that the critical edition of Reformation church orders begun in 1902 by Emil Sehling has now reached its sixteenth large volume.[1] Other responses came from evangelicals ranging from Thomas Müntzer to various Anabaptist groups, as well as Roman Catholic theologians.

"The church orders of the Reformation ... constitute a touchstone for the reality-changing elements of Luther's theology."[2] Although it is impossible within the space of a chapter to do more than survey a selection of these ordinances, such a survey will suggest Luther's profound impact upon his society. The tremors of this impact traveled from town to town through printed media and Luther's extensive correspondence.[3]

---

1. E. Sehling, ed., *Die evangelischen Kirchenordnungen des 16. Jahrhunderts*, vols. 1–4 (Leipzig, 1902–1913), continued by R. Smend, O. Weber, E. Wolff (Tübingen: Mohr, 1955ff.). Gerta Scharffenorth, *Den Glauben ins Leben ziehen ... Studien zu Luthers Theologie* (Munich: Kaiser, 1982), 340–41, tabulated 54 of the more important of these. The term "church order" denotes legislation governing the life of the church and often the community that as a rule was established or at least promulgated by the secular magistrates. See Julius Bodensieck, ed., *The Encyclopedia of the Lutheran Church*, 3 vols. (Philadelphia: Fortress Press, 1965), vol. 1, 516.
2. Scharffenorth, *Den Glauben*, 73; 126 n. 9: "For the history of the effect of Reformation theology they are indispensable."
3. Nearly 25 percent, or 891, of the 3,599 pieces of correspondence in the Weimar

The Evangelical Church Orders

Although Luther was conscious of his dependence upon his prince, he hoped his movement would decisively take root in the cities. For all his intransigence in theological principles, he was concerned for the cities and grasped their problems. "The stylistic affinity of his epistles with the letters of Paul to urban congregations is the reproduction of a situation not merely literary imitation!"[4] The effects of this correspondence were multiplied by Luther's numerous students and friends in these cities. "Wittenberg consciously pursued a multiplicator policy. Members of the inner Wittenberg circle were continually sent out for the correct implementation of the Reformation in cities under the Saxon sphere of influence."[5] Luther was continually reassigning his colleagues to new situations that needed attention. As Luther wrote to Spalatin in mid-1522: "Everywhere people are thirsting for the gospel. On all sides they are asking us for evangelists."[6]

Because of his status as an imperial outlaw, Luther's personal contact was limited to Saxon cities. Here he assisted with advice and activity the introduction of the essence of the evangelical church in Altenburg (1522), Erfurt (1525, 1533), Halle (1527–28, 1534, 1542), Leipzig (1531–33), Naumberg (1536), and Freiberg (1538). Above all, Luther gave authoritative expression to the reorganization of the church's resources for social welfare. After the famous case of Leisnig in 1523 (see Chapter 2), Luther was concerned with Plauen, Zerbst, and Erfurt (1525), Eisenach (1534), Naumberg (1537), Belgern (1540), and Freiberg (1543).[7] Bugenhagen, Luther's Wittenberg colleague and pastor, continued the work of Luther in such northern German cities as Lübeck and Hamburg.

Altenburg

The Reformation took hold in Altenburg very early. Luther had preached there on his journey to Worms in 1521. In April 1522 the town council requested

---

edition of Luther's works are concerned with urban affairs. Wolfgang Reinhard, "Luther und die Städte," in Erwin Iserloh & Gerhard Müller, eds., Luther und die politische Welt (Stuttgart: Steiner, 1984), 88–90.
4. Ibid., 110.
5. Ibid., 105.
6. WA Br 2:580, 5–6. Cited in Martin Brecht, Martin Luther: Shaping and Defining the Reformation 1521–1532, trans. James Schaaf (Minneapolis: Fortress Press, 1990), 68. Brecht adds (pp. 68–69): "At that time the question of filling pastorates was more than an incidental administrative problem for Luther. In essence, it was associated with his views on the priesthood of all believers (allgemeines Priestertum), understood also as a general office of ministry (allgemeines Predigtamt), as he expressed them again and again in his sermons. Under extreme circumstances, Luther could even envision women preaching."
7. Reinhard, "Luther und die Städte," 103–4. For Luther's influence on the social welfare development in Hesse, see William J. Wright, "The Homberg Synod and Philip of Hesse's Plan for a New Church-State Settlement," SCJ 4 (1973), 27, 41–42.

Luther to send a pastor. Luther proposed Gabriel Zwilling, who had been involved in the recent disturbances in Wittenberg but was now aligned with Luther. The local conservative clergy opposed the town council's right to appoint the preacher of the parish church, and Elector Frederick was himself dubious about Zwilling. Frederick finally agreed with Luther's support of the town council and his view of the prince's responsibility to promote the gospel, but the elector requested Wenzeslaus Linck to fill the post of preacher at St. Bartholomew, one of the three major churches in the city.

Linck (1483–1547) was a lifelong friend and colleague of Luther, a fellow Augustinian who had also been influenced by Johann von Staupitz, Luther's father confessor. Linck had studied and taught at the University of Wittenberg from 1503 to 1515, and then became preacher in the Augustinian cloister in Nuremberg. In Nuremberg he was introduced to the humanist circle by Staupitz. In 1520 Linck left Nuremberg to become vicar-general of the Augustinians. In this brief period before being appointed preacher in Altenburg, he released the Wittenberg monks from their vows.[8] In Altenburg, Linck faced the powerful and antagonistic Franciscans as well as widespread impoverishment due to past destruction by fires.[9] It is in this context, as well as the larger theological context of the Reformation with its new attitudes to work and the poor, that Linck's major treatise, "On Work and Begging: How Laziness Should be Met and Everyone Drawn to Work,"[10] should be read.

Beyond the specific hardships of Altenburg, the broader social context of the times had already stimulated outbursts, tracts, and legislation against the idle. Eberlin von Günzberg had wondered that there was any money left in the country at all—only one person in fifteen, he claimed, did any work. More had suggested in his *Utopia* that healthy beggars should be compelled to work. Hans Sachs published his "Frau Work: A Lamentation on the Great Heaps of the Lazy." Luther had remarked that the papacy made begging a form of worship.[11] Nevertheless, if one is to speak of a work ethic among the Lutheran reformers, it is important to note both the context of their writings and the fact that they did not regard work simply as a value in and of itself. As Linck put it, work is a value because it "furthers the general welfare."

8. See Helmar Junghans, *Der junge Luther und die Humanisten* (Weimar: Böhlau, 1984), 291, 302; and Charles Daniels, "Hard Work, Good Work, and School Work: An Analysis of Wenzeslaus Linck's Conception of Civic Responsibility," in Lawrence Buck & Jonathon Zophy, eds., *The Social History of the Reformation* (Columbus: Ohio State Univ. Press, 1972), 41.
9. Jürgen Lortz, *Die Reformatorisches Wirken, Dr. Wenzeslaus Lincks in Altenburg und Nürnberg* (Nüremberg: Korn & Berg, 1978), 15–16; R. Bendixen, "Ein Büchlein Wenzeslaus Lincks von Arbeit und Betteln," *Zeitschrift für kirchliche Wissenschaft und kirchliches Leben* 6 (1885), 584; and R. Bendixen, "Wenzeslaus Linck," *Zeitschrift für kirchliche Wissenschaft und kirchliche Leben* 8 (1887), 139.
10. "Von Arbeyt und Betteln wie man solle der faulheyt vorkommen und yederman zu Arbeit ziehen" (Zwickau, 1523), printed in Laube, *Flugschriften* vol. 2, 1086–1108.
11. Bendixen, "Ein Buchlein," 584–85.

He changed from the traditional views of the age that work was the curse of mankind because of original sin. Linck incorporated work into God's plan of atonement. Work received new dignity because it was no longer degrading [to work]; it was part of the divine plan. By emphasizing the transcendent quality of labor, it was no longer an end in itself, but a means to an end. . . . The end of work, he preached, was not only earthly satisfaction but primarily a Christian life lived in accord with God's divine calling.[12]

That divine calling is not conceived of as privatistic but rather as centered in the community. Linck has no doubt, he says in the introduction to his tract, that "where one is truly devoted to such a community chest it shall benefit an obvious community need. Even though Altenburg is a poor city and nearly consumed by beggars and the lazy, it shall without doubt maintain its poor and not tolerate the foreign beggars and other swindlers who snatched bread from their mouths."[13] Echoing Luther, Linck uses a corporal analogy in advocating local responsibility for the poor:

It is just as when one member of the body is sick and cannot perform its customary function for the welfare of the others. When this happens, the other members help the sick member regain its strength, or at least make sure that it does not completely deteriorate. . . . All who bear common burdens share with each other both good and bad, fortune and injury, profit and trouble; for they are one body, whether it be a city, a village, a parish, a house, or another such assembly.[14]

The resources for this community welfare were the endowments given to the churches for memorial masses, vigils, and all the other late medieval gifts to the church. Linck addressed the use of these resources in his 1524 tract "On the Testaments of Dying People." Since salvation is by grace alone (*sola gratia*), the desire of dying persons to acquire certainty of salvation through endowing foundations and masses is wrong. The clear knowledge of justification *sola gratia* allows concern for the neighbor and service to the community to take the place of self-seeking. The famous catchall phrase *ad pias causas* (for religious causes) no longer is valid now that God's truth is revealed.[15] The faithful testator is to be responsible to his or her family and to the poor. Where this has not been the case, but the testator through the misleading of clerical advisors has given money to church endowments, Linck states that the executor is free to adjust the will to the new evangelical understanding.

12. Daniels, "Hard Work," 42–43.
13. Laube, *Flugschriften* vol. 2, 1087.
14. Ibid., 1096–97. Cited in translation by Steven Ozment, "The Social History of the Reformation: What Can We Learn from the Pamphlets?" in Hans-Joachim Köhler, ed., *Flugschriften als Massenmedium der Reformationszeit* (Stuttgart: Klett-Cotta, 1981), 186.
15. Lortz, *Reformatorische Wirken*, 37–40.

When a situation arises in which God has clearly commanded men to help one another, we should not hesitate to take the money that has been willed to churches, cloisters, and the like. For example, where there is famine and poor people suffer want.... The support of the poor, to which we are obligated by both divine and natural law, should be pursued with these funds, and the goods and treasures that remain over should be placed in a common chest and held there until needed again.[16]

Linck concluded with reference to Luther and the Leisnig ordinance: "But as to how the property shall be used according to Christian love, Dr. Martin Luther has precisely indicated in advice on how endowments are to be handled and his Order for a Common Chest."[17] Linck's attack upon endowed masses and bequests "had such a popular appeal to the townsmen that this sermon was reprinted in Nürnberg, Zwickau, and Magdeburg."[18]

Linck's efforts to reform the city of Altenburg lasted the whole three years he was there. Although the city was not completely in the evangelical fold by 1525, the year of Linck's departure, Linck has been credited with its turn to the Reformation.[19] Luther and the Wittenberg reforms were of course behind this success. The city council had asked Luther to send a pastor in the spring of 1522, and in the fall of 1522 some parishes in Altenburg followed Wittenberg's example and established a common chest. The 1527 Common Chest Order at Altenburg with few exceptions followed the measures of the common chest order in Wittenberg. "In other respects it shall also be obliged in all measures, as the Wittenberg Common Chest Order, supporting visitations of the sick, needy house-poor, beggars passing through, and poor people" (Sehling 1:515).

However, urban social welfare legislation did not occur in a linear progression stretching from Wittenberg to Leisnig to Altenburg to Zwickau, and so on. Wittenberg and Leisnig served as the initial models, common chest orders were developing simultaneously in various cities and, in the process, cross-fertilizing each other. Linck's ideas reflect those of another follower of Luther, Lazarus Spengler, who wrote the 1522 Nuremberg ordinance. "Whether he [Linck] first influenced Spengler or whether he was influenced by the ordinances is impossible to determine."[20]

16. Ozment, "Social History of the Reformation," 184.
17. Bendixen, "Ein Büchlein," 588.
18. Daniels, "Hard Work," 45. The town council in Zwickau was already "inspired by Luther's outline of a community chest for the city of Leisnig.... The first pertinent reference in the council minutes is to 'dy gemayne Buchsen' on 8 August 1523, and the second to 'der gemeyne kasten' on 19 August. All church funds were to be channeled into this chest." Susan Karant-Nunn, *Zwickau in Transition, 1500–1547: The Reformation as an Agent of Change* (Columbus: Ohio State Univ. Press, 1987), 131. On the decline of the effectiveness of Zwickau's common chest due to economic decline and failing motivation, see Karant-Nunn, *Zwickau,* 217–19, 230–31.
19. Bendixen, "Wenzeslaus Linck," 139.
20. Daniels, "Hard Work," 44. Daniels adds: "What is of importance is that Linck, from

Nuremberg

The importance of Luther's strategic personal contacts for the furtherance of welfare reform is equally obvious in the developments in Nuremberg. In 1525 Wenzeslaus Linck returned to Nuremberg to take the post of preacher at the New Hospital Church. The Nuremberg patrician and jurist Christoph Scheurl had been a university professor in Wittenberg and was a friend of Johann von Staupitz. Scheurl was a member of the Societas Staupitziana, a humanist circle that formed around the person of Staupitz, general vicar of the Augustinian Eremites in Nuremberg. This circle consisted of the most well known persons in Nuremberg's clerical, intellectual, and political life, including the secretary to the town council, Lazarus Spengler, the mayor, Kaspar Nützel, as well as the artist Albrecht Dürer. With Linck's return from Wittenberg (where as dean he had promoted Luther to the doctorate), the society was renamed the Societas Augustiniana. After Luther's two visits to Nuremberg on his way to and from Augsburg in 1518, the group was once more renamed; this time it became the Sodalitas Martiniana. The majority of the town council eventually sided with this circle. By 1520 Scheurl wrote that most of the city sided with Luther. At the Diet of Worms in 1521 Spengler was in personal contact with Luther. As preaching posts in the city became vacant they were filled by students and followers of Luther. Hector Pömer and Georg Besler, Luther's students, were installed as provosts of, respectively, the major churches of St. Lorenz and St. Sebald. When the preaching post at St. Sebald was vacated, Dominikus Schleupner was called to it on Luther's advice. In 1522 the preaching post of St. Lorenz was filled by the young Andreas Osiander, who was to be one of the most important of the Nuremberg reformers.[21]

One of the fruits of the evangelical sermons coming from these pulpits was the creation in July 1522 of a new welfare order modeled after the example of Wittenberg's *Ordnung des gemeinen Beutels*.[22] Osiander had been vigorously proclaiming that providing support for the poor was an essential responsibility of the church. After various additions and amendments, the new welfare order stemming from such preaching was printed at the end of August or the beginning of September 1523. This has been called "a fundamental overthrow of the medieval exercise of charity as a means for achieving one's own salvation," and the foundation of social welfare on gratitude for the grace of absolution (Sehling 11:17). In the perspective of the city council, this new order for poor relief was the first major step on the way to churchly reform.[23]

---

an evangelical pulpit, was preaching social concern." On the subject of priority, see also Lortz, *Reformatorische Wirken*, 15–16, and Bendixen, "Ein Büchlein," 588.

21. Sehling 11:14–17; Gottfried Seebass, "The Reformation in Nürnberg," in Lawrence Buck & Jonathon Zophy, eds., *The Social History of the Reformation* (Columbus: Ohio State Univ. Press, 1972), 20–22.

22. Sehling 11:17. Cf. Gottfried Seebass, *Das Reformatorische Werk des Andreas Osiander* (Nuremberg: Verein für Bayerische Kirchengeschichte, 1967), 181.

23. Otto Winckelmann, "Über die ältesten Armenordnungen der Reformationszeit (1522–1525)," *Historische Vierteljahrschrift* (1914): 214.

The preface of the new ordinance reflected the Lutheran preaching behind it by its extended commentary on Matt. 22:37–40.

> As Christ says in the gospel, faith and love are the two chief points of a right Christian existence, in which all the other commandments of God are included and on which depend all the law and the prophets. For to love and trust Christ, and to do to the neighbor as I believe Christ has done to me, this is the only right way to become pious and be saved; there is no other way. Through faith a person becomes righteous, living, and blessed. There is nothing more necessary than to manifest such faith. Indeed, where faith lives in a person it cannot remain hidden but is expressed openly in everything the person lives, works, and does. This he does for the need of the neighbor, to be wise and helpful to him, as he sees that Christ has been to him. (Sehling 11:23)

Referring to the parable of the last judgment (Matt. 25:31-46), the introduction continues:

> Every Christian shall have to give account at the last judgment whether for Christ's sake he has loved his needy and poor neighbors, fed them, given them to drink, clothed them, visited them, and in short been of help and assistance; he will not be asked whether he has endowed many masses, built churches, gone on pilgrimages, and done similar works that have not been commanded by Christ. (Sehling 11:29)

The order was to be administered by two chief overseers who belonged to the city council. Under them worked ten overseers drawn from the citizens, two of whom attended alternately to their duties for a half-year duration. This was an honorary post without salary. The overseers consulted with the council only on the most difficult questions. A salaried assistant for each of the four quarters of the city was assigned to the overseers. His responsibilities included calling on the poor in his quarter, inquiring after their reputation, confirming the number of their children, and evaluating the extent of support necessary. If the children were capable of gainful employment, work should be provided for them. If a poor person needed more help than initially allowed him or her, the decision was reserved to the overseers.

At the beginning "two pious priests" had offered to accompany the assistants on their rounds and to report the situations of the poor to the administrators. This provision was dropped from later editions of the order. To ensure the impartiality and fairness of the assistants, they were assigned to a different quarter of the city every week. Just as in the pre-Reformation begging orders, the poor being regularly supported had to wear identification on their clothes; they were not to be seen in taverns and "other unseemly places." However, the upright, deserving poor (in other words, the house poor) did not have to wear these badges; they were recorded on a special list and were supported discreetly. All begging was strictly forbidden.

Financial support for the welfare program was, the council hoped, to come from gifts, foundations, and legacies of the citizens. The preachers were to exhort their congregations continuously from their pulpits to support the poor-relief fund. Offertory boxes were set up in the churches, and these funds were collected at worship and placed on the altar. Later, collection bags were used. Actual church property at first remained untouched, but the council expressed hope that with time church resources would be added to the city's poor-relief fund. By the end of September the thirteen alms foundations of St. Sebald became part of the city's welfare fund, and new funds were directed to the city.[24]

Unlike the later Leisnig ordinance, the Nuremberg order made no provision for taxation to maintain the funding for the city's social welfare. However, the ordinance found such strong approval among the populace that in its first three years it received 13,000 gulden. The value of this may be estimated by noting that the average income for a beneficed cleric in Nuremberg at that time amounted to 45 gulden and lodging (Sehling 11:17). Thus Nuremberg became a model for other cities in terms of public welfare. The poor were provided with medical services including medicines and midwives without charge. A survey in 1522 showed that about 500 poor people must have been supported constantly and completely by the city; partial support extended to about 5,000. In particular emergency situations the city distributed bread, the so-called Lord's bread (*Herrenbrot*), to as many as 15,000 citizens (noncitizens were excluded). All this is not to say that Nuremberg was a perfect example of social harmony or the ideally ordered society as has sometimes been suggested. But the wise political tactics of the city council and the comparatively well constructed public welfare program contributed to the long-term stability of the city.[25]

The Nuremberg order attracted widespread attention as the first attempt by an imperial city in Germany to establish an obligatory, secular welfare system and to abolish begging. Nuremberg's contribution to social welfare drew interest from other cities not only because of the publicity given it by word of mouth and example, but also because it was widely distributed as a printed document.[26] Thus while the evangelically oriented magistrates of Kitzingen were aware of and probably influenced by the Wittenberg *Beutelordnung*, they followed almost literally the order of neighboring Nuremberg (Sehling 11:64; see 72–76 for the order itself).

---

24. Winckelmann, "Über die ältesten Armenordnungen," 216–19; Sehling 11:23–32.
25. Rudolf Endres, "Sozialstruktur Nürnbergs," in Gerhard Pfeiffer, ed., *Nürnberg—Geschichte einer europäischen Stadt* (Munich: Beck, 1971), 199.
26. Winckelmann, "Über die ältesten Armenordnungen," 221. Spengler, the city secretary, had ordered its printing in August 1523. Cf. Otto Winckelmann, "Die Armenordnungen von Nürnberg (1522), Kitzingen (1523) Regensburg (1523) und Ypern (1525)," ARG 10 (1912/13), 255.

Regensburg also appears to have literally followed Nuremberg's lead in developing an evangelical ordinance for poor relief.[27] However, a recent study by Kristin Zapalac of the iconography of social change in Reformation Regensburg raises the question of how much influence the evangelical movement had upon poor relief. Zapalac suggests the continuation of medieval Catholic motivation for poor relief. She refers to Nördlingen, a free imperial city about equidistant from both Nuremberg and Regensburg. "In Nördlingen the painting of Christ as the Man of Sorrows placed above the *Almosenkasten* in 1522 reminded the Bürger that donations to the *Almosenkasten* fed the poor (= fed the suffering Christ himself) and were acts of mercy in accordance with Matthew 25 and the teaching of the medieval church.[28]

In response it should be noted that the Nuremberg ordinance also referred to the famous Matthew 25 passage, and that following the commandments was as important to the evangelicals as it was to late medieval Catholics. The difference for Luther's understanding of the commandments is that they are no longer to be spiritualized for the acquisition of God's grace, but rather are the means for benefiting the neighbor with the God-given gifts of creation. Here, again, Luther understands service to the neighbor as service to God, as worship—*dienst Gottes* equals *Gottesdienst*. In his pamphlet, "Whether One May Flee from a Deadly Plague" (1527), Luther wrote:

> This I well know, that if it were Christ or his mother who were laid low by illness, everybody would be so solicitous and would gladly become a servant or helper. . . . And yet they don't hear what Christ himself says, "As you did it to one of the least, you did it to me" [Matt. 25:40]. When he speaks of the greatest commandment he says, "The other commandment is like unto it, you shall love your neighbor as yourself" [Matt 22:39]. There you hear that the command to love your neighbor is equal to the greatest commandment to love God, and that what you do or fail to do for your neighbor means doing the same to God. If you wish to serve Christ and wait on him, very well, you have your sick neighbor close at hand. Go to him and serve him, and you will surely find Christ in him, not outwardly but in his word. (LW 43:130)[29]

The evangelical theological judgment upon the medieval motivation for almsgiving corresponded to its judgment on righteousness of works. Alms are not given in order to acquire salvation, but as gratitude for experienced redemption. Thus on Sundays, alms were placed on the altar right after the

---

27. Winckelmann, "Armenordnungen," 256. The order itself is printed in Winckelmann's article (8-13), with notations on its parallels to the Nuremberg order.
28. Kristin Zapalac, "*In His Image and Likeness*": *Political Iconography and Religious Change in Regensburg, 1500–1600* (Ithaca, N.Y.: Cornell Univ. Press, 1990), 212 n. 100; see also p. 87.
29. See also Vilmos Vajta, *Die Theologie des Gottesdienstes bei Luther* (Stockholm: Svenska Kyrkans Diakonistyrelses Bok förlag, 1952), 315–16.

sermon, the proclamation of God's saving act, as a thanks offering.[30] Luther's concern was to free persons from unbiblical, medieval commands (such as endowments) for the biblical commands of faith to God and love of one's neighbor. Thus the Regensburg order repeats the Nuremberg Lutheran expression that being a Christian means living "solely by a genuine confidence and faith to God, and brotherly love to the neighbor."[31]

Far more significant than the apparently slavish imitation of the Nuremberg order in Kitzingen and Regensburg was the new regulation of social welfare in Strasbourg.[32]

Strasbourg

As in Nuremberg, so too in Strasbourg Luther's influence had a strong presence in both personal and printed sources.[33] Furthermore, the two cities had long had a close relationship.[34] It seems that Strasbourg used the Nuremberg order as the model for its own; the two versions agree on many points, and a contemporary copy of the Nuremberg order has been discovered in the Strasbourg archive.[35] This copy was apparently brought from Nuremberg to Strasbourg in October 1522 by Daniel Mieg. Mieg, regarded as one of the most capable of Strasbourg's citizens, was a member of the city council and an active adherent of the Reformation. He had been in Nuremberg as a Strasbourg delegate to a meeting of municipal authorities during the Imperial Diet.[36] On the basis of the Nuremberg model, the Strasbourg order was drafted by a committee of five city councillors, the most important of whom were Mieg, Mathis Pfarrer, and Jakob Meyer. Pfarrer, a zealous admirer of Luther, and next to Jakob Sturm the most prominent Strasbourg politician of the Reformation period, was the essential spirit of the committee.

It is of interest that the initiative for the restructuring of Strasbourg's social welfare came not from pastors and theologians but from the laity in its government. On the one hand this reflects the simple fact that apart from Matthew Zell, the evangelical pastors Wolfgang Capito, Martin Bucer, and

---

30. Mechtild Köhn, *Martin Bucers Entwurf einer Reformation des Erzstiftes Köln* (Witten: Luther Verlag, 1966), 181.
31. Winckelmann, "Über die ältesten Armenordnungen," 227.
32. Ibid., 361.
33. Francis Rapp, *Réformes et Réformation à Strasbourg: Église et société dans le diocèse de Strasbourg* (1450–1525) (Paris: Editions Ophrys, 1974), 472–73.
34. François-Joseph Fuchs, "Les relations commerciales entre Nuremberg et Strasbourg aux XVe et XVIe siècles," in *Hommage à Dürer: Strasbourg et Nuremberg dans la première moitié du XVIe siècle* (Strasbourg: Librairie Istra, 1972).
35. Winckelmann, "Über die ältesten Armenordnungen," 362; Winckelmann, *Das Fürsorgewesen der Stadt Strassburg vor und nach der Reformation bis zum Ausgang des sechzehnten Jahrhunderts* (Leipzig, 1922; reprint, New York: Johnson Reprint Corp., 1971), 78–79, and no. 40 in the collection of primary sources in the second part of the book.
36. Winckelmann, "Über die ältesten Armenordnungen," 362–63; Jean Rott, "La Réforme à Nuremberg et à Strasbourg: Contacts et Contrastes," in *Hommage à Dürer*, 100.

Caspar Hedio were not yet installed in city parishes. But on the other hand, this situation also reflects Luther's conviction that all Christians are called to exercise their faith in active love. (Similarly, the author of the introduction to the Nuremberg order was the layman Lazarus Spengler.)[37]

The Strasbourg order departed from its Nuremberg model in the development of the salaried office of alms steward (*Almosenschaffner*).[38] In its appointment of Lucas Hackfurt to this position, the city council further indicated its Reformation orientation. Hackfurt, a native of Strasbourg who had studied theology at Heidelberg, was one of the first priests in the city to enthusiastically embrace Luther's teaching. At this time he was directing a private Latin school in Strasbourg. "That the council entrusted the important alms stewardship to such a resolute adherent of the new [evangelical] orientation and harsh opponent of the Roman Church, exemplifies perhaps better than anything else the disposition from which the new Strasbourg poor order emerged."[39]

By all accounts, Hackfurt was an extremely hardworking, responsible, and sensitive administrator who faithfully served his city and its less fortunate citizens from his appointment in 1523 until his death in 1554.[40] Hackfurt soon developed a sense of the economic realities that were creating hardships for the poor and those living on the economic margins. He continually advised, admonished, requested, and exhorted the city council to provide more funds, regulate the economic inflation, provide public-works projects, and regulate the markets in real estate, grain, and wine. By 1530 a physician was assigned to care for the sick poor. God, Hackfurt said, had provided the city with great wealth, including that of the church's properties and monastic establishments. "The property was there because God wanted it to be distributed by the secular authorities to help the poor."[41]

The work of Hackfurt's office was furthered in 1530 with the development of the ministerial office of deacon, the foundation for which was set forth in Bucer's tract "Von der wahren Seelsorge" (On Genuine Pastoral Care).[42] Bucer,

---

37. On Spengler, see Harold Grimm, *Lazarus Spengler: A Lay Leader of the Reformation* (Columbus: Ohio State Univ. Press, 1978).
38. The order is printed in Winckelmann, *Fürsorgewesen*, no. 43 in the "Urkunden und Aktenstücke" section. See paragraphs 38–42 for the office of steward.
39. Winckelmann, *Fürsorgewesen*, 86.
40. Winckelmann, "Über die ältesten Armenordnungen," 367, claims that Hackfurt's service can hardly be overestimated.
41. Miriam Usher Chrisman, "Urban Poor in the Sixteenth Century: The Case of Strasbourg," in Miriam Usher Chrisman & Otto Grundler, eds., *Social Groups and Religious Ideas in the Sixteenth Century* (Kalamazoo: Medieval Institute, Western Michigan University, 1978), 66.
42. Robert Stupperich, "Bruderdienst und Nächstenhilfe in der deutschen Reformation," in Herbert Krimm, ed., *Das diakonische Amt der Kirche*, 2d ed. (Stuttgart: Evangelisches Verlagswerk, 1965), 185.

who became a follower of Luther after hearing him at the Heidelberg Disputation in 1518, became the most prominent Reformation leader in Strasbourg and southern Germany. He presented his theological justification of the welfare ordinance soon after its institution. This tract, perhaps influenced by Luther's 1520 "The Freedom of a Christian," was titled "Everyone Should Live Not for Himself but for Others" (1523).[43] Bucer's theme was that faith means to be active in brotherly love among all citizens. Bucer never tired of emphasizing that love as well as faith belongs to the church. What Bucer learned of social welfare in Strasbourg, he translated to the context of England in his *De Regno Christi* (On the Kingdom of Christ), written after he became a professor at the University of Cambridge in 1549.[44]

Hamburg

Just as Nuremberg served as a model for social welfare orders in the south of Germany, so Hamburg served as a model in the north of Germany and in Scandinavia. Luther's strategically placed students, colleagues, and friends were instrumental for the developments in northern Germany as they were in southern Germany. However, one person stands out beyond all the others in these northern developments: Johannes Bugenhagen (1485–1558).

It was Bugenhagen[45] who translated Luther's theology of poor relief into practical legislation. Although in later histories of the Reformation Bugenhagen has been overshadowed by his friend and colleague Luther, his organizational genius was highly esteemed by his evangelical contemporaries. Upon becoming pastor of the City Church in Wittenberg, he was instrumental in the reconstruction of the church in Wittenberg after the disturbances there in 1522. He was in constant demand by cities, areas, and countries throughout northern Europe for help in instituting the Reformation. He himself wrote or edited church orders for Braunschweig (1528), Hamburg (1529), Lübeck (1531),

43. Robert Stupperich, ed., *Martin Bucers Deutsche Schriften*, vol. 1 (Gütersloh: Mohn, 1960), 29–67. A modern English translation is in Paul Fuhrmann, *Instruction in Christian Love* (Richmond: John Knox Press, 1952).
44. See Wilhelm Pauck in collaboration with Paul Larkin, trans., "De Regno Christi," in Wilhelm Pauck, ed., *Melanchthon and Bucer* (Philadelphia: Westminster Press, 1969), 256–59 ("Care for the Needy"), 295–306 ("Claiming Ecclesiastical Goods for Christ the Lord, and their pious use"), 306–15 ("Poor Relief").
45. A priest and educator in his home country of Pomerania, hence later called Pomeranus and Dr. Pommer, Bugenhagen moved to Wittenberg and enrolled in the university there in April 1521 after reading some of Luther's writings. He soon became a friend and colleague of both Luther and Melanchthon. In 1523 he became pastor of the City Church and thus also Luther's pastor as well as spiritual advisor. He became a doctor of theology in 1533 and a professor in 1535. He published a number of biblical commentaries, theological tracts, a Low German translation of the entire Bible, and a popular harmony of the four Gospels. See Hans Hermann Holfelder, "Bugenhagen," *TRE* 7 (1981).

Pomerania (1535), Denmark (1537), Schleswig-Holstein (1542), Braunschweig-Wolfenbüttel (1543), and Hildesheim (1544).[46] This "Reformer of the North," as he is sometimes called, ranked after Luther as a theologian and after Melanchthon as an educator. His specific genius was to bind theology to exegesis and ecclesial praxis to the application of Scripture. In his originality and historical effect, he must be ranked with the great South German reformers Zwingli, Bucer, Osiander, and Brenz.[47]

Bugenhagen was so effective in translating Reformation theology into legislation that until recently most research has focused on his practical accomplishments to the neglect of their theological foundation. It is equally important to emphasize that Bugenhagen's contributions to poor-relief legislation and its enactment were embedded in the doctrine he learned from Luther. For Bugenhagen, Reformation doctrine and its institutionalization belong together as "constitutive factors for the progress of the Reformation."[48]

Bugenhagen's grasp of Luther's theology is evident already in his emphasis upon Christ's justification of the sinner in the open letter he wrote in 1520 to his Treptow students. Scripture is now to be read from the perspective of the doctrine of justification; Scripture and justifying faith in Christ are related exclusively to each other. It is not surprising that this theological commitment was strengthened and deepened after Bugenhagen's arrival in 1521 in Wittenberg. In consort with Luther, Bugenhagen centered his theology on Christ as mediator between God and humankind, and understood justification by faith to impel the Christian in the power of the Spirit to serve the neighbor.[49]

This fundamental theological orientation received clear and programmatic articulation in the long open letter Bugenhagen wrote to the city of Hamburg. In 1525 he was called to become the pastor of the St. Nicholas Church in Hamburg. However, his Wittenberg congregation was reluctant to let him go, and a shift in the Hamburg city council's attitude to the evangelical movement made acceptance impossible. Thus, in the manner of the apostles and Luther, Bugenhagen wrote an epistle to Hamburg titled: "To the Honorable City of Hamburg concerning the Christian Faith and True Good Works in Opposition to False Faith and Imaginary Good Works, Thereto, How This shall

46. With the exception of Denmark and Schleswig-Holstein, these and other church orders have been printed in Sehling. See Kurt Hendel, "The Care of the Poor: An Evangelical Perspective," *Currents in Theology and Mission* 15 (1988); Frank Lane, "Johannes Bugenhagen und die Armenfürsorge in der Reformationszeit," *Braunschweigisches Jahrbuch* 64 (1983); and Lane, *Poverty and Poor Relief*.
47. Wolf-Dieter Hauschild, ed., *Lübecker Kirchenordnung von Johannes Bugenhagen 1531* (Lübeck: Schmidt-Römhild, 1981), xxvi.
48. Holfelder, "Bugenhagen," 358.
49. Hans Holfelder, "Bugenhagens Theologie—Anfänge, Entwicklungen und Ausbildungen bis zum Römerbriefkolleg," *Luther* 57 (1986), 67–68, 77–79.

Be Prepared by Good Preachers, in Order That Such [True] Faith and Works Be Preached."[50]

The Scriptures make it clear, Bugenhagen affirms, that salvation is by God's grace alone apart from all works and merit; indeed, apart from faith, all human works are sins.[51] "Faith active in love is the theological basis and practical motivation for the care of the poor in Bugenhagen's theology. He approaches the problems of poverty and poor relief primarily from a theological, not a social or economic, perspective, and maintains that caring for the poor is not a matter of free choice for the Christian but a clear expectation."[52] This is clearly expressed in the following citation from his letter to Hamburg in which he evangelically recasts the medieval perspective on Matt. 25:40.

> Here one sees very well how the hearts of Christians are disposed to everything good that they know according to God's Word pleases him. And they think nothing at all of all these things that they accomplish. As we have already said, they also do not think to become pious by this activity, for they are already pious and Christians before they do such good works. For Christ says that they are blessed by their heavenly Father, that is, they are redeemed from their condemnation (into which all persons are born, live, and die), and blessed not through their merits and works, but rather by the heavenly Father who has made them his children and brothers of the Lord Christ. As he [Christ] says, what you did to one of the least of these my brethren [you have done to me, Matt. 25:40], etc. Thus he says, receive your inheritance that is to be possessed for eternity, the kingdom that was prepared for you from the foundation of the world. If God prepared this eternal kingdom for you, then certainly you yourself did not prepare this kingdom with your works. If it was prepared for you from the foundation of the world, how could we then prepare it with our works and merits? What could you prepare when you were not even there? Then why did they do such works? They did them not to merit the eternal kingdom of God which was given to them by grace without [their] merit, but rather to honor Christ alone and to serve the neighbor, as Christ says: What you did to the least of these my brethren, you did to me.[53]

Throughout this entire text on Christian faith and true good works, Bugenhagen repeatedly emphasizes that salvation is solely by the grace of God

---

50. "Von dem christlichen Glauben und rechten guten Werke wider den falschen Glauben und erdichtete gute Werke gepredigt werden, an die ehrenreiche Stadt Hamburg," 1526. Printed in Karl A. T. Vogt, *Johannes Bugenhagen Pomeranus: Leben und ausgewählte Schriften* (Elberfeld, 1867), 101–267.
51. Vogt, *Johannes Bugenhagen*, 170.
52. Hendel, "Care of the Poor," 527.
53. Vogt, *Johannes Bugenhagen*, 172–73.

alone, and that service to the neighbor is the human response to the gift of salvation. "In sum, the hypocrites make an idol of their works, but the Christians do many good works. However, Christians do not rely upon their works but upon Jesus Christ alone, the only Mediator, through whom alone and by nothing else we come to the Father."[54] "Christ's salvific role became the basis for Bugenhagen's application of faith to human behavior. His social ethics may be sought in various humanistic writings and contemporary practices but in vain. His social ethics flow from his understanding of Christ's role in man's justification."[55]

Since my focus is on poor relief, I will not recount Bugenhagen's consequent explanation of how the gospel informs service to others in every area of personal and social life. With regard to poor relief, however, Bugenhagen echoes the suggestions Luther had been advancing since 1519.

> If such [service to others] is to be accomplished, combine together all the goods such as those from benefices and other charitable foundations that with time have become free through the dying off of persons, and those goods that may be appropriated with good conscience when the truth is brought to light (with all that pious people also give and with all the testaments that were given for charity). [With these resources] establish a common chest for dependent widows, orphans, the poor, the sick, the needy house-poor, poor maidens, and the like to whom honest citizens can determine on the basis of their need what is to be given or loaned, and how it is to be appropriately sent to them.[56]

Bugenhagen's 1526 tract to Hamburg was the theological basis for his 1528 Braunschweig church order, the first and then formative model for his later church orders. To him, a responsible church order cannot be independent of its theological substance,[57] and thus the introduction to the Braunschweig order repeats the theme of his earlier tract:

> If we wish to be Christians we must be aware of the consequences. We must avoid monkish charades and penitential liturgies lest God despise us. God has not commanded us to perform any of these. We must carry out the true worship of God, that is, true good works of faith which were first commanded us by Christ. This is primarily that we bear the burden

54. Ibid., 175.
55. Lane, *Poverty and Poor Relief*, 143f. See also Hendel, "Care of the Poor," 527.
56. Vogt, *Johannes Bugenhagen*, 261.
57. Hans-Günter Leder, "Leben und Werk des Reformators Johannes Bugenhagen," in H.-G. Leder & Norbert Buske, eds., *Johannes Bugenhagen und die Reformation im Herzogtum Pommern* (Berlin: Evangelisches Verlagsanstalt, 1985), 31.

of our neighbors' needs as Jesus said [John 13:35]: "So will all people know that you are my followers if you always love one another."[58]

Here, as in his earlier tract, Bugenhagen is emphasizing that good works are not the prerequisite but rather the consequence of salvation. Thus the description of Christian social ethics as the "liturgy after the liturgy" is as applicable to Bugenhagen as it is to Luther. "Bugenhagen made it clear that obedience was worship."[59] He contrasted the Reformation recovery of the gospel to that of the late medieval church, in which he believed worship was falsified by efforts to acquire merit through charity.

Before men gave the monks many coins, they gave so much to Vigil masses, masses for the dead and other masses and bleatings. They gave without limit for marriages, funerals, baptisms, feasts of the Apostles, Marian devotions. They gave for pictures, plaques, bells, organs, and innumerable vigil lights both in churches and in their homes. We don't even mention the needless benefices, memorials, confraternities, letters of indulgences, pilgrimages, etc.[60]

Now, however, the false worship and misplaced good works of exchanging money for merit are to be displaced by true worship and the good works of serving the poor.

Bugenhagen's 1529 Hamburg church order [61] was preceded by the establishment of a common chest (*Kistenordnung*) in the St. Nicholas parish in 1527. This order, influenced by Luther's Leisnig order,[62] also presents the evangelical commandment to love the neighbor in place of salvation by works, which as the motive for medieval charity was also the major cause of its inadequacy. This new relief system raised poor relief from a vehicle of individual salvation to a Christian responsibility of the parish for all the needy without distinction.

58. Hans Lietzmann, ed., *Johannes Bugenhagens Braunschweiger Kirchenordnung* 1528 (Bonn: Marcus & Weber, 1912), 135. Cited by Lane, *Poverty and Poor Relief*, 141. See Sehling 6/1:445.

59. Lane, *Poverty and Poor Relief*, 154, 157f.

60. Lietzmann, *Braunschweiger Kirchenordnung*, 137, cited by Lane, *Poverty and Poor Relief*, 159.

61. A modern German edition is in Hanns Wenn, ed. & trans., *Johannes Bugenhagen: Der Ehrbaren Stadt Hamburg Christliche Ordnung 1529. De Ordeninge Pomerani* (Hamburg: Wittig Verlag, 1976), 211–57.

62. Rainer Postel, *Die Reformation in Hamburg*, 1517–1528 (Gütersloh: Mohn, 1986), 276–78; see 278–81 for a modern German edition of the order. Cf. also Paul Philippi, *Vorreformatorische Diakonie: Die Kirche in der hamburgischen Sozialgeschichte bis zum Ende des Reformationsjahrhunderts* (Stuttgart: Verlagswerk der Diakonie, 1984), 51–54; and Rainer Postel, "Zur Bedeutung der Reformation für das religiöse und soziale Verhalten des Bürgertums in Hamburg," in Bernd Moeller, *Stadt und Kirche im 16. Jahrhundert* (Gütersloh: Mohn, 1978), 171–72.

This effort to help the needy stand on their own feet corresponded to evangelical teaching (cf. Matt. 10:10, 20:1-16, 25:14-30; Luke 10:7; Eph. 4:28; 1 Thess. 4:11-12; 2 Thess. 3:6-12; 1 Tim. 5:18) and made economic sense. Above all it presupposed that those who were supported were not to be seen as impersonal objects of good works, but rather as independent members of the parish. This new poor relief thus had a communal aspect.[63]

Bugenhagen's church order for Lübeck (1531) follows the form of his earlier work. He begins by stating that Christians are to support themselves and their families according to Paul's injunction in 1 Tim. 5:8, 16. Those who are able should also assist their poor servants, relatives, neighbors, and other poor people who are known to them (1 Tim. 6:9, 17; Matt. 6:24). Preachers are to exhort not only the rich to help the worthy poor, but also craftsmen blessed by good fortune, as Paul teaches (Eph. 4:28). "We will no longer tolerate money-preachers who do not preach the gospel and saving doctrine, but rather preach such doctrine as is advantageous to themselves. For these are the fellows who held purgatory masses and sold us indulgences, etc."[64] The preachers can boldly appeal for social welfare because people will know the clergy are not lining their own pockets now that they are honorably supported by salaries. In this regard, Bugenhagen's genius was to separate the fund for poor relief (*Armenkasten*) from the fund for schools, pastors' salaries, and the maintenance of the church (*Schatzkasten*). A further advantage of this arrangement was to establish the independent financing of the church, and thereby make an effort to preserve the independence of the preacher with regard to the political authorities.[65]

Bugenhagen recognized the existence of many needy people whose poverty is not readily known. These "worthy poor," as Bugenhagen termed them, are decent, honorable people who through misfortune, unemployment, or underemployment suffer demonstrable need through no fault of their own.

> We are to care for the worthy poor just as we would have others come to our aid in our need. Before they even approach us, we should see to their need out of Christian love alone for God's sake and to honor the holy gospel. Christ will indeed remember these things on the last day even if we have already forgotten them, for true Christians do many good works and help others to blessedness and in bodily need, but nevertheless do not rely upon such good works, but rather upon the pure grace of God in Christ. This may be read in Matt. 25(:31-46).[66]

Bugenhagen's point is that up to now everyone has been taken in by the many beautiful objects in the churches and the numerous other means for

63. Postel, *Reformation in Hamburg*, 281–83.
64. Hauschild, *Lübecker Kirchenordnung*, 10.
65. Winckelmann, "Über die ältesten Armenordnungen," 225; Philippi, *Vorreformatorische Diakonie*, 57.
66. Hauschild, *Lübecker Kirchenordnung*, 12.

acquiring merit before God, such as indulgences, masses, special pilgrimages, brotherhoods, and ways to participate in all the good works taking place in the cloisters and in the monastic orders. All these efforts to find something special to help one's own blessedness were not only without God's Word, but even against God's Word.[67] Now, in light of the gospel, "we must diligently care for the worthy poor and thus aspire to true worship of God, the worship that Christ deems of value at the day of judgment. No Christian can disapprove of this unless he or she would forget all integrity, and no pope and council may make this otherwise."[68]

That such preaching was not without social effect is suggested by the testament of Anna Büring, the aged and wealthy widow of the Hamburg mayor. In 1535 she changed the will she had drafted in 1503. In her earlier testament, she declared, she had left her money to purchase vigils, masses for her soul, and numerous other good works in order to avoid the pain of purgatory. Now, however, having heard God's Word and holy gospel, she renounced this earlier orientation. Since she now believed she was saved by grace alone, she decided to provide for her family and then to leave the rest of her fortune for the sick and the needy. Provisions included establishing housing for the poor and a scholarship for a five-year study at a Christian university. Smaller bequests went to the church for construction and to the city for the common good. "Testaments give particularly serious and heartfelt witness to personal convictions. The relatively broad tradition shows that that of Anna Büring is representative for the change which occurred with the Reformation. At the same time it demonstrates some of its social-historical dimensions."[69]

Bugenhagen's basic principle for formulating church orders was to link theological argumentation and its practical-legal consequences. He expressed his theological basis in a sermonic style intended to make the order plausible to the community. To Bugenhagen, the reform of the church was not just to be a legal decree from above; it was to engage the whole urban community in the reform of worship, the development of schools, and the creation of a new social welfare program. All of these efforts were perceived to be central to Christian responsibility and to be the duty of the entire city. The writings of Luther find expression in Bugenhagen's application of Christian faith to the totality of daily life, exploding the late medieval concentration on the cultic as expressly Christian. The church was no longer defined and organized by the priestly office but as the assembled community under God's Word and around Christ's sacrament. "Poor relief was an act of charity done joyfully for God's sake by men justified and happy in Christ. It was, in fact, a 'Gottesdienst,' an act of worship, of divine service."[70]

---

67. Ibid., 12–13.
68. Ibid., 15.
69. Rainer Postel, "Sozialgeschichtliche Folgewirkungen der Reformation in Hamburg," in Wenzel Lohff, ed., *450 Jahre Reformation in Hamburg: Eine Festschrift* (Hamburg: Agentur des Rauhen Hauses, 1980), 63–64.
70. Lane, *Poverty and Poor Relief*, 174.

Roman Catholic Reactions

In light of the medieval theology of almsgiving, it is no surprise that Roman Catholic theologians did not understand the Reformation contributions to social welfare to be divine service. Roman Catholic cities, however, were quite willing to adapt Lutheran social innovations. All early modern cities, regardless of religious orientation, were faced with the same social issues. The Catholic city of Ypres is exemplary for the development of social welfare legislation.

The Social Legislation of Ypres

When Ypres published its Poor Ordinance[71] in 1525 it was a Roman Catholic city. Furthermore, within months of this ordinance the Catholic humanist Juan Luis Vives published his own program for poor relief at the behest of the mayor of the neighboring city of Bruges. This coincidence in time and structure of programs would seem to indicate either mutual or reciprocal influences. The Sorbonne gave its approval to the Ypres plan in 1531; both the diocesan bishop, the Cardinal of Lorraine, and the papal legate, Campeggio, granted indulgences to Ypres in the same year for the support of poor relief. The order was characterized as a pious and holy undertaking. In 1531, Emperor Charles V requested a copy of the statute from the magistrates so that he could use it as a model for his forthcoming decree on poor relief in the empire.[72]

In the late fall of 1525 the magistrates of Ypres, with the cooperation of citizens and clergy, composed a plan for poor relief to take effect on 3 December. The goal was to consolidate charitable resources and regulate their distribution under civil authority. Article 21 eliminated all begging: "No one, whoever it may be, may demand alms either within or outside the city, at tables, streets, churches, or before the houses of the people in any manner; and whoever shall be found acting against this shall be sharply punished according to the measure of his offense."

Following a description of the hardships that unrestrained begging imposed upon the city in general and the poor in particular, the decree set forth administrative details. "Four good men" chosen by the magistrates were to

---

71. The Flemish original is printed in I. L. A. Diegerick, ed., *Inventaire des chartes et documents appartenant aux archives de la ville d'Ypres*, vol. 5 (1860), 290ff. A German translation is in Winckelmann, "Armenordnungen von Nürnberg," 13–18. See also Part Two, section 7.2, of this volume.

72. J. Nolf, *La réforme de la bienfaisance publique à Ypres au XVIe siècle* (Ghent, 1915). W. J. Ashley, *An Introduction to English Economic History* (London, 1920), 2:347f.: "The peculiar importance of the Ypres ordinance lies in the fact that it led to a discussion of principle by the very highest tribunal in the Roman obedience." Charles V's ordinance in French is printed in Carl Steinbicker, *Poor Relief in the Sixteenth Century* (Washington, D.C.: Catholic Univ. of America, 1937), 245–48.

oversee the program. Four men from each parish, under these supervisors, would ascertain the state of the poor in their respective areas. Each parish would record these investigations in a book; along with the input of local social workers, this record would be the basis for the weekly distribution of aid to the poor. The city's charitable resources (incomes from almsgiving, foundations, and churches) were to be gathered into a common purse; an exception was foundation income specifically designated for the clergy or persons mentioned in the "letter of foundation." Further resources were to come from donations received by delegated officials in the streets, collection boxes placed in the parishes, and, if need be, weekly door-to-door collections in every parish. The officials were to be responsible for a monthly accounting in every parish and a biannual accounting to the magistrates. The clergy were directed to promote the order through their preaching and counseling. The four city supervisors would hold sessions to hear and discuss complaints on Mondays and Fridays.

The ordinance expressed concern for the education, health, and training of poor children and young women. Begging was forbidden on pain of punishment; poor travelers could stay in the city overnight and then would be aided on their way. All foreign poor living off alms had to be out of the city by 3 December 1525 or they would be imprisoned on bread and water. Lest beggars were to think they could circumvent these rules by sending their children into the streets to beg, child begging was clearly prohibited. As a further stricture on foreign poor, the law prohibited the rental of housing to foreigners without prior clearance by the magistrates. Finally, all citizens were to render help in fulfilling this ordinance or face appropriate punishment.

Some time after the enforcement of this ordinance, certain members of the clergy objected to its provision for a common purse; in addition they condemned the prohibition of begging as conformity to Lutheran doctrine. Hoping to resolve these clerical polemics against the new regulation, the magistrates met with the superiors of the four mendicant orders, the Franciscans, Carmelites, Augustinians, and Dominicans. Shortly thereafter the mendicants presented a written copy of their complaints. They charged that the ordinance did not take account of mendicants and other religious who had taken vows of poverty; they rejected the common purse and the prohibition of begging; they claimed that the virtuous poor were being neglected either through the ignorance or the partiality of the administrators and their assistants; and they argued that the religious, sick, infirm, disabled, and blind should be able to beg in freedom. Certainly begging from laziness was sin, they acknowledged, but even this form of begging provided the opportunity to give alms for God's sake, which is a meritorious act. They held up to the magistrates the example of Saint Alexius, who begged before his father's palace and was rewarded with sainthood for his renunciation and humiliation. Even if most beggars begged out of laziness, there might be an Alexius among them, and therefore begging must not be abolished. In short, the mendicants argued that lay control of charitable establishments was impious, prejudicial to the preexisting foundations established for the care of the poor and pilgrims, and contrary to divine law.[73] These critiques or variations of them were to be repeated across the continent in the next decades by Catholic opponents of social welfare reform.

The magistrates of Ypres examined and refuted these charges and denied that they had introduced heresy. They observed that during that very year (1530), the city had aided 1,600 to 1,800 poor persons and placed numerous children in school or trades. Clearly, the magistrates claimed, these results should demonstrate that the ordinance was a forceful work against deprivation and immorality. Believing they could overcome the obstinacy of the clergy, the magistrates in December 1530 requested Jean Crocius, a Dominican, and Jacques de Pape, master of the Latin school in Ypres and a Latin poet, to appeal on their behalf to the Sorbonne. The appeal referred to a recent theologian of the Sorbonne, John Major, who in his commentary on the Sentences (c. 1516) had said: "If the prince or community should decree that there should be no beggars in the country, and should provide for the impotent, the action would be praiseworthy and lawful."[74]

The dean of the theology faculty responded with the Sorbonne decision on 16 January 1531. "We hold that the system of poor relief which the magistrates of Ypres have instituted is severe but valuable; it is healthy and pious, and not inconsistent either with the Gospel or with the example of the Apostles or of our forefathers."[75] The judgment proposed certain limitations on the Ypres ordinance, however. First of all, the support of the poor should be arranged so that no foreign or domestic poor could fall into extreme need. In case the common purse did not suffice to meet needs, public begging could not be forbidden. No one should be hindered from publicly or privately distributing alms. Church goods were not to be drawn into the common purse, and the begging orders could not be forbidden to beg. Finally, the poor of neighboring places should also be supported and allowed to beg. "The secular magistrates are to take care that they do not presume under the cloak of piety or help for the poor to embark on sacrilege and take to themselves the goods and revenues of the churches or priests; for this would be the part not of good Catholics but of impious heretics, Waldensians, Wycliffites or Lutherans."[76]

Meanwhile the city was beginning to attract less qualified praise from elsewhere. The most important among requests for copies of the ordinance came from Charles V, who used it for the basis of his Pragmatic Decree of 6 October 1531. However, the controversy with the mendicant orders and the response of the Sorbonne led the city magistrates to revise and expand their

73. Nolf, *Réforme de la bienfaisance*, 50, 51, 69.
74. Cited by Ashley, *An Introduction*, 341.
75. F. R. Salter, ed., *Some Early Tracts on Poor Relief* (London, 1926), 76f.
76. Salter, *Some Early Tracts*, 77.

order under the title *Forma subventionis pauperum* (The Form of Assistance of the Poor).[77]

This 1531 ordinance shows the influence not only of the preceding developments but also that of Juan Luis Vives. In response to the Roman Catholic pressures, the revision reflected more sensitivity to the views of the mendicants than did the 1525 ordinance. The virtue of voluntary poverty is expressly recognized with reference to the saints Alexius and Fabiola. Neither voluntary poverty nor private almsgiving was forbidden, and the medieval ideological linkage of rich and poor was expressly recognized.

> The poor man again loves the rich man as his benefactor from whom he has his living and by whose aid he is helped, he thanks him for all that he has, he gives to him many blessings and good prayers as a token of gratitude and he renders them heartily and as liberally as he can. For no other cause did nature mingle rich and poor together but that the poor men shall receive benefits of rich men. And the rich should take of God the fruit of the benefits with much money and increase. . . . God has given us the poor to exercise the works of virtue upon.[78]

The order made appeals to canon law, the church fathers, John Major, and participation in Christ's mystical body. The clergy were included as advocates of the poor and exhorters of the citizens to this good work.

The scholarly confusion of this 1531 order with that of 1525 has led some critics to attribute the Ypres developments to Vives. However, Vives's book on supporting the poor did not appear until six months after the 1525 order; moreover, Vives had done his best while working on it to conceal its subject matter from even his closest associates.[79] Although Vives advocated the abolition of begging, he did not suggest confiscation of church income for support of the poor, nor did he depart from the medieval rationale for private almsgiving. In terms of theory, Vives maintained poverty as a highly valued divine ordinance because it can strengthen faith and personal ethics.

It seems plausible that the first Ypres order was a development in the context of late medieval urban change that utilized the insights of the evangelical poor orders already instituted in Germany. The Ypres magistrates need not have accepted the theological motivation in order to recognize the viability of the new orders for social welfare established in Nuremberg and Strasbourg, cities with trade connections to Ypres.[80] However, the recognition that new

---

77. *Forma subventionis pauperum quae Hyperas Flandorum urbem viget universae reipublicae longe utilissima*, 1531. A copy is in Harvard University's Houghton Library. The 1535 English translation by William Marshall is in Salter, *Some Early Tracts*, 36–76.
78. Salter, *Some Early Tracts*, 70ff.; *Forma subventionis*, Ciin.
79. Alice Tobriner, *A Sixteenth-Century Urban Report* (Chicago: Univ. of Chicago Press, 1971), 15ff.; Carlos G. Noreña, *Juan Luis Vives* (The Hague: Nijhoff, 1970), 2, 96, 98, 146, 196f.
80. See Fuchs, "Relations commerciales entre Nuremberg et Strasbourg," 77.

social orders could bring with them new theological legitimations—that is, Lutheran theology—is no doubt behind the mendicants' charge that the 1525 order introduces Lutheran heresy. The reform of poor relief in the Low Countries was a "curious and doubtless generally unconscious introduction of Lutheran principles into the legislation of Catholic cities and countries."[81]

There may also be a more direct connection between Ypres and Wittenberg. This connection may have been mediated by Jakob Propst, a native of Ypres, a student and friend of Luther, and the reformer of poor relief in Bremen. An Augustinian, Propst had studied with Luther in Wittenberg and went from there to become the prior of the new Augustinian cloister in Antwerp in 1519. In 1521 he went back to Wittenberg for his baccalaureate, then returned to Antwerp at the end of the year. By this time the Wittenberg *Beutelordnung* had appeared; shortly after Propst's departure, both the new Wittenberg order and Karlstadt's tract on poor relief had been published. In Antwerp in February 1522, under pressure from the Inquisition, Propst renounced his evangelical faith. He then went to Ypres, where his preaching became increasingly evangelical; he was again imprisoned in May. Among other things, Propst accused the mendicants of money-grubbing. He escaped prison and fled to Wittenberg. In 1524 he went to Bremen as preacher and reformer. In 1525 he authored a new church order for Bremen that included reform of poor relief and the schools. His Bremen order referred to the models Luther had developed in 1522–23 in Wittenberg and Leisnig.[82] Propst may also have had an influence on the 1525 development in Ypres.[83]

In light of these urban and personal connections, it is more difficult to conceive of the 1525 Ypres order developing independently than it is to conceive of it developing in relation to Lutheran influences. There is no reason not to take the concerns of both the mendicant orders and the Sorbonne seriously. The charge of Lutheran heresy may be a recognition of the connection between theology and changing social values. The increasing visibility of the Lutheran heresy (its first martyrs were in the Low Countries),[84] culminating in the Augsburg Confession in 1530, could very well have affected the initial clerical openness to social change and replaced it with concern for the restoration of the prior status quo. This development seems to be reflected in the Roman Catholic polemics against Vives, the decree of Charles

81. Paul Bonenfant, "Les origines et le caractère," 230. Cf. also Herman van der Wee, *The Growth of the Antwerp Market and the European Economy (Fourteenth to Sixteenth Centuries),* 2 vols. (The Hague: Nijhoff, 1963), 2:162–63.
82. Ortwin Rudloff, *Bonae Litterae et Lutherus: Texte und Untersuchungen zu den Aufängen der Theologie des Bremers Reformators Jakob Propst* (Bremen: Hauschild, 1985), 203, 215.
83. Ernst Büttner, "Das Buch der 'Armenkiste an unser Lieben Frauen Kirche' zu Bremen (1525 bis 1580), sein Bedeutung und sein mutmassliche Beziehung zu der Armenordnung in Ypern," *Archiv für Kulturgeschichte* 12 (1916), 359–61.
84. See Luther's letter of consolation: "The Burning of Brother Henry" (1525), LW 32:261–86.

V, and the Bruges ordinance instituted in 1560 that was attacked by the Augustinian monk Villavicencio as heretical.

Roman Catholic Demurrals

Charles V's advocacy of poor-relief reform in the Empire took effect in Spain in the royal decree of 1540. This decree, among other things, stimulated the famous debate between the Catholic theologians Juan de Robles (also known as Juan de Medina) and Domingo de Soto. Although Charles V had no intention of arrogating poor-relief duties and rights from the Roman Catholic Church, that is how Soto viewed the royal decree.[85]

Soto, a Dominican, rejected all governmental strictures on public begging. In his 1545 treatise, *Deliberación en la causa de los pobres* (Deliberation on the Cause of the Poor), "he challenged the precepts and goals underlying all the early sixteenth-century welfare reforms and any authority—the theologians of the Sorbonne, the decisions of past church councils and even the pope— to sanction the permanent prohibition of begging in a Catholic state."[86] Soto defended begging as a moral right for the poor and a stimulus to compassion for the rich. "But Soto's most devastating argument, reiterated throughout his treatise, was based upon the accepted dictum of the Catholic church that alms should be given voluntarily to be meritorious."[87] The response in defense of the new government program by the Benedictine abbot, Robles, was that the critical issue was not compassion for the poor but rather their actual relief. But it was Soto, not Robles, who represented the Catholic opinion of the day.[88]

Soto and Robles agreed on at least two points: "almsgiving bestowed on the giver a special form of grace," and "poor relief should be administered

---

85. See Maureen Flynn, *Sacred Charity: Confraternities and Social Welfare in Spain 1400–1700* (Ithaca, N.Y.: Cornell Univ. Press, 1989), 90; and Linda Martz, *Poverty and Welfare in Hapsburg Spain: The Example of Toledo* (Cambridge: Cambridge Univ. Press, 1983), 20–21. Flynn (88–98) and Martz (22–30) describe in detail the controversy between Soto and Robles.

86. Martz, *Poverty and Welfare*, 23. "For those who favoured reform it was unfortunate that Soto, whose fame was such that it was said 'Qui soit Sotum soit totum' [He who knows Soto, knows everything], should be an opponent."

87. Ibid., 26.

88. Flynn, *Sacred Charity*, 98, points out that some contemporary commentators "disparage the claims of Soto as unrepresentative of Catholic opinion. But if we compare the two men's views with the actual practice of relief in Spain, it is clear that Soto's position dominated." This is true elsewhere than Spain in the sixteenth century. In eighteenth-century France, "A donor was invited to form a '*société d'action* with God and the angels,' the most profitable of speculations an investor could hope to make." Cissie C. Fairchilds, *Poverty and Charity in Aix-en-Provence 1640–1789* (Baltimore: Johns Hopkins Univ. Press, 1976), 27. The Roman Catholic Steinbicker comments in his 1937 study, *Poor Relief*, 118: "[Vives's] object of civil supremacy in the field of poor relief was wrong. Christian charity aims not only towards a better life here on earth, but essentially towards the best life in eternity."

and implemented by ecclesiastics."[89] The latter point is the central concern of the Spanish Augustinian, Lorenzo Villavicencio. He was sent to the Netherlands by Philip II as a preacher, writer, and organizer against the growth of Protestantism.

Villavicencio's strong attack on humanist and evangelical programs for social welfare, *De oeconomia sacra circa pauperam curam* (On the Sacred Economy concerning Care of the Poor) (1564), was in response to the Bruges city senate effort two years earlier to take over the charitable institutions of the city in order to control begging. Villavicencio, echoing the concerns of the Council of Trent, was against any civic usurpation of ecclesial and especially episcopal rights.[90] He wrote:

> A Senate which secretly favors Lutheranism or paganism, since it would not dare to invade the rights of the Church openly, fearing the Catholic people and Princes, nevertheless does so obscurely and secretly. The Senators wish to bring ecclesiastical jurisdiction and property within their power. . . . In spite of the fact that the possession, disposition and administration of the "patrimony of the poor" pertains to the Divine society, the civil magistrates wish to determine where and how much of it is spent. . . . They want this authority over poor-relief so that afterwards they may be able to bring within their power many other ecclesiastical things, and finally command the whole ecclesiastical organization.[91]

For Villavicencio, the bishop alone as *pater pauperum* (father of the poor) is finally responsible for the care of the poor. Of course, the laity are responsible for personal charity, but the laicization of social welfare is nothing other than the disguised greed of the princes and merchants who want to get their hands on the church's wealth. What else can one expect, he asks, from such heretics as Luther, Melanchthon, Brenz, and Calvin? Since these heretics have broken with the Bride of Christ, it is not surprising that they are pushing the true, living representatives of Christ, the poor, out of society and wanting to imprison the poor "like wild animals in cages."[92]

The work of Villavicencio witnesses to the intense self-examination by the Tridentine church of its essence and responsibilities.[93] He was intensely aware that social issues always involve fundamental values and theological commitments. He also, along with such persons as Soto, Robles, Erasmus, More, and Vives, exemplifies the divided mind among Catholics faced by the

---

89. Martz, *Poverty and Welfare*, 25, 28.
90. Karl Dueringer, "Lorenzo de Villavicencio als Anwalt der kirchlichen Armenpflege im Zeitalter der Tridentinischen Reform," *Gesammelte Aufsätze zur Kulturgeschichte Spaniens* (Münster: Aschendorff, 1963), 332.
91. Book 3, chap. 3, cited by Steinbicker, *Poor Relief*, 127–28.
92. Dueringer, "Lorenzo de Villavicencio," 332–35.
93. Ibid., 337.

social and theological challenges of the sixteenth century. But then, the evangelicals were not of one mind either.

Radical Evangelical Reactions

Scholars of the Reformation have long recognized the heterogeneity of the early Reformation movements and their leaders. George H. Williams's *The Radical Reformation*[94] is one of the most ambitious and noteworthy of the numerous terminological efforts that have been advanced to create some order out of the diversity of evangelical positions. In an elegant paragraph, Hans J. Hillerbrand summarizes this plurality:

> During those years [of the early Reformation], the *causa Lutheri* increasingly turned into a widespread and ubiquitous desire for renewal and reform. Political, economic, and social goals no less than religious and theological ones were advocated. Earlier reform proposals and grievances were echoed. It was a polyphonic choir, and not all sang out of the same hymnal.[95]

A review of all these voices is beyond the scope of this study. I shall focus on the themes of communalism and voluntary charity expressed by some of the so-called radical reformers (ranging from Thomas Müntzer to the Anabaptist movements) in opposition to the social welfare models stemming from Luther.

Thomas Müntzer's Criticisms

Müntzer has been a notorious and controversial figure since his involvement in the Peasants' revolts of the 1520s. Initially he viewed Luther as a comrade-in-arms, but Müntzer soon turned his considerable firepower against Luther, whom he came to consider a perverter of the gospel, a willing tool of the princes, a "carrion crow," "Father Pussyfoot," "Dr. Liar," "the Wittenberg Pope," "archdevil," and a "rabid fox," to mention a few of his epithets. To Müntzer, Luther was "the personification of a corrupt, self-indulgent society."[96]

Luther, himself no slouch at invective, in turn labeled Müntzer a bloodthirsty rioter possessed by the devil who was hell-bent on destroying both

94. George H. Williams, *The Radical Reformation* (Philadelphia: Westminster Press, 1962). A revised edition is forthcoming from Sixteenth Century Journal Publishers.
95. Hans J. Hillerbrand, "Radicalism in the Early Reformation: Varieties of Reformation in Church and Society," in Hans J. Hillerbrand, ed., *Radical Tendencies in the Reformation: Divergent Perspectives* (Kirksville, Mo.: Sixteenth Century Journal Publishers, 1988), 25. See also in the same volume Adolf Laube, "Radicalism as a Research Problem in the History of the Early Reformation."
96. Peter Matheson, "Thomas Müntzer's *Vindication and Refutation*: A Language for the Common People?" SCJ 20 (1989), 611.

church and state, a man born for heresies and schisms (LW 40:45–49). Thus began the Protestant historiography of Müntzer and, by association, of all the so-called radical reformers and Anabaptist groups. Müntzer became the strongest symbol of the dissent and heresy that logically led to the horrors of the Peasants' War of 1525 as well as the 1534–35 disaster of the city of Münster. The modern stimulus for Müntzer research has come from Marxist historians who took their cue from Friedrich Engels's reinterpretation of Müntzer as a revolutionary forerunner of liberation from social and political oppression. This viewpoint is summarized by the pamphlet prepared in East Germany for the 1989 quincentenary of Müntzer's birth.

> The GDR ... has understood itself as a state living up to the idea of Thomas Müntzer's that "power shall be given to the common folk." As a man who fought with dedicated self-sacrifice for the goal of building a new society in the interests of the common people, Müntzer's example demonstrates ethical and moral values that have borne and still bear fruit in creating the foundations of socialism.... Müntzer's legacy lives on in socialist society and, as Erich Honecker commented, it is particularly dear to us.[97]

From this perspective it was Müntzer who was the reformatory social revolutionary and champion of the poor.[98] Recent research on Müntzer questions this evaluation, however, by pointing out that aspects of his championing of the poor are more legend than fact.[99] It appears that "Müntzer belongs to the historical personalities who have become known more through the history of their reception than through their own works."[100]

Müntzer's early life is obscure, but recent research cogently argues that his social origins among prosperous urban craftsmen and entrepreneurs were similar to Luther's.[101] Some of Müntzer's relatives and friends were partial to a kind of self-renunciation characteristic of early capitalists concerned that their new worldly success would dull their hearing the voice of God. The

97. *Theses Concerning Thomas Müntzer* 1489–1989 (Berlin: Panorama DDR, 1989), 6–7.
98. See Carter Lindberg, "Theology and Politics: Luther the Radical and Müntzer the Reactionary," *Encounter* 37 (1976). For overviews of recent Müntzer studies see Carter Lindberg, "Müntzeriana," LQ 4 (1990); and James Stayer, "Thomas Müntzer in 1989: A Review Article," SCJ 21 (1990).
99. Cf. Helmar Junghans, "Der Wandel des Müntzerbildes in der DDR von 1951/52 bis 1989," *Luther* 60 (1989), 104, 125. Junghans, 128, makes the interesting observation that although the older research presents Müntzer as a social revolutionary, liberation theology has responded positively to Luther but hardly included Müntzer.
100. Siegfried Bräuer, "Die Theologie Thomas Müntzers als Grundlage seiner sozi-alethischen Impulse," *Evangelische Monatsschrift Standpunkt* 70/3 (1989), 63.
101. See Ulrich Bubenheimer, *Thomas Müntzer: Herkunft und Bildung* (Leiden: Brill, 1989); and Tom Scott, *Thomas Müntzer: Theology and Revolution in the German Reformation* (New York: St. Martin's Press, 1989). For much of what follows I am dependent upon the work of Bubenheimer.

medieval judgment that salvation for merchants was unlikely and condemnation for usurers was certain continued to echo in their ears. Müntzer's demand for an ascetic structure of life developed in this socioeconomic context. "The mentality of the merchant-traders keyed to growth, expansion, and capital-accumulation was considered as fleshly 'desire' in the horizon of asceticism demanded by Müntzer."[102]

At the same time, Müntzer's intimate involvement in these circles may be behind his sharp attack on Luther's criticism of merchants in his 1524 tract "Trade and Usury." Whereas Luther perceived the basic threat to the common good in the new capitalism, Müntzer saw it in the old order of feudalism. So Müntzer condemned Luther as an opportunistic toady of the princes. Indeed, Müntzer charged, Luther had bought the favor of the princes by legitimating their expropriation of church property.[103] In his 1524 "Vindication and Refutation" Müntzer wrote:

> You should be ashamed of yourself, you arch-wretch! Are you trying to patch up a hypocritical accommodation with this erring world?... The poor monks and priests and merchants cannot defend themselves. So it is easy for you to insult them! But the godless rulers are to be immune from criticism, even if they tread Christ underfoot.... But though you have scolded the princes you can give them fresh courage again, you new pope, by presenting them with monasteries and churches....
>
> That you stood up at Worms before the Empire is to the credit of the German nobility, whose great mouths you smeared with honey, for they were quite sure that your preaching would present them with monasteries and foundations on the Bohemian pattern [i.e., secularization of church property].[104]

According to Müntzer, the essential authors of usury and robbery are the princes who oppress the merchants as well as the poor. His orientation here has specific biographical background: at the time he was having his "Vindication and Refutation" printed in Nuremberg, Müntzer was in communication with Christoph Fürer, a participant in the leading Nuremberg mining society. Luther had rejected exactly such societies that were pushing toward becoming monopolies.[105]

To Müntzer it was the rulers who assumed that everything belonged to them: "The fish in the water, the birds in the air, the plants on the face of the earth—it all has to belong to them!" Hence, "There is no greater abomination on earth than the fact that no one is prepared to take up the cause

102. Bubenheimer, *Thomas Müntzer*, 119.
103. Luther's preface to the Leisnig order expresses concern that this *not* take place.
104. "A highly provoked Vindication and Refutation of the unspiritual soft-living Flesh in Wittenberg, whose robbery and distortion of Scripture has so grievously polluted our wretched Christian Church," in CW 324–50, 342–43, 348.
105. Cf. Bubenheimer, *Thomas Müntzer*, 141–44.

of the needy. The great do whatever they please, as Job describes in chapter 41."[106] The world is corrupt because everyone cares only for material goods; clinging to their creaturely desires, people strive to acquire riches and power. "The first Christian awareness cannot be attained without suffering. For the heart has to be torn away from clinging to this world by wretchedness and pain, until it becomes altogether hostile to this life."[107]

To Müntzer, Luther was the preacher of a fictitious faith in a honey-sweet Christ who had fulfilled the law for us. True faith, however, rested not in a substitutionary atonement but in discipleship that proved itself in life. To Müntzer, Christ therefore is the moral example whom Christians are called to emulate by following in the footsteps of Jesus, fulfilling the law, and becoming like God. To Luther this was a disastrous illusion, the exact opposite of his understanding of the gospel. In a letter to Spalatin concerning Melanchthon's anxiety at the 1530 Diet of Augsburg, Luther wrote:

He [God], however, who has begun this work, certainly has begun it without our counsel and effort.... He it is who will complete and close it outside and beyond our counsel and effort; concerning this I have not the slightest doubt....

Be strong in the Lord, and on my behalf continuously admonish Philip not to become like God, but to fight that innate ambition to be like God, which was planted in us in paradise by the devil.... In summary: we are to be men and not God; it will not be otherwise, or eternal anxiety and affliction will be our reward. (LW 49:337)[108]

Müntzer soon took up the "cause of the needy," as he saw it, by joining with the peasant revolt. Captured and tortured after the failure of the peasants at Frankenhausen, Müntzer confessed that what he and they "held and sought to put into practice were: All things are to be held in common and distribution should be to each according to his need, as occasion arises. Any prince, count, or gentleman who refused to do this should first be given a warning, but then one should cut off his head or hang him."[109]

Müntzer's contrast of creaturely self-interest to the good of the community (*Eigennutz vs. Gemeinnutz*), and his forced confession of Christian equality (*omnia*

106. "Vindication and Refutation," CW 335.
107. CW 98. Cf. Günter Vogler, "Sozialethische Vorstellungen und Lebensweisen von Täufergruppen—Thomas Müntzer und die Täufer im Vergleich," *Evangelische Monatsschrift Standpunkt* 70/3 (1989), 75, 78.
108. Cf. Klaus Deppermann, "Thomas Müntzer—Bahnbrecher der Neuzeit?" in Klaus Deppermann et al., *Thomas Müntzer: Ein streitbarer Theologe zwischen Mystik und Revolution* (Karlsruhe: Schriftenreihe der Evangelischen Akademie Baden, 1990), vol. 68: 9, 18–21.
109. CW 437. On Müntzer's support for community of goods, see Hans-Dieter Plümper, *Die Gütergemeinschaft bei den Täufern des 16. Jahrhunderts* (Göttingen: Kümmerle, 1972), 18–23.

sunt communia), are echoes of medieval slogans and utopian visions rather than a blueprint for social change.[110] "In that sense, therefore, he had no real 'theory of society.'"[111] Luther's practical advice for developing social welfare, evident in his *To the Christian Nobility*, "is totally absent in Müntzer."[112]

Luther's writings against usury and his proposals for social welfare legislation make it clear that he did not advocate any utopian plans for simple redistribution of wealth. In his tract *Against the Robbing and Murdering Hordes of Peasants* (1525), Luther stated:

> It does not help the peasants when they pretend that according to Genesis 1 and 2 all things were created free and common, and that all of us alike have been baptized. For under the New Testament, Moses does not count; for there stands our Master Christ, and subjects us, along with our bodies and our property, to the emperor and the law of this world, when he says, "Render to Caesar the things that are Caesar's." . . . For baptism does not make men free in body and property, but in soul; and the gospel does not make goods common, except in the case of those who, of their own free will, do what the apostles and disciples did in Acts 4. (LW 46:51)[113]

Years later Luther reiterated this point in his *Preface to the Acts of the Apostles*: even though "St. Augustine and many others have looked upon the fact that the apostles had all things in common with Christians [Acts 2:44–45; 4:32–37] as the best example which the book contains," this is not the point of the book. "Rather it should be noted that by this book St. Luke teaches the whole of Christendom, even to the end of the world, that the true and chief article of Christian doctrine is this: We must all be justified alone by faith in Jesus Christ, without any contribution from the law or help from our works" (LW 35:363).

This argument is not meant to detract from Müntzer's perceptive insight that poverty does not necessarily prepare one to receive the gospel but may, in fact, have the opposite effect: "The poor man is too worried about getting

110. Dieter Fauth, "Das Menschenbild bei Thomas Müntzer," in Siegfried Bräuer & Helmar Junghans, eds., *Der Theologe Thomas Müntzer: Untersuchung zu seiner Entwicklung und Lehre* (Berlin: Evangelische Verlagsanstalt, 1989), 46: "In terms of intellectual history we also see Müntzer standing in the utopian tradition. Thus it is exemplarily clear that his anthropology also included utopian elements." Cf. also Hans-Jürgen Goertz, "Spiritualität und revolutionäres Engagement. Thomas Müntzer: Ein Revolutionär zwischen Mittelalter und Neuzeit," in Deppermann et al., *Thomas Müntzer*, 52.
111. Scott, *Thomas Müntzer*, 171–72; see also 138, 184–85.
112. Bräuer, "Theologie Thomas Müntzers," 63. Vogler, "Sozialethische Vorstellungen," 75, points out that a basic reason Müntzer's social-ethical conceptions remained on the level of postulates was that he lacked a community of adherents or an institutional church to realize them.
113. Cf. also Günther Rudolph, "Thomas Müntzers sozialökonomische Konzeption und das Traditionsbewusstsein der sozialistischen Arbeiterbewegung," *Deutsche Zeitschrift für Philosophie* 23 (1975), 560–61.

his food to have time to learn to read [the Bible]."[114] But while Müntzer opposed oppression and social misery because they hindered the peasants from coming to faith, it is important to note that he turned to the peasants as a last recourse for his program of reform after it was rejected by the princes and the magistrates. Further, an examination of Müntzer's vocabulary shows that he mainly used the terms "poor" and "needy" in a spiritual rather than in a material, social sense.[115] "Müntzer's intentions were not aimed at any reform of existing conditions, or the restitution of past conditions, but at a complete revolution in order to bring about the immediate rule of God and the establishment of Christian freedom and equality on earth."[116]

As Müntzer realized at the end of his life, the bread that interested the peasants was not that of the Word. In his last letter to his followers, written after his capture at the disastrous battle of Frankenhausen, Müntzer said that the people had not understood him, "for they sought only their own interests and the divine truth was defeated as a result."[117] His vision of social equality wherein all things were held in common foundered on his followers' creaturely materialism, their *Eigennutz*.[118]

Anabaptist Preclusions

Müntzer's dearly won insight about human selfishness was also perceived by the Hutterites, the Anabaptist community that developed the rule of a total community of goods as a condition of membership.[119] They believed that private property and selfishness went hand in hand, as expressed in their familiar jingle:

"Communal living would not be hard
If there were not such self-regard"[120]

While Müntzer discovered that self-regard precluded the imposition of the community of goods on the whole society, the Anabaptists moved to control

114. CW 272. Cf. Scott, *Thomas Müntzer*, 101–2.
115. See Hans Otto Spillmann, *Untersuchungen zum Wortschatz in Thomas Müntzers deutschen Schriften* (Berlin: Walter de Gruyter, 1971), 75–80.
116. Laube, "Radicalism as a Research Problem," 20. See also Lindberg, "Theology and Politics," 370–71.
117. CW 160; also 161: "Everyone was more concerned with his own self-interest than in bringing justice to the Christian people."
118. See Vogler, "Gemeinnutz und Eigennutz," 188–91.
119. Donald F. Durnbaugh, ed., *Every Need Supplied: Mutual Aid and Christian Community in the Free Churches, 1525–1675* (Philadelphia: Temple Univ. Press, 1974), 14.
120. *"Die Gemeinschaft wär nicht schwer/Wenn nur der Eigennutz nit wär."* Cited by Robert Friedmann, "The Christian Communism of the Hutterite Brethren," ARG 46 (1955), 208; and Peter James Klassen, *The Economics of Anabaptism 1525–1560* (The Hague: Mouton, 1964), 74.

self-regard by the alternative of closed communities of goods apart from the larger society.

Recent research has highlighted the pluralistic origins of the Anabaptists and sharply questioned the older notion that Anabaptism was "the Protestantism of the poor."[121] Anabaptists were drawn from all levels of society, including prominent intellectuals, although the greatest numbers came from the urban craftsmen and then from the peasantry after persecution drove many from the cities.[122] Indeed, the late medieval urban guild experience may have been a source for the Hutterite development of a communism of production as well as consumption.[123] Other suggestions for the inspiration of the community of goods range from the necessity for mutual aid due to persecution as well as an ecclesial separatism from the world to medieval monastic models.[124]

The theological legitimation for the Hutterites draws on the theme of complete surrender to God (*Gelassenheit*) that found expression in medieval mystics and Karlstadt and Müntzer. Indeed, much of the Hutterite article, "True Surrender [*Gelassenheit*] and the Christian Community of Goods," echoes the favorite biblical passages Karlstadt used in his tract "There Should Be No Beggars among Christians."[125] Communal Anabaptism was not dependent solely upon the example of the communism of the primitive church described in Acts, but found biblical warrants and models from ancient Israel up to its present.[126] The Bible was not merely the norm of faith and life but the blueprint for the restitution of the early Christian community. The question of the true church is to be decided not by doctrine but in the life of the community. For the communal Anabaptists, that life was to be a stark alternative to the larger society—a self-contained, voluntary community of goods.[127] This alternative was based in a personal love ethic that rejected all personal gain.

This communal living was altogether at variance with the goals of either the Peasants' Revolt or the Münster kingdom, for, by its very nature, it

121. Cf. James M. Stayer, "The Anabaptists," in Steven Ozment, ed., *Reformation Europe: A Guide to Research* (St. Louis: Center for Reformation Research, 1982), 144.
122. Klassen, *Economics of Anabaptism*, 83.
123. See Plümper, *Gütergemeinschaft*, 148.
124. Williams, *Radical Reformation*, 429–34. Stayer, "Christianity in One City," 126–28, discusses the development of community of goods in Anabaptist Münster as a response to the crisis of its military siege.
125. E.g., the Deuteronomic injunctions of the sabbatical year and that there be no poor among the people. The article in English translation is in *The Chronicle of the Hutterian Brethren*, trans. and ed. by the Hutterian Brethren (Rifton, N.Y.: Plough Publishing House, 1987), vol. 1:265–75. For the argument for Karlstadt's influence, see Calvin Pater, *Karlstadt as the Father of the Baptist Movements* (Toronto: Univ. of Toronto Press, 1983).
126. See Klassen, *Economics of Anabaptism*, 64–82.
127. Hans-Jürgen Goertz, *Die Täufer: Geschichte und Deutung* (Berlin: Evangelische Verlagsanstalt, 1988), 120, 31–33.

could never be coercive. There was to be an economic equality based on voluntarism, not compulsion. Furthermore, the community of goods was regarded as an expression of the love ethic for a spiritually-united group, and was never intended for society as a whole. Those practicing this communitarianism were convinced that true community of goods pre-supposed a spiritual fellowship, and thus could be applied only in the group. Since the foundation of this communal living was strictly a spiritual one, references to society as a whole were out of the question.[128]

The irony here is that the Anabaptist emphasis upon a visible church precluded the development of a social ethic that could legislate welfare; whereas Luther's emphasis upon the hiddenness of the church impelled such a development.

128. Klassen, *Economics of Anabaptism*, 64.

Chapter 4

Social Reform
beyond Charity
for the Poor

MARTIN LUTHER is not usually thought of as a major social ethicist, let alone an initiator of social welfare policies. This ignorance or forgetfulness of Luther's major contributions to the theology and praxis of social welfare is to some extent due to a scholarly neglect of the legislative developments of the Reformation. As Gerta Scharffenorth has noted, the church orders are an indispensable resource for evaluating the social effect of Reformation theology, but a complete scholarly edition was not begun until the turn of the twentieth century, and not much research has been devoted to them.[1] The powerful influence of Ernst Troeltsch also cannot be ignored as a reason for the assumption that Luther's reform did not affect social structures. The all too common portrayal of Luther as a conservative ethicist who separated public and private morality, advocated an "ethic of disposition," and dualistically decreed "an inward morality for the individual and an external 'official' morality" indifferent to social structures and institutions stems from Troeltsch's famous work, *The Social Teaching of the Christian Churches*.[2] This evaluation was uncritically taken up by Reinhold Niebuhr, who condemned Luther's "quietistic tendencies" and "defeatism." It was evident to Niebuhr that for Luther "no obligation rests upon the Christian to change social structures so that they might conform more perfectly to the requirements of brotherhood."[3]

1. Gerta Scharffenorth, *Den Glauben ins Leben ziehen . . . Studien zu Luthers Theologie* (Munich: Kaiser, 1982), 126.
2. Ernst Troeltsch, *The Social Teaching of the Christian Churches*, 2 vols. (New York: Harper & Row, 1960), vol. 2, 472, 508, 510–11.
3. Reinhold Niebuhr, *The Nature and Destiny of Man*, 2 vols. (New York: Scribner's, 1964), vol. 2, 192–93.

That these judgments of Troeltsch and Niebuhr have become the received tradition is illustrated by a study by a past president of the Society of Christian Ethics, Max Stackhouse. According to Stackhouse, Luther "was primarily engaged in a spiritual and narrowly conceived ecclesiastical revolution. He was quite unsympathetic to the political and social movements [of his time]." Furthermore, "Lutheranism did not develop a genuinely urban base which would allow appropriations of notions of civil rights, corporate independencies, or cosmopolitan values."[4] Helmer Junghans cites Heinz Schilling as an example of this same widely held interpretation of Luther: "'In his nearly monomaniacal concentration upon the cardinal problem of the individual-personal gaining of grace, Luther worked continually throughout his life on the inner, religious kernel of the Reformation. He left the organization of the world, and indeed almost the organization of the visible church to others.'"[5]

While these distortions of Luther's theology and praxis are unlikely to be laid to rest by this brief study, I do hope this volume stimulates a fresh look at Luther's contributions to social ethics. This is important not only for scholarship but for the life of the church, especially those churches—and not just Lutheran ones—that acknowledge Luther as their "father in the faith."[6] To dismiss Luther's contributions to social ethics in general and to the development of early modern social welfare in particular without a rereading of the sources and their context has become a deficit in the contemporary life of the church. I do not wish to romanticize and idealize Luther's contributions nor to suggest they be repristinated. He was neither the first nor the only later medieval thinker to struggle with the issue of relating the gospel to social justice. Nor were his programs always accepted or completely carried out. But Luther does provide a clear model not only for the crucial role of the theological application of faith to society, but more importantly for the locus in Scripture of that theology. Luther was effective not because he told people what they ought to do, but because he first told them what God has done for them. The trend in contemporary theology has been to reverse this order, to make the world itself the source and locus of faith.

The "Boston Declaration" of January 1976 ... says this without reservations: The places where "the transforming reality of God's reign is found

---

4. Max Stackhouse, *Creeds, Society, and Human Rights: A Study in Three Cultures* (Grand Rapids, Mich.: Eerdmans, 1984), 54–55.
5. Heinz Schilling, "Die 'Zweite Reformation' als Kategorie der Geschichtswissenschaft," in Heinz Schilling, ed., *Die reformierte Konfessionalisierung in Deutschland—Das Problem der "Zweiten Reformation"* (Gütersloh, 1986), 413, cited by Junghans, "Sozialethisches Denken," 67. Cf. Strohm, "Martin Luthers Sozialethik," 68–69, 88–89.
6. This is the ecumenically felicitous phrase of the Roman Catholic Luther scholar Peter Manns. See Peter Manns, *Martin Luther: An Illustrated Biography* (New York: Crossroad, 1982), 217; Peter Manns, *Martin Luther—Ketzer oder Vater im Glauben?* (Hannover: Lutherhaus Verlag, 1980); Peter Manns & Harding Meyer, eds., in collaboration with Carter Lindberg & Harry McSorley, *Luther's Ecumenical Significance: An Interconfessional Consultation* (Philadelphia/New York: Fortress Press/Paulist Press, 1984), 20–22.

today," are "the struggles of the poor" for just distribution of goods, the "drive for ethnic dignity" against all racism, the struggle of women against "sexist subordination," and many similar points. Without doubt the Christian must take up solidarity with the poor, the oppressed and those discriminated against, and must engage with whole heart and both hands for their struggle for freedom. But certainly not in order to recognize there God's revelation and to experience God in his reign! To the contrary, he can only participate in the struggles of the poor and the oppressed because *already elsewhere*—in Jesus of Nazareth and in the testimony to him—he *has* authoritatively heard of God as the God of the poor and oppressed and at the same time *has become* freed and authoritatively called to engagement for the poor and oppressed.[7]

Luther had the boldness to address structural sources of injustice and to advocate legislative redress of them because his social ethics was rooted in the worship and proclamation of the community. The congregation is the local source in which God "creates a new world."[8]

Focusing on Service to the Neighbor

Certainly the impressions of Troeltsch and his followers can no longer be seriously maintained in light of the actualization of Luther's theology in the social legislation and programs of the church orders. Perhaps some of the confusion arises from the anachronism of speaking of "social ethics" with regard to Luther, since social ethics as an academic discipline or field is a late nineteenth-century category.[9] Luther does not speak of social ethics per se, but that does not mean that in our sense of the phrase he did not develop it.

What Luther does speak of is service to the neighbor, service that is inseparable from service to God—indeed, *is* service to God. The German language allows expression of the multiple facets of this service to appear: *dienst Gottes* is serving God in Christian vocation, benefiting the neighbor; *Gottesdienst* is translated literally as worship, but it conveys for Luther God's

7. Harding Meyer, " 'Delectari assertionibus' on the Issue of the Authority of Christian Testimony," in Lindberg, *Piety, Politics, and Ethics: Reformation Studies in Honor of George Wolfgang Forell* (Kirksville, Mo.: Sixteenth Century Publishers, 1984), 14. This displacement of authority from God to the world of the Christian was Luther's critique of Karlstadt and Müntzer. Cf. Carter Lindberg, "Theory and Practice: Reformation Models of Ministry as Resource for the Present," LQ 27 (1975), 35; and Lindberg, "Müntzeriana," 202–3.
8. Theodor Strohm, " 'Theologie der Diakonie,' in der Perspektive der Reformation," in Paul Philippi & Theodor Strohm, eds., *Theolgie der Diakonie* (Heidelberg: Heidelberger Verlagsandstalt, 1989), 182. Cf. Luther's exegesis of Psalm 82, LW 13:46–47.
9. Siegfried Bräuer, "Die Theologie Thomas Müntzers als Grundlage seiner sozialethischen Impulse," *Evangelische Monatsschrift Standpunkt* 70/3 (1989), 63.

service—that is, God's creative, giving love in creation and redemption. It is because God serves us that we serve others. As Vilmos Vajta has emphasized in his thorough study of Luther's theology of worship, worship and service to others are inseparable.[10] There is no doubt then that both worship and service are corporate and communal. Luther is not just parroting empty words when in his tract "Concerning the Order of Public Worship," written for the Leisnig community, he admonishes participation in daily worship services not "for the sake of reward, temporal or eternal, but alone to the glory of God and the neighbor's good" (LW 53:15).[11] The reform of worship included the renewal of social life.[12]

Recall that Luther replaced the medieval sacrifice of the mass by communion. It is no accident or whim that Luther's social-ethical critique of the brotherhoods and his suggestions for a common chest are part of his treatise on the Lord's Supper, "The Blessed Sacrament of the Holy and True Body of Christ, and the Brotherhoods" (1519). Luther never tired of focusing attention upon the relationship between worship and social ethics. We have seen how Luther interpreted the collect of the mass as the point in worship for dedication of material goods for distribution to the needy, and how the church orders place offerings on the altar after the proclamation of the gospel.[13] And we may recall once more Luther's affirmation in his "Preface" to the Leisnig order: "Now there is no greater service of God [*gottis dienst*] than Christian love which helps and serves the needy" (LW 45:172; WA 12, 13, 26f). Worship creates the community and the community serves others. The work of the people does not stop at worship but rather begins there as the work of the people for the benefit of others—in what has been called "the liturgy after the liturgy."[14]

The theology and praxis of Luther's social ethics are interrelated and complementary. I began this study by using the formulation of Robert Wuthnow that Luther's theology "was inherently articulated with practical circumstances and yet capable of casting these circumstances in a critical light. He created, as it were, a *discursive field* in which to bring together in imaginative ways the practical realities of institutional life on the one hand and the ideals

10. Vilmos Vajta, *Die Theologie des Gottesdienstes bei Luther* (Stockholm: Svenska Kyrkans Diakonistyrelses Bokförlag, 1952), passim.
11. A recent study of the Lutheran Pietist A. H. Francke (d. 1727), who was active in developing the charitable institutions of Halle, uses this phrase for its title: Gary R. Sattler, *God's Glory, Neighbor's Good* (Chicago: Covenant Press, 1982).
12. Wilhelm Maurer, *Historischer Kommentar zur Confessio Augustana* (Gütersloh, 1978), vol. 2: 177ff.
13. Cf. Vajta, *Theologie des Gottesdienstes*, 310, 110.
14. The useful term "liturgy after the liturgy" is the Orthodox tradition's understanding of ecclesial community marked by the Eucharist and directed toward service to others. This phrase has come into ecumenical service, especially in the World Council of Churches, through the encounter with the Orthodox churches. Cf. Theodor Strohm & Gerhard Schäfer, "Abschliessende Überlegungen: 'Theologie der Diakonie' als Aufgabe ökumenischer Studienarbeit," in Philippi & Strohm, *Theologie der Diakonie*, 240.

evident in Scripture on the other."[15] That discursive field was not buried in learned treatises for other professors but set forth in the vernacular, "for the laity," with suggestions for practical applications. Furthermore, the prime means of communication was oral—the discursive field was proclaimed in sermons and discussions, and inculcated by catechetical instruction. An excellent example of this is the dialogue on the common chest in Schwabach (included in Part Two of this volume).

Recasting Wealth, Poverty, and Salvation

The significance of this discursive field for the development of a new approach to social welfare was to break the grip of medieval theology on the societal understanding of the relationship between wealth, poverty, and salvation. The medieval interpretation and endorsement of poverty as a means to salvation for both rich and poor directed attention away from the social problems of poverty to the world beyond. I do not mean here to gainsay the motivation, inspiration, and spiritual athleticism of individuals—rich and poor—in the Middle Ages. But the medieval theological symbiosis of rich and poor expressed in individualistic charity was unable to constructively address the increasing vagabondage and widespread begging, let alone their underlying causes in the social problems of the day. Poverty and mendicancy were so integral to the theological superstructure that they proved intractable to the late medieval political and legislative efforts to resolve their social effects.

Luther's contribution to this discursive field was to remove the theological legitimation of poverty. If salvation is by grace alone, poverty no longer serves anyone. The poor no longer possess any special sanctity; they are sinners like their wealthier compatriots. With faith, not charity, as the locus for the relationship to God, attention could be focused on this-worldly problems and their causes. Because salvation was no longer understood to be the goal of life but rather the foundation of life, human energy and reason were liberated to this-worldly concerns. The importance of this Reformation shift in perspective is summarized by Adolf Laube:

> Because the entire social order derived its theoretical legitimacy largely from religious-theological notions and because the church, holding a monopoly of that ideology, established itself as the force that guaranteed order, any societal change required theological support in order to challenge the authority of the church. However intense the preparation of

15. Robert Wuthnow, *Communities of Discourse: Ideology and Social Structure in the Reformation, the Enlightenment and European Socialism* (Cambridge: Harvard Univ. Press, 1989), 134. For a fundamental presentation of Luther's law-gospel dialectic in service to his social ethics, see George W. Forell, *Faith Active in Love: An Investigation of the Principles Underlying Luther's Social Ethics* (Minneapolis: Augsburg, 1959).

Humanism, the *Devotio moderna*, conciliarism, and other reform movements, these neither reached the theological core of the dominant world
view, nor would and could they mobilize the masses against the old
powers. It is a characteristic feature of the Reformation that by resorting
to the final and supreme authority, the Word of God, it questioned the
existing societal conditions and thereby gained revolutionary thrust.[16]

Luther was self-conscious about this point. He saw that the root of the
crises of his time was not primarily immorality, lack of love, or personal and
corporate corruption. To be sure, these are all serious concerns and everyone
should work to correct them. But to assume that their correction will overcome
crisis is like assuming that the proverbial rearranging of deck chairs will keep
the Titanic afloat.

It is not the security of a new life, but the certainty of God's activity, that
will overcome crisis. Stated starkly, the issue for Luther was doctrine.

Doctrine and life are to be distinguished. Life is as bad among us as
among the papists. Hence we do not fight and damn them because of
their bad lives. Wycliffe and Hus, who fought over the moral quality of
life, failed to understand this. I do not consider myself to be pious. But
when it comes to whether one teaches correctly about the Word of God,
here I take my stand and fight. That is my calling. To contest doctrine
has never happened until now. Others have fought over life; but to take
on doctrine—that is to grab the goose by the neck! ... When the Word
of God remains pure, even if the quality of life fails us, life is placed in
a position to become what it ought to be. That is why everything hinges
on the purity of the Word. I have succeeded only if I have taught correctly.
(WA TR 1:294–295; LW 54:110)[17]

Luther had no illusions about the universality of sin and the pervasiveness
of evil, and thus he criticized social programs—humanist, Catholic, and Anabaptist—that rested upon the view that the transformation of individuals
would lead to the transformation of society or vice versa. That this insight
was not lost upon his followers is evident in Hans Sachs's dialogue of 1524,
"The Argument of the Romanists against the Profiteering and Other Public
Offenses of the Christian Comunity [of Nuremberg]." Here Romanus, the

16. Adolf Laube, "Radicalism as a Research Problem in the History of the Early
Reformation," in Hans J. Hillerbrand, ed., *Radical Tendencies in the Reformation: Divergent
Perspectives* (Kirksville, Mo.: Sixteenth Century Journal Publishers, 1988), 13.
17. Cited by Steven Ozment, "Humanism, Scholasticism, and the Intellectual Origins
of the Reformation," in F. Forrester Church & Timothy George, eds., *Continuity and
Discontinuity in Church History* (Leiden: Brill, 1979), 148. Cf. Lindberg, "Luther and the
Crises of the Late Medieval Era," 101–2; Lindberg, "Luther's Critique of the Ecumenical
Assumption that Doctrine Divides but Service Unites," *Journal of Ecumenical Studies* 27
(Fall 1990), 679–96, 682–85.

priest, challenges the wealthy evangelical citizen, Reichenburger, to defend the Lutheran movement's ethics and to answer for its failure to transform the city. Reichenburger responds by ascribing the limited moral improvement to the recalcitrance of the old church to change, and concludes by faulting Romanus "for believing in the possibility of a sinless society this side of eternity."[18] The pamphlet does not attest a distancing of the Reformation from social goals; just treatment of workers and generosity for the needy are concerns Reichenburger also shares. It rather suggests the rejection of a moral perfection Protestants did not believe society capable of attaining. As in the religious sphere, so also in the social sphere, the Reformation refused to sanction utopian standards; neither the individual nor the communal conscience was to be burdened by impossible ideals. This is the conviction that the renewal of worship and the renewal of social life are anchored in the gospel, the good news, that the Christian life is not governed by the demand to move from vice to virtue but rather lives from grace. This stands against the transformation of any social agenda, regardless of its merit, into a pseudo-gospel, an ersatz liturgy.

Beginning with Doctrine

The specifics of Luther's economic and social programs are not directly translatable to the present, but his point of departure—doctrine—is a salutary reminder to contemporary theologians and social advocates in the churches of the indispensable theological foundation for social ethics. "What must be seen above all, is how Luther sought to analyse and think through the political, social, and economic phenomena of his time from the perspective of Holy Scripture. On this every theologian in every time can learn from him."[19]

That Luther's point of departure was doctrine—*sacra doctrina*, Scripture—may be perceived as wrongheaded or even offensive to those who struggle to develop a social ethics "from below," from praxis, from social analysis. Luther's emphasis may also be misunderstood in our American culture that so prizes religious toleration on the one hand and moral activism on the other. For these reasons it must be emphasized that Luther's penetrating distinction between doctrine and life is made precisely for the sake of life: "When the Word of God remains pure . . . life is placed in a position to become what it ought to be" (WA TR 1:294–95). Without such a distinction, the twin

18. Steven Ozment, "The Social History of the Reformation: What Can We Learn from the Pamphlets?" in Hans-Joachim Köhler, ed., *Flugschriften als Massenmedium der Reformationszeit* (Stuttgart: Klett-Cotta, 1981), 198–202, citations from 201–2. For another discussion of this dialogue, see John Van Cleve, *The Problem of Wealth in the Literature of Luther's Germany* (Columbia, S.C.: Camden House, 1991), 137–54.
19. Helmar Junghans, "Sozialethisches Denken und Handeln bei Martin Luther," *Evangelische Monatsschrift Standpunkt* 70/3 (1989), 71.

consequences are cheap grace and works-righteousness. The function of doctrine is the proclaiming of the forgiveness of sin as unconditional promise. That is why the church stands or falls on the basis of its relation to the doctrine of justification by grace alone through faith alone.[20]

I hope, by the analysis of Luther's writings about economics in this volume, to make clear that his point of departure by no means excludes but rather demands social analysis from the midst of life. Again, this social analysis flows from Word and sacrament as the source for the identification with the needy. This is the very point being realized in the thousands of base communities in Latin America. "In a day in which the gospel was imprisoned by educated and clerical elites, Luther redeemed it as *viva vox* and gave it into the hands of the people. In Latin America the gospel is read and meditated on in tens of thousands of base Christian communities as the source of prophetic challenge to a system of exploitation and the source of liberating commitment."[21]

The early evangelical church orders made this same point, that it is in the communal hearing of the gospel that the good tree is formed that bears good fruit. So, according to the Braunschweig order, we hear that if we would be Christians we must manifest this in our fruits, the true good works of faith commanded by Christ, "namely that we attend to the needs of our neighbors. With such fruits we indeed testify that we have become the good trees through faith in Christ, and thereby do not deceive ourselves."[22]

The church orders express the inseparableness of obedient service to the neighbor and the liberating realization of faith. The expression of this inseparableness in the church orders' orientation to the needy led to the development of criteria that distinguished between those suffering the emergency contingencies of life and those who were marginalized. The former included the house poor—citizens impoverished through no fault of their own (for example, by an unjust credit system); tradesmen and day laborers who through accident or misfortune fell into hardship; the sick and the disabled who were unable to work; widows and orphans without relatives and friends to support them; poor women in childbed; poor students who had to beg to support themselves. These people were seen as the "legitimate poor" (*rechten Armen*), who must be supported for more or less time according to their situation.

---

20. Carter Lindberg, "Justification by Faith Alone: The Lutheran Proposal to the Churches," *New Conversations* 10/2 (1988), 31.

21. Leonardo Boff, "Luther, the Reformation, and Liberation," in Dow Kirkpatrick, ed., *Faith Born in the Struggle for Life: A Rereading of Protestant Faith in Latin America Today* (Grand Rapids, Mich.: Eerdmans, 1988), 211. The South African theologian Simon Maimela also emphasized the importance of social analysis in Luther's works; see Lindberg, "Luther on Property and Poverty," *Luther-Jahrbuch* 57 (1990), 251. For a presentation and discussion of Luther and liberation theology, see Scott W. Gustafson, "Some 'Lutheranisms' in Liberation Theology?" *Lutheran Theological Seminary Bulletin* 68 (1988): 34–51.

22. Sehling 6/1:445f. Cited by Scharffenorth, *Glauben ins Leben ziehen*, 113.

According to Bugenhagen, common sense can distinguish these legitimate poor from those who are lazy, drink too much, or in other ways waste their resources in an unseemly way and should not be supported.

The latter group, those marginalized in an urban society who should be helped, included endangered spouses and children in ruined marriages; sick or poor strangers with no place to turn; prisoners (because Christ said to visit them); and those awaiting capital punishment.

Congregational members are to be involved in helping the people in these two groups by putting all their own resources, their gifts from God, in service to the neighbor because contributions to the common chest will not be sufficient. The church orders catalog these forms of support in terms of food, money, clothing, and warm meals for the poor, sick, children, and women in childbirth; care of the elderly, house poor, children, and abandoned women; repayable interest-free loans to help people get established; loans, generally not repayable, to young tradesmen to enable marriage that otherwise would be impossible without a higher salary; dowries for single maidens; support for poor students; visiting services for the sick and imprisoned; and personal initiative to help those neighbors perceived to need it. In short, the church orders set forth a community diaconate that reflected what Luther had taught in his 1519 sermon on the Lord's Supper—everyone in need should bring his or her concerns before the community and be assisted.

These steps toward a more credible Christian community were taken under difficult external conditions that included counter-Reformation measures by ecclesial and worldly authorities, wars within the empire, threats of Turkish invasions and campaigns against the Turks, plagues, food shortages due to bad harvests, and the upheavals of the Reformation.[23] In many areas these conditions continued to worsen as the wars of religion raged until exhausted in the Thirty Years' War that ended in 1648. Nevertheless, the church order had given legislative forms to Luther's vision of the liturgy after the liturgy; in many cases these forms lasted into modern times. The attempt to resolve social problems in the cities was a constitutive component of the early Reformation, and the decisive theoretical breakthrough for the attempt goes back to Luther.[24]

---

23. Scharffenorth, *Glauben ins Leben Ziehen*, 115–18, with references to Sehling.
24. Adolf Laube, "Martin Luther und die Anfänge des städtischen Sozialréformen," paper presented at the Sixth International Congress for Luther Research, Erfurt, 1983; I am grateful to Professor Laube for sharing his paper with me. See also Laube, *Flugschriften*, vol. 2: 1003, 1011.

Part Two

Sources on Poverty and Social WELFARE

Chapter 5

Late Medieval Attitudes to Begging and Poverty

5.1 Canon Law (post-1140)

CANON LAW is the collection of ecclesial rules and decrees concerned with matters of faith, morals, and discipline that gradually accumulated in the Western church. The development of canon law is usually associated with the work of the twelfth-century Italian monk Gratian, whose "Concordance of Discordant Canons" (*Concordantia Discordantium Canonum* or *Decretum Gratiani*) of 1140 became the basic text for ecclesial law. The following brief passages illustrate the medieval efforts to discriminate between the deserving and undeserving poor.

Source: Georges Herzog, trans., appendix to Brian Tierney, "The Decretists and the 'Undeserving Poor,' " in *Comparative Studies in Society and History*, vol. 1 (London/New York: Cambridge Univ. Press, 1958–59), 371–73.

We should not show our liberality indifferently to all who come to us. But we should know that these four following aspects require our attention when we are giving hospitality: the quality of the beggar, the capacity of the donor, ... the reason for the demand, ... the quantity being requested....

The order of charity is indeed such that you first provide for your relatives and that you help them with kindness, but not that you make them rich.... Nothing should be given to simulators, harlots, and hunters of alms because when you give to them you give not to the person but to a most worthless species to which nothing should be given; unless they are in extreme necessity, in which case give to the person and not to the species. . . . The same can be said about heretics and the anathematized. . . .

In regard to these statements, it is evident that we should not show our liberality indiscriminately to all who come to us because they are different from each other. . . .

If, however, we are not able to give to everybody, the righteous should be preferred to the unrighteous, the good to the bad, the member of the family to the stranger, the religious to the non-religious, and it should be given to the best, the nearest member of the family or the most religious, rather than to the less good, or the one who is not from your near family or the less religious . . . unless this bad or sinful or foreign or irreligious or not so good or not so familiar or less religious person is in such a great indigence that he would die without our help. In this case, our help should go to them as prescribed in *Pasce* 86, and so all the authorities agree entirely when they speak of the manner to give alms or hospitality with discrimination or without discrimination.

5.2 Jacques de Vitry (d. c. 1240)

THE FOLLOWING SERMON illustration and the account of hospital care are by Jacques de Vitry, a French bishop, cardinal, and patriarch of Jerusalem. He was a world traveler and historian who wrote a great deal but left little autobiographical data. He is well known for his use of *exempla*, illustrative stories to drive home moral and religious convictions, and for his *Historia Occidentalis*, "History of the West." The latter work has been of value to historians interested in thirteenth-century European life and religion.

Sources: Marshall W. Baldwin, ed., *Christianity through the Thirteenth Century* (New York: Harper & Row, 1970), 396; John Frederick Hinnebusch, *The Historia Occidentalis of Jacques de Vitry: A Critical Edition*, trans. Carter Lindberg (Fribourg: University Press, 1972), 146–51.

A *Sermon* Illustration

Moreover, although poverty and other tribulations are advantageous, yet certain ones abuse them. Accordingly we read that when the body of Saint Martin was borne in procession it healed all the infirm who met it. Now there were near the church two wandering beggars, one blind, the other lame, who began to converse together and said, "See, the body of Saint Martin is now being borne in procession, and if it catches us we shall be healed immediately, and no one in the future will give us alms, but we shall have to work and labor with our hands." Then the blind man said to the lame, "Get up on my shoulders because I am strong, and you who see well can guide me." They did this; but when they wished to escape, the procession overtook them; and since, on account of the throng, they were not able to get away, they were healed against their will.

"Concerning Hospitals for the Poor and Homes for the Lepers"

In addition to the above, there are innumerable men as well as women in all the congregations of the West who, renouncing the world and living according to the rule, are living in homes for lepers or hospitals for the poor. In all these places they are ministering humbly and devoutly to the poor and the sick. They live according to the rule of Saint Augustine without anything of their own, and in common under obedience to one superior. And having taken up the religious habit, they promise to the Lord perpetual continence.

The men and the women eat and sleep separately from each other with all reverence and chastity. They do not neglect to hear the canonical hours of the day and night insofar as the hospitality and ministry to the poor of Christ permits. In the larger houses there is an assembly for worship, and numerous brothers and sisters frequently gather together in Chapter for correcting faults of negligence or for other necessary and honorable reasons. There are also frequent readings of divine scripture recited aloud to them at meals, and silence is observed in the refectory and other certain places and at established times. Sick men and healthy guests who are received in the house must eat and sleep separate from the women.

Their chaplains, ministering in spiritual matters with all humility and devotion to the poor and sick, instruct the ignorant by preaching the divine word, console the faint-hearted and feeble, and exhort them to endurance and actions of grace. They continually celebrate the divine office day and night in the common chapel, in order that all the sick who are strong enough may hear from their beds. They diligently and solicitously administer confession and extreme unction, and other sacraments to the sick, and burial to those who of necessity die.

These therefore are the ministers of Christ, sober and spare to themselves and very austere and severe to their own bodies, [but] deeply compassionate and feeling with respect to the poor and the sick, ministering to their needs according to their own powers. These ministers of Christ are all the more lowly in the house of the Lord as they are of higher degree in the world. Moreover for Christ's sake, very many of them suffer the filth of the sick and nearly intolerable annoyances, thereby inflicting outrages upon themselves to which no other kind of penitance may be conceived to compare to this martyrdom holy and precious in the sight of God. Therefore this filthy excrement by which their spirits are being fertilized toward fructification will be changed by the Lord into precious stones and it will bring forth a sweet fragrance.

Abuses by Some Congregations Yet this holy and God-pleasing hospital-order and religion of hospitality has been so corrupted in many places and houses, deplorably reduced to nothing, that the vile and abominable reprobate congregation offends not only those who have recognized their thorough wickedness but also the eyes of God. For under pretense of hospitality and feigning piety, they have become seekers of gain, liars, persons of deception using any means to extort money. Moreover they care not for the poor, but support themselves from the poor except when occasionally offering a small amount to the poor and sick in order, like cunning traders, to exact alms fraudulently from the faithful, and thereby to generate more for themselves. For they give a very little amount to the poor in order that they might receive abundantly; under pretext of alms they seek riches. They are hunters rather than mediating benefactors. Thus they seize things like wild beasts, like birds of prey, like fish. They put a few coins in the money sack in order to beg for more. They beg for alms with such persistency, irreverence, and agitation that respect of religion is confounded and rendered contemptible. It was against this that Saint Jerome said: "It is better not to have what is given than shamelessly to beg for it."

And also very often bearded brothers shamefully acquire much by outward hypocrisy, or by means of hired servants and lying chaplains who are not afraid to deceive the simple and to send their falcons into the harvest of another, or by misusing indulgence letters for shameful greed. That is to say nothing concerning the most evil crime of forging false letters and using stolen bulls to their perdition; they are not afraid of anything. Indeed, that which they shamefully amass they use up more shamefully "in reveling and drunkenness" (cf. Rom. 13:13), and other things done in secret and darkness.

But though they do these things shamelessly, it is a disgrace to us to utter these things now.

Those abusers living under religious rule and ordained to purity retain nothing but their outer religious garments, nearly all of them accept simony. They who shamefully become monks or nuns live together in the most scandalous imitation of others in the same place, in murmuring and dissension, in strife and sedition, in idleness and dissolution, in retention of purse and things, in bed chamber and impurity and all sorts of filthiness, without affection, without mercy, without covenant. They compound their ostentation and seduction in ornate beds emptied of the poor and sick. They convert the houses of hospitality and piety into dens of robbers, prostitutes, and synagogues of the Jews.

Praise for Other Congregations However, such noxious corruption and detestable hypocrisy does not fill all houses of hospitality. For some are congregations living under a religious rule, some originally places of worship, or principally hospitals in which fervent love, the unction of piety, seemly be-havior, and severe discipline are not wanting. Among these are the Hospital of the Holy Spirit in Rome, the Hospital of Saint Samson and the Hospital of Saint Anthony in Constantinople, and the Hospital of Saint Mary at Ron-cevalles in Navarre, and others that are pleasing to God and very necessary for poor pilgrims and the sick. Moreover in Paris and Noyon in France, Provins in Compania, Tournai in Flanders, Liège in Lorraine, and Brussels in Brabant, there are hospitals of piety and noble houses, workshops of sanctity, convents of comeliness and religion, refuges of the poor, aids of compassion, conso-lation to the mourning, refreshment to the hungry, and sweetness and sooth-ing to the sick.

5.3 John Hus (1371–1415)

HUS, BOHEMIAN reformer and martyr, stood in the tradition of a Czech reform movement dating back to about the mid-fourteenth century that emphasized "cultivation of the spiritual life, renunciation of the world, austerities of apostolic poverty, frequent communion, and the 'imitation of Christ.' " Thus while Luther admired Hus, it is misleading to posit a continuity between the Hussite reform movement and that of the six-teenth century. Hus expressed his attitude toward almsgiving and begging in his sharp attack on church immorality titled *On Simony* (1413). The following excerpt on charity trusts illustrates some of the abuses later attacked by sixteenth-century reformers.

Source: *The Library of Christian Classics*, vol. 14: *Advocates of Reform*, ed. Mat-thew Spinka (Philadelphia: Westminster Press, 1953), 259–60.

"On Charity Trusts" (1413)

As for the alms which were left in trust to be distributed among the poor, patrons sin gravely when they do not so distribute them. Some donors have specified by will that cloth be distributed among the poor, or certain food, or some other alms, but patrons keep it to themselves, or distribute it among their relatives or servants, or to others for favor's sake, as if they were giving of their own, desiring thus to gain praise; and to the very needy unfortunates they give nothing. This sin is particularly common among monks, priests, and burghers: for monks, collecting bequests enjoining them to distribute money, cloth, or food among the poor, do not do so; the priests, that they might feed the poor in lean days or at other times, do not feed them; and likewise the burghers. . . .

Hence, learn to know yourselves, ye robbers of the poor, murderers, thieves, and sacrilegious! . . . It is certain that they are robbers; for they dis-possess the poor of their property. Likewise it is evident that they are thieves, for they steal what belongs to others. They are also simoniacs and sacrilegious because they steal holy alms, which are called holy because they were dedicated to the Lord, who is holy above all that are holy, and because man gives to the poor in order to be holy. A reasonable man will perceive therefrom how gravely men sin in respect of alms, those that give them, those that manage them, as well as those who receive them: the first by giving out of ill-gotten wealth; the second by keeping it for themselves or by improper distribution; and the third by receiving it unworthily. For the last named are guilty of receiving alms unworthily if they have no need of it; or if they take too much; or if they waste it profligately; and all of them by generally wrangling about the alms.

It is best, therefore, that a man give alms while still alive, without aspiring to leave behind him a perpetual charity trust. For nowhere in the Scriptures is it stated that men should establish perpetual charity endowments, but it is stated that while living men ought to give alms to the poor, so that after they die they may immediately enjoy the reward of eternal bliss.... But a faithful lover of God gives the poor, while he is alive, whatever he can, in accordance with His command; for thus he lays up a treasure for himself which he can enjoy promptly after death. For he dispatches it on ahead, that it may be ready for him after he leaves the world. For the Lord Jesus, his apostles, and other saints, have not established perpetual charity trusts.

5.4 Johann Geiler of Kaysersberg (1445–1510)

A DOCTOR OF THEOLOGY and successful academic at the universities of Freiburg in Breisgau and Basel, Geiler accepted an official preaching position created for him in Strasbourg in 1478. As preacher in the famous cathedral of Strasbourg, he was also unofficial preacher for the diocese and an advocate of various reforms of the city and church. The following advice on poor relief is from his attack on the city authorities, *Die XXI Artikel.*

Source: Trans. Carter Lindberg, from Christoph Sachsse & Florian Tennstedt, eds., *Geschichte der Armenfürsorge in Deutschland: Vom Spätmittelalter bis zum 1. Weltkrieg* (Stuttgart: Kohlhammer, 1980), 56.

"Concerning Begging"

A necessary matter, not only here [Strasbourg] but throughout Christendom, would be to take care that alms be rightly dispensed to the poor and not given to the unworthy who need it least of all.... We owe it out of our own humanity to provide for the poor and to be zealous in this matter. Therefore the Emperor and the assembly of princes should take over this, as it has been suggested but in vain. Therefore it is necessary that every community support their own poor. By God's grace there is a large amount of alms in this city through various contributions. The difficulty, however, lies in their distribution. It would be necessary for this purpose that a few be chosen to take on the business of administration [of alms]. And an ordinance would be necessary according to which the able-bodied beggars or children who could earn their bread would be urged to work, and only those unable to work be provided with alms. Also, they [the poor] must be divided into six or seven groups with each group under the direction of one whose abilities are trusted It is too much to expect that one person would be able to keep things in order for six or seven groups. Other measures must be conceived whereby this inordinate mess can be straightened out.

5.5 Nuremberg Begging Order of 1478

AN EXAMPLE of Geiler's call for "other measures" is Nuremberg's effort to control begging. As early as 1370, Nuremberg prohibited strangers from begging in the city for more than three days. The spread of begging orders throughout the late medieval cities indicates how difficult begging was to control.

Source: Trans. Carter Lindberg, from Christoph Sachsse & Florian Tennstedt, eds., *Geschichte der Armenfürsorge in Deutschland: Vom Spätmittelalter bis zum 1. Weltkrieg* (Stuttgart: Kohlhammer, 1980), 64–66.

The honorable city council has been informed often and emphatically, fully and credibly that some beggars and beggaresses live a life without fear of God, even lives that are unseemly and unbecoming. Also that there are some who come here to Nuremberg for alms, demanding and taking them, even though they are not needy. And because alms, when they are given, are a particularly praiseworthy, meritorious, virtuous, and good work, and because those that take alms without need or falsely are thereby burdened by a heavy and manifest wrong, the above-named, our councillors, to the praise of God but also from necessity, undertake to prevent such dishonesty and danger from swindling whereby poor, distressed persons are deprived from their support by alms. To this end they desire to establish and earnestly command that the following ordinance, avoidance of which shall incur the herein contained penalties, shall be enforced and kept, according to which everyone is to comply:

First, our councillors direct, establish, and command that neither citizens nor visitors—men or women—in this city of Nuremberg may beg either day or night unless permission to do so is granted by the appropriate person appointed by the honorable council.

And whoever has received such permission shall not beg unless they openly wear the beggar's badge that is given them. Whoever begs without permission and the badge shall remain a year and a mile away from this city.

Beggars and beggaresses who are ashamed to beg by day and desire to beg only at night will be given a special badge. In the summer they are to beg no longer than two hours in the night, and in the winter no longer than three hours, and not without a light according to the law of the city ordinance.

Then each beggar and beggaress, before being given permission and the badge, shall inform in an appropriate manner the lords chosen [by the council] the truth of their condition, their health, whether married or single, and number of children in order to determine whether they are dependent or not on begging. Whoever holds back the truth shall remain a year and a mile outside the city. In addition, even if begging is necessary to such a person, permission will not be granted unless he brings at least every year from his father confessor a statement that he has at least confessed and received absolution.

Beggars will not be permitted to beg if they have children with them among whom one is eight years old and without disability because they could very well earn their own bread. However, if a man or woman beggar has four or five children, all under seven years, and also a child over eight to watch the rest, then the elected lords shall be entitled to make an allowance.

The names of such beggars' children who are over eight and are healthy, and who would not be helped by their parents to [find] work, shall be indicated to the bailiff. This is in order to be able to pick them up, make note of them, and determine whether they can be helped to employment here or in the countryside.

The beggars who are permitted to beg here and who are not cripples, lame, or blind shall not sit idly at the begging place in front of the church on any work day, but rather do spinning or other work they are able to perform in their situation. Whoever is discovered acting differently than this shall remain a mile outside the city for a month. The beggars and beggaresses who according to the above regulations are allowed to beg here shall not go into the churches to beg, but rather sit, stand, or walk around them. The churches of St. Moritz, St. Nicholas, and St. Kunigunde are excepted from this. And if it rains and storms, they may seek shelter in the other churches, sitting or standing in the area around the church doors so long as they do not request alms from anyone. Whoever disobeys this shall be banned from the city for a year.

Also, that beggar, be he citizen or visitor, who is permitted to beg, and who has a nasty looking injury on his body or his limbs, the sight of which could cause detriment [to the well-being] of pregnant women, shall cover such wounds and not allow them to be openly visible or displayed. Otherwise he shall be banned from the city for a year.

Also, neither a resident nor a visiting beggar who is permitted to beg shall sing, tell tales, or put on shows, be they paintings, images, miraculous animals, or other things, in a church or in any place in the city on the public streets; but he may stand there and request alms like the other poor people. An exception is if anyone keeps moving along the lanes singing begging songs; this shall be permitted. Those who violate this and are apprehended shall have their props taken away by the city servant or bailiff, including the money earned by singing or by exhibition; and this transgressor shall not return to the city for a year.

Those who are not citizens may also beg here, but, however, for not more than two days every quarter year. And they may not beg without the knowledge of the honorable council's elected commission, and they must be able to recite the Lord's Prayer, the Ave Maria, the Creed, and the Ten Commandments. The exceptions to this regulation are the three days before and after the presentations of the saints, All Saints' Day and All Souls' Day. Those discovered transgressing this regulation shall be prohibited from the city for a year.

Poor priests, including foreign and wandering priests, who because of failing eyesight or other bodily infirmities can no longer perform their priestly vocation, but who are honorable, may respectably request alms in front of the churches. However, it must be known beforehand that they are priests.

Everyone who is poor through his own fault shall not beg for more than a day here in the city if he wishes to avoid being prohibited for a year.

Likewise, recognized penitents whose penance was not imposed here shall not beg more than one day a year here in the city if they wish to avoid the city prohibition of a year.

Also the lepers, whether local or foreign, shall not go about the city begging. Local lepers especially shall confine themselves to their assigned places. And foreign lepers to whom this is communicated shall also behave this way under penalty of being banned from the city for a year. Only during Passion Week may the lepers enter as it has been the custom for some time.

If a student desires to seek alms here, he shall not be allowed unless he goes punctually to school and behaves as an obedient student. The schoolmaster shall appropriately punish students who behave otherwise. If there is a necessity, the honorable council will render help.

Our lords of the council determine and command, also from important motives, that no one among the citizens, neither a renter nor an innkeeper nor anyone else, shall maintain nor lodge a student for longer than three days who is not himself a citizen here or a child of a citizen, regularly goes to school, and conducts himself appropriately. Whoever violates this shall for penance bring twenty pounds each day to the Town Hall.

There shall also be no begging here by women in childbed; they shall not lie before the churches nor obstruct begging there unless it is allowed to the honorable women who are appointed to look after the women in childbed, and they have a badge made for this occasion. When the childbed period is over, the badge is to be returned. Whoever violates this law shall be banned from the city for a year.

Even so no one here in the churches, houses, nor in the lanes shall beg for a woman in childbed unless that woman and those who beg for her possess permission and the special badge for this. When the period of child-bed is then over, the badge must be returned. Everyone who violates this law shall be banned from the city for a year.

The honorable council will especially supervise the beggars, and if they are guilty of inappropriate behavior punish them as the council deems appropriate to their manner. Offenses are decreed.

Also, no pilgrims, residents, nor public innkeepers shall lodge or maintain any beggar longer than three days unless permission is obtained from the particular lords. Otherwise a pound of new pennies is due for each day for each person.

The Begging Judge or Begging Master depends upon exact information from those whom the honorable council entrust with the above described matters and thereby has instituted. When, outside the city servant or bailiff, one informs against or charges anyone and proves that one or more of the above presented offenses have been committed, he shall be rewarded with nine pennies for each individual case and each person.

This legal ordinance becomes effective on Laetare Sunday in the year 1478.

5.6 Martin Luther's "Foreword" to Mathias Hütlin, Liber Vagatorum (1510)

THE LIBER VAGATORUM ("The Book of Vagabonds") is discussed in Part One, chapter 1. The translation is based on both Luther's "Foreword" and edition in WA 26:638–51 and the modern German edition in Boehncke & Johannsmeier. I also compared my translation with that of D. B. Thomas in J. C. Hotten, *Liber Vagatorum: The Book of Vagabonds & Beggars* (London: Penguin, 1932). Georges Herzog's translation of this tract for my course at Boston University was also very helpful.

Source: Trans. Carter Lindberg, from Heiner Boehncke & Rolf Johannsmeier, *Das Buch der Vaganten, Spieler, Huren, Leutbetrüger* (Cologne: Prometh Verlag, 1987), 79–97.

This booklet about the trickery of beggars was first printed by someone who called himself "*Expertum in truffis*," that is, a fellow experienced in roguery. This booklet would have proved this even if he had not named himself. It seemed to me a good thing that this booklet should not be neglected but rather should become known everywhere so that one can see and understand how the devil rules so powerfully in the world, and so that it could help enlighten people to be on the lookout for him [the devil]. This Rotwelsch language is clearly from the Jews, for there are many Hebraic words in it, as those who know Hebrew will understand.

But the real understanding and the true admonition of this booklet is certainly this: that princes, lords, town councils, and everyone shall become wise and see and know the beggars. They should also learn that while people will not give to and help the house poor and the needy neighbor, as God has commanded; people will be stimulated by the devil for fear of God's judgment to give ten times too much to such depraved and unscrupulous tricksters, just like we have been doing up to now in giving to foundations, cloisters, churches, chapels, and mendicant monks, all the while forsaking the true poor.

Therefore every town and village should know and be acquainted with its own poor, listing them in a register so that they can help them. But foreign beggars ought not be tolerated without a letter or seal, for there is far too much roguery among them, as mentioned by this booklet. And if a town were aware of its poor, then such roguery would soon be discovered and forbidden. I myself in recent years have been fooled by these vagabonds and blabbermouths more than I wish to confess. Therefore, he who will be warned, be warned and do good to his neighbor according to Christian love, manner, and command. May God help us. Amen.

Honest Beggars (Bregern) The first chapter concerns the *breger*. These are beggars who do not wear any signs or only a few of the saints. They present themselves plainly and simply before people and ask alms only for the sake of God and the Virgin.

Some are among the house poor, a homeless man with children who is known in the village where he begs. And if they could make a comeback with their work or other honorable things, they would no doubt abandon begging. For there are many pious persons who beg unwillingly and who are ashamed before those they know, since earlier they had enough but now have to beg. If he could get ahead, he would give up begging. Conclusion: It is proper to give to these beggars because the money is well placed.

Falling Sickness (Grantnern) The eighth chapter concerns the *Grantnern*. They are beggars who say in the farmhouses, "Oh, my dear friend, look, I am afflicted with the falling sickness of Saint Valentine, or Saint Kurin, or Saint Vitus, or Saint Anthony, and I vowed to give to these beloved saints an offering of six pounds of wax, an altar cloth, and a silver salver (etc.). Now I have to get this from the contributions and help of pious people. Therefore, I beg you to contribute a penny, some flax or some yarn for the altar cloth. May God and the dear saints protect you well from plagues and days of illness." Note this false trick: some fall down even in front of churches, they take soap in their mouths in order to have foam come out as thick as a fist. And they pierce their nostrils with a straw to bleed as if they had the plague. And it's all knavery. These are vagabonds who infest all the countries. Likewise, many of them provide for themselves this way by saying: "Be aware, dear friend, that I am the son of a butcher, of an artisan. Once a beggar came to my father's house and begged for the sake of Saint Valentine. My father gave me a penny to give to him. I said, 'Father, this is a trick!' My father commanded me to give it to him, but I didn't. At that moment I got the falling sickness. I vowed to Saint Valentine to give three pounds of wax as well as a sung mass. And thus now I have to ask and beg this from pious people because I promised to do so. Otherwise I would have had enough by my own means. Therefore I beg you for your contribution and help, so that the dear Saint Valentine might protect and preserve."

Everything he says are lies. He has asked for more than twenty years for these three pounds of wax and the mass, but with the fruits of his begging he gambles, drinks, and buys women. And there are many who use even more subtle words than these noted here. Some have letters and seals confirming their situation is true.

Conclusion: If some *Grantner* comes to your house or is before the church, and begs plainly and simply for the sake of God, and does not use flowery words, then you should give to him because many people really are burdened with this difficult sickness of the saints.

But if the *Grantner* use many words and speak of great wonders and how they have taken vows; and if they use their tongues skillfully, that is a sign that they have been in this business a long time. They are no doubt false, for they talk up those who believe them and take a nut from their tree. Beware of them and don't give them anything.

Fake Begging Priests (*Schleppern*) The tenth chapter is about the *Schleppern*. They are learned beggars who present themselves as priests. They come to the houses accompanied by a student who carries their sack. They say, "I am an ordained priest with the name of Mr. Jörg Kessler from Kitzbühel (or whatever he likes to call himself), and I am from the village and family of such and such (they use well-known names), and I will celebrate my first mass at this village, and I am going to be ordained at the altar in the village or that church which now has no altar cloth or mass book. I will not be able to get these things without a special contribution and the help of everyone." And the donor helps himself toward the angels with thirty early masses in Advent for his gift, or he can liberate as many souls of his family as he gives pennies.

Likewise, they also enroll the peasants in a brotherhood, and say that it was authorized by the bishop with the blessing of grace and an indulgence of sins in order to complete the altar. These are the means to move the people. One gives yarn, the other fine linen or flax, one a tablecloth or towels or silver.

This is not a brotherhood like the others such as the mendicants had, because the others have inspectors coming every year, but the founder of this brotherhood never comes back (if he did he'd be drowned).

Likewise, this treachery is seen in nearly the entire Schwarzwald, and Brigenzerwald, in Kurwalen, in Bar, and in Allgäu, Etschland, and Switzerland where there are few priests, and where the churches and the farms are far apart.

Conclusion: Give nothing to these *Schleppern* or tramps because it's a bad affair. For example, one named Mansuetus invited peasants to come to see his first mass in St. Gall. They looked for him but couldn't find him. After lunch they found him in the whorehouse, but he escaped them.

Fake Salves (*Seffern*) The twenty-fifth chapter is concerned with the *Seffern*. These beggars cover themselves with a salve, layer on layer, and then they go and lie in front of the churches. It seems as if they have an illness because their face and mouth appear broken out in sores. But when they go to the bathhouse three days later, they are completely cured.

Fake Sickness (*Schweigern*) The twenty-sixth chapter deals with the *Schweigern*. These beggars take horse manure, mix it with water, and paint their hands and arms with it. They are thus transformed as if they had the yellow sickness [hepatitis?] or some other dread disease, which it is not. Thereby they delude the people and are thus called *Schweiger.*

Chapter 6

Renaissance and Reformation Perspectives

6.1 *Desiderius Erasmus* (c. 1469–1536)

"BEGGAR TALK" appeared in print in 1524. Thus it appeared after the major writings of Karlstadt and Luther, the social welfare orders of Leisnig, Nuremberg, and Strasbourg; and two years before the writing by Vives. Note that the beggars' ruses in this colloquy echo the descriptions of false beggars provided in the *Liber Vagatorum*. The names of the characters reflect their "trade"—Misoponus means "hater of work," and Irides means "son of Irus," the beggar in the *Odyssey*.

Source: Craig R. Thompson, trans. & ed., *The Colloquies of Erasmus* (Chicago: Univ. of Chicago Press, 1965), 250–54.

"*Beggar Talk*" (1524)

Irides: What strange bird do I see flying this way? The face I recognize, but the clothes don't suit. Either I'm simply doting or this is Misoponus. The chance must be taken: I'll accost the fellow, ragged as I am.—Greetings, Misoponus.
Misoponus: Irides, I see.
Irides: Greetings, Misoponus.
Misop.: Be quiet, I say.

Irides: What? You don't want to be greeted?

Misop.: Not by that name, certainly.

Irides: What's the matter? Aren't you the same person you had been? Or is your name changed along with your clothes?

Misop.: No, but I've got my old one back.

Irides: Who were you then?

Misop.: Apitius.

Irides: Don't be ashamed of your old pal if you've met with better luck. It wasn't very long ago that you were in our order.

Misop.: Come over here out of the way, if you please, and you'll hear the whole story. I'm not ashamed of your order but of the first order.

Irides: What order are you talking about, the Franciscan?

Misop.: Not at all, my good friend: the order of the down-and-out.

Irides: Well, you've plenty of company in *that* order!

Misop.: I was rich. I threw the money away. When it was gone, nobody knew Apitius. I ran away in disgrace and joined your club, preferring that to digging.

Irides: You were wise. But where did this strange sleekness come from? For your change of clothes isn't so surprising.

Misop.: Why?

Irides: Because the goddess Laverna enriches many men unexpectedly.

Misop.: Do you suppose I've become rich by stealth?

Irides: Perhaps by a lazier way, then—by open robbery.

Misop.: No, by your goddess Poverty! Neither by stealth nor by robbery. But first let me explain my handsomeness, which seems to surprise you so.

Irides: In our company you were covered all over with sores.

Misop.: Well, I've employed a very kind physician.

Irides: Who?

Misop.: None other than myself—unless you think there's anybody better disposed to myself than I am.

Irides: But I wasn't aware that you practiced medicine.

Misop.: All that decoration of mine I had put on with paints, turpentine, sulphur, resin, birdlime, linen cloth, and blood. When I felt like doing so, I took off what I had put on.

Irides: Imposter! There was nothing more wretched-looking than you were. You might have played Job in the tragedy.

Misop.: My need compelled it at the time; though Fortune too sometimes changes her skin.

Irides: Tell me about fortune, then. Did you find some treasure?

Misop.: No, but a more comfortable source of income than your slight one.

Irides: How could you make money when you had no stroke of luck?

Misop.: A profession's a livelihood anywhere.

Irides: I understand: you mean the profession of picking pockets.

Misop.: Don't put it like that. I mean the profession of alchemy.

Irides: It's hardly fifteen days since you left us, and have you mastered an art that others have scarcely learned in many years?

Misop.: I found a short cut.

Irides: What, I beg you?

Misop.: Your profession had brought me about four gold pieces. By good luck I fell in with an old crony who hadn't managed his fortune any better than I had mine. We had some drinks together. As often happens, he began to tell me his story. I struck a bargain with him: I'd pay for the drinks and he'd let me in on his trade secrets. He imparted them in good faith; now they're my means of support.

Irides: May not one learn them?

Misop.: I'll share them with you for auld lang syne. You know there are lots of people everywhere who are dying to learn this art.

Irides: I've heard that and I believe it.

Misop.: I worm my way into their company every chance I get. I boast of my art. When I see a sucker, I prepare the bait. . . .

Irides: Is your profit from this profession enough to support you?

Misop.: Oh, yes; in fine style, too. Hereafter, if you're smart, you'll give up this wretchedness and join my order.

Irides: Oh, no, I'd rather try to get you back into mine.

Misop.: What? Voluntarily return to what I've once fled from and give up the good thing I've found?

Irides: My profession has the advantage of becoming more attractive as you grow accustomed to it. Hence, though there are many men who quit the Franciscan or Benedictine order, did you ever see one who left mine after having lived in it for some time? For you could hardly taste the pleasures of begging in merely a few months.

Misop.: That taste taught me it's the most miserable thing there is.

Irides: Then why does nobody give it up?

Misop.: Maybe because some men are naturally miserable.

Irides: I wouldn't trade this "misery" even for king's wealth. For begging's the nearest thing to possessing a kingdom.

Misop.: What do I hear? Coal's the nearest thing to snow?

Irides: Tell me, in what respect are kings luckiest?

Misop.: In being free to do as they please.

Irides: This freedom, than which nothing is sweeter, belongs to no king more than it does to us. I don't doubt there are many kings who envy us. Whether there's war or peace, we're safe. We're not drafted for the army; we're not called to public offices; we're not taxed when the public is plundered by levies. No one investigates our lives. If any crime is committed, even an uncommonly savage one, who would think a beggar worth arresting? Even if we strike a man, he's ashamed to fight with a beggar. Neither in peace nor war may kings enjoy themselves, and the mightier they are the more men they fear. The common people have a superstitious dread of harming us, as though we were under God's protection.

Misop.: But meanwhile you live in filthy rags and huts.

Irides: What have these to do with true happiness? What you're talking about is external to man. To these rags we owe our happiness.

Misop.: But I'm afraid you're going to lose a good deal of this happiness before long.

Irides: How so?

Misop.: Because citizens are already muttering that beggars shouldn't be allowed to roam about at will, but that each city should support its own beggars and all the able-bodied ones forced to work.

Irides: Why are they planning this?

Misop.: Because they find prodigious crimes committed under pretext of begging. In the second place, there's not a little danger from your order.

Irides: I've often heard talk of this kind. It will be done at the Greek calends.

Misop.: Sooner than you'd like, perhaps.

6.2 Andreas Bodenstein von Karlstadt (c. 1480–1541)

THE FOLLOWING TRACT by Luther's Wittenberg colleague is the second half of a larger writing that advocates the abolition of both idolatrous images and begging, *Von abtuhung der Bylder und das keyn Bedtler unther den Christen seyn sollen*. Karlstadt clearly shares Luther's concern for preventive action against the causes of poverty and for increased effectiveness of social welfare; note also his suggestions for job training and start-up loans for business ventures.

Source: Carter Lindberg, ed. & trans., *Piety, Politics, and Ethics: Reformation Studies in Honor of George Wolfgang Forell* (Kirksville, Mo.: Sixteenth Century Journal Publishers, 1984), 157–66.

"There Should Be No Beggars among Christians" (1522)

I have said, and I will say it incessantly: beggars are a sure sign that no Christians or few and discouraged Christians are in a city in which beggars are seen. That is easily understood. Beggars are running all about after bread, begging in the streets, before the houses, or sitting before the churches. We should not tolerate but rather banish such people; not in an unreasonable and tyrannical manner but rather with willing help so that we Christians shall allow no one to come into such poverty and need that he is afflicted and caused to go and cry out after bread. Therefore I say that we always have poor brothers and sisters [Matt. 26:11] who are in need of our help and aid. But we should pay diligent heed to our neighbors and fellow Christians and come to help their need before they cry out to us. If we do not do this then we are not Christians. . . .

In short, I will introduce a beautiful text which is clear, and runs thus: There shall be no beggar among you because the Lord your God blessed you in the earth which he gave you to possess [Deut. 15:4]. Look how God has forbidden beggary to his faithful, and how he promises the blessed that they shall have no poor among them. The text continues [Deut. 15:7f.].

If one of your brothers who dwells in the gate of your city comes to poverty, you shall not harden and shut your heart; you shall also not close your hand but rather open it to the poor and lend him what he needs. This Scripture is bright, clear, and light, and understandable to us all: in every city you shall have consideration for its inhabitants. Thus where one falls into poverty, everyone, and in particular the highest civil authority, should have compassion upon the poor and no one should stop the heart, but rather open his hands and lend the poor brother what he needs. Therefore Christian magistrates should be particularly diligent to help our own, as Paul teaches, and deem fitting to have care for everyone, in what way ours shall be renewed. Not that we should suffer burdens and need ourselves, and the others live in pleasure. But rather in this way, we have food and drink and our wives, children, servants, relatives are also provided for, we shall have enough and be satisfied and help our fellow citizens and neighbors. The citizens in every city, and the farmers in every village, shall provide for their poor brethren, lending them what they need. Also princes, officials, mayors, judges, village-mayors, and other magistrates shall examine the way and comfortable means whereby the poor brothers and sisters, each according to his station, will be maintained, and that no one be allowed to run after bread. For this reason it is fitting that students who beg for their living be sent to their parents, for they learn much more roguery and indecency in beggary than virtue and learning. It is much better that they learn the craft of their parents than that they run after bread. Otherwise they serve nothing other than the papistic, unlearned, and deceitful priests.

It is proper that the highest civil authorities direct their attention to the strong beggars who are able to work, and force them to work in order to support themselves. But also that they give them aid and help to begin their craft or work. Whether one desires to be a printer, goldsmith, baker, tailor, shoemaker, or learn a similar craft, or to begin to employ and promote, they shall help everyone according to his requirements. For they shall lend their brethren what they need.

If it happens that one may return the help he received without burden, they shall take the same and help others. But if the former would be so burdened by returning what was lent him, the benefactor should not demand it or expect it for he has done good. . . .

In particular the mendicant cloisters are forbidden and should no longer exist. For begging is forbidden. It is no help at all that they are willing beggars. Their desire and action is unchristian, fraudulent, and noxious, for they have no pretext for their begging in Holy Scripture. They repeatedly deceive the poor and the rich about them, and they injure the poor with their demands for cheese, corn, bread, beer, wine and testament, and all sorts of things. Pluck the poor children out of their mouths, for they themselves have need of these things. Servants like this are concerned with beggary, thus the highest civil authority should soon banish it and help them to a better life.

A laudable way and means is at hand provided God would give his grant to accomplish such ways and means. And these means are undertaken: that one shall set up a common purse or chest, and therein include all the income of all the brotherhoods. Bear in mind that brotherhoods oppose divine glory and honor, that they make division in Christian unity, that they eat and drink like beasts, living as a fish in water and as a wall stands upon a rock. For they scorn all others, are full of slander, and have useless and devilish hopes.

Also the income from the parish endowments, when they are available through the renunciation or death of the priests, shall come into the above-mentioned chest to be lent by the council to everyone in the city. Consider that many endowments are founded and established on the Mass, for that is a devilish matter and against the nature of the holy sacrament. Consider also that there are too many priests who desire to serve neither God nor the neighbor, and will not even learn. . . .

Also I would like to see that the income of the stony churches be devoted to the above-mentioned chest and brotherly help. . . .

6.3 Martin Luther (1483–1546)

"That Clergy Should Preach against Usury" (1540)

THE SUBJECTS of poverty, social welfare, and economics are interwoven throughout Luther's writings. Most of this material is readily accessible in *Luther's Works* and will not be repeated here. However, Luther's exhortation to the clergy to preach against usury is, as far as I know, not accessible in any translation. Much of this tract repeats his earlier condemnations of and exhortations against exorbitant interest rates, that is, those beyond his suggested 5 percent ceiling. But he is clearly angrier here about unrestrained early capitalism, and he raises his condemnation to that of a *status confessionis*. The translation is of this section in WA 51:367–69.

Source: Carter Lindberg, trans., from Günter Fabiunke, *Martin Luther als Nationalökonom* (Berlin: Akademische Verlag, 1963), 207–8.

Because God wills it, we will let the princes do what they can or will. But it is not proper for us preachers to approve it [usury]. In this regard let us be bishops, i.e., be on guard and watch, for it concerns our salvation. First, we shall scold and condemn usury from the pulpit, and diligently and straight out repeat the text [cf. Neh. 5 et al.], namely: Whoever loans something and gets more in return is a usurer and is condemned as a thief, robber, and murderer. Secondly [consider this], if you clearly know and are acquainted with a usurer, do not administer the sacrament to him or grant him absolution as long as he does not repent! Otherwise you yourself participate in his usury and his sin. Then you also, on account of his sin, will go forth with him to the devil even if your own sins are [washed] as pure and holy as Saint John the Baptist. For Saint Paul's saying to Timothy is well known [1 Tim. 5:22], "Do not be hasty in the laying on of hands, nor participate in another man's sins!" Likewise in Romans 1[:32]: "Though they know God's decree that those who do such things deserve to die, they not only do them but approve those who practice them!" Third [give heed], that you let the usurer lie as a pagan in death, and do not bury him among other Christians! Also that you do not go with him to the grave if he had not earlier repented. But if you do this, then as said above, you participate in his sin. For because he is a usurer and idolater, because he serves mammon, he is unbelieving and he cannot have or receive the forgiveness of sins nor the grace of Christ nor the communion of the saints. He has condemned himself, separated and banned himself, so long as he does not confess his sins and repent.

This talk will perhaps seem to be somewhat harsh. Perhaps it will also be frightening to some. Above all it will appear frightening to the small usurers; I mean those who take only five or six percent. However, to the great devourers of the world, those who can never take a high enough percentage, one can never be sufficiently harsh, for they have given themselves over to mammon and the devil. They let us cry out and not once enquire about it. It is in particular of these I have spoken; they should be given over in life and death to the devil, and there should be no Christian fellowship with them.

6.4 "A Conversation concerning the Common Chest of Schwabach, Namely by Brother Heinrich, Knecht Ruprecht, Spuler, and Their Master of the Wool Cloth Trade" (1524)

SCHWABACH, about ten miles south of Nuremberg, belonged to the Margrave of Ansbach. The first evangelical services were opposed by the local priest and thus were held in homes and led by the city judge, Hans Herbst. A common chest was established in Schwabach on 5 February 1524, and a pamphlet authored by Herbst quickly made its institution popular (Sehling 11:65). I do not know if the following pamphlet is Herbst's; Schade states the author's identity is unknown. At any rate, the author of this dialogue pamphlet closely links the new social welfare of the common chest to evangelical preaching and worship based in the Scriptures. At the same time, the author reveals both the aspirations and the anxieties attendant on this new venture. The names reflect tasks in the wool cloth trade. Kemerin is probably a wool-carder and Spuler may be one who puts the wool on spools. Brother Heinrich is a monk who clearly has embraced evangelical reform. The translation is of the printed text, "Ein Gesprech von dem Gemeinen Schwabacher Kasten als durch Bruder Heinrich Knecht Ruprecht Kemerin Spuler und Irem Maister des Hantwerks der Wullen Tuchmacher."

Source: Carter Lindberg, trans., from Oskar Schade, ed., *Satiren und Pasquille aus der Reformationszeit*, vols. 1–3 (Hildesheim: Georg Olms, 1966 reprint of 2d ed. of 1863), vol. 3:196–206. Words and phrases in square brackets are my explanatory additions. In most cases I have translated the biblical quotations from the text, and have added full text references to the RSV.

Brother Heinrich: Good day.
Master: Same to you. I hope it's going well!
Brother: Thanks be to God. O Master, I have heard something good.
Master: What is it?
Brother: A common chest has been established.
Master: Praise and thanks be to God that even the poor are being considered! Who are the directors?
Brother: Hans Heller and Hans Volkmer. They have pledged and sworn to collect [resources] into the common chest, and the alms will be distributed to the poor on Walpurgis [May Day eve].
Kemerin: I'll bet! They will collect and distribute, all right; Heller to his belly and Volkmer to his beer needs.
Master: Oh, these two will not do that because they are good Lutherans.
Brother: It's not called Lutheran, but Christian or evangelical.[1] Anyway, one wouldn't collect for Saint John because he can neither eat nor drink.
Master: I hear you with pleasure.
Kemerin: How will the church be maintained?
Master: That [i.e., the church] means community when this little word stands by the other, as by chest or need. All the needs of the church and city can be met from this; otherwise [under the old system of begging] there would be no money left in existence.
Kemerin: There will be a lot of people who will buy useless things and then think, "So, I have nothing more; I shall get loans and help from the common chest." That's why this [common chest] will not last long, because no one will be willing to assist such rubbish.
Master: That's a concern, but I hope my lords and the community will hinder such filth.

---

1. In 1522 Luther made a vociferous attempt to discourage the use of the term "Lutheran." "I ask that men make no reference to my name; let them call themselves Christians not Lutherans" (LW 45:70).

Brother: For that reason God alone is to be beseeched, so that they consider the love of God and the neighbor as Christ says in John 15[:12-14], "This is my commandment, that you love one another as I have loved you. For no one has greater love than the one who offers his life [*seel*] for the friend. You are my friends if you do what I have commanded you."

Kemerin: Christ offered his life for us, but our lords would find that hard to do, and especially since my gracious lord the Margrave will be against it [the common chest].

Brother: Why will his grace be against it? Have not common chests been instituted in Onolzbach, Kitzingen, and perhaps other cities of his grace?

Kemerin: Oh, the parson won't tolerate it because he won't get the third penny from it. Therefore he will get his friends and strangers to oppose it.

Master: Indeed, the third penny from the fish followers [Roman Catholics]!

Brother: You're angry!

Master: Huh, our parson hasn't preached to us for many years.

Brother: Thus have the lazy shepherds dedicated themselves to us. Woe to them as Jeremiah 23 says [23:1 "Woe to the shepherds who destroy and scatter the sheep of my pasture!"], and it says in many other places in Holy Scripture.

Kemerin: Oh, go pull your own nose, you expelled monk!

Brother: Ha, ha, ha! I'm not ashamed of this. Truly, God knows nothing of the parsons, monks, and nuns, for they don't believe in Christ.

Kemerin: How so?

Brother: Each one has a disciplinarian who doesn't believe in Christ. And they in turn have disciplinarians such as the pope, cardinals, bishops, etc., and therefore they don't believe in Christ.

Kemerin: Where is that written?

Brother: In Galatians 2[:23-29]: "The law was our disciplinarian until Christ that we might be justified by faith. But now that faith has come, we are no longer under the disciplinarian, for you are all God's children through faith in Jesus Christ. For as many [of you as] are baptized, have put on Christ. Here there is no Jew nor Greek; here there is no slave nor free; here there is no man nor woman; for you are all one in Christ Jesus. You are all Christ's, so you are Abraham's seed and heirs according to the promise."

Kemerin: Oh, you don't persuade me with your silly preaching [*genspredig = goose-preaching*].

Brother: That's what your useless folks do who desire to hinder the common chest. Who knows, such people might be still more needier for alms than a poor beggar. For today one is a jailbird, the other robs, and the third is burdened by disease such as syphilis and the like. No one [of these people] has letter and seal for poverty [i.e., city permission to beg].

Kemerin: Well, that's true. But some will want to designate their alms.

Brother: Yes, the godless beggars of whom Paul writes in 1 Tim. 5[:13], "They are idlers and go about from house to house. Not only are they lazy, but gossips and busybodies, saying what they should not."

Kemerin: But the common chest will still make poor people because many will give to it what might be necessary for his own needs. Also, many will give up his own inheritance.

Knecht Ruprecht: That is something to be concerned about.

Master: Yes, if our lords desire to act as our parsons, monks, and nuns who have done a good job attracting the people and given nothing in return no matter how poor and wretched the people become. But my lords will act more wisely and with understanding.

Brother: Therefore we shall beseech God for understanding and wisdom, so we shall receive from God as it is written in James 1[:5-6]: "So if one is lacking wisdom he should ask God who gives abundantly to everyone, and reproaches no one, so he will give it to him. But let him ask in faith and not in doubt."

Master: It's high time we ask God so that the devil with his false spirit does not harm us in the love to God and the neighbor.

Knecht: Yes, it is also of necessity a good thing that one decree more than two overseers [for the common chest].

Brother: Also, so that my lords not be suspect in this [venture], the overseers should solemnly vow and make no accounts without the will and knowledge of the whole community, or be permitted to do their accounting before twelve or sixteen citizens, elected from the community. Also, the overseers shall be relieved each year, except for the eldest, and others be appointed in their place.

Knecht: Thus the community shall willingly help with body and goods.

Master: Without any doubt my lords will consider all these needs in an orderly manner.

Brother: I ask you, dear Master, read the booklet by Luther on the order of the common chest.[2]

Master: I will read it.

Knecht: I would very much like to know whether a brotherhood, as they say, will be created.

Brother: Oh, it would be evangelical that there should be a brotherhood, but not called Saint Anne's Brotherhood or Saint John's Brotherhood, and the like, but rather only Christ's Brotherhood, as Paul says in 1 Cor. 1[9-10]: "For God is faithful through whom you are called to the fellowship, that is to the brotherhood of his Son, Jesus Christ, that you all are one, and there be no dissension among you but that you all be completely of one mind and in one judgment."

Master: In view of that, it certainly is good that a common chest has been established.

Brother: Indeed; as is often expressed in Scripture, the faithful had all things in common, as in Acts 4[:32]: "The faithful were of one heart and one mind." No one, as much as he might have had, said that it was his own but rather all things were in common for these people.

---

2. Luther's Preface to the Leisnig order, 1523 (LW 45:159–76).

Master: O that my lords and community would be united in godly and brotherly love; no one would be against it!

Brother: Thus says Paul to the Romans in chapter 8[:31], "So if God be for us who can be against us."

Master: I believe we must have love, which is the root of all things.

Brother: Yes, Paul in 1 Cor. 13[:1ff.] said this, "If I speak with the tongues of men and angels and have not love, so I would be a noisy gong or a clanging cymbal. And if I could prophesy and knew all mysteries, even all knowledge, and had all faith that I could move mountains, and had not love, then I would be nothing."

Master: O what a powerful thing is love.

Brother: Indeed, it is also in this chapter [1 Cor. 13:4-7] that love is patient, friendly, not jealous or boastful; it is not puffed up; it seeks not its own but the [good of the] neighbor; it does not think bad things; it does not rejoice over unrighteousness but rather rejoices with the truth; it bears all, it believes all, it hopes all, it endures all, and the like.

Master: O blessed is the person who considers the fruits of love and lives by it.

Brother: Paul says also in Romans 13[:8], "Owe no one anything than that you love one another." Therefore we beseech God through Jesus Christ that he bestow the grace of the Holy Spirit on our lords and the community, that godly and brotherly love be considered. Without any doubt our petition will be heard, for Christ said in John 16[:23], "Truly, truly, I say to you, if you ask anything of the Father in my name, that will he give you." God also spoke to Jeremiah in chapter 32[:39], "I will give them one heart and one way that they may fear me forever, and it will be for their own good and that of their children," etc.

Master: Therefore one may not exercise great knowledge or art in our faith, but rather let love alone appear from faith.

Brother: That's true, for as one believes in Christ so one lets love flow to the neighbor; also as one helps the neighbor so Christ brings one to faith, which is faith alone in Christ and in his Word.

Knecht: Now I will also help in this; all the money in our brotherhood will be brought into the common chest.

Kemerin: O you big fool to let yourself be persuaded! Haven't you heard that only the house poor will be helped? Why would strangers be helped by it? Thus no trust and help is given.

Brother: That would be unevangelical, for it is written in Galatians 6[:2], "You shall bear one another's burdens." Also in Matthew 7[:12, conflated with Luke 6:27ff.], "Everything that you desire people would do to you, that shall you also do, not only to your friends but also to your enemies. Love one another, thereby you are known as my disciples."

Master: I hope my lords will seriously consider this too.

Knecht: I am concerned that some of the town council may not be good evangelicals.

Brother: Concerning those who are not good evangelicals, it is written in Acts 28[:26ff.] and Isaiah 6[:9-10] that they shall hear with their ears and not understand; they shall see with their eyes and not comprehend, for the heart of this people is hardened.

Master: Everything does not depend upon the papists.

Kemerin: Yes, dear Master, it's never happened that if someone in a high office establishes something, then another comes along and tears it down.

Master: Well then, it must be properly established.

Kemerin: Sure, if there were no self-interest then many would apply to be overseers so that it should be supported. Thus only the rich will benefit.

Knecht: It would be good to prevent this.

Brother: Oh, God's help alone is needed, as it is written in John 15[:5], "Without me you can do nothing."

Knecht: It would be good that with God's help the mass would be reduced to singing and reading.

Master: I won't advise on this, for the pious Luther writes very shocking and terrible things concerning the misuse of the mass.

Knecht: Yes, if it were true.

Brother: Oh, it's unfortunately too true.

Kemerin: I would the devil take Luther body and soul.

Brother: May God protect him and all lovers of the evangelical truth!

Master: Amen.

Spuler: Oh, all the parsons and monks should be killed.

Kemerin: You should be struck in the mouth with peasant shit.

Spuler: Sure, I mean you'd rather have the parsons and monks than God's Word and the common chest.

Brother: One should not kill the parsons and monks but rather petition God for them and have patience with them.

Spuler: But one can no longer fully bear with them, for they desire to be lords and are nothing but beggars.

Brother: You're right. But one should not kill them but rather refuse to give them anything, like other beggars who go door to door, because God in the Holy Scripture has forbidden begging as in Deuteronomy 15, Proverbs 30, Timothy 16 [sic; probably means 6], Isaiah 6, and the like.

Knecht: Haven't I heard that you should give to those who ask?

Brother: That's in Luke 6[:30], "Whoever asks of you, give to him." Also Tobit taught his son, Tobit 4[:7], "You shall not turn your face away from the poor," etc. This is not to be understood as if one must have to give sufficient to everyone because no one's avarice can be satisfied, but that one should help those, as Christ says in Matthew 25[:40], "Truly I say to you, what you have done to one of these the least of my brethren, you have done to me."

Knecht: It would be good if the lazy beggars were expelled from the country or driven to work.

Brother: God has also commanded in Genesis 3[:19], "You shall earn your bread by the sweat of your brow." But if one is sick or unable to return to his own country without alms, then we should do as the Samaritan in Luke 10.

Knecht: But people want to be seen and praised for giving alms.

Brother: Sure, as the hypocrite in Luke 18[:9ff.], who said, "God, I thank you that I am not like other men, etc." But it is written in Matthew 6[:1-4], "When you give alms, do not let your left hand know what the right hand does, so that your alms are hidden and your Father who sees in secret will reward you openly." Oh, we cannot come before God's face, as it is written in Genesis 43[:5] unless we bring our least brother with us. God will not be honored and loved without love and service to the neighbor.

Knecht: Oh, if we had an evangelical preacher, all these matters would then be good.

Kemerin: What's lacking to you in our preacher?

Knecht: Oh, he can't preach anything other than "this is written in the first distinction, or the other distinction."

Brother: Ugh, he's too full of juristry and sophistry, that's why it's so difficult for him to preach evangelically; it would take him a year to prepare one [evangelical sermon].

Master: It's not easy to paint white over black.

Brother: Christ has truly warned us in Philippians and Colossians 2[:8], saying: "Beware that no one makes a prey of you by philosophy and unnecessarily seduces you by human opinions, and not according to Christ's teaching."

Kemerin: Oh, the new teaching will still create great strife and rebellion.

Master: Sure, to those who do not receive God's Word and rarely or do not at all go to preaching. Therefore, my dear Kemerin, give up your useless chatter!

Brother: Yes, useless chatter is forbidden as it is written in Ephesians 4[:29], "Let no idle chatter come from your mouths." For all such talk is called the empty words of the devil, as Saint Peter, so they would hinder godly and brotherly love.

Knecht: Was Saint Peter then a devil?

Brother: Sure as it's written in Matthew 16[:22] where Christ revealed his future passion to his disciples. And Saint Peter said to him, "Lord, God forbid! This shall never happen to you!" But Christ turned to him and said, "Get away from me, Satan! You are an offense to me, for you think not according to God but according to men."

Master: Did you hear this, Kemerin? So be warned!

Kemerin: Yes, I've heard it. But if all those who oppose the new teaching and the common chest should be devils, there would be many here.

Brother: Christ, not I, said this.

Master: Don't you know, my dear Kemerin, you are responsible for your own guilt?

Kemerin: Sure I know, give me the responsibility.

Master: Then don't speak any more against the Holy Scriptures and the common chest.

Kemerin: I will no longer speak against it as long as I live.

Master: You've called Brother Heinrich an expelled monk. Apologize to him!

Kemerin: I have spoken in anger, dear Brother Heinrich. Forgive me, and next Sunday drink with us! I will give you a measure of wine.

Brother: Well! I'll do it, but according to the words of 1 Thessalonians 5[:14f.], "We beseech you dear brethren, exhort the idle, comfort the fainthearted, help the weak, be patient with everyone." Oh, it's time for me to go home.

Knecht: Oh, stay a little while and tell me whether I should go to the sacrament if it is not given in both forms [bread and wine].

Brother: I'll talk about that on Sunday. I must go home now. But we shall all beseech God the Almighty that he will impart his strength, grace, and wisdom to our lords and the entire community so that godly and brotherly love will be taken into consideration with a good beginning, better middle, and the very best conclusion. Thereto help God the Father, God the Son, and God the Holy Spirit. Amen. Therewith may God protect you and preserve me from evil!

Master and Knecht: God preserve us from evil and God protect you too!

Brother: Amen. My dear Kemerin, speak no more against the common chest but as it is written in Matthew 9 [*sic*; actually 19:21], sell what is yours and give it to the poor people.

Kemerin: I will happily follow you otherwise, but that I should sell what is mine and give to the poor, that I'll have to sleep on.

Brother: God enlighten you and us all!

Kemerin: Amen.

Knecht: Praise and thanks be to God that you two are united again.

Kemerin: My dear Master and my dear Knecht Ruprecht, I ask you for God's sake, forgive me for having angered you.

Master and Knecht: God forgive us our sin!

Kemerin: Amen!

Master: I'll go to communion on Friday also.

Knecht: So, I will get a measure of beer, and cheese and bread, and we will eat.

Kemerin: You haven't eaten well today. Get a pint of beer and I'll make a beer soup and bake a small cake.

Knecht: Get going, Spuler, and get us the beer.

Kemerin: Get going, dear son, and forgive me also! I will do nothing more against you.

Spuler: Yes, my dear Kemerin, and forgive me too!

Kemerin: Oh yes, happily.

Knecht: Give thanks, my dear Brother Heinrich, that you have also united us.

Master: Thus has God's Word worked. Praise, honor, and thanks be to God! Amen.

Chapter 7

Social Welfare Legislation

7.1 Order of the City of Wittenberg (1522)

THIS THE FIRST of the two earliest examples of social welfare legislation.

Sources: Carter Lindberg, trans., from Hans Lietzmann, ed., *Die Wittenberger und Leisniger Kastenordnung* (Berlin: de Gruyter, 1935); also in Emil Sehling, ed., *Die evangelischen Kirchenordnung des 16. Jahrhundert*, vol. 1 (Tübingen: Mohr, 1902), 697–98.

1. It is unanimously resolved that all income from the churches, all of the brotherhoods, and the guilds shall be collected together and brought into a common chest. Two from the city council, two from the community, and a secretary are to be delegated who shall receive and possess such income in order to provide for the poor people.

2. Moreover, henceforth the endowed income of priests, when it is freed through the death of a priest, will also be collected in the same common chest; and henceforth no one [no other priest] will be endowed by it.

3. Likewise, no beggars shall be tolerated in our city, rather one shall urge them to work or expel them from the city. But they who because of age or sickness or other misfortune have fallen into poverty shall be provided for from the common chest through the appropriate delegated manner.

4. Likewise, there shall be no *Terminey* [wandering mendicants] among us.

5. Likewise, no monks shall be allowed to beg in our city, but rather they are allowed the income they now have. In addition they shall [henceforth] support and maintain themselves by the work of their hands.

6. Likewise, everything which the cloisters among us now have is to be inventoried, such as chalices, *pacificale* [a silver liturgical piece], monstrances, and the like; also to be listed are the incomes they possess and collect yearly.

7. Likewise, no foreign students will be allowed in our city. If one or more desire to study with us, then they must provide themselves with food and drink, for we will allow no one to beg nor to ask for alms.

8. Likewise, neither wandering begging monks with relics [*Stacionierer*] nor any kind of monks begging alms for building churches [*kirchenbitter*] shall be tolerated in view of the fact that all the churches are finished, and more than enough are built, etc.

9. Likewise, loans shall be made from the common chest to poor artisans who without this are unable to support themselve daily by their trade, in order that they may be able to provide for themselves. When they are established, however, they can repay the loan without any interest; but if they are unable to repay the loan, it shall be pardoned for God's sake.

10. Likewise, the common chest shall provide for poor orphans, the children of poor people, and maidens who shall be given an appropriate dowry for marriage.

11. Moreover, where such income is not sufficient for such good works or does not extend itself far enough, then shall others, be they priests or citizens, according to what they have, yearly contribute a sum of money for the maintenance of the multitude of the poor.

12. Likewise, the priests whom we now have, since their income also is collected into the common chest, shall be supported yearly with six gulden, although yearly they have before received eight gulden from the Vigils they kept. Seeing that the Mass and Vigils lapse, they may request the same money for poor sick people, and comfort them in their need. They shall encourage no one, however, to make a testament [will] to their advantage.

13. Likewise, the images and altars in the churches shall be done away with in order to avoid idolatry, for three altars without images are enough.

14. Likewise, the Mass shall not be held other than as Christ instituted it at the Last Supper. For the sake of the weak in the faith, however, singing is allowed. Only the first part of the Missal containing the *missae de tempore* shall be used, not the second part of the Mass of the saints, and the *introit, kyrie, gloria in excelsis et in terra*, the collect or *preces*, epistle, gradual, without the sequence, the gospel, creed, offertory, preface, *sanctus* without the major and minor canons [i.e., *Canon Missae* and offertory prayer] so long as they are

not out of accord with the Scriptures. After this begins the evangelical mass; if there are communicants the priest consecrates; if there are not communicants, the priest consecrates and summarizes it with prayers for that purpose. Thereafter he concludes with the collect without the *Ite missa est*. Also the communicant may take the consecrated host in the hand and himself put it in his mouth; the same may be done with the cup, hence drinking from it.

15. We also will not permit unchaste persons to be supported by us; they should have recourse to marriage. If they will not do this but are residents they shall be banished. If they are not residents they shall be severely punished according to their particular offense; beyond this anyone devoting himself to unchaste relationships or living shall be expelled from the city.

16. In case our fellow citizens and residents are burdened by interest rates that are too high, for example, five to six percent, or do not have the means for a deposit, we will loan them the main sum from the common chest, and they will repay the capital at four percent annually until it is repaid. But we convey to the clergy among us this confidence that they will also devote themselves herein in Christian love, and submit voluntarily in these particular things.

17. Likewise, particular regard shall be given to the children of poor people. Boys sent to school and studies who because of poverty are unable to remain there, shall be given the means [to remain in school] so that at all times there will not be lacking learned people to preach the Holy Gospel and the Scriptures, and also in worldly government. Those not sent to school shall be supported [in studying] trades and crafts, for in such things particular care is needed.

7.2 The Poor Order of Ypres (1525)

Source: Carter Lindberg, trans., from Otto Winckelmann, "Die Armenordnungen von Nürnberg (1522), Kitzingen (1923), Regensburg (1523) und Ypern (1525)," *Archiv für Reformationsgeschichte* 11 (1914): 13–18.

1. Whereas the magistrates and jurists of the city of Ypres are completely informed about the various troubles, abuses, and irregularities reported about the common poor receiving alms in the city, that some of them employing cunning and misrepresentation derive great benefit, and others are able to gain little or nothing, that even many of these same persons in order to support themselves by alms go out daily to the tables, streets, and churches, thus maintaining themselves in idleness and indolence, who nevertheless, if they would present themselves for service or work should be able to support themselves honestly, all of which proves to be a great burden and hardship to the inhabitants of this city; whereas further, this is contrary to the proclamation and mandates of our illustrious lords and the various commands

our lords' forefathers decreed lawful in earlier times; therefore in order to prevent these things and in order to create order and law so that henceforth alms will be better and more reliably distributed for the support of those who need them and to no others:

2. The magistrates and jurists have taken this matter upon themselves and with careful deliberation by the city council have chosen four good men to be over the entire city, requesting them, for God's sake and on behalf of the welfare of the city and its inhabitants, to be ready to undertake and attend this matter and charge, that rule and order shall be brought about among the poor, and they have authorized the same [four men] with such authority as they themselves have.

3. And these aforementioned four men, earnestly applying themselves, have sent for another four men from each parish, which generally have had the burden of the poor, commissioning these same [men], that they should, each in his own parish, ascertain the state of the poor, what vocation they practice, how old they are, what obligations they have concerning children, sickness, etc.; likewise which trade they carry on, whether they are peaceful or drunkards, gamblers, indolent, or bread-beggars, etc.

4. Moreover, these four persons from each parish receiving this charge have done this well and truly, and made a book for each parish that contains the aforementioned investigation with a good explanation.

5. Moreover, after this is done, the aforementioned four men in the presence of the visitors [i.e., the social workers] have scrutinized the afore-mentioned book, and according to its judgments have conferred something to every household according to its need, income, burdens, and condition; and this is to be discharged weekly, since it would be too great a sum by the month.

6. Moreover, after the inspection, if the case is found and considered to be difficult and burdensome, as to how one should raise these funds, it is recognized as necessary that one find the means to bring all the alms which are given or endowed into a common purse, in order that henceforth through it the men in every parish may distribute according to the number of their poor. They are to distribute weekly in money, bread, wood, and in other respects according to discretion and according to the circumstances and burdens of the poor. No money shall be given to the wicked, disorderly, and drunkards for the support of wives and children, but rather bread, wood, and other commodities which are necessary for them, nevertheless compelling by all means, by threat of punishment and loss of their maintenance, these same [wicked poor] to work and to bring home their earnings.

7. Moreover, all tables, Holy Spirit houses, guilds, and other places of worship which have annual incomes and distribute gifts shall in the future dispense only the established alms to clerical persons, like mendicants, and all persons mentioned in the letter of foundation. Those [foundations] wherein it is stated in general [that their incomes] are to be distributed to the poor shall have their funds brought into the common purse.

8. Moreover, in order to be able to begin to put into effect this matter, it is considered necessary for the four aforementioned men first and foremost to make a purse of the good great sum of money, which they shall obtain for God's sake partly from places of worship, tables, and other persons, namely by charity; partly also thereby, that two elected men are in all the main streets of the city who hopefully have implored those whom they know disposed to this cause, in order to have additional support, which has greatly helped to bring these things to realization.

9. Moreover, that one shall set up collection boxes in every parish so that each one can put in his private alms, and that in every church this common purse may be passed around, saying: "For God's sake for the poor of this city."

10. Moreover, if this is still not sufficient, one shall in every parish once weekly for a time openly collect from door to door for support of all the poor of the city.

11. Moreover, the four men of every parish shall give an account every month before the four men of the city authority about everything that they shall have received and dispersed, specifically in order to know the state of things.

12. And these same four men of the city authority shall return to the aforementioned persons such a sum of money as they think appropriate for distribution and provisions to the poor in the next month.

13. Similarly, the four men of the city authority shall give account to the city council every half year of their income and expenditures.

14. Moreover, one shall earnestly request the parsons and preachers to promote the matter, calling it to the people's attention and recommending it, especially in preaching and wills; if these proclaim well their diligence, it may be hoped that with the grace of God the matter will advance.

15. Moreover, every preacher, whether secular or in orders, is not to forget to request funds. If they should hear a few complaints from the poor about the order, they themselves should not support these complaints, but rather comfort the poor with friendly words and direct them to bring forth their complaints in order to effect care, as is suitable. And also in order to effect care, we intend to know whether the alms to some persons will not be well-employed or whether some out of shame might not reveal their need. This is to be brought to attention, namely to the place where the four men of the city authority hold session twice weekly, namely Mondays and Fridays, in order to hear and discuss each person's complaints.

16. Moreover, as the children of all the poor of the city have up to now forlornly run about and remained in begging, one shall restrain them, some to go to school, some to go to a trade and service; and one must clothe them in order that they might be received in citizens' houses. For this the masters have sundry sums of money for the assistance and support of the same in trades.

17. There are also those among the deserving poor who have wounds, so let them be cleaned and healed, and similarly devote much cost for the support of these poor.

18. Moreover, according to the way that all these things have been brought forward by the magistrates and thoroughly considered by the citizens, they have been approved and certified with the good knowledge and will of the clerical estates in hopes of great benefit and gain which the city shall receive therefrom; namely, that alms will be better invested, and the evil and undeserving will have no part, and the deserving and the modest will not be forgotten.

19. Moreover, therewith young daughters, who frequently are ruined by poverty, shall have no reason to wander but rather on the contrary shall be watched over and instructed, and the citizens find servant girls; for it has been found that many fathers and mothers would rather have their children begging for the sake of the profits they get from them, than that they should come to honor in the service of good people.

20. Moreover, also that beggars now are better able to care for their salvation, whereas earlier they had great difficulty caring for their sustenance and could hardly be reckoned among Christians, then one did not see many of them go to church and the sacrament.

21. Moreover, thus, the aforementioned, according to the way that these things have been assigned to them by the city authority and granted by the community, have decreed a general mandate in the following form: henceforth, namely, from Sunday evening 3 December 1525, it is commanded that no one, whoever it may be, may demand alms either within or outside the city, at tables, streets, churches, or before the houses of the people in any manner; and whoever shall be found acting against this shall be sharply punished according to the measure of his offense.

22. In like manner, anyone coming from outside the city, whoever it may be, venturing to go begging in the city, and also anyone from the city area who ventures outside the city to beg [will receive] the same punishment; nevertheless it is indeed understood that people passing through, going on their way, shall be permitted to lodge one night in the inns of the city, in conformity to the mandate of our gracious Emperor in the year 1509; there one shall care for their pressing need; nevertheless if they are concerned to stay longer in the city or for begging before the churches and houses, they shall be punished as above. And persons traveling through who do not stay overnight in the city shall be given alms so that they might continue.

23. It is also commanded of everyone who has children that he does not allow his children to go begging in the street, and that the children also shall be corrected with switches or in another manner according to the discretion of the magistrates.

24. Moreover, that all beggars, male and female, idlers, and others living from the alms of good people, who now are in this city whether it be in houses of worship or other places, take off and leave the city between now

and the coming Sunday of 3 December 1525. If they are found here after that, the punishment shall be imprisonment on bread and water. Specifically, this is because one finds from good experience that many different families come here in order to establish themselves, who often have been expelled from abroad because they have fallen out with the people and been charged with penalties or offenses, meanwhile leaving behind wife and children without witness from their parsons where they were residing. These people come in such great numbers that the overburdening of all is no longer to be tolerated.

25. And should it occur because of this that this order might miscarry and be discontinued, the magistrates with the community council have ordered, commanded, and mandated that no inhabitant of the city, whoever he be, let housing or room, giving up to or letting have the use of in any way with their household to any persons coming from abroad, unless they indicate it beforehand to the magistrates in order that instruction and command first be given as the case demands it in connection with appropriate punishment; the persons who before the instruction of the general order would be considered as dwelling here, shall not, however, be included in this article, but rather shall remain where they previously were tolerated.

26. Further, it is commanded that every inhabitant of this city who is requested by the officials and deputies of this city render help and assistance in the fulfillment of this order, considering appropriate punishment if |such help| is wanting.

Bibliography

Abel, Wilhelm. *Agrarkrisen und Agrarkonjunktur in Mitteleuropa vom 13. bis zum 19. Jahrhundert*. Berlin, 1935.

————. *Massenarmut und Hungerkrisen im vorindustriellen Deutschland*. 3d ed. Göttingen: Vandenhoeck & Ruprecht, 1986.

Adams, Robert. "Designs by More and Erasmus for a New Social Order." *Studies in Philology* 42 (1945): 131–45.

Alves, Abel. "The Christian Social Organism and Social Welfare: The Case of Vives, Calvin, and Loyola." *Sixteenth Century Journal* 20 (1989): 3–21.

Amundsen, Darrel W., & Gary B. Ferngren. "Medicine and Religion: Early Christianity through the Middle Ages." In Martin E. Marty and Kenneth L. Vaux, eds., *Health/Medicine and the Faith Traditions: An Inquiry into Religion and Medicine*, 93–131. Philadelphia: Fortress Press, 1982.

Aquinas, Thomas. *Summa Theologiae*. II–II, q. 23. New York: McGraw-Hill; London: Eyre & Spottiswoode, 1975.

Arduini, Maria Lodovica. "Biblische Kategorien und mittelalterliche Gesellschaft: 'Potens' und 'Pauper' bei Rupert von Deutz und Hildegard von Bingen (XI bzw. XII Jh.)." In Albert Zimmermann, ed., *Soziale Ordnungen im Selbstverständnis des Mittelalters. Miscellanea Mediaevalia* 12/2: 467–97. Berlin: de Gruyter, 1980.

Aries, Philippe. "Richesse et pauvreté devant la mort." In Michel Mollat, ed., *Études sur l'histoire de la pauvreté*, vol. 2, 519–33. Paris, 1974.

Ashley, W. J. *An Introduction to English Economic History*. 2 vols. London, 1920.

Assion, P. "Matthias Hütlin und sein Gaunerbuchlein, 'de Liber Vagatorum.'" *Alemannisches Jahrbuch* (1971/72): 74–92.

Aston, Margaret. " 'Caim's Castles': Poverty, Politics, and Disendowment." In Barrie Dobson, ed., *The Church, Politics, and Patronage in the Fifteenth Century*, 45–81. New York: St. Martin's Press, 1984.

Augustine. *The City of God.* New York: Modern Library, 1950.

———. *The Confessions of Saint Augustine.* New York: Collier Books, 1966.

———. *De doctrina Christiana. Patrologia cursus completus, series latina,* vol. 34. Ed. P. Migne. Paris, 1844–55.

———. *Enarrationes in Psalmos* 85:3. *Patrologia cursus completus, series latina,* vols. 36–37. Ed. P. Migne. Paris, 1844–55.

Baldwin, Marshall, ed. *Christianity through the Thirteenth Century.* New York: Harper & Row, 1970.

Barge, Hermann. *Andreas Bodenstein von Karlstadt.* 2 vols. Leipzig: Brandstetter, 1905, reprint 1968.

———. *Jakob Strauss: ein Kämpfer für das Evangelium in Tirol, Thüringen und Süddeutschland.* Leipzig: Heinsius, 1937.

———. *Luther und der Frühkapitalismus.* Gütersloh: Bertelsmann, 1951.

Baron, Hans. "Franciscan Poverty and Civic Wealth as Factors in the Rise of Humanistic Thought." *Speculum* 13/1 (1938): 1–37.

Bataillon, Marcel. "J. L. Vivès: Réformateur de la bienfaisance." *Bibliothéque d'humanisme et Renaissance* 14 (1952): 141–59.

Bauer, Clemens. "Conrad Peutingers Gutachten zur Monopolfrage: Eine Untersuchung zur Wandlungen der Wirtschaftsanschauungen im Zeitalter der Reformation." *Archiv für Reformationsgeschichte* 45 (1954): 1–42, 145–95.

Bayer, Oswald. "Luther's Ethics as Pastoral Care." *Lutheran Quarterly* 4 (1990): 125–42.

Beckerman, Wilfred. "The Measurement of Poverty." In Thomas Riis, ed., *Aspects of Poverty in Early Modern Europe,* vol. 1, 47–63. Stuttgart: Klett-Cotta, 1981.

Beier, A. L. *Masterless Men: The Vagrancy Problem in England 1560–1640.* London and New York: Methuen, 1985.

Bell, Susan. "Johann Eberlin von Günzburg's Wolfaria: The First Protestant Utopia." *Church History* 36 (1967): 122–39.

Bendixen, R. "Ein Büchlein Wenzeslaus Lincks von Arbeit und Betteln." *Zeitschrift für kirchliche Wissenschaft und kirchliches Leben* 6 (1885): 584–92.

———. "Wenzeslaus Linck." *Zeitschrift für kirchliche Wissenschaft und kirchliches Leben* 8 (1887): 138–53.

Berger, Peter. *The Sacred Canopy: Elements of a Sociological Theory of Religion.* New York: Anchor Books, 1969.

Berman, Harold J. *Law and Revolution: The Formation of the Western Legal Tradition.* Cambridge: Harvard University Press, 1983.

Beyer, Michael. "Die Neuordnung des Kirchenguts." In Helmar Junghans, ed., *Des Jahrhundert der Reformation in Sachsen,* 91–112. Berlin: Evangelische Verlagsanstalt, 1989.

Black, Christopher. *Italian Confraternities in the Sixteenth Century.* Cambridge: Cambridge University Press, 1989.

Blaschke, Karlheinz. "Die Auswirkung der Reformation auf die städtischen Kirchenverfassung in Sachsen." In Bernd Moeller, ed., *Stadt und Kirche im 16. Jahrhundert.* Gütersloh: Mohn, 1978, 162–67.

Blickle, Peter. *Gemeindereformation: Die Menschen des 16. Jahrhunderts auf dem Weg zum Heil.* Munich: Oldenbourg, 1987.

——. *The Revolution of 1525: The German Peasants' War from a New Perspective.* Trans. T. Brady & H. C. E. Midelfort. Baltimore: Johns Hopkins University Press, 1985.

——. "Die soziale Dialektik der reformatorischen Bewegung." In Peter Blickle, ed., *Zwingli und Europa*, 71–89. Zurich: Vandenhoeck & Ruprecht, 1985.

Blockmans, W. P., & W. Prevenier. "Poverty in Flanders and Brabant from the Fourteenth to the Mid-Sixteenth Century: Sources and Problems." *Acta Historiae Neerlandicae*, 10: 2–57. The Hague: Nijhoff, 1978.

Bodensieck, Julius, ed. *The Encyclopedia of the Lutheran Church.* 3 vols. Philadelphia: Fortress Press, 1965.

Boehncke, Heiner, & Rolf Johannsmeier. *Das Buch der Vaganten, Spieler, Huren, Leutbetrüger.* Cologne: Prometh Verlag, 1987.

Boesch, Bruno. "Zu Sprache und Wortschatz der alemannischen Dichtung 'Von des tüfels segi' (Teufels Netz)." *Alemannisches Jahrbuch* (1971/72): 46–73.

Boff, Leonardo. "Luther, the Reformation, and Liberation." In Dow Kirkpatrick, ed., *Faith Born in the Struggle for Life: A Rereading of Protestant Faith in Latin America Today*, 195–212. Grand Rapids, Mich.: Eerdmans, 1988.

Böhmer, Wolfgang, & Friedrich Kirsten. "Der gemeine Kasten und seine Bedeutung für das kommunale Gesundheitswesen Wittenbergs." *Wissenschaftliche Zeitschrift: Martin-Luther-Universität: Mathematisches Naturwissenschaftliches Reihe* 34/2 (1985): 49–56.

Bonenfant, Paul. "Les origines et le caractère de la réforme de la bienfaisance publique aux Pays-Bas sous le règne de Charles-Quint." *Revue belge de philosophie et d'histoire* 5 (1926): 887–904; 6 (1927): 207–30.

Bornkamm, Heinrich. *Luther in Mid-Career, 1521–1530.* Philadelphia: Fortress Press, 1983.

Bosl, Karl. "Gesellschaftsentwicklung 500–900" and "Gesellschaftsentwicklung 900–1350." In *Handbuch der deutschen Wirtschafts- und Sozialgeschichte*, vol. 1. Stuttgart: Union Verlag, 1971. 133–69, 226–73.

——. "Potens und Pauper: Begriffgeschichtliche Studien zur gesellschaftlichen Differenzierung im frühen Mittelalter zum 'Pauperismus' des Hochmittelalters." In Karl Bosl, *Frühformen der Gesellschaft im mittelalterlichen Europa*, 106–34. Munich: Oldenbourg, 1964.

Bossy, John. *Christianity in the West 1400–1700.* Oxford: Oxford University Press, 1985.

Brady, Thomas. Review of *Obrigkeitliche Armenfürsorge* by Robert Jütte. *Sixteenth Century Journal* 17/3 (1986): 390–91.

——. *Ruling Class, Regime and Reformation at Strasbourg 1520–1555.* Leiden: Brill, 1978.

——. *Turning Swiss: City and Empire, 1450–1550.* Cambridge: Cambridge University Press, 1985.

Brandt, Ahasver von. "Mittelalterliches Bürgertestamente." *Stiftungsberichte der Heidelberger Akademie der Wissenschaften: Philosophische-historische Klasse* 3 (1973): 5–29.

———. *Regesten der Lübecker Bürgertestamente des Mittelalters.* Lübeck: Schmidt-Römhild, 1964.

Braudel, Fernand. "History and the Social Sciences." In Peter Burke, ed., *Economy and Society in Early Modern Europe*, 11–42. New York: Harper & Row, 1972.

Bräuer, Siegfried. "Die Theologie Thomas Müntzers als Grundlage seiner sozialethischen Impulse." *Evangelische Monatsschrift Standpunkt* 70/3 (1989): 62–67.

Brecht, Martin. "Luthertum als politische und soziale Kraft in den Städten." In Franz Petri, ed., *Kirche und gesellschaftlicher Wandel in deutschen und niederländischen Städten der werdenden Neuzeit*, 1–21. Cologne: Böhlau, 1980.

———. *Martin Luther: Shaping and Defining the Reformation 1521–1532*. Trans. James Schaaf. Minneapolis: Fortress Press, 1990.

Brown, Peter. *Augustine of Hippo*. Berkeley: University of California Press, 1969.

"Bruderschaften." *Theologische Realenzyklopädie*, vol. 7, 196–99. Berlin and New York: de Gruyter, 1981.

Brummel, Bonnie Lee. "Luther and the Biblical Language of Poverty." *Ecumenical Review* 32 (1980): 40–58.

———. "Luther on Poverty and the Poor." Ph.D. diss. Columbia University, 1979.

Bubenheimer, Ulrich. "Andreas Rudolff Bodenstein von Karlstadt." In Wolfgang Merklein, ed., *Andreas Bodenstein von Karlstadt: 1480–1541*, 5–58. Karlstadt, 1980.

———. *Thomas Müntzer: Herkunft und Bildung*. Leiden: Brill, 1989.

Bucer, Martin. "De Regno Christi." In Wilhelm Pauck, ed. & trans., *Melanchthon and Bucer*. Philadelphia: Westminster Press, 1969.

———. *Deutsches Schriften*. Vol. 1. Gütersloh: Mohn, 1960.

———. *Instruction in Christian Love*. Trans. Paul Fuhrmann. Richmond: John Knox Press, 1952.

Burrell, Sidney. "Calvinism, Capitalism, and the Middle Classes: Some Afterthoughts on an Old Problem." In S. N. Eisenstadt, ed., *The Protestant Ethic and Modernization: A Comparative View*, 135–54. New York: Basic Books, 1968.

Büttner, Ernst. "Das Buch der 'Armenkiste an unser Lieben Frauen Kirche' zu Bremen (1525 bis 1580), sein Bedeutung und sein mutmassliche Beziehung zu der Armenordnung in Ypern." *Archiv für Kulturgeschichte* 12 (1916): 345–62.

Camporesi, Piero. *Il libro dei vagabondi*. Turin: Einandi, 1973.

Caprivi, Leopold von. "Mit scharfen ökonomischen Blick: Luthers Schrift vom Kaufhandel und Wucher bleibt aktuell." *Lutherische Monatshefte* 21 (1982): 382–85.

Carmichael, Ann G. *Plague and the Poor in Renaissance Florence*. Cambridge: Cambridge University Press, 1986.

Chaney, Edward P. de G. " 'Philanthropy in Italy': English Observations on Italian Hospitals, 1545–1789," in Thomas Riis, ed., *Aspects of Poverty in Early Modern Europe*, vol. 1, 183–217. Stuttgart: Klett-Cotta, 1981.

Chatellier, Louis. *The Europe of the Devout: The Catholic Reformation and the Formation of a New Society*. Cambridge: Cambridge University Press; Paris: Editions de la Maison des Sciences de l'Homme, 1989.

Chiffoleau, Jacques. *La comptabilité de l'au-delà: Les hommes, la mort et la religion dans la région d'Avignon à la fin du Moyen Age (vers 1320–vers 1480)*. Rome: École Française de Rome, 1980.

Chill, Emanuel. "Religion and Mendicity in Seventeenth-Century France." *International Review of Social History* 7 (1962): 400–25.

Chilton, David. *Productive Christians in an Age of Guilt-Manipulators*. Tyler, Tex.: Institute for Christian Economics, 1982.

Chrisman, Miriam Usher. *Lay Culture, Learned Culture: Books and Social Change in Strasbourg, 1480–1599*. New Haven: Yale University Press, 1982.

———. "Urban Poor in the Sixteenth Century: The Case of Strasbourg." In Miriam Usher Chrisman & Otto Gründler, eds., *Social Groups and Religious Ideas in the Sixteenth Century*, 59–67, 169–71. Kalamazoo: Medieval Institute, Western Michigan University, 1978.

Cipolla, Carlo M. "Economic Fluctuations, the Poor, and Public Policy (Italy, 16th and 17th Centuries)." In Thomas Riis, ed., *Aspects of Poverty in Early Modern Europe*, vol. 1, 65–77. Stuttgart: Klett-Cotta, 1981.

———. *Public Health and the Medical Profession in the Renaissance*. Cambridge: Cambridge Univ. Press, 1976.

Clay, Rotha M. *The Hospitals of Medieval England*. London, 1909.

Clement of Alexandria. "Who Is the Rich Man That Shall Be Saved?" In *Ante-Nicene Fathers*, vol. 2, 591–604. Grand Rapids, Mich.: Eerdmans, 1956.

Cohn, Norman. *The Pursuit of the Millennium*. New York: Harper & Row, 1961.

Courtenay, William J. "Token Coinage and the Administration of Poor Relief during the Late Middle Ages." *Traditio* 3/2, (1972): 275–95.

Cunnington, P., & C. Lucas. *Charity Costumes of Children, Scholars, Almsfolk, Pensioners*. London: A. & C. Black, 1978.

Daniels, Charles. "Hard Work, Good Work, and School Work: An Analysis of Wenzeslaus Linck's Conception of Civic Responsibility." In Lawrence Buck & Jonathon Zophy, eds., *The Social History of the Reformation*, 41–51. Columbus: Ohio State University Press, 1972.

Davis, Natalie Zemon. "Gregory Nazianzen in the Service of Humanist Social Reform." *Renaissance Quarterly* 20/4 (1967): 455–64.

———. "Poor Relief, Humanism, and Heresy: The Case of Lyons." In W. H. Bowsky, ed., *Studies in Medieval and Renaissance History*, vol. 5, 215–75. Lincoln: University of Nebraska Press, 1968.

———. *Society and Culture in Early Modern France*. Stanford: Stanford University Press, 1975.

Deppermann Klaus. "Thomas Müntzer—Bahnbrecher der Neuzeit?" In Klaus Deppermann et al., *Thomas Müntzer: Ein streitbarer Theologe zwischen Mystik und Revolution*, vol. 68, 7–21. Karlsruhe: Schriftenreihe der Evangelischen Akademie Baden, 1990.

Dickens, A. G. *The German Nation and Martin Luther.* London: Arnold, 1974.

Dirlmeier, Ulf. *Untersuchungen zu Einkommensverhältnissen und Lebenshaltungskosten in oberdeutschen Städten des Spätmittelalters (Mitte 14. bis Anfang 16. Jahrhundert).* Heidelberg: Winter Universitätsverlag, 1978.

Dolan, John P., trans. *Erasmus: Handbook of the Militant Christian.* Notre Dame, Ind.: Fides Publishers, 1962.

Douglas, James. *Why Charity? The Case for a Third Sector.* Beverly Hills: Sage Publications, 1983.

Duchrow, Ulrich. *Christenheit und Weltverantwortung.* Stuttgart: Klett-Cotta, 1970.

Dueringer, Karl. "Lorenzo de Villavicencio als Anwalt der kirchliche Armenpflege im Zeitalter der Tridentinischen Reform." *Gesammelte Aufsätze zur Kulturgeschichte Spaniens.* Münster: Aschendorff (1963): 327–39.

Dummler, Karl. "Die Leisniger Kastenordnung von 1523." *Zeitschrift für evangelisches Kirchenrecht* (1984): 337–53.

Durkin, John. "Care of the Poor: Pre-Reformation Hospitals." In David Roberts, ed., *Essays on the Scottish Reformation 1513–1625*, 116–28. Glasgow: Burns, 1962.

Durnbaugh, Donald, ed. *Every Need Supplied: Mutual Aid and Christian Community in the Free Churches*, 1525–1675. Philadelphia: Temple University Press, 1974.

Edwards, Mark U., Jr. "Statistics on Sixteenth-Century Printing." In Philip Bebb & Sherrin Marshall, eds., *The Process of Change in Early Modern Europe: Essays in Honor of Miriam Usher Chrisman*, 149–63. Athens: Ohio University Press, 1988.

Ehrle, Franz. "Die Armenordnungen von Nürnberg (1522) und von Ypern I (1525)." *Historisches Jahrbuch der Görres-Gesellschaft* 9 (1888): 450–79.

———. *Beiträge zur Geschichte und Reform der Armenpflege.* Freiburg im Breisgau, 1881.

Eire, Carlos M. N. *War against the Idols: The Reformation of Worship from Erasmus to Calvin.* Cambridge: Cambridge University Press, 1986.

Elert, Werner. *Morphologie des Luthertums.* 2 vols. Munich: Beck, 1958.

Endres, Rudolf. "Sozialstruktur Nürnbergs." In Gerhard Pfeiffer, ed., *Nürnberg—Geschichte einer europäischen Stadt*, 194–99. Munich: Beck, 1971.

Epstein, Steven. *Wills and Wealth in Medieval Genoa*, 1150–1250. Cambridge: Harvard University Press, 1984.

Fabiunke, Günter. *Martin Luther als Nationalökonom.* Berlin: Akademische Verlag, 1963.

Fairchilds, Cissie C. *Poverty and Charity in Aix-en-Provence 1640-1789.* Baltimore: Johns Hopkins University Press, 1976.

The Fathers of the Catholic Church, vol. 11. Washington, D.C.: Catholic University Press, 1963.

Fauth, Dieter. "Das Menschenbild bei Thomas Müntzer." In Siegfried Bräuer & Helmar Junghans, eds., *Der Theologe Thomas Müntzer: Untersuchung zu seiner Entwicklung und Lehre*, 39–61. Berlin: Evangelische Verlagsanstalt, 1989.

Feger, Otto, ed. *Vom Richterbrief zum Roten Buch: Die älterer Konstanzer Ratsgesetzgebung.* Constance, 1955.

Feuchtwanger, L. "Geschichte der sozialen Politik und des Armenwesens im Zeitalter der Reformation." *Jahrbuch für Gesetzgebung, Verwaltung, und Volkswirtschaft im Deutschen Reich* 32 (1908): 167–204; 33 (1909): 191–228.

Fideler, Paul. "Christian Humanism and Poor Law Reform in Early Tudor England." *Societas—A Review of Social History* 4 (1974): 269–85.

Fischer, Thomas. "Der Beginn frühmoderner Sozialpolitik in deutschen Städten des 16. Jahrhunderts." In *Arbeitspapiere des Forschungsschwerpunktes Reproduktionsrisiken, soziale Bewegungen und Sozialpolitik,* vol. 3, 1–29. Universität Bremen, 1980.

———. *Städtische Armut und Armenfürsorge im 15. und 16. Jahrhundert.* Göttingen: Schwartz, 1979.

Fischer, Wolfram. *Armut in der Geschichte.* Göttingen: Vandenhoeck & Ruprecht, 1982.

Fischoff, Ephraim. "The Protestant Ethic and the Spirit of Capitalism: The History of a Controversy." In S. N. Eisenstadt, ed., *The Protestant Ethic and Modernization: A Comparative View,* 67–86. New York: Basic Books, 1968.

Flynn, Maureen. "Charitable Ritual in Late Medieval and Early Modern Spain." *Sixteenth Century Journal* 16/3 (1985), 335–48.

———. *Sacred Charity: Confraternities and Social Welfare in Spain, 1400–1700.* Ithaca, N.Y.: Cornell University Press, 1989.

Forell, George W. *Faith Active in Love: An Investigation of the Principles Underlying Luther's Social Ethics.* Minneapolis: Augsburg, 1959.

Forma subventionis pauperum que Hyperas Flandorum urbem viget universae reipublicae longe utilissima. 1531. (Houghton Library, Harvard University.)

Frank, Ross H. "An Interpretation of *Land of Cockaigne* (1567) by Pieter Breugel the Elder." *Sixteenth Century Journal* (1991), 299–329.

Frey, Christofer. "Die Reformation Luthers in ihrer Bedeutung für die moderne Arbeits- und Berufswelt." In Hartmut Löwe & Claus-Jürgen Roepke, eds., *Luther und die Folge,* 110–34. Munich: Kaiser, 1983.

Friedmann, Robert. "The Christian Communism of the Hutterite Brethren." *Archiv für Reformationsgeschichte* 46 (1955): 196–209.

Frostin, Per. "The Hermeneutics of the Poor—The Epistemological 'Break' in Third World Theologies." *Studia Theologica* 39 (1985): 127–50.

Fuchs, François-Joseph. "Les relations commerciales entre Nuremberg et Strasbourg aux XVe et XVIe siècles." In *Hommage à Dürer: Strasbourg et Nuremberg dans la première moitié du XVIe siècle,* 77–90. Strasbourg: Librairie Istra, 1972.

Fügedi, Erik. "Steuerlisten, Vermögen und soziale Gruppen in mittelalterlichen Städten." In Ingrid Bátori, ed., *Städtische Gesellschaft und Reformation,* 58–96. Stuttgart: Klett-Cotta, 1980.

Geiger, Gottfried. "Die reformatorischen Initia Johann Eberlins von Günzburg nach seinen Flugschriften." In Horst Rabe, H. Molitar, & H.-C. Rublack, eds., *Festgabe für Ernst Walter Zeeden,* 178–201. Münster: Aschendorff, 1976.

214   *Beyond Charity*

Geist, Hildeberg. "Arbeit: Die Entscheidung eines Wortwertes durch Luther." *Luther-Jahrbuch* 13 (1931): 83–113.

Geremek, Bronislaw. *The Margins of Society in Late Medieval Paris.* Trans. Jean Birrell. Cambridge: Cambridge University Press, 1987.

————. *La potence ou la pitié.* Paris: Gallimard, 1987.

————. "Renfermement des pauvres en Italie (XIV–XVIIᵉ siècle): Remarques préliminaires." In *Histoire économique du monde Méditerranéen 1450–1650*, 205–17. Toulouse: Privat, 1973.

————. *Truands et misérables dans l'Europe moderne, 1350–1600.* Paris: Gallimard, 1980.

Gierra, Peter. "Luthers reformatorische Erkenntnis als Anstoss zum Aufbau der Armenfürsorge." In Peter Gierra, ed., *Impulse zur Diakonie in der Lutherstadt Wittenberg*, 5–15. Berlin: Evangelische Verlagsanstalt, 1983.

Gilchrist, John. *The Church and Economic Activity in the Middle Ages.* London: Macmillan, 1969.

Gilder, George. *Wealth and Poverty.* New York: Basic Books, 1981.

Glazer, Nona, & Carol Creedon, eds. *Children and Poverty: Some Sociological and Psychological Perspectives.* Chicago: Rand McNally, 1970..

Goertz, Hans-Jürgen. "Eigentum: Mittelalter." In *Theologische Realenzyklopädie*, vol. 9, 417–23. Berlin and New York: de Gruyter, 1982.

————. "Spiritualität und revolutionäres Engagement. Thomas Müntzer: Ein Revolutionär zwischen Mittelalter und Neuzeit." In Klaus Deppermann et al., *Thomas Müntzer: Ein streitbarer Theologe zwischen Mystik und Revolution*, vol. 68, 42–54. Karlsruhe: Schriftenreihe der Evangelischen Akademie Baden, 1990.

————. *Die Täufer: Geschichte und Deutung.* Berlin: Evangelische Verlagsanstalt, 1988.

Graham, Gordon. *The Idea of Christian Charity: A Critique of Some Contemporary Conceptions.* Notre Dame, Ind.: University of Notre Dame Press, 1990.

Graus, F. "The Late Medieval Poor in Town and Countryside." In Sylvia Thrupp, ed., *Change in Medieval Society*, 314–24. New York: Appleton-Century-Crofts, 1964.

Greyerz, Kaspar von. "Stadt und Reformation: Stand und Aufgaben der Forschung." *Archiv für Reformationsgeschichte* 76 (1985): 6–63.

Griffen, Clyde. "Rich Laymen and Early Social Christianity." *Church History* 36 (1967): 45–65.

Grimm, Harold. *Lazarus Spengler: A Lay Leader of the Reformation.* Columbus: Ohio State University Press, 1978.

————. "Luther's Contributions to Sixteenth Century Organization of Poor Relief." *Archiv für Reformationsgeschichte* 81 (1970): 222–34.

Grossmann, Maria. *Humanism in Wittenberg 1485–1517.* Nieuwkoop: de Graaf, 1975.

Guy, Alain. *Vives ou l'Humanisme engagé.* Paris: Seghers, 1972.

Haile, H. G. *Luther: An Experiment in Biography.* Princeton: Princeton University Press, 1983.

Hall, Basil. "The Reformation City." *Bulletin of the John Rylands Library* 54 (1971/72): 103–48.

Hartmann, Robert, ed. *Poverty and Economic Justice: A Philosophical Approach.* Ramsey, N.J.: Paulist Press, 1984.

Hauschild, Wolf-Dieter, ed. *Lübecker Kirchenordnung von Johannes Bugenhagen 1531.* Lübeck: Schmidt-Römhild, 1981.

Hendel, Kurt. "The Care of the Poor: An Evangelical Perspective." *Currents in Theology and Mission* 15 (1988): 526–32.

Hendrix, Scott. "Luther's Impact on the Sixteenth Century." *Sixteenth Century Journal* 16 (1985): 3–14.

Hering, H. "Die Liebesthätigkeit der deutschen Reformation." *Theologische Studien und Kritiken* 56 (1883): 661–729.

Herlihy, David. "Alienation in Medieval Culture and Society." In Frank Johnson, ed., *Alienation: Concept, Term, and Meanings*, 125–41. New York: Seminar Press, 1973.

Hesse, Helmut. "Über Luthers 'Von Kauffshandlung und Wucher.'" In Helmut Hesse & Gerhard Müller, eds., *Über Luthers "Von Kauffshandlung und Wucher,"* 25–57. Frankfurt am Main: Verlag Wirtschaft und Finanzen, 1987.

Hillerbrand, Hans J. "Radicalism in the Early Reformation: Varieties of Reformation in Church and Society." In H. J. Hillerbrand, ed., *Radical Tendencies in the Reformation: Divergent Perspectives*, 25–41. Kirksville, Mo.: Sixteenth Century Journal Publishers, 1988.

Hilton, Boyd. *The Age of Atonement: The Influence of Evangelicalism on Social and Economic Thought, 1795–1865.* New York: Clarendon Press, 1988.

Himmelfarb, Gertrude. *The Idea of Poverty: England in the Early Industrial Age.* New York: Knopf, 1984.

Hinnebusch, John F. *The Historia Occidentalis of Jacques de Vitry: A Critical Edition.* Fribourg: University Press, 1972.

Holfelder, Hans Hermann. "Bugenhagen." *Theologische Realenzyklopädie*, vol. 7, 354–63. Berlin and New York: de Gruyter, 1981.

———. "Bugenhagens Theologie—Anfänge, Entwicklungen, und Ausbildungen bis zum Römerbriefkolleg." *Luther* 57 (1986): 65–80.

Holleman, Warren. "Welfare Reform, Helmut Thielicke, and Secular Humanism." *Dialog* 28 (1989): 289–92.

Hsia R. Po-Chia. "Civic Wills as Sources for the Study of Piety in Muenster, 1530–1618." *Sixteenth Century Journal* 14/3 (1983): 321–48.

Hunecke, Volker. "Überlegungen zur Geschichte der Armut im vorindustriellen Europa." *Geschichte und Gesellschaft* 9 (1982): 480–512.

Hutterian Brethren, eds. & trans. *The Chronicle of the Hutterian Brethren.* Rifton, N.Y.: Plough Publishing House, 1987.

Irsigler, Franz. "Bettler und Dirnen in der städtischen Gesellschaft des 14.–16. Jahrhunderts." In Thomas Riis, ed., *Aspects of Poverty in Early Modern Europe*, vol. 2, 179–91. Odense: Odense University Press, 1986.

Irsigler, Franz, & Arnold Lassotta. *Bettler und Gaukler, Dirnen und Henker: Randgruppen und Aussenseiter in Köln 1300–1600.* Cologne: Graven Verlag, 1984.

Jaritz, Gerhard. "Die Realienkundliche Aussage der sogenannten 'Wiener Testamentsbücher.' " In *Das Leben in der Stadt des Spätmittelalters*, 171–90. Vienna: Verlag der Österreichischen Akademie der Wissenschaften, 1977.

————. "Seelenheil und Sachkultur." In *Europäisches Sachkultur des Mittelalters*, 57–81. Vienna: Verlag der Österreichischen Akademie der Wissenschaften, 1980.

Jetter, Dieter. *Geschichte des Hospitals*, vol. 1: *Westdeutschland von den Anfängen bis 1850*. Wiesbaden: Steiner, 1966.

Johannsmeier, Rolf. "Die Angst vor den Armen: Bettlerszenen vom Oberrhein." In Heiner Boehncke & Rolf Johannsmeier, *Das Buch der Vaganten, Spieler, Huren, Leutbetrüger*, 7–41. Cologne: Prometh Verlag, 1987.

Jordan, W. K. *The Charities of London, 1480–1660*. London: Allen & Unwin, 1960.

————. *The Charities of Rural England, 1480-1660*. New York: Russell Sage Foundation, 1961.

————. *Philanthropy in England, 1480–1660*. London: Allen & Unwin, 1959.

Junghans, Helmar. *Der junge Luther und die Humanisten*. Weimar: Böhlau, 1984.

————. "Sozialethisches Denken und Handeln bei Martin Luther." *Evangelische Monatsschrift Standpunkt* 70/3 (1989): 67–71.

————. "Der Wandel des Müntzerbildes in der DDR von 1951/52 bis 1989." *Luther* 60 (1989): 102–30.

Justin Martyr. "First Apology." In Cyril Richardson, ed., *Early Christian Fathers*, 225–89. Philadelphia: Westminster Press, 1953.

Jütte, Robert. *Abbild und Soziale Wirklichkeit des Bettler- und Gaunertums zu Beginn der Neuzeit: Sozial-, Mentalitäts- und Sprachgeschichtliche Studien zum Liber Vagatorum (1510)*. Cologne and Vienna: Böhlau, 1988.

————. *Obrigkeitliche Armenfürsorge in Deutschen Reichsstädten der frühen Neuzeit*. Cologne: Böhlau, 1986.

————. "Poor Relief and Social Discipline in Sixteenth Century Europe." *European Studies Review* 11 (1981): 25–52.

————. "Vagantentum und Bettlerwesen bei Hans Jakob Christoffel von Grimmelshausen." *Daphnis* 9 (1980): 109–31.

Kahl, Gisela. "Martin Luther, 'der älteste deutsche Nationalökonom.' " In *Martin Luther: Leistungen und Wirkungen Wissenschaftliche Zeitschrift* (Gesellschaftswissenschaftliche Reihe. Friedrich-Schiller-Universität Jena) 33/3 (1984): 315–26.

Kamen, Henry. *The Iron Century: Social Change in Europe 1550–1660*. New York: Praeger, 1971.

Karant-Nunn, Susan. *Zwickau in Transition, 1500–1547: The Reformation as Agent of Change*. Columbus: Ohio State University Press, 1987.

Katz, Michael B. *In the Shadow of the Poorhouse: A Social History of Welfare in America*. New York: Basic Books, 1986.

Kawarau, G. "Zur Leisniger Kastenordnung." *Neues Archiv für sächsische Geschichte und Altertumskunde* 3 (1880): 78–85.

Kiessling, Rolf. *Bürgerliche Gesellschaft und Kirche in Augsburg im Spätmittelalter*. Augsburg: Mühlberger, 1971.

Kiss, Igor. "Luthers Bemühungen um eine sozial gerechtere Welt." *Zeichen der Zeit* (1985), 59–65.

Kittelson, James. "Humanism and the Reformation in Germany." *Central European History* 9 (1976): 303–22.

Klassen, Peter James. *The Economics of Anabaptism 1525–1560.* The Hague: Mouton, 1964.

Kohls, Ernst-Wilhelm. "Evangelische Bewegung und Kirchenordnung in oberdeutschen Reichsstädten." *Zeitschrift der Savigny-Stiftung für Rechtsgeschichte, Kanonistische Abteilung* 53 (1967), 110–34.

———. *Die Schule bei Martin Bucer in ihrem Verhältnis zu Kirche und Obrigkeit.* Heidelberg: Quelle & Meyer, 1963.

Köhn, Mechtild. *Martin Bucers Entwurf einer Reformation des Erzstiftes Köln.* Witten: Luther Verlag, 1966.

Kunst, Hermann. *Evangelischer Glaube und politischer Verantwortung.* Stuttgart: Evangelisches Verlagswerk, 1976.

Ladner, Gerhart B. "*Homo Viator*: Medieval Ideas on Alienation and Order." *Speculum* 42 (1967): 233–59.

Lane, Frank. "Johannes Bugenhagen und die Armenfürsorge in der Reformationszeit." *Braunschweigisches Jahrbuch* 64 (1983): 147–56.

———. "Poverty and Poor Relief in the German Church Orders of Johann Bugenhagen, 1485–1558." Ph.D. diss. Ohio State University, 1973.

Laube, Adolf. *Flugschriften der frühen Reformationsbewegung* (1518–1524). 2 vols. Berlin: Akademie Verlag, 1983.

———. "Martin Luther und die Anfänge des städtischen Sozialreformen." Paper presented at the Sixth International Congress for Luther Research, Erfurt, 1983.

———. "Radicalism as a Research Problem in the History of the Early Reformation." In Hans J. Hillerbrand, ed., *Radical Tendencies in the Reformation: Divergent Perspectives*, 9–23. Kirksville, Mo.: Sixteenth Century Journal Publishers, 1988.

Leclère, Françoise. "Recherches sur la charité des bourgeois envers les pauvres au XIVᵉ siècle à Douai." *Revue du Nord* 48 (1966): 139–54.

Leder, Hans-Günter. "Leben und Werk des Reformators Johannes Bugenhagen." In H.-G. Leder & Norbert Buske, eds., *Johannes Bugenhagen und die Reformation im Herzogtum Pommern*, 9–45. Berlin: Evangelisches Verlagsanstalt, 1985.

Le Goff, Jacques. *Your Money or Your Life: Economy and Religion in the Middle Ages.* New York: Zone Books, 1988.

Lehmann, Hermann. "Luthers Platz in der Geschichte der politischen Ökonomie." In Günter Vogler et al., *Martin Luther: Leben–Werke–Wirkung.* 2d ed., 279–94. Berlin: Akademie Verlag, 1986.

Lentze, Hans. "Das Seelgerät im mittelalterlichen Wien." *Zeitschrift der Savigny-Stiftung für Rechtsgeschichte, Kanonistiche Abteilung* 44 (1958): 37–103.

Lesnick, David. *Preaching in Medieval Florence: The Social World of Franciscan and Dominican Spirituality.* Athens: University of Georgia Press, 1989.

Liber Vagatorum: The Book of Vagabonds. Trans. J. C. Hotten; revised by D. B. Thomas. London: Penguin, 1932.

Liermann, Hans. *Handbuch des Stiftungsrechtes.* Tübingen, 1963.

Lietzmann, Hans, ed. *Von Abtuhung der Bilder und das keyn Bedtler unther den Christen seyn sollen* (Kleine Texte 74). Bonn, 1911.

———. *Die Wittenberger und Leisniger Kastenordnung* (Kleine Texte 21). Berlin: de Gruyter, 1935.

Lindberg, Carter. "The Conception of the Eucharist According to Erasmus and Karlstadt." In Marc Lienhard, ed., *Les dissidents du XVIe siècle entre l'Humanisme et le Catholicisme,* 79–94. Baden-Baden: Koerner, 1983.

———. "Conflicting Models of Ministry—Luther, Karlstadt, and Muentzer." *Concordia Theological Quarterly* 41/4 (1977): 35–50.

———. "Justification by Faith Alone: The Lutheran Proposal to the Churches." *New Conversations* 10/2 (1988): 31–41.

———. "Karlstadt, Luther, and the Origins of Protestant Poor Relief." *Church History* 46 (1977): 313–34.

———. "Karlstadt's 'Dialogue' on the Lord's Supper." *Mennonite Quarterly Review* 53 (1979): 35–77.

———. "Luther and the Crises of the Late Medieval Era: An Historical Interpretation." *African Theological Journal* 13/2 (1984): 92–104.

———. "Luther on Property and Poverty." *Luther-Jahrbuch* 57 (1990): 251–53.

———. "Müntzeriana." *Lutheran Quarterly* 4 (1990): 195–214.

———. "Prierias and his Significance for Luther's Development." *Sixteenth Century Journal* 3/2 (1972): 45–64.

———. "Reformation Initiatives for Social Welfare." In D. M. Yeager, ed., *The Annual of the Society of Christian Ethics 1987,* 79–99. Washington, D.C.: Georgetown University Press, 1987.

———. "La théologie et l'assistance publique, le cas d'Ypres (1525–1531)." *Revue d'histoire et de philosophie religieuses* 61 (1981): 23–36.

———. "Theology and Politics: Luther the Radical and Müntzer the Reactionary." *Encounter* 37 (1976): 356–71.

———. "Theory and Practice: Reformation Models of Ministry as Resource for the Present." *Lutheran Quarterly* 27 (1975): 27–35.

———. "'There Should Be No Beggars among Christians': An Early Reformation Tract on Social Welfare by Andreas Karlstadt." In Carter Lindberg, ed., *Piety, Politics, and Ethics: Reformation Studies in Honor of George Wolfgang Forell,* 157–66. Kirksville, Mo.: Sixteenth Century Journal Publishers, 1984.

———. "Through a Glass Darkly: A History of the Church's Vision of the Poor and Poverty." *Ecumenical Review* 33 (1981): 37–52.

Lindgren, Uta. "Avicenna und die Grundprinzipien des Gemeinwesens in Francesc Eiximenis 'Regiment de la Cosa Pública' (Valencia 1383)." In Albert Zimmermann, ed., *Soziale Ordnungen im Selbstverständnis des Mittelalters. Miscellanea Mediaevalia* 12/2: 449–59. Berlin: de Gruyter, 1980.

———. "Europas Armut: Probleme, Methoden, Ergebnisse einer Untersuchungsserie." *Saeculum* 28 (1977): 396–418.

Lis, Catherina, & Hugo Soly. *Poverty and Capitalism in Pre-Industrial Europe.* Atlantic Highlands, N.J.: Humanities Press, 1979.

Little, Lester K. "Evangelical Poverty, the New Money Economy and Violence." In David Flood, ed., *Poverty in the Middle Ages,* 11–26. Werl: Dietrich-Coelde, 1975.

————. *Liberty, Charity, Fraternity: Lay Religious Confraternities at Bergamo in the Age of the Commune.* Northampton, Mass.: Smith College, 1988.

————. "Pride Goes before Avarice: Social Change and the Vices in Latin Christendom." *American Historical Review* 76/1 (1971): 16–49.

————. *Religious Poverty and the Profit Economy in Medieval Europe.* Ithaca, N.Y.: Cornell University Press, 1978.

————. "L'utilité sociale de la pauvreté volontaire." In Michel Mollat, ed., *Études sur l'histoire de la pauvreté,* vol. 1, 447–59. Paris, 1974.

Lohse, Bernhard. *Martin Luther: An Introduction to His Life and Work.* Philadelphia: Fortress Press, 1986.

Lorenz, Eckehart, ed. *The Debate on "Status Confessionis": Studies in Christian Political Theology.* Geneva: Lutheran World Federation, 1983.

Lortz, Jürgen. *Die reformatorische Wirken Dr. Wenzeslaus Lincks in Altenburg und Nürnberg.* Nuremberg: Korn & Berg, 1978.

Lütge, Friedrich. "The Fourteenth and Fifteenth Centuries in Social and Economic History." In Gerald Strauss, ed., *Pre-Reformation Germany,* 316–79. New York: Harper & Row, 1972.

Manns, Peter. *Martin Luther: An Illustrated Biography.* New York: Crossroad, 1982.

————. *Martin Luther—Ketzer oder Vater im Glauben?* Hannover: Lutherhaus Verlag, 1980.

Manns, Peter, & Harding Meyer, eds., in collaboration with Carter Lindberg & Harry McSorley. *Luther's Ecumenical Significance: An Interconfessional Consultation.* Philadelphia: Fortress Press; New York: Paulist Press, 1984.

Maron, Gottfried. " 'Niemand soll sein eigner Richter sein': Eine Bemerkung zu Luthers Haltung im Bauernkrieg." *Luther* 46 (1975): 60–75.

Martz, Linda. *Poverty and Welfare in Hapsburg Spain: The Example of Toledo.* Cambridge: Cambridge University Press, 1983.

Maschke, Erich. "Die Unterschichten der mittelalterlichen Städte Deutschlands." In Erich Maschke & Jürgen Sydow, eds., *Gesellschaftlichen Unterschichten in den sudwestdeutschen Städten,* 1–74. Stuttgart: Kohlhammer, 1967.

Matheson, Peter. "Adam's Burden: Diagnoses of Poverty in Post-Medieval Europe and the Third World Now." *Tijdschrift voor Geschiednis* 89/2 (1976): 149–60.

————. "Thomas Müntzer's *Vindication and Refutation*: A Language for the Common People." *Sixteenth Century Journal* 20 (1989): 603–15.

McGrath, Alister. *The Intellectual Origins of the European Reformation.* Oxford, England: Basil Blackwell, 1987.

McKee, Elsie. "John Calvin on the Diaconate and Liturgical Almsgiving." Ph.D. diss. Princeton University, 1982; since published by Librairie Droz, Geneva, 1984.

Meyer, Hans Bernhard. *Luther und die Messe.* Paderborn: Bonifacius, 1965.

Meyer, Harding. " 'Delectari assertionibus' On the Issue of the Authority of Christian Testimony." In Carter Lindberg, ed., *Piety, Politics, and Ethics: Reformation Studies in Honor of George Wolfgang Forell,* 1–14. Kirksville, Mo.: Sixteenth Century Journal Publishers, 1984.

Miller, Timothy. *The Birth of the Hospital in the Byzantine Empire.* Baltimore: Johns Hopkins University Press, 1985.

Moeller, Bernd. *Imperial Cities and the Reformation.* Philadelphia: Fortress Press, 1972.

―――. "Korreferat zu Wolfgang Reinhard: Luther und die Städte." In Erwin Iserloh & Gerhard Müller, eds., *Luther und die politische Welt,* 113–21. Stuttgart: Steiner, 1984.

―――. "Luther und die Städte." In *Aus der Lutherforschung: Drei Vorträge,* 9–26. Opladen: Westdeutschen Verlag, 1983.

―――. "Piety in Germany around 1500." In Steven Ozment, ed., *The Reformation in Medieval Perspective,* 50–75. Chicago: Quadrangle Books, 1971.

―――. *Reichsstadt und Reformation.* Revised ed. Berlin: Evangelische Verlagsanstalt, 1987.

―――. "Stadt und Buch: Bemerkungen zur Struktur der reformatorischen Bewegung in Deutschland." In Wolfgang Mommsen et al., eds., *Stadtbürgertum und Adel in der Reformation,* 25–39. Stuttgart, 1979.

―――. "The Town in Church History." In Derek Baker, ed., *The Church in Town and Countryside,* 257–68. Oxford, England: Basil Blackwell, 1979.

Mohl, Ruth. *The Three Estates in Medieval and Renaissance Literature.* New York: Columbia University Press, 1933.

Moisa, Maria. "Fourteenth-Century Preachers' Views of the Poor: Class or Status Group?" In Raphael Samuel & Gareth Jones, eds., *Culture, Ideology, and Politics: Essays for Eric Hobsbawm,* 160–75. London: Routledge & Kegan Paul, 1982.

Mollat, Michel, ed. *Études sur l'histoire de la pauvreté.* 2 vols. Paris, 1974.

―――. "Hospitalité et assistance au début du XIIIᵉ siècle." In David Flood, ed., *Poverty in the Middle Ages,* 37–51. Werl: Coelde, 1975.

―――. "La notion de pauvreté au Moyen Age: position de problémes." *Revue d'histoire de l'Église de France* 70 (1966): 6–23.

―――. *Les pauvres au Moyen Age.* Paris: Hachette, 1978.

―――. "The Poor in the Middle Ages: The Experience of a Research Project." In Thomas Riis, ed., *Aspects of Poverty in Early Modern Europe,* vol. 1, 29–37. Stuttgart: Klett-Cotta, 1981.

―――. "Les réactions des pauvres à la pauvreté en France au bas Moyen Age." In Thomas Riis, ed., *Aspects of Poverty in Early Modern Europe,* vol. 2, 77–88. Odense: Odense University Press, 1986.

Mollat, Michel, & Philippe Wolff. *The Popular Revolutions of the Middle Ages.* London: Allen & Unwin, 1973.

Mone, F. J. "Armen- und Krankenpflege vom 13. bis 16. Jahrhundert." *Zeitschrift für die Geschichte des Oberrheins* 12 (1861): 5–53.

————. "Ueber die Armenpflege vom 13. bis 16. Jahrhundert." *Zeitschrift für die Geschichte des Oberrheins* 1 (1850): 129–63.

More, Thomas. *Utopia: A New Translation, Backgrounds, Criticism.* Robert M. Adams, trans. & ed. New York: W. W. Norton, 1975.

Muchembled, Robert. Review of P. Brachin, trans. & ed., *Van Hout et Coornhert: Bienfaisance et répression au XVIe siècle.* Paris: Vrin, 1984; in *Revue du Nord* 69 (1987): 446–47.

Mueller, Reinhold C. "Charitable Institutions, the Jewish Community, and Venetian Society: A Discussion of the Recent Volume by Brian Pullan." *Studi Veneziani* 14 (1972): 37–81.

Müller, Gerhard. "Zu Luthers Sozialethik." In Helmut Hesse & Gerhard Müller, eds., *Über Martin Luthers "Von Kauffshandlung und Wucher,"* 59–79. Frankfürt am Main: Verlag Wirtschaft und Finanzen, 1987.

Mundy, John H. "Charity and Social Work in Toulouse, 1100–1250." *Traditio* 22 (1966): 203–87.

————. "Hospitals and Leprosaries in Twelfth- and Early Thirteenth-Century Toulouse." In J. H. Mundy, R. Emery, & B. N. Nelson, eds., *Essays in Medieval Life and Thought,* 181–205. New York: Columbia University Press, 1955.

Murken, Axel. "Von den ersten Hospitälern bis zum modernen Krankenhaus." In Carl Meckseper, ed., *Stadt im Wandel: Kunst und Kultur des Bürgertums in Norddeutschland 1150–1650,* vol. 3, 189–217. Stuttgart-Bad Canstatt: Edition Cantz, 1984.

Murray, Alexander. "Religion among the Poor in Thirteenth-Century France: The Testimony of Humbert de Romans." *Traditio* 30 (1974): 285–324.

Nelson, Benjamin. *The Idea of Usury: From Tribal Brotherhood to Universal Otherhood.* 2d ed. Chicago: University of Chicago Press, 1969.

Nipperdey, Thomas. "Die Utopia des Thomas Morus und der Beginn der Neuzeit." In T. Nipperdey, *Reformation, Revolution, Utopie,* 113–42. Göttingen: Vandenhoeck & Ruprecht, 1975.

Nolf, J. *La réforme de la bienfaisance publique à Ypres au XVIe siècle.* Ghent, 1915.

Noonan, John T. *The Scholastic Analysis of Usury.* Cambridge: Harvard University Press, 1957.

Noreña, Carlos G. *Juan Luis Vives.* The Hague: Nijhoff, 1970.

Nucé de Lamothe, M.-S. de. "Piété et charité publique à Toulouse de la fin du XIIIe siècle d'après les testaments." *Annales du Midi* 76 (1964): 5–39.

Oberman, Heiko A. *The Dawn of the Reformation.* Edinburgh: T. & T. Clark, 1986.

————. "The Shape of Late Medieval Thought: The Birthpangs of the Modern Era." *Archiv für Reformationsgeschichte* 64 (1973): 13–33.

————. *Werden und Wertung der Reformation.* Tübingen: Mohr, 1977.

Oexle, Otto G. "Die mittelalterlichen Gilden: Ihre Selbstdeutung und ihr Beitrag zur Formung sozialen Strukturen." In Albert Zimmermann, ed., *Soziale Ordnungen im Selbstverständnis des Mittelalters. Miscellanea Mediaevalia* 12/1: 203–26. Berlin: de Gruyter, 1979.

Ozment, Steven. "Humanism, Scholasticism, and the Intellectual Origins of the Reformation." In F. Forrester Church & Timothy George, eds., *Continuity and Discontinuity in Church History,* 133–49. Leiden: Brill, 1979.

———. "Pamphlets as a Source: Comments on Bernd Moeller's 'Stadt und Buch.'" In W. Mommson, ed., *Stadtbürgertum und Adel in der Reformation,* 79. Stuttgart, 1979.

———. *The Reformation in the Cities.* New Haven: Yale University Press, 1975.

———. "The Social History of the Reformation: What Can We Learn from the Pamphlets?" In Hans-Joachim Köhler, ed., *Flugschriften als Massenmedium der Reformationszeit,* 171–203. Stuttgart: Klett-Cotta, 1981.

Park, Katherine. *Doctors and Medicine in Early Renaissance Florence.* Princeton: Princeton University Press, 1985.

Pater, Calvin. *Karlstadt as the Father of the Baptist Movements.* Toronto: University of Toronto Press, 1983.

Pawlas, Andreas. "Zur Kalkulation einer 'gerechten' Preis bei Luther." *Luther* 60 (1989): 87–99.

Peters, Albrecht. *Kommentar zu Luthers Katechismen: Die Zehn Gebote.* Göttingen: Vandenhoeck & Ruprecht, 1990, 255–78: "Das Siebte Gebot."

Philippi, Paul. *Vorreformatorische Diakonie: Die Kirche in der hamburgischen Sozialgeschichte bis zum ende des Reformationsjahrhunderts.* Stuttgart: Verlagswerk der Diakonie, 1984.

Pirenne, Henri. *Histoire de Belgique,* vol. 3. Brussels: Lamertin, 1907.

Pischel, Felix. "Die ersten Armenordnungen der Reformationszeit." *Deutsches Geschichtsblätter* 17 (1916): 317–29.

Piven, Frances Fox, & Richard A. Cloward. *Poor People's Movements: Why They Succeed, How They Fail.* New York: Vintage Books, 1979.

———. *Regulating the Poor: The Functions of Public Welfare.* New York: Vintage Books, 1971.

Plath, Uwe. "Der Durchbruch der Reformation in Lüneburg." In G. Korner et al., eds., *Reformation vor 450 Jahren,* 25–69. Lüneburg, 1980.

Plümper, Hans-Dieter. *Die Gütergemeinschaft bei den Täufern des 16. Jahrhunderts.* Göppingen: Kümmerle, 1972.

Pope, Stephen. "Aquinas on Almsgiving, Justice, and Charity: An Interpretation and Reassessment." *Heythrop Journal* 32 (1991): 167–91.

Postel, Rainer. *Die Reformation in Hamburg, 1517–1528.* Gütersloh: Mohn, 1986.

———. "Sozialgeschichtliche Folgewirkungen der Reformation in Hamburg." In Wenzel Lohff, ed., *450 Jahre Reformation in Hamburg: Eine Festschrift,* 63–84. Hamburg: Agentur des Rauhen Hauses, 1980.

———. "Zur Bedeutung der Reformation für das religiöse und soziale Verhalten des Bürgertums in Hamburg." In Bernd Moeller, ed., *Stadt und Kirche im 16. Jahrhundert,* 168–76. Gütersloh: Mohn, 1978.

Pound, John. *Poverty and Vagrancy in Tudor England.* London: Longman, 1971.

Press, Volker. "Martin Luther und die sozialen Kräfte seiner Zeit." In Erwin Iserloh & Gerhard Müller, eds., *Luther und die politische Welt,* 189–217. Stuttgart: Steiner, 1984.

————. "Reformatorische Bewegung und Reichsverfassung." In Volker Press & Dieter Stievermann, eds., *Martin Luther: Probleme seiner Zeit*, 11–42. Stuttgart: Klett-Cotta, 1986.

Pullan, Brian. "Catholics and the Poor in Early Modern Europe." *Transactions of the Royal Historical Society.* 5th Series. 26 (1976): 15–34.

————. *Rich and Poor in Renaissance Venice: The Social Institutions of a Catholic State to 1620.* Cambridge: Harvard University Press, 1971.

Rapp, Francis. "L'Église et les pauvres à la fin du Moyen Age." *Revue d'histoire de l'Église de France* 52 (1966): 39–46.

————. *Réformes et Réformation à Strasbourg: Église et société dans le diocèse de Strasbourg (1450–1525).* Paris: Editions Ophrys, 1974.

Ratzinger, Georg. *Geschichte der kirchlichen Armenpflege.* Freiburg im Breisgau, 1868; 2d ed., 1884.

Reicke, Siegfried. *Das deutsche Spital und sein Recht im Mittelalter.* 2 vols. Stuttgart: Enke, 1932.

Rein, Martin. "Problems in the Definition and Measurement of Poverty." In Peter Townsend, ed., *The Concept of Poverty: Working Papers on Methods of Investigation and Life-Styles of the Poor in Different Countries*, 46–63. New York: American Elsevier, 1970.

Reinhard, Wolfgang. "Luther und die Städte." In Erwin Iserloh & Gerhard Müller, eds., *Luther und die politische Welt* (Stuttgart: Steiner, 1984). 87–112.

————. "Möglichkeiten und Grenzen der Verbindung von Kirchengeschichte mit Sozial- und Wirtschaftsgeschichte." In Gerta Klingenstein & Heinrich Lutz, eds., *Spezialforschung und "Gesamtgeschichte,"* 243–78. Munich: Oldenbourg, 1982.

Riis, Thomas. "Poverty and Urban Development in Early Modern Europe (15th–18th/19th Centuries): A General View." In Thomas Riis, ed., *Aspects of Poverty in Early Modern Europe*, vol. 1, 1–28. Stuttgart: Klett-Cotta, 1981.

Robertson, D. W. "The Doctrine of Charity in Medieval Literary Gardens," *Speculum* 26 (1951): 24–29.

Roche, Daniel. "A Pauper Capital: Some Reflections on the Parisian Poor in the Seventeenth and Eighteenth Centuries." *French History* 1/2 (1987): 182–209.

Rochefort, David. "Progressive and Social Control Perspectives on Social Welfare." *Social Science Review* (December 1981): 568–92.

Rochler, Wolfgang. *Martin Luther und die Reformation als Laienbewegung.* Wiesbaden: Steiner, 1981.

Roncière, Charles-M. de la. "Pauvres et pauvreté à Florence au XIVe siècle." In Michel Mollat, ed., *Études sur l'histoire de la pauvreté*, vol. 2., 661–745.

Rosenthal, Joel. *The Purchase of Paradise: Gift Giving and the Aristocracy, 1307–1485.* London: Routledge & Kegan Paul; Toronto: University of Toronto Press, 1972.

Rott, Jean. "La Réforme à Nuremberg et à Strasbourg: Contacts et contrastes." In *Hommage a Dürer: Strasbourg et Nuremberg dans la première moitié du XVIe siècle*, 91–142. Strasbourg: Librairie Istra, 1972.

Rowan, Stephen. *Ulrich Zasius: A Jurist in the German Renaissance, 1461–1535.* Frankfurt: Klostermann, 1987.

Rubin, Miri. *Charity and Community in Medieval Cambridge.* Cambridge: Cambridge University Press, 1987.

Rublack, Hans-Christoph. "Forschungsbericht Stadt und Reformation." In Bernd Moeller, ed., *Stadt und Kirche im 16. Jahrhundert,* 9–26. Gütersloh: Mohn, 1978.

———. "Grundwerte in der Reichsstadt im Spätmittelalter und in der frühen Neuzeit." In Horst Brunner, ed., *Literatur in der Stadt,* 9–36. Göttingen: Kümmerle, 1982.

———. "Reformation and Society." In Manfred Hoffman, ed., *Martin Luther and the Modern Mind,* 237–78. New York: Mellen Press, 1985.

———. "Reformatorische Bewegung und städtische Kirchenpolitik in Esslingen." In Ingrid Bátori, ed., *Städtische Gesellschaften und Reformation,* 191–220. Stuttgart: Klett-Cotta, 1980.

Rücklin-Teuscher, Gertrud. *Religiöses Volksleben des ausgehenden Mittelalters in den Reichsstädten Hall und Heilbronn.* Berlin: Ebering, 1933.

Rudloff, Ortwin. *Bonae Litterae et Lutherus: Texte und Untersuchungen zu den Anfängen der Theologie des Bremers Reformators Jakob Propst.* Bremen: Hauschild, 1985.

Rudolph, Conrad. *The "Things of Greater Importance": Bernard of Clairvaux's "Apologia" and the Medieval Attitude toward Art.* Philadelphia: University of Pennsylvania Press, 1990.

Rudolph, Günther. "Thomas Müntzers sozialökonomische Konzeption und das Traditionsbewusstsein der sozialistischen Arbeiterbewegung." *Deutsche Zeitschrift für Philosophie* 23 (1975): 558–69.

Rüger, Willi. *Mittelalterliches Almosenwesen: Die Almosen Ordnungen der Reichsstadt Nürnberg.* Nuremberg, 1932.

Sachsse, Christoph, & Florian Tennstedt, eds., *Geschichte der Armenfürsorge in Deutschland: Vom Spätmittelalter bis zum 1. Weltkrieg.* Stuttgart: Kohlhammer, 1980.

Salter, F. R., ed. *Some Early Tracts on Poor Relief.* London, 1926.

Samuel, Raphael, & Gareth Jones, eds. *Culture, Ideology, and Politics: Essays for Eric Hobsbawm.* London: Routledge & Kegan Paul, 1982.

Santa Ana, Julio de. *Good News to the Poor: The Challenge of the Poor in the History of the Church.* Geneva: World Council of Churches, 1977.

———, ed. *Separation without Hope? Essays on the Relation between the Church and the Poor during the Industrial Revolution and the Western Colonial Expansion.* Geneva: World Council of Churches, 1978.

———. *Towards a Church of the Poor.* Geneva: World Council of Churches, 1979.

Sattler, Gary R. *God's Glory, Neighbor's Good.* Chicago: Covenant Press, 1982.

Schade, Oskar, ed. *Satiren und Pasquille aus der Reformationszeit.* Vols. 1–3. 1863; reprint, Hildesheim: Georg Olms, 1966.

Scharffenorth, Gerta. *Den Glauben ins Leben ziehen . . . Studien zu Luthers Theologie.* Munich: Kaiser, 1982.

Schendel, Eberhard. "Martin Luther und die Armen." In *Lutherischen Kirche in der Welt* 36 (1989): 112–24.

Scherpner, Hans. *Theorie der Fürsorge*. Göttingen, 1962.

———. "Die Reformation in den Reichsstädten und die Kirchengüter." In Jürgen Sydow, ed., *Bürgerschaft und Kirche*, 67–88. Sigmarinen: Thorbecke, 1980.

Schindling, Anton. "Kirche, Gesellschaft, Politik, und Bildung in Strasbourg." In Grete Klingenstein & Heinrich Lutz, eds., *Spezialforschung und "Gesamtgeschichte,"* 169–88. Munich: Oldenbourg, 1982.

Schmidt, Heinrich. *Reichsstädten, Reich und Reformation*. Stuttgart: Steiner, 1986.

Schulze, Winfried. "Vom Gemeinnutz zum Eigennutz: Über den Normenwandel in der ständischen Gesellschaft der frühen Neuzeit." *Historische Zeitschrift* 243 (1986): 591–626.

Schweicher, Curt. "Werke der Barmherzigkeit." In Engelbert Kirschbaum, ed., *Lexikon der christlichen Ikonographie*, vol. 1, 245–51. Rome: Herder, 1968.

Schwiebert, E. G. *Luther and His Times*. St. Louis: Concordia, 1950.

Scott, Tom. *Thomas Müntzer: Theology and Revolution in the German Reformation*. New York: St. Martin's Press, 1989.

Scribner, Robert. "The *Mordbrenner* Fear in Sixteenth-Century Germany: Political Paranoia or the Revenge of the Outcast?" In Richard J. Evans, ed., *The German Underworld: Deviants and Outcasts in German History*, 29–56. London & New York: Routledge, 1988.

———. *Popular Culture and Popular Movements in Reformation Germany*. London & Ronceverte: Hambledon Press, 1987.

———. "Sozialkontrolle und die Möglichkeit einer städtische Reformation." In Bernd Moeller, *Stadt und Kirche im 16. Jahrhundert*, 57–65. Gütersloh: Mohn, 1978.

Seebass, Gottfried. "The Reformation in Nürnberg." In Lawrence Buck & Jonathon Zophy, eds., *The Social History of the Reformation*, 17–40. Columbus: Ohio State University Press, 1972.

———. *Das reformatorische Werk des Andreas Osiander*. Nuremberg: Verein für Bayerische Kirchengeschichte, 1967.

———. "Stadt und Kirche in Nürnberg im Zeitalter der Reformation." In Bernd Moeller, *Stadt und Kirche im 16. Jahrhundert*, 66–86. Gütersloh: Mohn, 1978.

Shapiro, Jacob. *Social Reform and the Reformation*. 1909; reprint, New York: AMS Press, 1970.

"Shepherd, The." *Ante-Nicene Fathers*, vol. 2. Grand Rapids, Mich.: Eerdmans, 1956.

Shewring, Walter, ed. *Rich and Poor in Christian Tradition*. London: Barnes, Oates & Washbourne, 1948.

Sider, Ronald J. *Andreas Bodenstein von Karlstadt*. Leiden: Brill, 1974.

———. *Evangelicals and Development: Toward a Technology of Social Change*. Philadelphia: Westminster Press, 1981.

Slack, Paul. "The Reactions of the Poor to Poverty in England c. 1500–1750." In Thomas Riis, ed., *Aspects of Poverty in Early Modern Europe*, vol. 2, 19–29. Odense: Odense University Press, 1986.

Smalley, Beryl. *The Study of the Bible in the Middle Ages.* Notre Dame: Univ. of Notre Dame Press, 1964.

Speakman, Elizabeth. "Mediaeval Hospitals." *Dublin Review* 133 (1903): 283–96.

Spicciani, Amleto. "The 'Poveri Vergognosi' in Fifteenth-Century Florence." In Thomas Riis, ed., *Aspects of Poverty in Early Modern Europe*, vol. 1, 119–82. Stuttgart: Klett-Cotta, 1981.

Spillmann, Hans Otto. *Untersuchungen zum Wortschatz in Thomas Müntzers deutsche Schriften.* Berlin: de Gruyter, 1971.

Spinka, Matthew, ed. *Advocates of Reform.* Philadelphia: Westminster Press, 1953.

Sprengler-Ruppenthal, Annaliese. *Mysterium und Riten: Nach der Londoner Kirchenordnung der Niederländer (ca. 1550 bis 1566).* Cologne: Böhlau, 1967.

Stackhouse, Max. *Creeds, Society, and Human Rights: A Study in Three Cultures.* Grand Rapids, Mich.: Eerdmans, 1984.

Stayer, James M. "The Anabaptists." In Steven Ozment, ed., *Reformation Europe: A Guide to Research*, 135–59. St. Louis: Center for Reformation Research, 1982.

———. "Christianity in One City: Anabaptist Münster, 1534–1535." In Hans J. Hillerbrand, ed., *Radical Tendencies in the Reformation: Divergent Perspectives*, 117–34. Kirksville, Mo.: Sixteenth Century Journal Publishers, 1988.

———. "Thomas Müntzer in 1989: A Review Article." *Sixteenth Century Journal* 21 (1990): 655–70.

Steinbicker, Carl. *Poor Relief in the Sixteenth Century.* Washington, D.C.: Catholic University of America, 1937.

Steinmetz, David. *Luther in Context.* Bloomington: Indiana University Press, 1986.

Steinmetz, Max, ed. *Hans Hergot und die Flugschrift "Von der newen Wandlungen eynes christlichen Lebens."* Leipzig: VEB Fachbuchverlag, 1977.

Stock, Ursala. *Die Bedeutung der Sakramente in Luthers Sermonen von 1519.* Leiden: Brill, 1982.

Strohm, Theodor. "Luthers Wirtschafts- und Sozialethik." In Helmar Junghans, ed., *Leben und Werk Martin Luthers von 1526 bis 1546*, vol. 2, 205–23. Berlin: Evangelische Verlagsanstalt, 1983.

———. "Martin Luthers Sozialethik und ihre Bedeutung für die Gegenwart." In Hans Süssmuth, ed., *Das Luther-Erbe in Deutschland: Vermittlung zwischen Wissenschaft und Öffentlichkeit*, 68–91. Düsseldorf: Droste Verlag, 1985.

———. " 'Theologie der Diakonie' in der Perspektive der Reformation." In Paul Philippi & Theodor Strohm, eds., *Theologie der Diakonie*, 175–208. Heidelberg: Heidelberger Verlagsanstalt, 1989.

Strohm, Theodor, & Gerhard Schäfer. "Abschliessende Überlegungen: 'Theologie der Diakonie' als Aufgabe ökumenischer Studienarbeit." In Paul

Philippi & Theodor Strohm, eds., *Theologie der Diakonie*, 233–46. Heidelberg: Heidelberger Verlagsanstalt, 1989.

Stupperich, Robert. "Bruderdienst und Nächstenhilfe in der deutschen Reformation." In Herbert Krimm, ed., *Das diakonische Amt der Kirche*, 2d ed., 167–96. Stuttgart: Evangelisches Verlagswerk, 1965.

———. "Das Enchiridion militis christiani des Erasmus von Rotterdam nach seiner Enstehung, seinem Sinn und Charakter." *Archiv für Reformationgeschichte* 69 (1978): 5–23.

———. "Das Problem der Armenfürsorge bei Juan Luis Vives." In August Buck, ed., *Juan Luis Vives*, 49–62. Hamburg: Hauswedell, 1981.

Süssmuth, Hans. *Studien zur Utopia des Thomas Morus*. Münster: Aschendorff, 1967.

Sydow, Jürgen. *Bürgerschaft und Kirche*. Sigmarinen: Thorbecke, 1980.

Tawney, R. H. *Religion and the Rise of Capitalism*. Harmondsworth, England: Pelikan, 1977.

Tertullian. "Apology." *Ante-Nicene Fathers* 3 (1953), 46.

Théral, Marie-Louise. "Caritas et paupertas dans l'iconographie médiévale inspirée de la psychomachie." In Michel Mollat, ed., *Études sur l'histoire de la pauvreté*, vol. 1, 295–317. Paris: 1974.

Theses Concerning Thomas Müntzer 1489–1989. Berlin: Panorama DDR, 1989.

Thompson, Craig R., ed. & trans. *The Colloquies of Erasmus*. Chicago: University of Chicago Press, 1965.

Tierney, Brian. "The Decretists and the 'Undeserving Poor.'" *Comparative Studies in Society and History*, vol. 1, 371–73. London: Cambridge Univ. Press, 1958–59.

———. *Medieval Poor Law: A Sketch of Canonical Theory and Its Application in England*. Berkeley and Los Angeles: University of California Press, 1959.

Tietz-Strödel, Marion. *Die Fuggerei in Augsburg: Studien zur Entwicklung des sozialen Stiftungsbaus im 15. und 16. Jahrhundert*. Tübingen: Mohr, 1982.

Tobriner, Alice. *A Sixteenth-Century Urban Report*. Chicago: University of Chicago Press, 1971.

Todd, Margo. *Christian Humanism and the Puritan Social Order*. Cambridge: Cambridge University Press, 1987.

Trevor-Roper, H. R. *Religion, the Reformation, and Social Change*. London: Macmillan, 1967.

Trexler, Richard C. "Charity and the Defense of Urban Elites in the Italian Communes." In Frederic C. Jaher, ed., *The Rich, the Well Born, and the Powerful: Elites and Upper Classes in History*, 64–109. Urbana: University of Illinois Press, 1973.

Troeltsch, Ernst. *The Social Teaching of the Christian Churches*. 2 vols. New York: Harper & Row, 1960. 461–576.

Tronrud, Thorold J. "Dispelling the Gloom. The Extent of Poverty in Tudor and Early Stuart Towns: Some Kentish Evidence." *Canadian Journal of History* 20 (1985): 1–21.

Trüdinger, Karl. *Luthers Briefe und Gutachten an weltliche Obrigkeiten*. Münster: Aschendorff, 1975.

————. *Stadt und Kirche im Spätmittelalterlichen Würzburg*. Stuttgart: Klett-Cotta, 1978.

Uhlhorn, Gerhard. *Die christliche Liebesthätigkeit*. 3 vols. Stuttgart, 1882–90; reprint, 3 vols. in 1; Stuttgart: Gundert, 1895.

————. *Schriften zur Sozialethik und Diakonie*. Ed. Martin Cordes & Hans Otte in collaboration with Elke Rothämel. Hannover: Lutherische Verlagshaus, 1990.

————. "Vorstudien zu einer Geschichte der Liebesthätigkeit im Mittelalter." *Zeitschrift für Kirchengeschichte* 4 (1881): 44–76.

Vajta, Vilmos. *Die Theologie des Gottesdienstes bei Luther*. Stockholm: Svenska Kyrkans Diakonistyrelses Bokförlag, 1952.

Van Cleve, John. *The Problem of Wealth in the Literature of Luther's Germany*. Columbia, S.C.: Camden House, 1991.

Varga, Ivan. "Capitalism and the Return to Religion." *Ecumenist* 18/4 (1980): 54–59.

Vauchez, André. "Confraternities and Guilds in the Middle Ages." In Carter Lindberg & Emily Albu Hanawalt, eds., *Through the Eye of a Needle: Judeo-Christian Roots of Social Welfare*. Kirksville, Mo.: Thomas Jefferson University Press, forthcoming.

————. "Le peuple au Moyen Age: du 'Populus Christianus' aux classes dangereuses." In Thomas Riis, ed., *Aspects of Poverty in Early Modern Europe*, vol. 2, 9–18. Odense: Odense University Press, 1981.

Vicaire, M.-H. "La Place des oeuvres de miséricorde dans la pastorale en pays d'oc." In *Assistance et charité*, Cahiers de Fanjeaux 13. Fanjeaux: Privat, 1978, 21–44.

Vischer, Lukas, ed. *Church History in Ecumenical Perspective* (Papers and Reports of an International Ecumenical Consultation held in Basel, October 12–17, 1981). Bern: Evangelische Arbeitsstelle Oekumene Schweiz, 1982.

Vocht, Henry de, ed. *Literae virorum eruditorum ad Franciscum Cranveldium* (1522–1528). Louvain, 1928.

Vogler, Günter. "Gemeinnutz und Eigennutz bei Thomas Müntzer." In Siegfried Bräuer & Helmar Junghans, ed., *Der Theologe Thomas Müntzer*, 174–94. Berlin: Evangelische Verlagsanstalt, 1989.

————. *Nürnberg, 1524/25: Studien zur Geschichte der reformatorischen und sozialen Bewegung in der Reichsstadt*. Berlin: Deutschen Verlag der Wissenschaften, 1982.

————. "Reformation als 'frühbürgerliche Revolution': Eine Konzeption in Meinungstreit." In Peter Blickle, ed., *Zwingli und Europa*, 47–69. Zurich: Vandenhoeck & Ruprecht, 1985.

————. "Sozialethisches Vorstellungen und Lebensweisen von Täufergruppen—Thomas Müntzer und die Täufer im Vergleich." *Evangelische Monatsschrift Standpunkt* 70/3 (1989); 75–79.

————. "Von Eberlin zu Stiblinus—Utopisches Denken zwischen 1521 und 1555." In Siegfried Hoyer, ed., *Reform, Reformation, Revolution*, 143–50. Leipzig: Karl Marx Universität, 1980.

Vogt, Karl A. T. *Johannes Bugenhagen Pomeranus: Leben und ausgewählte Schriften.* Elberfeld, 1867.

Wallasch, Joachim. "Konventsstärke und Armenfürsorge in mittelalterlichen Klöstern, Zeugnisse und Fragen." *Saeculum* 39 (1988): 184–99.

Wandel, Lee Palmer. "Images of the Poor in Reformation Zurich." Ph.D. diss. University of Michigan, 1985. Since published as *Always among Us: Images of the Poor in Zwingli's Zürich.* Cambridge: Cambridge University Press, 1990.

Wee, Herman van der. *The Growth of the Antwerp Market and the European Economy (Fourteenth to Sixteenth Centuries).* 2 vols. The Hague: Nijhoff, 1963.

Weitzmann, Wilhelm. *Die soziale Bedeutung des Humanisten Vives.* Borna-Leipzig, 1905.

Wenn, Hanns, ed. & trans. *Johannes Bugenhagen: Der Ehrbaren Stadt Hamburg Christliche Ordnung 1529. De Ordeninge Pomerani.* Hamburg: Wittig Verlag, 1976.

White, Helen C. *Social Criticism in Popular Religious Literature of the Sixteenth Century.* New York: Octagon Books, 1973.

Wilks, Michael. *The Problem of Sovereignty in the Later Middle Ages.* London: Cambridge University Press, 1963.

Williams, George H. *The Radical Reformation.* Philadelphia: Westminster Press, 1962.

Winckelmann, Otto. "Die Armenordnungen von Nürnberg (1522), Kitzingen (1523), Regensburg (1523) und Ypern (1525)." *Archiv für Reformationsgeschichte* 10 (1912/13): 242–80; 11 (1914): 1–18.

————. *Das Fürsorgewesen der Stadt Strassburg vor und nach der Reformation bis zum Ausgang des sechzehnten Jahrhunderts.* Leipzig, 1922; reprint, New York: Johnson Reprint Corp., 1971.

————. "Über die ältesten Armenordnungen der Reformationszeit (1522–1525)." *Historische Vierteljahrschrift* (1914): 187–228, 361–400.

Wright, William J. *Capitalism, the State, and the Lutheran Reformation: Sixteenth Century Hesse.* Athens: Ohio State University Press, 1988.

————. "The Homberg Synod and Philip of Hesse's Plan for a New Church-State Settlement." *Sixteenth Century Journal* 4 (1973): 23–46.

Wuthnow, Robert. *Communities of Discourse: Ideology and Social Structure in the Reformation, the Enlightenment, and European Socialism.* Cambridge: Harvard University Press, 1989.

Zapalac, Kristin. *"In His Image and Likeness": Political Iconography and Religious Change in Regensburg, 1500–1600.* Ithaca, N.Y.: Cornell University Press, 1990.

Zeydel, Edwin H., trans. & ed. *The Ship of Fools by Sebastian Brant.* New York: Dover, 1962.

Index

Agricultural crisis, 38
Alain of Lille, 29
Alexius, St., 147, 149
Almosenkasten. *See* Common chest
Alms, 28, 29, 31–32, 34, 42, 45–46, 56–66, 81, 148, 174, 176–77, 179, 194, 202–3, 205
  legislation, 87
  merit of, 50, 68–69, 97, 151
  redeem from sin, 68–69
  steward of, 138
  See also Works of mercy
Almsgiving, 24, 27–29, 43, 51, 81, 99, 136, 146–47, 149, 151
  See also Charity
Altenburg, 129–32
Ambrose, St., 99
Anabaptists, 74, 128, 153, 158–60, 166
Anabaptists, Münster, 115 n.149
Antwerp, 150
Aragon, Cortes of, 45
Archbishop Henry II, 47
Armenkasten. *See* Common chest
Asceticism, 108–9
Atonement, 131, 156
Augsburg, 41, 43, 50, 52, 112, 133
Augustine, St., 23–24, 29–30, 78, 157, 175

The City of God, 78
Augustinians, 130, 133, 147, 150
Avarice, 25, 40, 113
Avicenna, 78 n.31

Baptism, 99
Barcelona, 55
Base communities, 168
Basel, 43–45, 77
Bataillon, M., 83
Bautzen, 41
Beggars, 37, 42–46, 53, 72, 131, 179, 205
  able-bodied, 45
  argot of, 49, 49 n.124; *See also* Rotwelsch
  badges of, 46, 134, 180–82, 194
  false, 47–51
  foreign, 81, 131
  literature on, 50
  native, 81
Begging, 32, 39, 43, 47, 69, 165
  abolition of, 75, 80, 105–6, 125, 146–47, 149, 190, 200
  and the plague, 79–80
  depiction of, 121
  false, 121
  legislation of, 47, 66, 69
  licensing of. *See* Beggars, badges of
  techniques of, 47–48, 176, 179, 182–89

Belgern, 129
Belgium, 83
Benedictine Rule, 25, 58
Benedictines, 25–26
Berger, P., 23
Besler, G., 133
Bible, 18, 27, 110, 116, 144, 159
  See also Ecclesiasticus; Tobit; Last judgment; Magnificat; Scripture
Bismarck, O., 110 n.136
Blockmans and Prevenier, 36
Boff, L., 168 n.21
Boston Declaration, 162
Brady, T., 90
Brant, S., 48
  Ship of Fools, 48
Braudel, F., 6
Braunschweig, 54
Braunschweig church order, 139, 142, 168
Braunschweig–Wolfenbüttel church order, 140
Bremen, 84, 84 n.48, 92, 150
Bremen church order, 150
Brenz, J., 140
Brotherhoods, 44, 92, 95, 101, 103–4, 121, 195–96, 200
  See also Confraternities
Bruges Ordinance, 151
Bruges, 77, 79, 82–83, 146, 152
Bucer, M., 94, 97 n.100, 137–40

230